'A tale of vision, determination a[...]
It's a fascina[...]
The Sund[...]

'It is a sympathetic picture, but not sycophantic. Space is
given to the critics ... a well-written account of the early
years of this significant and encouraging Christian enterprise.'
Church Times

'Alpha has become a global phenomenon and, in this
well-researched and compelling account, it has now
found its historian.'
TLS

'A riveting and well-written story'
★★★★★
Premier Christianity

'Andrew Atherstone's contribution makes clear how
the Alpha brand has changed the landscape of
modern Christianity.'
Inspire Magazine

Repackaging Christianity

Alpha and the building of a global brand

ANDREW ATHERSTONE

HODDER

First published in Great Britain in 2022 by Hodder & Stoughton
An Hachette UK company

This paperback edition first published in 2023

1

A CIP catalogue record for this title is available from the British Library

Paperback ISBN 978 1 399 80153 9
eBook ISBN 978 1 399 80152 2

Typeset in Bembo MT by Hewer Text UK Ltd, Edinburgh
Printed and bound in Great Britain by Clays Ltd, Elcograf S.p.A.

Hodder & Stoughton policy is to use papers that are natural, renewable
and recyclable products and made from wood grown in sustainable
forests. The logging and manufacturing processes are expected to
conform to the environmental regulations of the country of origin.

Hodder & Stoughton Ltd
Carmelite House
50 Victoria Embankment
London EC4Y 0DZ

www.hodderfaith.com

In memory of
Michael Green (1930–2019),
senior research fellow at Wycliffe Hall, Oxford,
one of the world's great Christian evangelists

Contents

Acknowledgements

ALPHA IS A global phenomenon, one of the best-known brands in Christian evangelism, adopted in multiple languages and cultures across the world. It has attracted the attention of the global media, politicians and celebrities, with profiles in glossy fashion magazines and scholarly journals. It has been the focus of numerous theological and sociological critiques, including book-length studies such as Stephen Hunt's *The Alpha Enterprise* (2004), Andrew Brookes's *The Alpha Phenomenon* (2007), James Heard's *Inside Alpha* (2009) and Stephen Brian's *Assessing Alpha* (2010).[1] But there has never yet been a history. The retirement in 2022 of Alpha's presiding genius, Nicky Gumbel, from his position as vicar of Holy Trinity Brompton (the birthplace of Alpha) – followed in 2023 by the thirtieth anniversary of Alpha's global launch and the publication of its key text, *Questions of Life* – is an opportune moment to begin historical analysis. Alpha in the 2020s remains vibrant, frequently refreshed and reinvented for new audiences, in new digital media, reaching many new communities. But after three decades, enough time has now elapsed for historians to set to work, examining Alpha in its cultural environment from its earliest origins to its latest evolutions. The story of Alpha is of major significance for understanding the place of religious faith in the modern world, but that story has never before been told.

As a history, this book is distinguished from previous studies by diving deep into the original archives. I am especially grateful to Alpha International and Holy Trinity Brompton for granting me privileged access to their abundant archives. This is not an authorised narrative, but it would have been impossible to research effectively without their goodwill. Mark Elsdon-Dew has been a wonderfully generous and knowledgeable guide to the sources, and trusted me with his precious and unique set of *Alpha News* and *HTB in Focus* newspapers.[2] Nicky Gumbel, a key subject in this study, has also kindly granted me access to some of his personal Alpha files and archive boxes, including his appointment diaries.

I am grateful to those who have granted interviews towards this book, including Peter Blundell, Chuck and Carol Butler, Charlie Colchester, Ken Costa, Al Gordon, Nicky and Pippa Gumbel, Jeremy Jennings, J.John, Kitty Kay-Shuttleworth, Philip Lawson-Johnston, Nicky and Sila Lee, Sandy Millar, Henry Montgomery, David Payne, Gordon and Sally Scutt, Charles Whitehead, Emmy Wilson and Bonnie Yule-Kuehne. Others have provided important documents or answered queries, including Jonathan Aitken, Adam Atkinson, Stephen Brian, Kristina Cooper (archives from the Catholic Charismatic Renewal), Sister Mary Paul Friemel (custodian of Peter Hocken's archives at the Mysterium Christi community, Hainburg an der Donau, Austria), Charles Freebury, Mike Frith, Mark Ireland, David MacInnes (archives from the 1974 CICCU mission), Charles and Tricia Marnham, Nick McKinnel (archives from the 1979 Step Forward mission), Tricia Neill, Tony Payne, Jackie Pullinger, Rodney Radcliffe, Neil Richardson, William Scholes, Nigel Skelsey, Patrick Whitworth (archives from HTB's *Lighthouse* course) and Edward Wright. Members of the Alpha International and HTB staff have been unfailingly helpful – thanks especially to Catherine Clark, Phil Dhillon-James, Chloe Harrison, Rachel Liebetrau, Chloe Lyward, Jane McKeever, Sam Prior, Ros Suni and Kathryn Taylor. Thanks also to Kensington Central Library (which has an excellent set of HTB parish magazines), Lambeth Palace Library, London Metropolitan Archives and Westminster Diocesan Archives for access to original materials. I am grateful also to Andy Lyon, Jessica Lacey and the team at Hodder & Stoughton for their enthusiasm for this project.

I

Rebirth and Renewal

HOLY TRINITY BROMPTON – known globally as HTB – is one of the world's leading hubs of Christian evangelism, church planting and spiritual renewal, famous as the birthplace of Alpha. Its waves of influence permeate not only the Church of England but many churches and denominations across the world. It stands at the centre of a nexus of significant transnational relationships and innovations that shape the expression of modern religious culture in multiple contexts and communities. Alpha, alongside other branded ministries within the HTB family, has become by the 2020s a powerful driver of Christian resurgence, experimentation and expansion on a global scale. But Alpha's roots stretch back to the 1970s, when a confluence of different factors led to HTB's emergence as a seedbed for renewal.

HTB is located in one of the most elegant and famed parts of central London. Within the boundaries of the parish, on Exhibition Road, lie three of the great museums of Victorian Britain – the Victoria and Albert Museum, the Science Museum and the Natural History Museum – which draw millions of visitors a year. Just along the Brompton Road is Harrods, an icon of luxury, the largest department store in Europe with 23 acres of floor space. In the early 1980s, Harrods boasted 214 departments, six restaurants, and a staff of over 5,000 (rising to 7,000 at Christmas), making it practically the size of a parish in its own right, and one of the HTB curates was deployed as Harrods chaplain.[1] The area is awash with students from nearby Imperial College London, just beyond which are Hyde Park, the Royal Albert Hall and Kensington Palace. Embassies and hotels jostle alongside each other. HTB itself was built by the Georgians in the 1820s, when Brompton was still a village surrounded by fields, not yet gobbled up by London's sprawl. It stands back from the Brompton

Road, down a tree-lined avenue, now partially hidden from view by the imposing neo-classical Brompton Oratory.

For much of the twentieth century, HTB was a 'society' church, where the elite of Knightsbridge mingled at weddings and christenings, or at memorial services for titled nobility. Its ethos mirrored the cultured Anglicanism of many public school or Oxbridge chapels. The established HTB tradition by the mid-1970s, in the words of vicar John Morris, was 'a very traditional form of worship, in which preaching and good music have formed a major part. It offers one of the finest forms of old-fashioned matins services in the metropolis.'[2] Music was taken especially seriously. Choral anthems and organ voluntaries were announced in advance in the *Brompton Broadsheet* (the parish newsletter) to whet the congregation's appetite and in 1975 (for example) included compositions by John Taverner, Thomas Tallis, William Byrd, Johann Sebastian Bach, Samuel Wesley, Felix Mendelssohn and many others. Twentieth-century music was supplied by the likes of Sergei Rachmaninoff, Ralph Vaughan Williams, Herbert Howells, Maurice Duruflé, Olivier Messiaen and Benjamin Britten. There was not a guitar in sight.

Nevertheless, even within this traditionalist environment, there were signs of spiritual renewal beginning to break through. Since the early 1950s HTB had hosted the London branch of the Divine Healing Mission, an organisation founded at Crowhurst in Sussex in the early twentieth century to encourage prayer for healing. Each Wednesday there was a 'healing service' at HTB in the context of holy communion, with the laying-on-of-hands offered at the communion rail. This was followed by a picnic lunch and teaching about healing or other aspects of the Holy Spirit's ministry.[3] Thus a steady stream of renewalist pioneers spoke at HTB under the auspices of the Divine Healing Mission, including in the late 1960s and early 1970s Church of England clergymen like Michael Harper and Colin Urquhart, and Episcopalian visitors from the United States such as Agnes Sanford and Rufus Womble.[4] Their books were marketed on the HTB bookstall and the *Brompton Broadsheet* recommended other paperbacks like Nicky Cruz's *Run Baby Run* (1968), Maynard James's *I Believe in the Holy Ghost* (1969), Basilea Schlink's *Ruled by the Spirit* (1969), Corrie ten Boom's *The Hiding Place* (1971) and Cardinal Léon

Joseph Suenens's *A New Pentecost?* (1975).[5] HTB congregation member Rodney Radcliffe reported on his tour of churches in the United States during a business trip, including to the pioneering Church of the Redeemer in Houston, Texas, which had been profiled on the HTB bookstall in Harper's *A New Way of Living* (1973).[6] Radcliffe also attended a meeting of the Full Gospel Business Men's Fellowship International in New York in November 1974, where he encountered the healing evangelist Kathryn Kuhlman. He enthused about it in the *Brompton Broadsheet*:

> Quite plainly, I saw miracles – the mighty works of the Lord. Cripples walked and leaped out of chairs; some, blind for years, were suddenly able to see; the deaf began to hear; those with cancer, multiple sclerosis and other illnesses were cured . . . God's power was released to work, and seemed to touch anyone who came.[7]

Yet these remained minority interests at HTB. Renewal was emerging around the edges of the congregation, in midweek meetings, but made little impact upon the main Sunday ministry. It was promoted by the London chaplain to the Divine Healing Mission, Nicholas Rivett-Carnac (HTB curate from 1968 to 1972), but otherwise received little public backing from the church's leadership.[8] According to one tribute, it was Rivett-Carnac who 'laid the foundations in intercession and prayer' for the spiritual life at HTB that followed in subsequent decades.[9]

Sandy and Annette Millar

Among the small number of young graduates connected with HTB from the early 1960s was Alexander ('Sandy') Millar, who later played a major role in Alpha's global expansion.[10]

Sandy Millar was born in London in November 1939, of Scottish descent. He lived a nomadic childhood as his father was a professional soldier, Major-General Robert Kirkpatrick Millar of Orton, engineer-in-chief in the Pakistan Army. Educated at Eton and Trinity College, Cambridge, Millar returned to London to pursue his childhood ambition to work as a criminal barrister. Legal training ran in the family – his grandfather John Hepburn Millar (1864–1929) was Professor of Constitutional Law and Constitutional History at the University of Edinburgh, and his great-grandfather John Millar, Lord Craighill (1817–88) was Solicitor General for Scotland. Called to the bar in 1964, aged 24, Sandy Millar's chambers were headed by Mervyn Griffith-Jones, famous for leading the prosecution of Penguin Books for obscenity in 1960 after the publication of *Lady Chatterley's Lover*, and of Stephen Ward in 1963 during the fallout from the Profumo Affair. With lodgings at Cadogan Place in Belgravia, Millar joined HTB and served on the Parochial Church Council (PCC), though he did not attend on Sundays very often. Despite his occasional church involvement, he lacked personal Christian faith. He did, however, believe in life after death – to persuade two cynical friends, also barristers, Millar took them to the headquarters of the Spiritualist Association of Great Britain in Belgrave Square, and paid for a medium to conjure up the spirits in a séance, though nothing happened. He knew that the Church of England disapproved of spiritualism, but put that down to 'professional jealousy'.

In July 1967, Millar was invited to a weekend house party by Annette Fisher, a young schoolteacher living in Kensington. She had experienced evangelical conversion in her first week at the University of St Andrews in 1959 through a Christian Union mission, but it was not until she was prayed for in the mid-1960s by Edgar Trout (a Methodist evangelist) to be 'filled with the Spirit' that she discovered a new boldness in evangelism. She sent a postcard to about 30 of her friends, inviting them to bring a tennis racquet and a Bible to the Manor House at Stoke Poges in Buckinghamshire. Millar enjoyed these social opportunities and was confident that, as a barrister, he would be able to resist the Christian agenda. Yet to his surprise, he found himself 'rivetted' by the speaker, David MacInnes (curate at St Helen's, Bishopsgate), who explained the Christian message in a way that Millar understood for the first time. When Millar asked about spiritualism, MacInnes encouraged him to read Raphael Gasson's *The Challenging Counterfeit* (1966), a popular charismatic paperback by a former medium who converted to Christianity. Millar was intrigued, but not yet persuaded.

A few months later, Millar was travelling to the Old Bailey in the morning rush hour on the London Underground. The carriage was packed, but a City worker who had recently become a Christian, and who Millar knew vaguely, looked at him across the crowd and called out, 'Do you realise that Jesus is alive?' The barrister felt acutely embarrassed and self-conscious, and quickly replied, 'Yes, yes I do', hoping that would end the conversation. But then the train stopped between stations, and the man asked again, 'Does that make any difference to your life?' Millar sensed the other commuters listening in, as they read their newspapers, and retorted, 'Oh yes, yes, yes', before he got off, flustered and blushing, at the next stop. He had 'never been so relieved to get out of a train'. In retrospect, however, that awkward public encounter was 'absolutely formative'. Millar worried about the conversation, especially the fact that he could not think of any substantial difference Jesus made to his life, and that he felt socially obliged to answer 'yes' when he really meant 'no'.[11] Resolved not to be caught in the same situation again, he bought a copy of the New Testament in modern translation (the *New English Bible*) and 'devoured' it, reading it from cover to cover. In the Gospels he discovered Jesus to be very different to the tame portraits propagated by school chapel and stained-glass windows. 'I just fell in love with Jesus', Millar recalled. 'I discovered for the first time what an astonishing man he is – an extraordinary figure, a leader, a man amongst men.'[12]

The following summer 1968, Fisher held a second house party at Stoke Poges. This time she struggled to find a speaker until John Collins (vicar of St Mark's, Gillingham) persuaded his curate, John Freeth, to attend at very short notice and with almost no time for preparation. Whereas MacInnes, the previous year, had been highly polished, Freeth stumbled through his presentations. He would begin a sentence and not finish it, or begin a story and not remember the ending. Nevertheless, Millar was struck by the fact that, although MacInnes and Freeth were entirely different characters, their message was the same. 'It was the same Jesus, the same gospel.' That evening at supper, as Millar was handing around salad, the penny dropped and he suddenly thought 'this is true'. As he later explained, 'I gave my life to the Lord that night.'[13] Fisher had been 'praying and praying like mad' for Millar's conversion. She also wanted to introduce him to the wider ministry of the Holy Spirit, so she invited him to one of the regular Fountain Trust meetings at the Metropolitan Tabernacle (Charles Spurgeon's former chapel) to hear David du Plessis, a South African evangelist and Pentecostal pioneer. At the end of the meeting, Millar went to the front for prayer, where du Plessis recalled Jesus's promise, 'Ask, and it shall be given you' (Luke 11:9), and prayed 'Come, Holy Spirit'. That evening, as Millar knelt alone by his bed praising God, he began to speak in tongues.[14]

Still a member at HTB, Millar's perspective on church life was now transformed. He threw himself into wider Christian activities, including the Divine Healing Mission and the Stewards' Trust (a network of Bible studies and house parties for young professionals in London, founded in 1954). He was introduced, for example, to the American charismatic pioneer Jean Darnall at a crowded meeting in Fisher's flat. The attenders, according to Nicholas Rivett-Carnac, 'would have looked more at home with a champagne cocktail in their hand than a Bible', but they were enraptured as Darnall spoke for two hours, and Millar hung upon her every word.[15] Millar also occasionally attended the lunchtime Bible expositions for City workers by Dick Lucas at St Helen's, Bishopsgate, calculating that he could dash there and back in a taxi from the High Court. After Millar and Fisher were married in October 1971, they started a Bible study in their home, though it was treated with some suspicion as a novelty by the congregation at HTB.

In his work as a barrister, Millar was increasingly perturbed by the devastating impact of drug addiction in the early 1970s as a major contributor to criminality. When visiting the cells, he longed to share the Christian message with those on trial, but was paid to provide legal advice, not spiritual wisdom. In his free time, he began to volunteer with the Association for the Prevention of Addiction (founded in 1967), but its secular basis again restricted gospel proclamation. Finally, in 1971, Millar discovered a little mission hall at Short's Gardens, in the Seven Dials district near Covent Garden, where Christian outreach to drug addicts and the homeless was run by the London City Mission, overseen by missionary Lionel Ball. Millar recruited a team of 15 friends from HTB and the Stewards' Trust – including Nicholas Rivett-Carnac, Rodney Radcliffe and Annette Fisher – who joined

Ball's endeavours each Thursday evening. They served meals, sang choruses on the piano, gave short talks from the Bible, engaged in conversations, and prayed with the alcoholics, addicts, ex-convicts and gang members who came in off the streets.[16] Jean Darnall brought 'a word from the Lord' for each member of the team, and encouraged them all: 'If you sit with these people in their distress and weep with them and hurt with them, and love them with the compassion of Jesus, you will see many changed lives and miracles of liberation and healing worked in the power of the Holy Spirit.'[17] The hall was officially called the London Medical Mission, but became known in Soho as the London Miracle Mission. This experience was critical in Millar's call to ordination. Through the London City Mission he witnessed 'God's love for the poor' in action, combining practical service with evangelism and prayer. Although the Short's Gardens outreach was difficult and sometimes dangerous, he had a growing sense that this was what he wanted to do with the rest of his life.[18] In October 1974 the Millars, with their young children, bade farewell to London and HTB, to train for ordination at Cranmer Hall in Durham.

The Kitchen and Cloud

Young people converged on the capital in September 1972 for the five-day London Festival for Jesus, organised by the Nationwide Festival of Light morality campaign, a British parallel to the Jesus People festivals in the United States.[19] The event combined street evangelism with Christian rock concerts, teach-ins, and practical service in 'Operation Clean-Up'. There were rallies at Tower Hill, Hyde Park and Trafalgar Square, and a flotilla of boats motored down the River Thames draped with 'Jesus is Alive Today' banners. At Hyde Park, 5,000 sat on the grass in the sunshine listening to Christian musicians from both sides of the Atlantic including Dana, Cliff Richard, Gordon Giltrap, Larry Norman and Californian band Country Faith. 'Light Up the Fire', a hit by Liverpool folk band Parchment, was the festival's theme song.[20]

Wanting to continue their festival experience, a group of seven young London friends looked for a permanent meeting place, where they could enjoy fellowship and food, and 'where the love of God could be felt and shared'.[21] The leader among them, older than the rest, was 29-year-old Michael Anstruther-Gough-Calthorpe – known as Mickie Calthorpe – an artist and designer who came from one of the wealthiest aristocratic families in Britain. His family owned the Calthorpe Estate, covering 1,600 acres of prime residential and commercial land in the fashionable Edgbaston district of Birmingham.[22] Calthorpe lived in a small mews house in Kensington, at 16 Petersham Place, and his mews garage was identified as the ideal location for this new project. However, at first it seemed impossible because the garage was tied up in a long-term lease to another tenant, who stored his car there, but the tenant died suddenly, thus terminating the contract. 'This was sad news', acknowledged Calthorpe, 'but to us it was a joyful confirmation.'[23] The garage was converted into 'The Kitchen', launched in April 1974, open for lunches and suppers from Monday to Thursday, staffed mostly by volunteers. The food was simple – typically a 'ploughman's lunch' (soup, homemade bread, Wensleydale cheese and fresh fruit), with stew in the evenings (sometimes rabbit) cooked on the Aga.[24] There was no charge and donations were placed in a basket. The Kitchen was described as 'an expression of love',[25] seeking to model God's welcome to allcomers. As early as 1975 it was hailed as 'an outstanding means of reaching outsiders', and many young people became Christians through its activities.[26] Here was the ethos of Alpha in bud – conversations about the Christian faith, with friends, around a meal, in an informal relaxed atmosphere. For those who wanted to take the discussion further, there were several Bible study groups affiliated with the Kitchen, including one in Calthorpe's flat.

The Kitchen was also conceived as a venue 'to nurture artistic talent to the glory of God', with engravings, pottery, needlework and paintings offered for sale to support the project. As the seven originators prayed and fasted about their shared vision, they were 'blessed by innumerable confirmations from the Scriptures', especially concerning the building of King Solomon's Temple in the Book of Chronicles.[27] Calthorpe used some of those biblical details as the inspiration for the Kitchen's colour scheme, cushions and artistic flourishes. Sometimes as many as 80 people crammed into the venue.

Music was provided by a homegrown Christian band called 'Cloud', founded in October 1973 and named after the cloud of God's glory that filled the Temple when the Levites raised songs of praise accompanied by trumpets, cymbals and other musical instruments (2 Chronicles 5:12–14). The name was chosen to signify the importance of worship and of entering the presence of God.[28]

Cloud's leader was Philip Lawson-Johnston. His mother was an Anstruther-Gough-Calthorpe (Mickie's aunt) and his businessman father, Baron Luke, was chairman of Bovril, the family firm. After leaving Eton College in 1968, Lawson-Johnston studied the history of art at the Inchbald School of Design before taking up glass engraving. His journey to Christian faith was 'a series of stepping-stones': he went forward at a Billy Graham rally at Wembley Stadium in 1966, and prayed a prayer of commitment after hearing David MacInnes preach at Chelsea Town Hall in 1968, but he felt sorely out of place when introduced to a Stewards' Trust Bible study group. The other members were barristers and stockbrokers in the City, while Lawson-Johnston was a long-haired, pot-smoking, wannabee rock musician.[29] In February 1972 he was invited to Calthorpe's flat to hear an address by Sandy Millar, and there Lawson-Johnston 'finally surrendered my heart fully to Jesus'. Calthorpe and another friend prayed for him that evening to be filled with the Holy Spirit:

> No drama or fireworks, but a penetrating peace entered me as the conflict and troubled thoughts of the previous years just lifted off me and I could understand with sudden clarity why Jesus died for me personally. It all began to make sense not just in a cerebral and intellectual way, but it was as if my heart came alive for the first time. I went away full of a sense of freedom and calm, knowing that something had happened deep inside.[30]

The Bible 'came alive' for Lawson-Johnston and he began to turn his new Christian faith into song. His first tutorials in worship music were from Californian songwriter and guitarist Chuck Butler of Country Faith who (with his young wife Carol Butler) was part of the early planning for the Kitchen in 1973.[31] As so often in the history of Christian renewal, where California led, Kensington followed.

Cloud's membership fluctuated between three and twenty people. It mostly comprised singers, led by acoustic guitar, but also integrated classical instruments – including, at various times, double bass, percussion, cello, violin, viola, flute, oboe, clarinet, French horn, trumpet and piano. Lawson-Johnston summed up the Cloud genre as 'a strong classical influence . . . mixed with a blend of folk and light rock'.[32] They toured Britain, leading worship for churches, conferences and schools, and played at the Christian rock festival, Greenbelt, which from 1975 was held on the Lawson-Johnston family estate at Odell in Bedfordshire.[33] Cloud also recorded their own albums, seven in total, beginning with *Free to Fly*, which sold 2,000 copies by Christmas 1975.[34] However, when the Kitchen launched an informal Service of Praise on Sunday evenings, led by Cloud, some grew concerned that it was 'setting itself up as a church', in rivalry to local churches. The Kitchen preferred to define itself as 'a large house group, and not a church', and believed it was fulfilling a need not provided for elsewhere.[35] Calthorpe, in particular, was wary of institutional churches. Nevertheless, Cloud decided in 1975 that they should be properly connected with a local church, so as a group they joined St Paul's, Onslow Square, a Victorian offshoot of HTB.

St Paul's was a conservative evangelical congregation, with a particular ministry to students and young people. It was considerably smaller than the two major Anglican evangelical congregations in central London – All Souls, Langham Place, under John Stott, and St Helen's, Bishopsgate, under Dick Lucas – but stood in the same tradition. When Raymond Turvey was appointed vicar in 1972, the parish profile insisted that their new incumbent must be 'a preacher and teacher, of conservative evangelical convictions, able to warm hearts'.[36] But when Cloud and other members of the Kitchen joined St Paul's, they brought with them a flavour of the Jesus Revolution and a hunger for renewal. Turvey allowed them to lead worship once a month on Sunday evenings, a sharp break in style from St Paul's usual hymnbook, *Psalm Praise* (1973), modern settings of the psalter. Cloud broke the mould. They pushed informality and a contemporary vibe more akin to a gentle rock concert than an organ recital. This appealed to the younger demographic at St Paul's and sowed the seeds of renewal. Soon these principles were embedded also into

HTB, when St Paul's was merged in 1976 with HTB, taking Cloud with them.

Cambridge Conversions

During the same period, in the mid-1970s, a remarkable series of Christian conversions took place at the University of Cambridge, which in due course had a major impact upon the future direction of HTB and Alpha. Among the thousands of new undergraduates who arrived in October 1973 were two young friends at Trinity College – Nicky Gumbel and Nicky Lee – who had been schoolboys together at Eton College and discovered to their surprise that they had been assigned rooms next to each other in Trinity's Whewell's Court.

Nicky Gumbel's family home was in Ovington Square, Kensington, a short walk from HTB, but he was baptised as an infant at the Anglo-Catholic congregation of St Paul's, Knightsbridge, in February 1956.[37] He came from a family of barristers, including both grandfathers. His father, Walter Gumbel, was a German Jew from Stuttgart who had fled the Nazi regime and made a new life in England, where he was called to the bar in 1935. Walter's cousin, Professor Emil J. Gumbel, was a prominent mathematician, pacifist and anti-Nazi campaigner, forced into exile in Paris and later New York.[38] Walter managed to get his parents and sister out of Germany just before the Second World War, but other members of the wider Gumbel clan perished in the concentration camps. Nicky's mother, Muriel Gumbel née Glyn, was also a barrister and Conservative Party politician, serving on the Greater London Council and during 1971–2 as mayor of the Royal Borough of Kensington and Chelsea. Her barrister brother, Sir Alan Glyn, was Conservative MP for Windsor. Nicky's elder sister, Lizanne Gumbel, followed in the family tradition, called to the bar in 1974, and it was assumed that Nicky would do the same. Indeed, soon after Nicky was born, his father put his name down at a set of tax chambers.[39]

When it came to religion, the Gumbels were notionally members of the Church of England, but seldom attended. Nicky's involvement in church was limited to 'midnight mass every other year'.[40] Eton school chapel was 'very dull' and left him with the impression that the Christian faith was 'dreary and uninspiring'.[41] During his gap year travelling in the United States, he lost his rucksack in Tallahassee, Florida, and was offered hospitality by a community of lively young evangelical Christians, probably part of the Jesus People movement, but was put off by 'their tendency to smile so much' and fled when they began to pray.[42] By the time Gumbel reached Cambridge he liked to call himself a 'logical determinist', believing that all human actions were predetermined by birth and environment, leaving no possibility for free moral choices.[43] He was 'at times an atheist and at times an agnostic, unsure of what I believed'.[44] In another place he described his outlook differently, as 'an atheist in my head and a nominal Christian in my heart (just to keep the options open). Outwardly life was full of excitements but inside things were very different.'[45]

Nicky Lee, son of a London stockbroker, was raised in rural Hampshire and attended the local village church at Christmas and occasionally at Easter.[46] Compared to Gumbel, he was much more open to the Christian message. In his first week at Cambridge, he met John Hamilton, a young Trinity graduate who was training for ordination at Ridley Hall. Hamilton visited many of the Trinity Freshers and knocked on Lee's door to invite him to an evangelistic address by the Cambridge Inter-Collegiate Christian Union (CICCU). Lee had always thought of God as 'a very mysterious spiritual being' and was intrigued by the way Hamilton spoke of a personal relationship with Jesus Christ. He occasionally attended the weekly CICCU evangelistic addresses on Sunday evenings, but worried that if he became a Christian he would have to break up with his 18-year-old girlfriend, Alison ('Sila') Callander, with whom he was head-over-heels in love. 'If any of those born-again Christians come anywhere near your room, don't let them in,' Gumbel advised Lee. 'Talk to them through a crack in the door because if you let them in you won't be able to get rid of them.'[47]

In the middle of their second term, the CICCU organised a major week-long mission called *Christ Alive* from 10 to 16 February 1974, in the Cambridge Guildhall, led by David MacInnes. Gumbel joined the crowd of undergraduates at the mission one evening, but it made no impact on him. Lee, by contrast, was deeply impressed by MacInnes's preaching and, although he sat at the back of the Guildhall, he had 'never heard someone speak with more power in my life'. Lee was increasingly persuaded by the evidence for Christianity and on the penultimate evening of the mission, Friday 15 February, when he met Callander off the train from London he took her straight to the Guildhall. She too was fascinated with what MacInnes had to say. Although she had been raised as a child in the Scottish Episcopal Church, and believed in God, she had 'never heard anybody talk about Jesus Christ like this' in all her years at church or boarding school chapel. 'Nobody had ever said you could have a relationship with Jesus Christ,' she recalled. 'For me relationship was everything and suddenly this was making sense.'[48]

The next morning, Saturday 16 February, Lee and Callander attended an evangelistic breakfast at Queens' College organised by their friend Stephen Ruttle (a future barrister), who was encouraging them towards Christian faith.[49] That evening they went to Great St Mary's, the University Church, for the final mission event. It began with 25 minutes of testimony and singing by American musician Barry McGuire – best known for his youth protest song 'Eve of Destruction' (1965) – who had become a Christian in 1971. McGuire stood on the chancel steps in bare feet and tattered jeans, with long hair and beard, holding his guitar, and riveted the audience with tales of his encounters with Jimi Hendrix and Jesus.[50] Then MacInnes preached about the crucifixion. Callander remembered:

> It was a revelation to me. I kept saying to myself, 'Why did nobody ever tell me before *why* Jesus died on the cross?' It was as if everything I had ever known fitted together, not just intellectually, but also emotionally and spiritually. Everything made sense when the cross was explained.[51]

When MacInnes invited anyone who wanted to respond to the gospel message to come to the front, Lee and Callander were quickly out of their seats, with about 50 other young people. Although Callander's life up to that point had been 'totally and utterly fulfilled and happy' – full of joy, friendship, family, love, privilege and opportunity – she nonetheless summed up the 'radical change' of Christian conversion as like the transformation of 'a black and white still photograph' that was suddenly now 'in glorious Technicolour, a moving motion picture'. It was the turning point of their lives.[52]

Lee and Callander returned excitedly to college, where Gumbel had been dancing at the Trinity Valentine Ball, and they all talked together late into the night. Gumbel was deeply suspicious of his friends' conversion and feared they were falling into the hands of 'a cult'.[53] Determined to investigate these questions for himself, his immediate ambition was to read books about competing philosophies and ideologies like Marxism, existentialism, Islam and Christianity. But the only relevant book he had to hand that Saturday night was his old school Bible (the Authorised Version), so he began to read the Gospels of Matthew, Mark, Luke, and reached about halfway through John, falling asleep at 3 o'clock in the morning. When he woke up, he picked up where he had left off, reading through the whole New Testament over the next couple of days. This encounter with Scripture was critical in Gumbel's sudden and unexpected conversion. In the best-known version of his testimony – published worldwide in the 1990s as part of Alpha – he explained: 'I was completely gripped by what I read. I had read it before and it had meant virtually nothing to me. This time it came alive and I could not put it down. It had a ring of truth about it. I knew as I read it that I had to respond because it spoke so powerfully to me.'[54]

Gumbel's gradual spiritual awakening had begun, stimulated by the Bible, though he still wanted to protect Lee and Callander from falling under MacInnes's sway. On Sunday 17 February, the evangelist was invited to lunch in their rooms at Trinity, where they fed him meagre fare of bread, cheese and cheap wine. Gumbel was so impressed with their guest's graciousness that his hostility thawed and he agreed to hear MacInnes preach that evening at Great St Mary's (a post-mission service). Gumbel went forward at the end of the service to find out more, increasingly intrigued but not yet fully persuaded.[55] For further advice, he sought out Jonathan Fletcher (son of former Labour MP, Baron Fletcher), the 31-year-old curate at Cambridge's Round Church. Fletcher instructed him that becoming a Christian entailed three decisions: to give up everything he knew was wrong, to be known publicly as a follower of Christ, and to 'hand over the driving seat of his life to Christ'. But Gumbel baulked at the idea of surrender to God, especially given his 'wild social life', and thought perhaps he would postpone the decision until his deathbed:

> I sensed it was true but the implications for my life were such that I thought it would be ruined. Then I sensed (and now, looking back, I think it was God speaking to me): 'If you don't do it now, you never will.' So basically I just said, 'Yes, OK.' And at that moment everything clicked into place. Suddenly I understood what life was about. I suppose I found what I'd been looking for unconsciously all my life.[56]

Elsewhere he wrote: 'I realised that Jesus *is* rather than Jesus *was* and with much hesitation and great reluctance . . . I abandoned the struggle and immediately found my life radically and wonderfully changed.'[57] This decisive conclusion is difficult to date precisely, but probably occurred on Monday 18 February 1974, as Gumbel wrestled with all he had heard and read during the previous weekend.

These Christian conversions were transformative in several ways. One immediate moral implication was that Lee and Callander concluded they must stop sleeping together, a painful decision involving many tears.[58] However, brimming with excitement at what they had discovered, the friends also now had an irrepressible passion to share their new-found Christian faith with others. Gumbel and Lee grew beards, to look more like Jesus, and began talking about being ordained. Gumbel carried pockets full of evangelistic tracts to distribute to all and sundry, and was mocked by some undergraduates as 'the divinely inspired Mr Nicholas Gumbel'.[59] Charles Moore, another Old Etonian at Trinity College (later editor of *The Spectator* and the *Daily Telegraph*), recalled that 'Two of the Nickys used to invite me to hearty and delicious teas (evangelicals love buns and crumpets) and talk to me about Jesus, sometimes playing me tapes of sermons by prominent preachers.'[60] A few days after his conversion, Gumbel attended a house party where he saw a young acquaintance, 19-year-old Pippa Hislop, dancing and approached her with the words, 'You look awful. You really need Jesus.' If this was intended to convince her of her need of the Christian gospel, it backfired spectacularly, and she thought he had 'gone mad'. At the next party, he went armed with numerous tracts and a New Testament. He invited 17-year-old Mary Rose Chichester (a baronet's daughter) to dance but it proved difficult when weighed down by so much literature, so they sat together and Gumbel soon brought the subject round to Christianity. For every question she asked, he produced a tract from one of his pockets. The next day, on a boat to France, Chichester was reading one of these tracts when suddenly she understood the message of Jesus and turning to a friend said, 'I have just become a Christian.' In the Alpha course, Gumbel used these anecdotes of his early enthusiasm as examples of insensitive evangelism. He came to realise that there were more winsome ways to share the Christian message, and that being passion-ate about evangelism did not mean charging around 'like a bull in a china shop'.[61]

Some weeks after her house party encounter with Gumbel, Pippa Hislop was converted independently of him. Born in Germany, the daughter of a colonel in the Royal Artillery, she was educated at an Anglican convent boarding school in East Grinstead with obligatory chapel twice a day, but had no real concept of relationship with Jesus. After college and secretarial training, she moved to Kensington and worked for an estate agent, though life mostly revolved around parties. She felt 'aimless and lost', but when invited to the Kitchen (newly launched in spring 1974) was struck by its friendliness. She was intrigued by the Christians who ran the Kitchen and conversations often turned to questions of faith. One day Mickie Calthorpe sat down with Hislop, opened the Bible and read John 10:10 ('I have come that they may have life, and have it abundantly'). The moment Calthorpe read that verse, it 'shot off the page' for Hislop. She went back to her shared flat, knelt down, and committed her life to Jesus.[62]

The first person that Gumbel himself led to Christ, in September 1974, was 20-year-old Henry Montgomery (grandson of the Second World War hero Field Marshal Montgomery) who had been recuper-ating from glandular fever at Lillestrøm, near Oslo, at the home of his mother and stepfather. Gumbel was also in Norway, for a conference led by Bible smuggler Brother Andrew, and was encouraged by Montgomery's sister (a friend in Cambridge) to contact him. Montgomery was very unenthusiastic about hosting Gumbel and decided to test his mettle by hiking him through the Norwegian mountains. For three days they trekked across the beautiful but wild terrain of Rondane National Park, clambering over rocks and boulders and discussing the meaning of life. Montgomery was especially impressed by Gumbel's integrity and 'sense of purpose'. On the three-hour return journey to Lillestrøm, sitting in a railway carriage by themselves, Gumbel led Montgomery in a prayer of repentance and commitment to Christ, a life-transforming decision.[63] Gumbel later wrote: 'There is no greater privilege and no greater joy than enabling someone to find out about Jesus Christ.'[64]

Another new believer in this wide network of friends was Ken Costa, who arrived in Cambridge from Johannesburg in October 1974, aged 25, as a graduate law student at Queens' College. Costa was a South African of Lebanese descent, raised on his family farm in the Transvaal. He attended a Roman Catholic boarding school in Pretoria, but as an undergraduate at Witwatersrand University he turned to Marxism through the writings of atheist philosopher Erich Fromm. With a 'burning passion for justice', and as president of the Witwatersrand student council, Costa threw himself into anti-apartheid agitation. Friends and fellow activists were placed under house arrest or imprisoned, and one of them, Ahmed Timol, was murdered in police custody in Johannesburg in 1971.[65] Costa grew hostile to all religion through witnessing 'the interlinking of the horrors of apartheid and warped theology' whereby conservative churches in South Africa often supported the Nationalist government.[66] As a young Marxist, he believed that justice would be established 'by the struggle of the people' and that salvation meant 'the reform of social structures'. Christianity, he declared, was 'for emotional cripples and I was not one'.[67] However, soon after his arrival in Cambridge, Costa 'embraced the faith' after reading through Mark's Gospel one evening, attracted to the character and claims of Jesus Christ.[68] Another new Cambridge student in October 1974 was Justin Welby (later Archbishop of Canterbury), a year behind Gumbel and Lee at Trinity College. Baptised at HTB as an infant, Welby like Gumbel had been raised in Kensington and educated at Eton. At the start of his second year as an undergraduate, he too committed his life to Christ, aged 19, through the witness of friends in the CICCU.[69]

The worlds of Cambridge and Kensington were closely intertwined. In Cambridge, the new converts were schooled in conservative evangelicalism through the CICCU and the Round Church. They volunteered as helpers at Scripture Union house parties in the Dorset village of Iwerne Minster, known as 'Bash camps' after their originator, Anglican clergyman E. J. H. Nash (nicknamed 'Bash').[70] The camp emphasis was upon Bible teaching, evangelism and the training of young leaders. Nash's strategy was to evangelise the elite public schools, knowing that they would supply many of Britain's future leaders, and he had a 'major impact' on Gumbel's life.[71] In Kensington, St Paul's, Onslow Square, offered similar teaching within a conservative evangelical framework.

However, at the Kitchen, where many of the Cambridge converts congregated during the vacations, renewal was breaking forth. It was there in summer 1974 that Gumbel asked friends to pray for him to be filled with the Holy Spirit and to receive the gift of tongues. He had previously been taught that 'the gifts of the Spirit had gone out with the apostolic age', but changed his mind when he witnessed the 'new radiance' of those filled with the Spirit.[72] This new spiritual experience had direct consequences for Gumbel's urgency in evangelism, at a deep emotional level, as he recalled:

> When I became a Christian I remember being convinced in my mind that Jesus was alive. After experiencing the power of the Holy Spirit this knowledge dropped from my head down to my heart as well. He gave me a deep inner certainty that Christianity was true and filled me with joy. A few days later I found myself weeping as I realised that if it was true this had implications for those people I knew and loved who were not following Jesus.[73]

Eager to experience more of the Holy Spirit's ministry, Gumbel, Lee and Costa occasionally attended St Matthew's Church in Cambridge, where renewal was pioneered in the 1970s under vicar Sidney Sims.[74] In Kensington, Sandy and Annette Millar provided a similar focal point when they returned in 1976 from Durham. Millar, a natural evangelist, was appointed curate at HTB, aged 36, and soon gathered around him a circle of young people seeking renewal. He and Annette started a Bible study group in their home, where 18-year-old Caroline Eaton, a stockbroker's daughter, was the first to commit her life to Christ in September 1976, shortly before beginning her Cambridge degree. At the Millars' request, Justin Welby promised to look after Caroline at university and within a few months they were dating, and later married.[75] Meanwhile, many of the Cambridge graduates settled in London, looking to make their mark in secular professions – Nicky Gumbel (who married Pippa Hislop) in law, Nicky Lee (who married Sila Callander) in teaching, and Ken Costa in investment banking. They were all strongly attracted by Sandy Millar's ministry and gravitated into his orbit.

New Beginnings

Despite some signs of renewal and growth, both HTB and St Paul's, Onslow Square, were in serious financial difficulties. With a steadily declining, elderly congregation, HTB was 'but a shadow of our former selves'.[76] It claimed an electoral roll of 365 (only 36 of whom lived in the parish), but on Sundays there were only 80 at the main morning service and 10 in the evening, in a building that could seat 1,200.[77] For several years it had been running at a deficit. HTB's total income in 1975 was just £14,000, outpaced by expenditure, and it had exhausted all its reserves.[78] St Paul's was younger and healthier, but its building was in poor repair – the stonework was decaying, the walls were permanently damp, the plaster had perished, there was dry rot in the roof timbers, the chancel arch was cracked, the electrical wiring and heating system were defunct, and the organ needed a complete overhaul.[79] These repairs would cost £80,000 but even then, vicar Raymond Turvey mourned, 'we would only have restored an archaic building which is totally unsuited for the present and future needs of a comparatively small Christian fellowship'.[80] St Paul's could seat 1,600, but there were only 150 attenders on Sunday mornings and 120 in the evenings. As the Bishop of Kensington provocatively reminded them, they often worshipped with 1,500 empty seats.[81] Turvey also doubted whether it was morally right to spend 'vast sums of money to prop up a decaying building in the face of all the crying needs of the Third World'.[82] An alternative proposal was to demolish the church (apart from the tower and spire) and replace it with luxury flats and a much smaller worship space, though this alarmed some older members. One complained that Onslow Square residents would 'deplore the pulling down of the building, and its replacement with some concrete horror'.[83] They sought help from the Victorian Society and Sir John Betjeman, among others, to save the church from the bulldozers.[84]

Both HTB and St Paul's therefore faced a troubled future. By coincidence, the Bishop of Kensington was approached – on the same day, within half an hour of each other – by both John Morris, announcing his retirement from HTB, and Raymond Turvey, lamenting that the St Paul's building was no longer viable.[85] The bishop himself was under pressure from the Church of England's new deployment strategy (the so-called 'Sheffield quota'), which required London diocese to reduce its full-time clergy from 752 in 1973 to 567 by 1980, a drop of almost a quarter.[86] London's mission strategy for the 1980s, in the face of drastic decline across the whole Church of England, was fewer church buildings and fewer (but better paid) clergy. Thus a merger between HTB and St Paul's solved three dilemmas at one stroke. Rather than two vicars, each with two curates, there would now be only one vicar with three curates, combined on the HTB site. St Paul's would gain a structurally sound building and HTB would receive an injection of enthusiastic young people.

Morris retired in November 1975 and the two parishes were gradually integrated under Turvey's leadership. It was a marriage of convenience and the union was stressful. Turvey was left feeling 'schizophrenic' when trying to hold together the formality and dignity of HTB with the 'informal friendliness' of St Paul's.[87] He likened it to dragging a mule forward with one hand, while attempting to restrain an impatient horse with the other (Psalm 32:9).[88] 'Let's face it,' Turvey confessed, 'both churches are obviously frightened that union will present a threat to their established and traditional way of worship.'[89] To begin with, the services at HTB remained unchanged, and incomers from St Paul's struggled with the older language of the 1662 *Book of Common Prayer* and the amount of chanting at matins. As a concession to the influx of young people, HTB agreed to start offering coffee after the service, not only sherry.[90] On Sunday evenings, greater informality and innovation was permitted, with occasional contributions from Cloud alongside the organ, and the introduction of dance and drama.[91]

Gradually the culture of HTB began to change. It seemed like the dawn of a new day. Preaching in 1976, Turvey proclaimed that the Church of England for too many decades had excused its 'landslide of decline' with mottos like 'quality not quantity' and 'small is beautiful'. He urged:

> These are half truths. Of course small can be beautiful, but the great can be magnificent. Heaven rejoices over one sinner repenting, but how much more when there are 'multitudes, multitudes in the valley of decision'. Scripture IS interested in numbers . . . When the Holy Spirit is at work it is growth and expansion all the time.[92]

The whole British nation in the mid-1970s was 'plunging into moral and economic chaos', a sign of divine judgement, Turvey declared, but if the Church turned back in repentance then God would open 'the floodgates of blessing':

> I believe the Holy Spirit of God is moving throughout our land in a new way: some churches are empty, but many are full. Some, like ours, are half-way. A pessimist would say it is half empty; those with faith know that it's half full . . . I feel sure that God is going to do great things for us during the next few years . . . I cannot believe that God intends the church which He has placed so strategically in the West End and which He has blessed so greatly in the past, to wither away into obscurity. There can only be one way ahead and that is forward. We must plan for advance and growth.[93]

In this context of hopeful new beginnings, Alpha was born. In the summer of 1977, Turvey was approached by a younger member of the congregation, Tricia Algeo, a 29-year-old trainee solicitor, with a proposal for a new discipleship course. She noticed that people were regularly becoming Christians through the ministry of HTB and needed nurture. Daughter of Sir Arthur Algeo (a prominent Ulster businessman, well known in farming and public affairs), she had been raised in Northern Ireland among the Reformed Presbyterians, a conservative denomination with roots in the Scottish Covenanters. Following a period of intense doubt, after reading Miguel de Unamuno's novella *San Manuel Bueno, Mártir* (1931) about a Spanish priest who lost his faith, Algeo had recommitted her life to Christ as a student at the University of St Andrews. On arrival in London in 1969, she joined St Paul's, Onslow Square, and Annette Fisher's Bible study group connected to the Stewards' Trust. Algeo worked from 1971 to 1974 as a 'travelling secretary' for the Inter-Varsity Fellowship supporting the Christian Unions across 19 colleges of London University and at Brunel, City, Reading, and Sussex universities. She then spent a year in Brussels with the Billy Graham Evangelistic Association working on the programme for *Eurofest '75*, a major evangelistic campaign and international youth congress. Therefore, Algeo had a particular concern for evangelism and the discipleship of young converts.[94]

Turvey liked the idea of an HTB discipleship course and gave responsibility to his newest curate, Charles Marnham, ordained in June 1977, aged 26. Marnham, the son of a distinguished barrister and QC, had read law at Jesus College, Cambridge, where he committed his life to Christ in January 1971 after reading John Stott's *Basic Christianity* (1958) and working through a six-week Bible study on the cross with Mark Ruston, vicar of the Round Church. The revolutionary moment for Marnham was to realise that the death of Jesus for the sins of the world was not just a theological truth but applied to him individually, and that he could enjoy 'a personal relationship with Jesus'.[95] After graduation he joined St Paul's, Onslow Square, and started training as a solicitor at the College of Law, but he soon changed track to ordination, joining the same cohort as Sandy Millar at Cranmer Hall, Durham, in 1974.

Both Algeo and Marnham were well equipped to lead a group for new Christians – both had experienced the radical difference between a church upbringing and personal Christian faith; both could testify to a turning point of conversion or recommitment at university, in the midst of wrestling over doubts or questions; and both had benefitted from nurture by older mentors. As they met over a long breakfast to discuss the idea, Algeo proposed the name 'Alpha' to symbolise new beginnings. It also had special biblical resonance in the Book of Revelation as one of the titles of Christ, the 'Alpha and Omega' who makes 'all things new' (Revelation 21:5, 22:13). Together they launched Alpha in November 1977, running over six Thursday evenings in Marnham's flat above the HTB church hall, with about six attenders at the first course. Algeo was an experienced speaker through her ministry with the Inter-Varsity Fellowship, so she and Marnham shared the talks between them, with occasional help in succeeding terms from other lay members of the congregation.

The first programme announced Alpha as 'a course on Christian foundations . . . designed to help those who want to go on in the Christian life', with six sessions:

1. Assurance and spiritual warfare
2. How should we read the Bible and why pray?
3. God the Father
4. The person and work of Jesus Christ
5. The person and work of the Holy Spirit
6. What is a *Christian* lifestyle?[96]

The heart of the course was clearly Trinitarian, with an emphasis on practical and distinctive Christian living. Supper was provided beforehand, because young professionals from HTB often arrived straight from work without time to eat. By summer 1978, each evening was reshaped as a succinct question:

1. What is God like?
2. Who is Man?
3. What did Jesus do?
4. Who needs the Spirit?
5. Why pray, read the Bible or go to Church?
6. Tricky questions.[97]

From his own searching for Christian faith in Cambridge and his one-to-one Bible studies with Ruston, Marnham knew the benefit of being allowed to ask questions. Therefore, he instituted a rule at

Alpha that all questions were welcome, no matter how difficult or apparently foolish. The course was advertised as well suited to those who 'want to start from scratch in re-thinking their Christian faith'.[98]

By 1980 the Alpha programme had been honed further, now 'designed to help those who have just begun the Christian life':

1. How can I be sure?
2. What did Jesus do?
3. What is God like?
4. Who needs the Spirit?
5. How can I know Christ better?
6. Why go to Church?[99]

The opening session on Christian assurance was especially appropriate for new converts, who may have prayed a prayer of personal commitment to Christ and were now trying to make sense of their experience or wondering whether anything had really changed after all. The programme was also now more explicitly Christocentric, beginning with the person of Jesus before discussion of God's character more broadly, and emphasising that the purpose of prayer and Bible reading was to 'know Christ better'. However, Algeo and Marnham quickly discovered that, although some who came on Alpha were new Christians, others were not yet Christians, and others perhaps were simply confused. It was not possible to draw clear lines between them and Alpha needed to cater for all these spiritual enquirers. The boundary between discipleship and evangelism was blurred from the beginning.

Soon the course began to grow and divided into smaller discussion groups after the talk, squeezed into the sitting room, the study, and two bedrooms of Marnham's flat. Marnham's lodger in 1979 returned one evening to find he could not use the bathroom because there was an Alpha small group meeting there too.[100] There were also some early Alpha romances, including between Algeo and Marnham, who were dating by January 1978 and married at HTB in December 1979. Alpha's global significance could not, of course, be seen at the time, but it was part of the fruit of spiritual renewal beginning to sweep through the congregation. The Marnhams later spoke of 'the privilege of planting the acorn'.[101]

Supper Party Evangelism

The year 1979 was the 150th anniversary of the founding of HTB in 1829, so was dedicated as a year of celebrations and intentional evangelism, seeking to use the opportunity 'to proclaim the Gospel of Jesus Christ' to friends and neighbours. There was an art exhibition, a festival of flowers and music, lunches and concerts (including with Cliff Richard), culminating in a two-week parish mission in October 1979.[102] Turvey initially invited the renowned evangelist David Watson (vicar of St Michael le Belfrey in York) to lead the mission, but he declined because he would only lead an area-wide mission, not a local parish one.[103] Instead the missioner was John Collins (vicar of Canford Magna in Dorset, formerly of Gillingham), with his wife Diana.

The initiative was called Step Forward and was designed around evening supper parties, a familiar aspect of Kensington social life. Members of the congregation invited their friends to a meal, at which there would be an explanation of the Christian faith and one or two Christian testimonies. The emphasis was upon informality, friendship, food, and conversations about Christianity in a relaxed environment – key components of what would later become the Alpha ethos. Turvey called it 'low-key evangelism'.[104] He exhorted his congregation:

> Our aim is to make Christ known. We are ambassadors for Christ. If you feel diffident remember that what Jesus said to his disciples he says to us today: 'You shall receive power after the Holy Spirit is come upon you and you shall be my witnesses even unto the ends of the earth.' So may I urge you to open your life fully to the power of God so that he can master you and use you. Remember he has promised to give his Holy Spirit to you if you will but have the courage to ask him.[105]

There were 105 supper parties during the fortnight and the fruit of the mission was seen in a fresh crop of new Christians.[106] About 40 people went forward at the final service when Collins invited them to respond to the gospel.[107] Turvey celebrated: 'Many people have taken the great step forward of personal commitment to Jesus Christ as their redeemer and master and are already experiencing a new sense of his presence and his power in their lives.'[108] For these new converts, Alpha was already up and running. Those who had not yet made a profession of faith, but wanted to discover more, were directed instead to a new discussion group called 'Enquirers'.[109]

Turvey's ambition was for evangelistic outreach to become a natural part of HTB's life, embedded within its DNA. Step Forward proved an essential part of that reorientation, and taught members of the congregation 'to talk simply and personally about our faith'.[110] It was followed in May 1980 by an area-wide mission called To London with Love, dubbed a 'festival of praise', led by David Watson. Three evenings in Chelsea Town Hall were followed by three evenings in the Royal Albert Hall, including music from the All Souls Orchestra, drama from Riding Lights theatre company, and evangelistic appeals. It was an ecumenical initiative sponsored by the Chelsea Council of Churches, encompassing many denominations including Anglicans, Roman Catholics, Methodists and Moravians, but HTB took the lead. The threefold aims of the festival, Watson explained, were renewal of local church life, unity among Christians, and evangelism to those outside the church – 'three inseparable strands of Christian mission'. It was also designed to help Christians talk about their faith. 'Would you be able to tell a friend from the Bible how he or she could find Christ for themselves?' asked the HTB magazine.[111] The congregation were trained in personal evangelism and encouraged to arrange more supper parties in their homes, as well as to invite their friends to Watson's large-scale events. Mission advertising included posters displayed at nearby London Underground stations – a strategy adopted by Alpha two decades later.[112]

Peregrine Worsthorne of the *Sunday Telegraph* was amazed to see the Royal Albert Hall (capacity 5,000) packed with young people, 'a great milling throng', though without 'razzamatazz': 'Truth to tell, Mr Watson is something rather special – a spellbinder without histrionic tricks, simply a conventional clergyman with a gift for preaching.' With sharp political edge, Worsthorne wondered whether the 1980s would witness a revival of orthodox Christianity, hand in hand with Thatcherism, in place of failed 'secular panaceas' like socialism, materialism, hedonism, liberalism and progress. He viewed Watson's mission as a foretaste of this coming evangelical revival:

> What made him extraordinary was his naturalness; his gift for talking about God as if he did not feel the need to put on a special ecclesiastical voice; nor to associate God with fashionable good causes. Unlike so much that passes for Christian teaching today there was no mention of the Third World, unemployment, racial discrimination, poverty, sexual equality or any other contemporary 'burning issue'. The audience were not asked to enlist in some collective crusade against this or that social injustice; merely to open their hearts and minds to the grace of Jesus Christ, by which act they would attain eternal life. Forget about putting the world to rights; concentrate instead on personal salvation. So old-fashioned, even archaic, is this message that it came across like a flash of revelation, filling the Albert Hall with a dazzling radiance.[113]

To London with Love was deemed a great success. Approximately 18,000 people attended the various events at HTB, Chelsea Town Hall and the Royal Albert Hall.[114] About 150 people responded to the evangelistic appeals and went forward to be 'counselled' during the mission.[115]

There was a growing sense of excitement about what lay ahead for HTB. Sandy Millar discerned that the Holy Spirit was beginning to renew the congregation, bringing 'a new freedom, a new love, a new joy and a new power', and was opening up 'wholly new and largely unexplored territory both in our worship of God and in our ministry to others'.[116] At the annual church weekend at Ashburnham Place in Sussex, in February 1978, Lucie Bell (a missionary in Burundi) offered a prophetic picture that HTB would become 'a jewel in Knightsbridge'.[117] As the 1980s dawned, this prophecy was remembered as a promise from God that 'very special' days lay ahead.[118]

Growing God's Family

In July 1980, Raymond Turvey was forced to take early retirement, on doctor's orders, suffering from debilitating arthritis in his neck.[119] This presented a crucial moment for the future direction of HTB. Some older members of the congregation hoped the next vicar would re-establish HTB's Anglican choral tradition. Others wanted a preacher in the classic evangelical mould of John Stott and Dick Lucas, while still others longed for the early signs of renewal to be fanned into flame. As a united benefice, the appointment lay jointly in the hands of the Bishop of London (patron of HTB) and the Church Pastoral Aid Society (patron of St Paul's, Onslow Square). The two churchwardens, Charlie Colchester and David Orton, drafted a careful statement of needs to guide the patrons. The next vicar must be 'a man of vision and proven leadership', with the gifts to oversee a rapidly growing congregation. He must accept the final authority of the Bible in all matters of teaching and conduct. He must be able to hold together the breadth of HTB's diverse liturgical traditions, while also being sufficiently 'socially flexible' to minister among young professionals and established Kensington residents. Most importantly – in a phrase hotly debated by the PCC – he must be 'a conservative evangelical personally committed to and experienced in leadership within the charismatic movement'.[120] Here for the first time was an explicit merging of two streams within modern evangelicalism – 'conservative' and 'charismatic'. It was the reference to charismatic renewal that worried some, but the PCC eventually agreed it, and it proved critical for HTB's future trajectory.[121]

John Collins, fresh from the Step Forward mission, was the ideal candidate. Aged 55, he was closely connected with the post-war evangelical resurgence in the Church of England. His conservative credentials were impeccable – nurtured by the Bash camps, president of the CICCU, curate from 1951 to 1957 under John Stott at All Souls, Langham Place. Collins had strong gifts in evangelism – among the many he led to Christian faith were David Sheppard (later Bishop of Liverpool) and David Watson.[122] And yet Collins had also eagerly embraced renewal during the 1960s and 1970s, as vicar in Gillingham and Canford Magna.[123] He was known to be an excellent trainer of leaders and a succession of his curates – David MacInnes, David Watson and John Mumford – themselves became prominent in charismatic evangelism and church growth. Sandy Millar called Collins the 'man who probably knows more about renewal than anyone else' in Anglican circles.[124] The HTB churchwardens were determined that Collins should be appointed and resisted all attempts by the patrons to nominate other people. Informal prayer meetings at HTB beseeched God to sovereignly overrule the patrons' plans, and Charlie Colchester rejoiced with the PCC that their prayers for the negotiations were being 'answered in a remarkable way'.[125] Soon afterwards, Collins's appointment was announced, and he was inducted in September 1980. According to one rumour, the Bishop of London only agreed to the nomination because he mistakenly assumed that the clergyman in question was the more famous Canon John Collins of St Paul's Cathedral, a radical clergyman, pacifist and political campaigner.

By the early 1980s, HTB was 'growing and expanding in every direction'.[126] Growth should be the experience of every Christian community, Collins insisted, even in modern secular Britain. 'God multiplies', he taught; 'God wants his family to grow.'[127] Like many city-centre churches, there was a constant turnover of HTB's younger and highly mobile membership, which created an expectation of regular renewal and a constant stream of new faces and new ideas. This included a growing number of university students from nearby institutions such as Imperial College and the Royal College of Music, though they only stayed for three years before dispersing across the country. Young married couples living in central London often moved away from HTB when the arrival of children and high property prices drove them out into the suburbs or the countryside in search of larger affordable homes. Yet, despite this constant cycle, HTB's base membership continued to expand. In 1980 there were 41 Bible study groups, rising to 69 by 1983 when the electoral roll topped 800 for the first time.[128] There was now such a predominance of young people that some began to worry whether HTB was still able to meet the needs of the over-40s.[129]

One of the drivers for growth was Collins's insistence upon a regular pattern of evangelism as integral to HTB's life – not modelled only by the clergy, but by every member of the congregation. Supper parties remained a key component of that strategy. Building on the Step Forward mission, there was another fortnight of focused supper-party evangelism in November and December 1981 under the banner 'Holy Trinity at Home'. Congregation members were encouraged to arrange a meal for their friends at which someone would give a brief talk about the Christian faith. As Collins explained: 'All of us have charming friends who would be unlikely to respond to an invitation to church; but, mellowed by a delicious meal, they might well be prepared to listen to a short and, we hope, attractive presentation of Christianity.' This would hopefully pave the way for further conversations on spiritual topics and perhaps an invitation to an evangelistic 'guest service' at HTB.[130] The pattern was repeated in November 1982, with a team of 50 members of the congregation trained as supper-party speakers. 'How can I introduce my friends to the blessings of God's kingdom?' asked Collins. There were of course many possible methods, he explained, but 'there is no doubt that a carefully prepared supper party is particularly suitable for this area of London'.[131]

Collins also wanted HTB to help resource other parishes for mission, so that growth would be multiplied across the Church of England. A new training course called *Lighthouse* was introduced in 1980, led by curate Patrick Whitworth (who had previously been David Watson's curate in York), to provide both a grounding in biblical doctrine and practical skills in evangelism and public speaking.[132] But this training was not restricted to the classroom. Course members all took part in short parish missions and teams were regularly sent out from HTB. Collins saw this as one of the most effective methods to combine discipleship and evangelism, modelled on the way Jesus trained the apostles.[133] This ministry was coordinated with Watson's city-wide festivals. HTB mission teams went to the same locations as Watson, as preparation or follow-up to the main event, helping local churches. Watson returned to the Royal Albert Hall for a 'Festival of Christ' in May 1982, hosted jointly by the four largest Anglican evangelical congregations in central London – HTB; All Souls, Langham Place; St Helen's, Bishopsgate; and St Michael's, Chester Square.[134] But Collins's ambition was that HTB would send out 20 mission teams a year and thus make a significant contribution to evangelism and renewal across the whole nation.[135] 'We dare to believe', he proclaimed, 'that God wants us to achieve great things for him.'[136]

When Watson decided to move his base of international operations from York to London, he naturally chose to join HTB, warmly welcomed by his old friend and mentor Collins. He was licensed as a 'public preacher' in London diocese in September 1982, attached to HTB, though not on the staff. However, there was no time for this promising relationship to develop and it ended almost as soon as it began. In January 1983, aged 49, Watson was diagnosed with inoperable cancer. He and his family found it difficult to settle at HTB, and during a brief period of remission he concluded that God was calling him 'to a change of direction', not attached to any one particular church, so the formal link was ended.[137] Watson's death in February 1984 robbed the Church of England of one of its greatest twentieth-century evangelists. It was thus to be another renewalist pioneer and church planter who decisively shaped HTB's theological trajectory during the 1980s: Watson's Californian friend, John Wimber.

2

Californian Catalyst

WHEN SANDY MILLAR was asked in the early 2000s to name the three outside influences that had most shaped the ethos of HTB, he replied, 'John Wimber, John Wimber and John Wimber.'[1] Elsewhere he declared that the churches in Britain owed more to Wimber than to any single man since John Wesley.[2] Wimber – a Californian musician, pastor, evangelist and church planter, born in rural Missouri – pioneered the rapid global expansion of the Vineyard network throughout the 1980s and early 1990s. Best known for his emphasis on miraculous 'signs and wonders' as a tool for church growth, he was a leading proponent of the so-called 'Third Wave' of renewal that swept through the churches in the last quarter of the twentieth century. Wimber planted a congregation in 1977 near Los Angeles, associated with the Calvary Chapels and the Jesus People movement, but in 1982 it went independent as 'Vineyard' and became the nucleus for a new denomination.

When David Watson visited California on a lecture tour in 1980 he was deeply impressed by his encounter with the Vineyard, especially 'the indisputable evidence of God's power to heal, coupled with a lot of biblical wisdom and human sanity'.[3] The following year, in June 1981, Wimber was invited to England with a team of young volunteers for ministry at St Michael le Belfrey, York, and St Andrew's, Chorleywood. These early transatlantic engagements were memorable and sometimes dramatic – at Chorleywood, for example, there was 'holy chaos' as many fell down in the pews when hippy evangelist and Jesus People veteran Lonnie Frisbee (part of Wimber's team) invoked the Holy Spirit.[4] Wimber returned the following summer for similar introductions to HTB and to a handful of Baptist churches in Lancashire and London. Nigel Wright (pastor of Ansdell Baptist Church, Lytham

St Anne's) described Wimber's visit on 19 June 1982 as the occasion when 'the experience of Pentecost became a contemporary reality' for his congregation, which had already embraced renewal 'but this was like going into overdrive'. After a dull lecture by Wimber on the benefits of 'power evangelism' as contrasted with 'programme evangelism', Wright began to wonder what the fuss was about:

> But then it happened. After lunch John cut short his lecture proclaiming that it was time to have some fun. He had even brought along his personal funmaker in the guise of an aging hippy called Lonnie Frisbee. Lonnie encouraged us to sing 'Majesty' twice and after praying simply invited the Holy Spirit to come. What then happened is exceedingly difficult to describe. Within seconds the inside of our attractive, Edwardian Baptist chapel was transformed into something resembling a battlefield. Holy carnage reigned. Not that I saw much of it because by this time I was flat on my back shaking under the power of the Holy Spirit and calling upon the name of the Lord as I had never done before. Half the church was doing something similar.[5]

Many of the congregation were 'trembling and shaking, speaking in tongues, calling on the Lord, prophesying', and some were 'flapping up and down like fish upon the floor'.[6] Men were 'reeling round as though they were drunk'.[7]

Ten days later, Wimber and his team of about 20 Californians arrived at HTB for two evenings of teaching and ministry, on Monday and Tuesday, 28 and 29 June 1982.[8] He came strongly recommended to John Collins by David Watson. Renewal was already gathering pace at HTB under Collins's leadership, and the previous year, for example, he had encouraged the congregation to read about the miracles in the New Testament and say to themselves, 'This could happen to me.'[9] Talks on healing were nothing new, promoted for many years at HTB through the Divine Healing Mission. Nevertheless, the encounter with Wimber was transformative, opening new vistas of possibility, and quickly became part of HTB folklore. The dramatic events became globally famous via the Alpha videos on 'Does God heal today?', and were often recounted by Nicky Gumbel and Sandy Millar to full comic effect.

On the first evening, HTB's lay pastors and Bible study leaders gathered in the church's crypt, in a room called 'The Spring'. The space had recently been redesigned by Mickie Calthorpe as a 'little amphitheatre' with banked seating, ideal for smaller gatherings, named 'The Spring' in the hope it would be 'a constant hidden source of refreshment and strength to the church above'.[10] The room was full, with 70 or 80 people, and Wimber began with a short, unexceptional talk on healing. But then he surprised everyone by announcing that they would 'do some'. Many at HTB were already familiar with the theory – as Millar quipped, 'I've got an attic full of notes on talks on healing' – but they had seldom been asked to put it into practice in a seminar context.[11] This was Wimber's standard *modus operandi*. His popular lectures on 'signs, wonders and church growth' at Fuller Theological Seminary in California were always followed by an optional 'clinic' where students put the lessons into practice, to the consternation of the resident academics.[12] In The Spring at HTB, Wimber read out a dozen prophetic 'words of knowledge' that had been given to his Californian team, concerning miscellaneous illnesses and injuries, and invited people to respond. One was for an injured elbow, another for a damaged back. But there was an awkward and embarrassed silence when he offered a word of knowledge for 'a barren woman' who was trying to conceive. That subject might have been acceptable in laid-back California, but in Kensington it was strictly taboo. Unexpectedly, 25-year-old Sarah Wright stepped forward and said, 'I think that must be me.' Her husband, 28-year-old Edward Wright (a chartered surveyor), was as surprised as anyone. They had been married for only three years, and had not yet spoken together about the difficulties of conception, though Sarah had privately begun to worry there might be a problem.[13] Wimber's prayer was simple but startlingly anatomical, naming her fallopian tubes. He laid a hand on Sarah's head and commanded healing in the name of Jesus. In retrospect, Millar believed that this encounter was a turning point for HTB: 'I think that was the moment when our church began to grow up. Suddenly it became possible for a beautiful woman in a beautiful church in a beautiful setting to say, in front of all her friends, "All is not well and I would love your help. Please pray for me."'[14] Nine months later, in March 1983, the Wrights celebrated the birth of a baby boy, the first of five children.

Although many HTB lay leaders experienced increasing faith in God's miraculous power to heal, others were perturbed by the events in The Spring. The prayers of Frisbee were especially alarming, leading to physical manifestations such as shaking, crying and hyperventilating.[15] Nicky Gumbel went home 'deeply cynical' about what he had witnessed. On the following evening, 250 people crowded into Church House (HTB's church hall) to hear Wimber. Nicky and Pippa Gumbel arrived late and the only available seats were in the front row. After a day in court as a barrister, Gumbel was wearing a three-piece pinstripe suit and stiff white collar, and looked, in his own words, 'very pompous'. The culture clash with the casual style of the Californians was palpable. Again there were words of knowledge, including for ten people with athlete's foot. Nine stood, but an embarrassed Gumbel, who was also suffering from the ailment, resisted the call and remained firmly seated until Pippa dug him in the ribs. When a member of Wimber's team approached to offer prayer for healing, Gumbel refused and instead asked for prayer, more generically, 'for the power of the Holy Spirit in my life'.[16] Power was a central theme in Wimber's teaching, as expressed in his bestselling books *Power Evangelism* (1985) and *Power Healing* (1986), and was a major renewal motif.[17] So the American volunteer prayed a simple petition for power. Gumbel recalled: 'What I experienced was like ten thousand volts going through my body. And every time he prayed his prayer, "More power, Lord", the voltage was turned up and eventually I was saying, "*No more power.*"' A form of shouting match ensued between them. Gumbel was oblivious to anything happening around him and the noise was so disruptive that Wimber instructed, 'Take him out.' Overcome by these physical manifestations, Gumbel was carried out through the French windows of Church House into the churchyard. Lest anyone should worry about what was happening, Wimber announced as Gumbel was removed: 'God's giving him the gift of evangelism.'[18]

Gumbel had been called to the bar in July 1977, aged 22 – following the career path mapped out for him by his parents – but although he enjoyed the work, he felt increasingly called instead to ordination.

His father's death in January 1981 released him to consider the possibility more seriously. On at least 15 occasions, as Gumbel read the Bible, he sensed God speaking to him about a change in direction, through texts such as 'How can they believe in the one of whom they have not heard? And how can they hear without someone preaching to them?' (Romans 10:14).[19] What particularly excited him about ordination was its potential for evangelism.[20] Millar had been through an identical dilemma a few years earlier and advised Gumbel to imagine himself towards the end of his career as a QC or high court judge. Would he be satisfied with how he had spent his life?[21] Gumbel's 'power encounter' during the Vineyard visit in June 1982, and Wimber's declaration that he was being specially anointed for evangelism, were strong confirmation of this call to pursue ordination. The following year the Gumbels left HTB for theological college.

Wimber's visit had 'a profound effect' on many at HTB, Collins observed. Those who heard the Californian, especially in The Spring, 'will never forget that evening. It seemed as if for an hour or two we were back in New Testament days watching our Lord's disciples at work.' Some had been physically healed and others, Collins continued, had

> launched out in faith and seen remarkable answers to their prayers. So the tide of faith is coming in. The goal which I and many others have pursued for the last twenty years seems much closer – that is to see a church so filled with the Spirit of God that all the beauty of Christ and all the power of Christ begins to emerge.[22]

It was the first of many visits by Wimber and other members of his rapidly growing Vineyard movement. He returned soon to HTB for a weekend of ministry in October 1982 (including preaching at the Sunday evening service), and often thereafter.[23] Wimber's early visits led, in Collins's words, to 'a surge of faith and love' across the congregation with 'extraordinary stories of people coming into God's kingdom, being healed, and being filled with the Holy Spirit'. Collins sat in the top back row at one of Wimber's meetings in The Spring, and was thus able to see the faces of those being 'touched by the

Spirit of God. There was a breath of heaven about them. It was beautiful to see, and I shall never forget it.'[24]

Eager to learn more, members of HTB travelled across the Atlantic in the opposite direction, to experience Vineyard in its original Californian context. In February 1983, John and Diana Collins attended the Presidential Prayer Breakfast in Washington DC where John Collins was seated next to David du Plessis, the Pentecostal ecumenist, 'who between mouthfuls of muffins and mushrooms regaled me with stories of the last few Popes'.[25] Next they flew to Los Angeles and spent time with the Vineyard congregations pastored by Wimber at Anaheim and John McClure at La Habra. Both were thriving churches with over 2,000 members, compared to which HTB was 'a mere minnow'.[26] Collins rejoiced in their ministry, in which the gifts of the Holy Spirit were 'so powerfully and effectively displayed', and found it 'thrilling' to witness miracles of healing.[27] That autumn, in September 1983, McClure was in London to teach seminars at HTB, and the following week Sandy Millar and Patrick Whitworth led a group of 25 from HTB to a Vineyard conference for international pastors in Palm Springs, California.[28] Among the party were Justin and Caroline Welby, who had recently re-joined HTB after returning to London from Paris.[29]

The Palm Springs event was held in the Sheraton Hotel in the Californian sunshine, complete with swimming pool and jacuzzi, a far cry from the damp and depressing conditions of most Christian conference centres in Britain. After enjoying Vineyard worship and ministry, the HTB pilgrims returned to Kensington with a new vision, 'deeply dissatisfied with "normal" church life as we had experienced it hitherto'. Millar liked to quote the old music-hall song from the 1920s, 'How ya gonna' keep 'em down on the farm, after they've seen Paree?', about American soldiers in the First World War who did not want to return to their old rural way of life after having their eyes opened to European culture in cities like Paris. This encapsulated the mood of the British visitors as they returned home from California. Their eyes had been opened to new possibilities.[30] Millar reckoned that by taking 25 people who now became vocal advocates for Vineyard principles, including many key lay leaders, HTB had saved seven years in its development.[31] He pointed especially to

Wimber's emphasis on intimacy with God and with fellow believers; informal worship; practical demonstration of 'signs and wonders'; generosity in resourcing other churches; ecumenical instinct; simplicity and lack of pretentiousness, without 'hype' or emotional pressure; and inclusion of every Christian in evangelism and prayer ministry without reliance on 'experts'. Vineyard provided an attractive and highly portable model of renewal that could be transplanted into a Church of England context and showed HTB a path to follow. For four years in a row Millar returned to California, where he 'tasted freedom' with the Vineyard, part of the constant transatlantic flow of charismatic personnel.[32] From 1984, Wimber also began a regular public conference ministry in Britain, influencing thousands within the old mainline denominations and establishing a platform for Vineyard's European expansion.[33]

It seemed to Collins that God was opening a 'wide door' for HTB's ministry. The congregations were growing, demand for prayer ministry was overwhelming (especially on Sunday evenings), and there was a notable change of attitude within the Anglican hierarchy of London diocese, who treated HTB with increasing goodwill instead of their usual cool ambivalence.[34] At this critical juncture in the church's life, Collins was determined to ensure these gains were not lost. Continuity of leadership was essential.[35] The Bishop of London had hoped to redeploy Millar elsewhere, proposing in 1981 that he become vicar of the village of Laleham near Staines, but Collins wanted to keep Millar at HTB.[36] Therefore, in September 1985, in a surprise move, Collins (aged 60) and Millar (aged 45) swapped places. Millar was inducted as the new vicar of HTB, and his former boss became one of his curates. This protected the line of succession for the next 20 years and Millar pushed ahead in embedding Wimber's renewalist principles deep within HTB's ethos.

London is Mine

HTB's strategic potential at the centre of one of the world's vibrant capital cities, and global transportation hubs, was increasingly evident. Sometimes this was emphasised by prophetic proclamation, like the prophecy announced in 1986 by Jeremy Jennings (HTB's pastoral director) concerning God's heart for London:

> London is mine, says the Lord. Where were you as it was prised out of my hand? My hand didn't open lightly or easily. But where were you, my people? It was like an oyster being opened with a knife, because I love the pearl within, and I want it back. Get on to your knees before me and don't let me rest until I have my pearl back in my hand where it belongs. Don't worry, because my power has not diminished and it is available today as it was in the past. So draw near to me and watch what I will do through you.[37]

This prophecy was widely publicised among the congregation. It was interpreted as a call to intercede for revival, and the need for fresh urgency in evangelism, since London belonged to God. Sometimes HTB's strategic location was highlighted in a more conventional manner via the pulpit. Vineyard pastor John McClure, preaching at HTB in 1991, spoke of the congregation's national significance:

> I want to call you to battle for Jesus Christ, I want to call you to a level of commitment to Jesus Christ beyond what you've known before. I believe this church is already a great church, and the intention of God is that it become a mighty church that shakes this city and profoundly affects this nation.[38]

Millar concurred. Echoing the prophet Ezekiel, he wrote in 1992 that across the United Kingdom there were many dead bones, but also some 'exhilarating signs of the beginning of new life'. He believed that HTB was called to take an active lead 'in the grand plan that God has for bringing thousands of people in this country to faith in the next few years. We are to prepare for revival!'[39] They must 'look for every possible way of bringing Jesus to every living person that is in some way within range of us'.[40] There were two main planks to HTB's revival strategy, in symbiotic relationship: church planting and Alpha.

The planting of new congregations was one of Wimber's key emphases. His friend and colleague in the church growth department at Fuller Theological Seminary, Professor C. Peter Wagner, famously asserted: 'Planting new churches is the most effective evangelistic methodology known under heaven.'[41] Millar likewise proclaimed that renewal and church planting were 'the way God has chosen, all over the world, to bring back life to his Church'. He lamented, however, that most Anglicans were oriented 'towards maintenance rather than mission' and had become 'keepers of an aquarium, rather than the fishers of men'.[42] The 1990s were hailed as 'the decade of evangelism', but Millar feared it would turn out to be 'the decade of delays'.[43] His own sense of urgency in evangelism was palpable. 'True Christian faith has never been able to stop taking opportunities to talk about Jesus!' he exclaimed.[44]

Some were beginning to advocate church planting across parish boundaries, and if necessary in defiance of the bishops. David Pytches (vicar of St Andrew's, Chorleywood, and founder of the New Wine movement) and his curate Brian Skinner had both witnessed the remarkable success of church planting as missionary bishops in South America. In 1992 they launched the Federation of Independent Anglican Churches to link together church plants operating without episcopal permission.[45] But the HTB policy, by contrast, was to work as closely as possible with diocesan authorities. This often required very patient negotiation and diplomacy, but had obvious benefits, not least potential access to numerous old church buildings that had fallen into a state of disrepair, with dwindling congregations, or had shut altogether. These buildings were a precious and untapped resource in the gift of the diocese.

HTB began planting in the mid-1980s, inspired by Wimber's example. Their first hope was to plant a new congregation south of the River Thames, in Southwark diocese, because many HTB members lived in the area around Balham and Clapham. They identified St Mark's, Battersea Rise, as an ideal location but the Bishop of Kingston resisted the idea and the Battersea clergy voted against it. John Collins observed in frustration that the focus of the whole Southwark diocese seemed to be upon implementation of the Church of England's 1985 *Faith in the City* report, a call to socio-political action, rather than upon evangelism and church planting.[46] So the first plant was instead north of the Thames, to St Barnabas, Kensington, where HTB sent 120 people in autumn 1985 led by curate and former barrister John Irvine (whose father, Sir Arthur Irvine, was a Labour MP and Solicitor General for England and Wales in Harold Wilson's government). At an embryonic stage the initiative was known as 'Barnabas Vineyard', seeking to embody Wimberite principles within Anglicanism.[47] The church plant to Battersea Rise eventually went ahead in 1987 with 50 people led by curate Paul Perkin, celebrated at HTB as 'a tremendous vindication of years of prayer and gentle persuasion'.[48]

HTB's third plant was closer to home, in its own parish. St Paul's, Onslow Square, had been declared 'redundant' in December 1978 and placed on the market by London diocese, but it was rescued from the developers at Millar's initiative and in March 1988 its 'redundant' status was officially revoked. 'We are on the verge of a great spiritual awakening', celebrated Millar. 'I hope redundant churches will be revived all over the country.'[49] Archdeacon Derek Hayward (general secretary of London diocese) attended the reopening, which he described as 'a very great occasion in the evangelical mould! Much shouting, cheering, hymn singing and so on – not really my idea of the C of E, but "by their fruits ye shall know them" and they certainly do pack the churches to the brim.'[50] Curate Nicky Lee led 200 members of HTB to St Paul's in 1990, which grew to 500 within two years.[51] The fourth plant was to another redundant church, St Stephen's, Westbourne Park, led by HTB curate Tom Gillum in 1994.[52] Meanwhile the plants themselves began to plant – from St Mark's to the Church of the Ascension in Balham, and from St Barnabas to the Oak Tree Anglican Fellowship in Acton (outside the parish system). 'HTB is to become a granny!' Millar rejoiced. 'How soon will it be before we're great-grannies?'[53]

In one sense, HTB itself had been re-planted in the mid-1970s by the influx of young, lively, new members from St Paul's, Onslow Square, led by Raymond Turvey. That formative history continued to shape its ethos two decades later. 'We were born out of planting and we live to plant,' Millar declared. It was part of HTB's 'genetic code'.[54] Although the process was very costly, in terms of giving away members, leaders and money, it proved an effective investment. Indeed, every time HTB gave away members to establish a new congregation, its own numbers were rapidly replenished.[55] As this strategy gathered momentum, the expanding network created its own identity as the HTB 'family of churches'.[56] Common vision and close partnerships were nurtured each year at Focus (or Home Focus), a summer celebration for the whole HTB network, launched in 1992. It took place at a Pontins holiday camp at Pakefield in Suffolk – 'where *Hi-de-Hi* meets the Holy Spirit', mused Gyles Brandreth[57] – before migrating to Mablethorpe in Lincolnshire, then to the Somerley Estate in Hampshire, then to Newark Showground in Nottinghamshire, as it grew and grew.

This expansionist strategy was not without its critics, especially those who disapproved of HTB's theology or felt threatened by its numerical success. One opponent likened it to the 'entryism' of Trotskyites in Militant Tendency, which attempted to infiltrate the Labour Party in the 1970s. In the same way, 'HTBers like to descend on thinly attended parish churches, swamp the resident congregation, elect themselves on to the Parish Synod and set up shop after their own fashion.'[58] At Westbourne Park, for example, former members of St Stephen's expressed their 'anger and disappointment' that London diocese had acquiesced in HTB's renewal scheme, which they feared would 'deal a blow to the Catholic tradition' in the parish, though the church building was derelict.[59] The deanery clergy also had 'considerable concerns' that HTB's plant would ride roughshod over parish boundaries and drain support from their own churches, while imposing an eclectic, middle-class congregation with teaching and worship that was not 'recognisably Anglican'.[60] Nevertheless, as the Archdeacon of Charing Cross explained to one discontented local vicar, without HTB's initiative St Stephen's would have to be pulled down: 'I cannot imagine anyone else in the world restoring that church.'[61] Many warmly welcomed the dynamic growth that such new congregations generated. Ruth Gledhill enthused in *The Times* that, 'like some fervid tree from the original garden of Eden, HTB seems unable to stop branching out'.[62]

Alpha's Global Launch

One of the few HTB curates not to lead a church plant was Nicky Gumbel. Instead, he pioneered the second key plank to HTB's revival strategy, masterminding Alpha's global expansion.

Gumbel and Millar had a great deal in common – both were schooled at Eton College, both were graduates of Trinity College, Cambridge, and both began their careers in the City of London as barristers. In many ways, Gumbel was walking in Millar's footsteps. When Gumbel wondered about becoming a clergyman, he sought Millar's counsel. When Gumbel planned for theological training in 1982, he applied to Millar's old college, Cranmer Hall in Durham. There the pattern faltered, however, because Cranmer Hall was unexpectedly full and although Gumbel was at the top of the waiting list and fully expected a place, none, surprisingly, became available. In retrospect, he saw this closed door as the gracious providence of God – if he had been ordained, as anticipated, in 1985, there would have been no opening at HTB, and therefore no involvement in Alpha. History would have taken a different direction.[63]

Gumbel trained instead at Wycliffe Hall in Oxford between 1983 and 1986. He appreciated the teaching of the college staff (including a new young tutor, Alister McGrath) and formed some lifelong friendships (including with one of his supervision partners, Graham Tomlin, later Dean of St Mellitus College and Bishop of Kensington). But the Oxford experience was generally a difficult, testing time. Having exchanged a barrister's prestige for the life of a humble ordinand, Gumbel struggled with 'lack of self-worth' and began to feel 'very insecure'.[64] He was no longer involved in regular Christian ministry, and long hours reading liberal theologians for his Oxford University degree unsettled his evangelical convictions. 'As I read a lot of books by scholars who were unorthodox in their beliefs and often hostile to biblical truths,' Gumbel recalled, 'I found my faith was under attack. My heart grew cold.'[65] The experience was 'spiritually oppressive' and for the first time since his conversion he was 'really beginning to doubt the things I had always believed'.[66] This put his spiritual life under 'great strain', eroding his confidence in God and impacting on his private devotions: 'All the time I was reading books which were undermining my faith and as I started to pray I could not get those thoughts out of my mind.'[67] The 'drip, drip of liberal theology' left him hanging on to Christian faith 'by my fingertips'.[68]

These difficulties were compounded by a new fearfulness in evangelism, Gumbel's chief calling. His former boldness, even brazenness, in telling others about Jesus suddenly evaporated. During a Wycliffe Hall mission to Allerton on the outskirts of Liverpool, Gumbel and fellow ordinand Rupert Charkham (later vicar of St Michael's, Chester Square) were sent to a supper party with a couple on the fringe of the church. Halfway through the main course, the husband, a non-Christian, asked what the mission was about. Gumbel 'stumbled, stammered, hesitated and prevaricated', and kept repeating the question, until eventually Charkham came to his rescue by providing a straight answer. 'I felt deeply embarrassed', Gumbel lamented, 'and hoped the ground would swallow us all up! I realised how frozen with fear I had become and that I was afraid even to take the name of Jesus on my lips.'[69]

In retrospect, however, Gumbel reflected that the Wycliffe experience helped to equip him for Alpha. It gave him time to examine questions in depth, to test and improve his theological assumptions, and to wrestle with the challenges of articulate liberal critics. When Alpha guests interrogated Gumbel, or when hostile observers pulled apart the course content, he had already faced more severe rigours in Oxford during his time of preparation.[70]

After college, Gumbel found it difficult to secure a curacy. He looked at nine possibilities, but none was a good fit and several turned him down. This threw his sense of calling into doubt again and the London diocesan director of ordinands suggested he return to the bar, though he had lost three crucial years from his career. In desperation he was reduced to signing on to the dole.[71] During the summer of 1986 the Gumbels spent seven weeks in California with John McClure's Vineyard congregation at Newport Beach, an important period of spiritual recovery after the strains of Oxford. Gumbel described it as a church that overflowed with love for God and for one another, and as he was 'soaked in their love', his heart was rekindled – it was 'like taking something out of a deep-freeze and defrosting it in the warm air'.[72] Meanwhile, back in London, Sandy Millar and John Collins advocated strongly on Gumbel's behalf with the diocesan authorities to permit him to serve his curacy at HTB. Ken Costa and other friends spent a weekend at Ashburnham Place in Sussex 'to pray against the bishop's resistance'.[73] Eventually the diocese relented, and Gumbel was ordained at HTB on 28 September 1986, aged 31.[74]

In September 1990, after four years on the HTB staff, Gumbel was given responsibility for Alpha. The course had evolved through the hands of a succession of curates since 1977, each of whom took their turn and adapted it in different ways. John Irvine (curate from 1981) lengthened Alpha from the original six weeks to ten weeks and introduced a weekend away focused on the Holy Spirit. During his time in charge there were about 30 on the course, which was still small enough to meet in the curate's flat.[75] Nicky Lee (curate from 1985) saw Alpha grow substantially, attracting a combination of new converts, older Christians who wanted to get back to 'basics', and outsiders eager to discover more about the Christian message. By 1987 there were over 100 on Alpha each term (a quarter of them HTB team), which stimulated the continual growth of the church as Alpha graduates formed new pastorates (a network of small groups).[76] One of Lee's innovations was an evangelistic supper party at the end of each course, so those who had just finished Alpha could invite their friends, and thus one course naturally fuelled the next.[77] Numbers rose again to 150 during 1989–90, partly the fruit of Billy Graham's London Crusade in July 1989 when the 70-year-old American revivalist addressed 400,000 people in a series of events at Earls Court and Wembley Stadium, relayed live to another 800,000 across the United Kingdom.[78] Yet Graham's crusade also symbolically marked a changing of the guard, his last crusade in Britain in a sequence stretching back to the 1950s. The evangelistic momentum soon passed to Alpha, a newer model of outreach, based not around football stadiums but supper parties.

Gumbel was reluctant to take charge of Alpha, because it was designed as a nurture course for new Christians and he wanted to focus instead on evangelism to those outside the church. In 1992 it was still being advertised at HTB as a course 'for beginners in the

Christian faith'.[79] But Gumbel quickly realised that Alpha also had excellent evangelistic potential. In one of his earliest small groups, most guests were not Christians and yet came to faith during Alpha.[80] He reordered the sequence of talks, to put more direct emphasis on Jesus at the beginning of the course, and reshaped each session as a question:

1. Who is Jesus?
2. Why did Jesus die?
3. How can I be sure of my faith?
4. Why and how should I read the Bible?
5. Why and how do I pray?
6. How can I resist evil?
7. How does God guide us?
8. Why and how should we tell others?
9. Does God heal today?
10. What about the church?

The Alpha weekend away, usually about halfway through the course, addressed three further questions: 'Who is the Holy Spirit?' 'What does the Holy Spirit do?' and 'How can I be filled with the Spirit?' There was also an introductory week ('Christianity: boring, untrue, and irrelevant?', later retitled 'Is there more to life than this?') and a final party week ('How can I make the most of the rest of my life?'), making 15 talks in total. The inherent tensions between a discipleship course and an evangelistic course persisted. Critics complained that as a model of evangelism Alpha moved too quickly from introducing Jesus to instruction in Christian lifestyle, thus assuming the faith of participants – but Alpha refused to draw tight boundaries and aimed to reach everyone on the spectrum from atheist to enquirer to new believer. Gumbel began to market the course as 'designed primarily for non-churchgoers and those who have recently become Christians'.[81]

Gumbel compared running Alpha to driving a sports car that belonged to somebody else and had several previous owners.[82] However, as soon as he took the steering wheel, Alpha accelerated rapidly. By his own admission, he was a Type A personality – inherently competitive, ambitious and prone to living life at top speed.[83]

Under Gumbel's leadership, numbers rose sharply. In spring 1992 there were over 200 at the Wednesday evening Alpha and another 40 on a new Wednesday morning Alpha (led by Deirdre Hurst and Annette Millar).[84] By the autumn there were 320 on the evening course, filling HTB's Church House to capacity, with four weekends away.[85] The old Victorian pews were removed from the church in 1993, transforming its potential as a much larger venue for Alpha banquets and other events.[86] This architectural restructuring was essential, Sandy Millar insisted, as 'paving the way for a more ambitious . . . period of growth'.[87]

Alpha began to spread by word of mouth to churches in Milton Keynes, Buckhurst Hill in Essex, Southampton, and Edinburgh, and Gordon Scutt of the Stewards' Trust ran the course at Malshanger near Basingstoke (HTB's Hampshire retreat house).[88] Soon Gumbel was fielding enquiries from churches around the country eager to borrow the Alpha materials. He therefore published his talks as *Questions of Life* in March 1993, followed two months later by the first Alpha conference to help church leaders set up their own courses. Over a thousand people packed HTB for the event, with delegates from across Britain and as far afield as France, Germany, Spain, Switzerland, Singapore, New Zealand and the United States of America.[89] The HTB bookshop took more than £10,000 during the two days.[90] This public launch marked the transformation of Alpha from a homegrown HTB resource into the start of a global phenomenon. Among the delegates was Justin Welby (curate in Coventry diocese), who took four members of his congregation and reported to Gumbel that they all returned home 'buzzing and excited'.[91]

Demand for Alpha was insatiable. Over the next 18 months there were Alpha conferences in Sheffield, Edinburgh, Birmingham, Norwich, Lincoln, Manchester, Hereford and Salisbury, with further events in Germany, Hong Kong and Norway. By spring 1994 there were 400 Alpha courses running across Britain, rising to 750 by the end of the year, with many more due to launch.[92] David Pytches encouraged Gumbel that Alpha was 'one of the most significant evangelistic enterprises since Billy Graham in the 1950s and we just thank God that he has raised you up at this time to "sell" it so well'.[93] Witnessing Alpha's sudden and unexpected growth, Millar excitedly exclaimed: '*Something is happening. The Spirit of God is on the move . . .*'[94]

HTB and Alpha were expanding rapidly in every direction, but this growth was largely reactive and uncoordinated, without proper strategic planning. Millar and Gumbel drove the vision, but as former barristers they lacked professional business and management expertise. A key new appointment as HTB's executive director was Tricia Neill, who was central to Alpha's subsequent ascendancy.[95] She joined the staff in April 1994, aged 44, and took charge of all Alpha conferences, masterminding its strategic growth. Neill was brought up in Northumberland in a Christian family and attended a Presbyterian church in North Shields throughout her youth, but as soon as she left home she gave up on church because she 'just didn't see the relevance of Christianity for my life'. After a decade as a schoolteacher, including seven years in Oman, she joined World Trade Promotions in 1985 as events director, responsible for organising major trade fairs across the globe in cities like Hong Kong, Chicago, Brussels and Cologne. Next she was headhunted in 1990 by Rupert Murdoch's News International (owner of *The Times*, *Sunday Times*, *Today*, *The Sun* and the *News of the World*) to run its exhibitions arm, responsible for large consumer events like the Schools Fair and the Sunday Times Festival of Fine Wine and Food. Neill enjoyed her fast-paced executive lifestyle, though she found London a lonely city and was involved in a series of destructive romantic relationships. She was left with a feeling that 'there must be more to life'. Two Christian friends at her tennis club invited Neill to an Alpha supper party at HTB in 1992, but she found Gumbel's talk challenging and resolved never to return.

Some months later, when Neill congratulated a neighbour on the birth of her first child, the young mother burst into tears, having just discovered her husband was having an affair. Neill did not know how to help, but found herself saying, 'You ought to go on an Alpha Course', and then added, to her own horror, 'And if you want I'll come with you and keep you company.' The two women attended Alpha at HTB in January 1993 and Neill's neighbour became a Christian after two weeks, followed a month later by Neill herself. Neill had begun reading the Bible, including Jesus's teaching on the cost of discipleship, and when sitting at her dining room table one morning, she decided, 'I want to be a Christian. I would give up everything and anything for that.' So she prayed a prayer of repentance and commitment to God: 'I gave my life to Jesus. I was so excited. It was like I was in love for the first time – an extraordinary feeling.' Neill was a volunteer helper on subsequent Alphas, though when Gumbel attempted to headhunt her for the HTB staff she turned him down flat. Her response changed after attending a friend's wedding where she was suddenly overcome by the realisation that it might be the last time in their lives that the wedding guests heard the Christian message. She began to cry and 'felt an overwhelming desire that everyone there should have the opportunity to do Alpha'. News International offered Neill promotion, with a large pay rise, but instead she joined HTB on a third of the salary and with no perks like a company car or bonuses. She was shocked to discover that HTB was so disorganised that on her first day at work she had no desk, no telephone and no computer. Gradually Neill built what Millar called 'a culture of professionalism' across all HTB's operations, including proper management structures and strategy.[96] Her business acumen, and the infrastructure she created, were critical for Alpha's global success.

Times of Refreshing

On Tuesday morning, 24 May 1994 – two days after Pentecost Sunday, and almost exactly a year after Alpha's global launch – Nicky and Pippa Gumbel were among a small group of church leaders who gathered in the home in Kingston upon Thames of John and Eleanor Mumford (founders of the South-West London Vineyard church), to hear about Eleanor's recent trip to the Airport Vineyard church in Toronto, Canada. A new spiritual 'outpouring' (nicknamed the 'Toronto Blessing') had begun there in January 1994, characterised by laughter, falling over, and 'drunkenness in the Spirit', attracting a growing number of Christian pilgrims from around the world.[97] After describing what she had witnessed in Toronto, Eleanor prayed for the leaders present and 'the Spirit fell in great power upon everyone there'.[98] At 2pm Gumbel returned to HTB, late for a lunchtime staff meeting in the crypt (the 'services committee'), which was just ending. With the staff in a hurry to get on with other tasks, Gumbel was asked to close the meeting with prayer, so he invited the Holy Spirit to fill everyone in the room in preparation for the afternoon ahead. According to one eyewitness account:

> The effect was instantaneous. People fell to the ground again and again. There were remarkable scenes as the Holy Spirit touched all those present in ways few had ever experienced or seen. Staff members walking past the room were also affected. Two hours later, some of those present went to tell others in different offices and prayed with them where they found them. They too were powerfully affected by the Holy Spirit – many falling to the ground. Prayer was still continuing after 5pm.[99]

One staff member, Emmy Wilson, testified that when Gumbel prayed, 'the Spirit came in power on all of us. I just felt I was falling in love with the Lord all over again . . . One moment I was laughing and then the next minute I was just weeping and weeping before the Lord.'[100] Millar was away at a meeting of the Evangelical Alliance, but was alerted by his incapacitated secretary, who crawled on her hands and knees to reach the telephone.[101] Tricia Neill, who had only joined the staff a few weeks earlier, was so alarmed by what was occurring across the HTB site that she locked herself in her office.[102]

In a hurriedly rearranged programme, Eleanor Mumford was invited to speak at the HTB services the following Sunday.[103] Again, when she invoked the Spirit, there was a remarkable response. Members of the congregation began to cry, or laugh, and many went forward for prayer ministry where they began 'to fall in the power of the Spirit'. 'Soon, the whole church was affected', reported the HTB newspaper, 'and there were scenes few could remember ever having seen before.' The children returning from their groups were also deeply affected and began to pray for each other. At the evening service, more than 100 went forward for prayer, and when 'the Spirit fell in great power' rows of chairs had to be removed to make room for all those lying prostrate on the floor. Two days later, Sandy Millar,

Jeremy Jennings and Emmy Wilson flew to Toronto for a three-day visit at the Airport Vineyard.[104]

Similar phenomena continued to break out, not only in HTB services but in the homes and offices of congregation members, and in other churches across London. Millar welcomed this 'astonishing outpouring' as a spontaneous work of the Holy Spirit, reminiscent of earlier revivals like those under Jonathan Edwards and Charles Finney in the eighteenth and nineteenth centuries.[105] It was front-page news in the *Church of England Newspaper*, which triggered a national media frenzy, with profiles in *The Times*, the *Sunday Telegraph*, the *Daily Mail* and elsewhere.[106] As a result, fresh crowds began to arrive at HTB, including visitors from across Britain. Before the Toronto Blessing, the Sunday evening service had a congregation of about 900 people, but now it regularly overflowed its 1,200 capacity. Even during August 1994, normally a quiet month, hundreds queued outside the church from as far as Lancashire, East Anglia and the West Country. Tickets had to be issued to regular members so they could secure a seat.[107] To cope with the numbers, HTB doubled its provision, launching two evening services from October 1994. That autumn's Alpha also broke records, with 500 on the evening course and 70 on the morning course.[108]

This excitement generated a continual flow of HTB members to Toronto. Ken Costa was initially sceptical and believed HTB had been struck by 'a mild dose of hysteria' that would soon pass. However, preaching at St Paul's, Onslow Square, he suddenly 'broke down in absolutely uncontrollable laughter' when he prayed for the Holy Spirit to come upon the congregation. He was laughing so much that he was physically unable to read the Bible passage. The curate who was meant to be leading the service was also incapacitated, having fallen to the floor. Shortly afterwards, on a business trip to New York, Costa visited Toronto Airport Vineyard where he 'started shaking in every part of my body and bouncing up and down like a pogo-stick'. He interpreted this as a visible sign of God seeking to grab his attention and shake his life.[109] Costa helped to persuade R. T. Kendall (minister of Westminster Chapel) that the Toronto Blessing was of divine origin, after Kendall had initially opposed it.[110] Glenda Waddell, an HTB staff member, found that for almost two months between

May and July 1994 she 'did nothing but laugh. I just laughed and laughed and laughed. Every time the Holy Spirit was anywhere near, I laughed.' At that summer's Focus week, during a time of prayer ministry, she began to roar loudly as she crawled around the floor, despite trying to resist the urge and praying, 'Oh Lord, I'll do anything but please, please, don't make me roar.' Similar events occurred during her holiday in Toronto, where a meeting for pastors at the Airport Vineyard sounded 'like a cross between a jungle and a farmyard', with a vast array of animal noises, including lions roaring, bulls bellowing, donkeys, a cockerel and song birds. Waddell felt the explanation was that God was stripping church leaders of their vanity and dignity, in order to prepare them for a more effective future ministry.[111] These phenomena excited many, but also caused widespread puzzlement, scepticism and alarm.

The transatlantic flow also took place in the opposite direction. For example, John Arnott (pastor of Toronto Airport Vineyard), with a team from Canada, spoke in London to HTB and its church plants in October 1994 and again in February 1995.[112] Meanwhile there was a stream of international pilgrims to Kensington, including the itinerant Pentecostal evangelist, Steve Hill, from Texas. Hill, a former drug addict and petty criminal, had been mentored by Pentecostal leaders David Wilkerson and Leonard Ravenhill, and by the revivalist Carlos Annacondia during seven years planting churches in Argentina. But Hill was surprised to read a profile in *Time* magazine of the 'laughing revival' taking place among 'straitlaced Anglicans' at HTB, where 'the youthful throng buzzes with an anticipation more common at a rock concert or rugby match'.[113] He therefore travelled to London in January 1995 and made a beeline for HTB, seeking out Sandy Millar for prayer. Hill recalled:

> When he touched me, the power of God swept through my body. I fell to the ground – I don't ever do that, ever. For 20 minutes rivers were flowing through me . . . I've been filled with the Holy Ghost, friends, I've seen everything a man can see in missions, [but] I got up 20 minutes later transformed. I was brand new! I was brand new! . . . I wasn't living in sin, friends, but little did I know how dry I was, until God soaked me.[114]

This testimony of Hill's 'power encounter' at HTB was a key part of his famous Father's Day sermon at Brownsville Assemblies of God church in Pensacola, Florida, in June 1995, which kick-started the so-called 'Pensacola Outpouring'. Brownsville became a centre of revivalist fervour for the next several years attracting millions of visitors from across the globe.[115] The outpourings in Toronto, Kensington and Brownsville were culturally and denominationally distinct, but there were important transatlantic linkages between them.

These 'times of refreshing' at HTB continued throughout 1994 and 1995. In November 1994, for example, 90 people gathered in Northampton for HTB's annual leaders' weekend. After a time of worship, Jeremy Jennings stood up to speak from Zechariah, but he had hardly begun when laughter broke out. First, Millar was 'quietly convulsed in laughter' and when the group prayed for him to be empowered for the work ahead, he 'fell to the floor, bent double with laughter'. Soon other leaders were affected in the same way. 'Within minutes, the room was "shaken" as dozens of people fell to the floor laughing, crying, and shaking.' Prayer ministry continued for more than three hours.[116] A journalist from the *Financial Times* who visited HTB described similar scenes at the end of a Sunday service, when Millar invoked the Holy Spirit and invited people to come forward for prayer:

> First, there was a gentle mewing, as of babies, from the gallery. Then came cries of women as if in labour. The girls who had gone forward subsided one after another to the floor where they lay moaning or silent. As for the men, they sat and sobbed or worked themselves into a frenzy of shaking, all the while groaning, shouting or laughing hysterically. It was as if they had been struck simultaneously by epilepsy.

'You can get to heaven without falling on the floor,' Millar explained. 'But it is what I would call "resting back": the sense of the presence of God is such that sometimes it takes too much energy to stay standing.'[117]

Media buzz was followed by more substantial theological commentary and critique. Early paperback assessments like Mike Fearon's *A Breath of Fresh Air* (1994), Patrick Dixon's *Signs of Revival* (1994), Dave

Roberts's *The 'Toronto' Blessing* (1994) and Rob Warner's *Prepare for Revival* (1995) all gave added publicity to HTB, burnishing its reputation as a global centre for renewal. But the Toronto Blessing also brought fresh scrutiny of HTB as a chief conduit and exporter of these phenomena to the British churches. When the septuagenarian clergyman John Papworth (honorary curate at St Mark's, Hamilton Terrace, St John's Wood) attended an HTB service, he was left 'deeply impressed and deeply shocked'. He suggested that HTB's attitude to the Holy Spirit demonstrated 'intellectual vacuity' and was 'simply not adult'. As members of the congregation shook uncontrollably, or fell to the floor, he thought that what they needed most of all was medical attention. Papworth admitted that St Mark's Church had crumbling buildings and 'zero attendance' for anything except its main Sunday service, but he dismissed HTB's huge popularity as the result of 'pseudo-revivalist emotional exploitation'.[118] Likewise, in the 1995 *Church of England Yearbook*, Robert Jeffery (Dean of Worcester) dismissed the Toronto Blessing as 'mass hysteria' that was undermining intellectually respectable faith.[119] Yet in reply the octogenarian missiologist Lesslie Newbigin (former Bishop of Madras and a regular speaker at HTB during his retirement) pointed to the 'genuine fruit of the Spirit' in the lives of those affected. He drew on his experience of Indian weather to describe this new move of the Holy Spirit, laying down a challenge to the Church of England's hostile leadership: 'I have the feeling that one gets when the monsoon breaks after a very dry summer. It would be sad (to put it mildly) if the response of churchmen were to be to shut the doors and windows.'[120]

Faced by fierce criticisms, which attributed the Toronto phenomena not to God but to psychological manipulation, auto-suggestion or even to the devil, Sandy Millar was a vocal advocate in defence of the movement. While some advised caution, he urged the opposite: 'We are living in the most eventful and exciting and challenging days that there have been for a long time. We need *more* of the Spirit, not less. We need more boldness and faith. We need to drink and drink and drink! We certainly don't need dreary lectures about being careful.'[121] Millar exhorted the HTB congregation not to draw back but to 'go deeper with God' and to 'go on drinking deeply of the water of life while this season continues'.[122] He celebrated 'the spontaneous bursting out of the Holy Spirit all over the place', and pleaded for the institutional church to take their hands off the controls, to allow new Christian life 'to blossom free from the restrictions and shop-steward type clerical sensitivities with which the modern church is riddled'.[123] As evidence for the goodness of these new waves of renewal, Millar often pointed to the spiritual fruit in people's lives – a new love for Jesus, for the Bible, for fellow Christians, and for walking with God, combined with a fresh joy, boldness and freedom in prayer.[124] Lives were being radically changed. 'What a thrilling time to be alive!'[125] In particular, he noticed that this new work of the Holy Spirit had increased HTB's zeal for evangelism, as witnessed by the large numbers coming to Christian faith through Alpha.[126]

Nevertheless, the relationship between Alpha and the Toronto Blessing – the two most famous products exported by HTB in the mid-1990s – was problematic for Alpha. They were permanently linked in the public imagination, and opponents of the 'gross heresy' of Toronto openly attacked Alpha, as if the two were synonymous.[127] Gumbel himself made the connection in a 1995 interview for *Renewal* magazine. He argued that it was 'no coincidence' that this new move-ment of the Holy Spirit from Toronto was simultaneous with the 'explosion' of Alpha: 'I think the two go together.'[128] Sometimes Toronto-style phenomena were in evidence at Alpha. For example, fitness executive Richard Ward was invited to HTB by a young woman he met rollerblading in Hyde Park. At the Alpha weekend at Chichester in spring 1995, he prayed a prayer of repentance, 'asked Jesus into my life', and then fell to the floor when Gumbel invoked the Holy Spirit. As Ward lay on the ground his tears turned to laugh-ter, and he spent the rest of the evening 'laughing and laughing', unable to stop.[129]

However, Alpha's association with the Toronto Blessing was unhelpful, given Toronto's negative publicity in many sections of the church, so Gumbel soon started to put clear distance between them. In May 1995, for example, he was due to take part in a theological discussion at Weston-super-Mare in Somerset, following the screen-ing of a BBC South film about Alpha. But when Gumbel previewed the film, he was disturbed to find that it made little mention of Alpha and instead used dramatic footage from a Pentecostal church of worshippers shaking and falling over. He therefore pulled out of the event at short notice, lest it damage the Alpha brand.[130] The first set of official Alpha videos (filmed at HTB's course in summer 1994) included a description of Eleanor Mumford's recent visit and its impact, but this acknowledgement of the Toronto link was soon erased.[131] Gumbel's talk on 'How can I be filled with the Holy Spirit?' was specially re-recorded in 1996, before the whole set was redone the following year.[132] In retrospect, a few years later, Gumbel observed of these phenomena: 'I don't talk about it now. It divides people. It splits churches. It is very controversial. But I'll tell you – I think the Toronto Blessing was a wonderful, wonderful thing.'[133] While the Toronto Blessing subsided and was deliberately removed from view, Alpha went from strength to strength.

Next Stop: The World

With HTB's influence extending rapidly in multiple directions, its Bible motto chosen for 1995 was from Isaiah 54:2–3: 'Enlarge the place of your tent, stretch your tent curtains wide, do not hold back; lengthen your cords, strengthen your stakes, for you will spread out to the right and to the left.' Millar insisted they had 'no delusions of grandeur' and 'no desire to build an empire', but simply wanted to play their part in extending the kingdom of God wherever God led them.[134] There was a world of difference between 'empire building' and 'kingdom building', Jennings reiterated.[135]

These expansive aspirations were encouraged by John Wimber in his final visit to HTB, as the keynote speaker at Focus in July 1995. It was his last opportunity to shape HTB's vision, 13 years after his memorable introduction in 1982. Wimber was a shadow of his former self, struggling with throat cancer and the effects of a recent stroke, but his optimism remained unbounded. He proclaimed that the HTB family of churches would transform London over the next 30 years, provided the devil did not stop them.[136] Furthermore, he urged them to look beyond the capital: 'God is calling you to shake this city and if you shake London, you will shake most of the world.' Wimber noted that the Church of England was losing ground and 'going out of business', closing churches every year, but that it was 'a ripe plum ready to [be] picked by the faithful'. He exhorted the HTB network to begin the work of multiplication by planting new churches outside London, into empty Anglican buildings in other cities across the United Kingdom.[137]

Millar likewise told Focus that God was laying before them 'a much bigger vision' than they had ever had before. He drew inspiration from Joshua in the Old Testament looking over the River Jordan towards the Promised Land, to 'practically the whole of the then known world'. Their call was to resource many others, internationally, especially by exporting Alpha. Alpha 'so clearly has the hallmarks, the fingerprints, the fragrance of Christ upon it', Millar asserted. 'It's so obviously a work and activity of the Spirit of God that we daren't not offer it to anybody who wants it.'[138] Building on these themes, Gumbel suggested that Alpha was key to HTB's global vision. In just two years, 9,000 church leaders had attended Alpha conferences and 1,500 courses were officially registered. New courses were being added at a rate of 100 each month, with 45 churches making contact every week to ask for details. Gumbel estimated that 100,000 people would attend Alpha in 1995, and perhaps 250,000 the following year. Within eight years, he calculated, there would be 200,000 Alpha courses spread across the globe. 'Next stop: the world', he declared.[139] From modest beginnings, Alpha had snowballed beyond HTB's wildest imagination and was gaining ground all the time. There seemed no limits to its global potential.

3

Building a Brand

ALPHA, AS A brand, is far more than a course. It encompasses a whole suite of resources – paperbacks, tracts, DVDs, conferences, podcasts, newspapers, magazines, cookbooks – constantly evolving to meet the appetites of a changing culture. At the core of Alpha's brand identity is a 'repackaging' of the Christian message for contemporary audiences, especially those disillusioned with church. During the 1990s, young people deserted the Church of England in droves, and the church's instinctive reaction, Nicky Gumbel observed, was to say: 'The message is not acceptable, so we must change the message.' On the contrary, he insisted, the gospel of Jesus Christ is always attractive to every culture and generation. What needed improvement was the external packaging – for example, by abandoning dull sermons and irrelevant music.[1] In *Questions of Life*, he explained:

> In both our worship and our witness we need to find a contemporary expression for eternal truths. God does not change; neither does the gospel. We cannot change our doctrine or our message just to suit passing fashions. But the way in which we worship and the way in which we communicate the gospel must resonate with modern men and women.[2]

This was Gumbel's reiterated theme. He emphasised the exclusive claims of Christianity: 'Jesus, the unique Son of God, the unique Saviour, the one uniquely raised from the dead, is the only way to God.' Therefore Christians must unashamedly proclaim Jesus, no matter how unpopular the message 'in an age when toleration, not truth, is the order of the day'.[3] 'It matters a great deal', Gumbel asserted, 'that people should hear the undistorted message of the gospel. The message is non-negotiable: we are not at liberty to tamper with it.' He reminded his readers of the Apostle Paul's startling anathema, that if anyone 'should preach a gospel other than the one we preached to you, let him be eternally condemned!' (Galatians 1:8).[4] Nevertheless, Gumbel urged that this unvarying gospel must be conveyed in a culturally attractive manner:

> We do not believe we have the liberty to tamper with the apostolic message. However, the message comes to us in a cultural packaging. Every generation has a duty to ensure that the packaging is not a stumbling block; to preserve the unchanging message but to change the packaging in order to make it understandable in the context of our own culture.[5]

Sandy Millar agreed: 'I feel very strongly that in church life today, you have to change. If you just want to stand still, if you preserve, you won't get new people. The only thing that should be preserved is the gospel.'[6] He praised Gumbel for 'stripping the gospel down to its bare essentials' in Alpha and for making Christianity 'accessible to this generation'.[7]

Dinner before Doctrine

To appeal to a young demographic, especially the under-35s, the Alpha brand focused upon relaxed informality. Part of its genius, according to evangelist Michael Green, was that it began not with doctrine, but with dinner.[8] Alpha's branding emphasis was friendship, food, and fun, in an easy-going, no-pressure environment, as conveyed by the Alpha mnemonic:

A – Anyone can come
L – Learning and laughter
P – Pasta (later expanded to 'pasta or potatoes or paella or pizza')[9]
H – Helping one another
A – Ask anything.[10]

Informality was *de rigueur*. 'People are sick of formality', agreed one Alpha insider. 'Even Jesus was sick of formality.'[11] Frequent jokes and humorous anecdotes were therefore an essential part of the formula, to demonstrate that 'laughter and faith in Jesus Christ are not incompatible'.[12] Alpha's centrepiece – the Holy Spirit weekend – encouraged intense spiritual experience, especially during the Saturday afternoon session on 'How can I be filled with the Spirit?', but this was usually immediately followed by a Saturday evening 'revue' of light-hearted entertainment and 'amusing sketches', with 'lots of laughter'.[13] Alpha billboards, and photographs of guests and conference delegates in *Alpha News*, very often showed people laughing and smiling.

When Gumbel took charge of Alpha, he paid meticulous attention to every detail, to make it as attractive as possible to younger guests. The standard of hospitality was key. At a typical Alpha evening there might be a glass of good wine, tablecloths, flower decorations, napkins, jazz music and low-level lighting. 'We expect people to feel offended by the Gospel', explained John Irvine at St Barnabas, Kensington, 'but we don't want them to be offended by anything else.'[14] Meanwhile at HTB's mid-morning Alpha, mainly aimed at young mothers, 'The tables, covered in white tablecloths, bow under the weight of grapes, flapjacks and biscuits, cafetières of fresh coffee, jugs of milk and turrets of cups and saucers.'[15] The quality of catering and the relaxed ambiance might only be the outer packaging of the product, but therein lay Alpha's success, suggested Damian Thompson in *The Times*: 'To a typical Church bureaucrat, this is an irrelevance: soggy quiche is good enough for the people of God. Alpha, in contrast, appropriates one of the most natural of all human instincts – the urge to entertain people nicely in your own home.' HTB had learnt, according to Thompson, that 'the secret of successful religion lies more in its ability to colonise social networks, or set up new ones, than in its ability to tailor doctrines to modern tastes'.[16]

Food and laughter conveyed a laid-back welcome. When asked to explain the secret of Alpha's success, Gumbel replied: 'Most Christians are so excited they just want to push the message down your throat. They act like they're trying to win an argument. They tell you what to believe. We don't do that. We don't push anybody into doing anything.'[17] 'It is right to persuade', Gumbel observed, 'but wrong to pressurise.'[18] Alpha eschewed an older style of 'crisis evangelism' – popular in the mid-twentieth century – where an itinerant revivalist urged instantaneous conversion upon a huge crowd at a special 'one night only' mission event in a football stadium. Alpha, by contrast, was the brand leader in low-key 'process evangelism', run in multiple smaller venues by local churches. There were still calls to Christian conversion, but they took place over a ten-week course, in gentler fashion. One of Alpha's guarantees was never to chase those who dropped out, which paradoxically gave more people confidence to attend. Its branded catchphrase was 'an opportunity to explore the meaning of life', a deliberately undogmatic approach. In earlier years, the talk was followed by Bible study, but when Gumbel took charge he replaced the Bible study with small-group discussion.[19] Alpha leaders were trained not to provide answers, but to ask guests, 'What do you think?' The model was 'not teacher–pupil, but host–guest'. Alpha small groups, according to the training manual, should be 'low key, relaxed and fun. Avoid intensity.'[20]

Christianity magazine praised Gumbel's presentations as 'lubricated with charisma. A credit to both the anointing of God and his legal training.'[21] But they were also the fruit of much toil. Every word was chosen with care, as Gumbel obsessively reworked his material. Night after night, he practised his talks upon his wife Pippa, sometimes with a group of friends, and if he lost their attention or the jokes fell flat, he rewrote those sections. Each talk was then committed to memory for easy delivery.[22] Gumbel's relaxed informality took hours of rehearsal. 'This is not Billy Graham-style oratory, designed to impress a stadium full of people', observed the American magazine *Christian Century*. 'It's more like a friendly conversation in Starbucks.'[23] The *Vancouver Sun* welcomed Alpha's approach as a refreshing departure from typical North American revivalism:

> The old ways of luring in converts are dead. Gone are in-your-face sidewalk preachers, fairground tents featuring sad hymns and miraculous healing, earnest people in nice clothes trudging door-to-door and even those sweaty preachers denouncing the devil from under hot TV camera lights.

Alpha by contrast, the newspaper approved, was 'wining and dining skeptics into the Christian family'.[24] All were welcomed, all questions were legitimate. 'There's no knocking on doors', Gumbel promised, 'but it's friends bringing friends.'[25] And as those friends in turn brought further friends, so the numbers grew.

Many testimonies from new converts spoke of the unpressured welcome they received at Alpha as a key part of its appeal. However, some Christians objected to this style of inoffensive evangelism. One Baptist critic complained at Alpha's 'softly-softly' approach, suggesting that Gumbel needed to work harder at 'smoking out sinners from their refuges of unbelief and sinful pride' and at striking fear into their hearts. He warned that the prevalence of humour throughout Alpha tended to create an atmosphere 'more akin to an after-dinner speech' and a fun evening out, not to seriousness and urgency.[26] 'Alpha bean bags launched', a comic quipped about Alpha's expanding product range. 'Critics claim content is too soft.'[27]

Non-Christian critics, conversely, warned that the attractive packaging hid an unpalatable product beneath the surface. *New Humanist* magazine dismissed Alpha as 'cuddly fundamentalism'.[28] Journalist A. A. Gill, famously acerbic, disparaged Alpha as

> more or less the same as American evangelism of the South Baptist type, but wrapped in a softly convivial, non-threatening English package. It's not money-grabbing, and it's not the Moonies . . . It's a slightly nerdy, harmless get-together for people who want a faith that matches their curtains and holiday plans, but underneath it is that old prescriptive chapter-and-verse absolutism that's going to send the rest of us to hell.[29]

The Guardian accused Alpha of 'love bombing', a technique employed by cults like Sun Myung Moon's Unification Church and David Berg's The Family of Love to manipulate new recruits by showering them with affection and false friendship.[30] Nikolai Segura (undergraduate at Imperial College, London, and founder of the Imperial College Secular Society) attended Alpha at HTB in 2001, aged 19, in order to analyse it from a secular perspective. He claimed that Alpha was guilty of targeting young, vulnerable people – newly separated from their parents and likely to be lonely and low on confidence – in an attempt to fill the empty pews of the Church of England . . . They use every cult tactic in the book: peer pressure; emotional blackmail; instant 'friends'; isolation; abstraction; fatigue – everything you'd expect from a well-oiled fundamentalist sect.

Lonely people with low self-esteem were most likely to respond to the promise of eternal life or the warm welcome of a Christian community, Segura declared, and the poorly educated would naively swallow Alpha's brand of 'paint-by-numbers Christianity'. He was particularly scared that Youth Alpha was attempting to infiltrate schools and youth groups to convert children, who were 'easy pickings for Alpha's professional indoctrinators'.[31] Others were also suspicious of Alpha's motives. Mike Norris, a 23-year-old City lawyer, attended Alpha at HTB in 1993, intrigued by the Christian message, but he was highly mistrustful and refused to eat the food for the first few weeks in case it was drugged. He was terrified, he later joked, that he might 'wake up in a bedsit in Hampstead with some cross-legged guru sitting at the end of my bed saying, "Thanks for the money, you know you're not going to see your family again and, by the way, your new name is Leonard."' Norris gradually overcame his suspicions, committed his life to Christ on the Alpha weekend, and became an Anglican clergyman and church planter.[32]

Gumbel's Image

Alpha's launch in 1993 and quick rise to dominance coincided with New Labour's sudden arrival on the British political scene in 1994 and subsequent landslide election victory. Both were involved in parallel projects, to rebrand an unpopular product to attract a new generation, and both struck a chord with the national mood at the end of the millennium. High church Anglicanism was often satirised as 'the Tory party at prayer', but Alpha, according to the *Evening Standard*, was 'New Labour at supper', with 'a smooth command of image and a radiant set of inner convictions'.[33] Nicky Gumbel was two years younger than Tony Blair, both in their early 40s when New Labour swept to power, and commentators often drew parallels between the two orators. To the *New Humanist* magazine, Gumbel was 'rather like Tony Blair on a fervent day'.[34] According to *The Observer*, they shared the 'same boyish sincerity, same halting but heartfelt delivery'.[35] Gyles Brandreth concurred, after hearing Gumbel at an Alpha celebration supper in 2001. 'When Gumbel spoke it was with easy charm and folksy sincerity', he noted. 'The style is modern: Blair and Portillo rather than Hague or Prescott.'[36] 'Gumbel reminded me irresistibly of Tony Blair', chimed in the *Evening Standard*. 'There was the otherworldly light dancing in the eyes, a mouth that was permanently on the verge of a reassuring smile, and a voice that quietly pleaded with you to believe it.'[37]

There were also striking parallels between Gumbel and Billy Graham, a generation apart. Although their methodologies were different, they both sought to repackage the Christian message for contemporary audiences and both were themselves central to their respective brands. As one historian put it: ' "Billy Graham" was not just a person. "Billy Graham" was a brand, a persona, an experience, and a product line of books and merchandise all rolled into one.'[38] Graham's personal appearance, well groomed and in smart suits, was key to building his image of professional respectability, in deliberate contrast to the unpolished appearance of earlier revivalists. 'Billy Graham is God's top salesman', wrote *Time* magazine in 1950. 'He looks like a salesman. Tall – six feet two inches. Handsome. Burning eyes. The sure gesture. The right phrase. The firm handclasp. Wherever Billy goes the celestial balance sheet shows a substantial profit.'[39] In the same way, Gumbel's persona was key to the Alpha brand. Like Graham, he stood six feet two inches tall, with good looks and a gleaming smile – telegenic, urbane, self-effacing. According to Canadian newspaper the *National Post*, Gumbel had 'the chiselled glam of a Hollywood player'.[40] He kept fit on the squash court and by cycling through London. His personal priorities for 1991 – recorded privately at the back of his diary – included one hour of prayer and one hour of exercise every day.[41] A middle-aged female admirer, Mary Killen (who later found fame on Channel 4's *Gogglebox*), interviewed Gumbel for *House & Garden* magazine and wrote of his 'taut physique, with washboard stomach' and his 'smouldering brown eyes'. 'Surely becoming a Christian should be a matter of free will rather than submission to charisma', she cooed.[42] As the primary face and voice of Alpha, Gumbel's image was essential in shaping Alpha's brand identity.

Alpha Merchandise

The core Alpha product was Nicky Gumbel's *Questions of Life* and the parallel ten-week course. But there was a burgeoning product range as Alpha tapped into a hungry Christian market and struggled to keep pace with demand. Apart from Gumbel's paperbacks, which were published by Kingsway, all other resources were produced in-house by Alpha Publishing. HTB's bookshop was quickly overwhelmed – 40 per cent of its business in 1993 was Alpha related, generating £50,000. But this was only a small token of things to come. There was soon a special 'Alpha Hotline' and a product distribution network around Britain.[43] Course manuals and audio cassettes of Gumbel's talks were followed in 1994 by videos, produced by a professional film company.[44] Within three years, 7,000 sets were in circulation. Always seeking to improve the product, the whole course was re-filmed in 1997 with more camera angles and a specially constructed set, and Gumbel received training from actor David Suchet.[45] Other merchandise included Alpha T-shirts, Alpha car stickers, Alpha balloons, Alpha banners, Alpha poster packs, Alpha wall planners, and an Alpha cookbook to help with menus – first proposed by a busy vicar's wife in Leicester.[46] There was a branded Alpha 'worship pack', with songs and hymns on CD or cassette, plus a songbook with piano score and guitar chords.[47] Resources were marketed to younger constituencies with the launch of Youth Alpha in 1996 and Student Alpha in 1998.[48] Office Alpha, or 'Alpha in the Workplace', for busy young professionals, was first pioneered among CEOs in a Vancouver boardroom in 1998, and 'Alpha Express' DVDs provided slimmed-down versions of Gumbel's talks to fit in a lunch hour.[49] Not forgetting the older population, Senior Alpha offered large-print manuals for use in residential care homes.[50] As the merchandise multiplied and sales rocketed, it soon became a multi-million-pound business, criticised by Martyn Percy (chaplain of Christ's College, Cambridge, and later dean of Christ Church, Oxford) as 'one of the slickest commodifications of the gospel'.[51] Unlike a regular business, however, any Alpha profits were reinvested back into the ministry.[52]

Alpha's logo was a colourful cartoon of a man struggling to carry a giant question mark. It was designed by Charlie Mackesy for the front cover of *Questions of Life* and became synonymous with the Alpha brand worldwide.[53] Mackesy was a close friend of the Gumbels and a member of St Paul's, Onslow Square. He characterised his school career as 'very restless and rebellious', a pattern of parties, drugs and drink. On one occasion he streaked naked at the Badminton horse trials and swam through the water jump, captured by the television cameras.[54] Twice he dropped out of university. But Mackesy's unconventionality and artistic talent were combined with a desire to promote the Christian message. An ITV documentary in 1990, *A Brush with God*, profiled his paintings and how 27-year-old Mackesy travelled the world 'spreading his own brand of Christianity with an infectious enthusiasm'.[55] His laid-back style made him a popular public speaker, especially among young people. Gumbel's books were all illustrated with Mackesy's humorous cartoons, an essential part of building Alpha's non-fusty image and a vital complement to Gumbel's carefully crafted prose. The cartoons helped to set the tone. Although Mackesy later found fame and fortune with his runaway bestseller, *The Boy, the Mole, the Fox and the Horse* (2019), it was through Alpha that he first became globally recognised.

After *Questions of Life*, Gumbel published a splurge of paperbacks in quick succession, as Alpha extended its product range. Three new books were published in 1994 alone – *Searching Issues* in January, *A Life Worth Living* in March, and *Telling Others* in October. *Searching Issues* addressed the seven most common questions raised by Alpha guests: suffering, other religions, sex before marriage, the New Age movement, homosexuality, science and faith, and the Trinity. *A Life Worth Living* began as an HTB sermon series on Philippians, which Gumbel dubbed St Paul's letter to Europe's first 'church plant'.[56] It covered practical topics such as responsibility, friendship, confidence, ambition and generosity. *Telling Others* was based on Gumbel's presentations to Alpha training conferences. It laid out the Alpha vision and offered nuts-and-bolts guidance on practicalities like pastoral care, small groups, giving talks and prayer ministry. After this initial frenetic flurry, the pace slowed. Two more Gumbel paperbacks were based on his Sunday preaching – *Challenging Lifestyle* (1996) on the ethical implications of the Sermon on the Mount, and *The Heart of Revival* (1997) on the prophet Isaiah – but there Gumbel laid down his busy pen. The main Alpha corpus was settled, built around these six books.

Brimming with ideas, Gumbel sketched out ideas for a seventh book on Galatians, entitled *Life in the Spirit*, and an eighth book on contentious theological issues such as abortion, marriage and divorce, women's ministry, baptism, heaven and hell, and war – but neither appeared.[57] After an exhausting few years as an author, one of Gumbel's personal resolutions for 1997 was 'Stop writing!'[58] Following his initial explosion of creativity, his energies turned instead to the work of embedding and disseminating the resources. One further product was added in 1999: *30 Days*, a month's worth of daily Bible notes, designed to help Alpha guests establish a pattern of regular Bible reading. Like all Gumbel's writings it sold briskly, shifting 35,000 copies in its first six months.[59]

There was such an appetite for Alpha that churches that ran the course faced the problem of repeat attenders, the 'Alphaholics'. *The Tablet* (a Roman Catholic magazine) carried a cartoon by Jonathan Pugh of a penitent kneeling in a confessional box, lamenting, 'I keep getting the temptation to do the Alpha Course again.'[60] Gumbel tried to dissuade people from repeating the course, unless they moved into new roles as helpers or discussion group leaders.[61] But those who had completed Alpha, and lapped it up, were left asking hungrily, 'What next?' From October 1995, HTB piloted Alpha II, another ten-week course, designed to help new Christians 'make the jump from Alpha into church life', with plans for a national roll-out in summer 1996.[62] It covered practical topics including worship, Christian community, handling money, the purpose of home groups, social action, sexual morality and work. The heart of the course, the Alpha II day, taught participants how to 'discover your gifts and God's call for your life' with the help of a detailed spiritual gifts questionnaire.[63] However,

Alpha II proved ineffective. Instead of helping to integrate Alpha graduates into church pastorates and home groups, it merely delayed the process, giving them a second bridge to cross and thus increasing the drop-out rate. HTB's policy, typically pragmatic, was never to offer something to the wider church, which sounded good in theory, without first proving it worked in practice. Therefore, Alpha II was never launched upon the market and was cancelled in 1999.[64] It was a rare example of an Alpha product that flopped even before it was released. Instead, the recommended follow-up to Alpha and *Questions of Life* were Gumbel's other paperbacks (each with their own branded guest manuals), which, taken together, provided a two-year programme in Christian adult education.[65]

Franchising the Product

For Alpha to grow, a national (and later international) infrastructure was essential. There was huge pressure on the Alpha office at HTB, with scores of enquiries every week from churches across Britain seeking advice on everything from menu planning to guest speakers.[66] To spread the load, 44 volunteer regional advisers were recruited in 1995 – including Justin Welby as Alpha adviser for Warwickshire.[67] This pool of Alpha advocates expanded to meet demand, with 120 regional advisers by 2000, and 270 by 2002.[68] Alpha churches were also encouraged to join an official register, published in *Alpha News*, so that enquirers could easily be connected with their nearest course.[69] The numbers grew so large that from 2002 the register was published as a separate directory, like a miniature *Yellow Pages*, running to 114 pages and 7,300 churches of all denominations.[70] Another target was to build a national network of strong Alpha churches that could help smaller or weaker churches in their region to run the course, through the sharing of expertise and personnel. These were initially called 'resource centres' and later, from 2002, 'resource churches'.[71] The language of 'resource church' became ubiquitous in the Church of England from the 2010s to mean a vibrant congregation helping to stimulate mission and church planting across a diocese, often funded with big budgets from the Church Commissioners.[72] But the concept was coined by HTB as one its strategic priorities. 'It is our vision', explained Tricia Neill, 'that there will be a strong Alpha church in each region' – a 'resource church' – helping to embed Alpha in local communities.[73]

Alpha, in effect, operated a franchise model. It manufactured a series of high-quality, attractive products that were then purchased and disseminated by a network of independent operators, all buying into a strong brand. By maximising the potential of tens of thousands of local churches, rather than one mass crusade, more people would be reached. As Gumbel put it: 'The more checkouts, the more customers.'[74] In an important 1998 analysis, Pete Ward (Archbishop of Canterbury's Adviser in Youth Ministry) drew parallels between Alpha and McDonald's. Both had global ambitions, relentlessly pursued efficiency, and provided a convenient, consistent, pre-packaged, simplified menu. 'In short, Alpha has done for evangelism what McDonald's has done for fast food.' However, Ward argued, Alpha, like the American restaurant chain, also suppressed creativity and diversity, propagating 'a uniform spirituality' devoid of contextualisation, a form of religious imperialism. 'Alpha is a work of God', Ward concluded, 'but it is also a religious cultural industry offering product to consumers.'[75] Sandy Millar objected strongly to the comparison, and to the implication that Alpha was superficial, monochrome or unhealthy, insisting that the only similarity between Alpha and McDonald's was that both had 'a desire to get the product out to as many people as possible'.[76]

With a franchise it was vital to protect the integrity of the product. As Alpha spread across the globe, local adaptations led to confusion and loss of brand identity. Gumbel and Neill repeatedly emphasised that for best results it was important to 'follow the recipe'.[77] In order to 'preserve confidence and quality control', HTB introduced a copyright clause in 1995 that permitted minor changes to the course (like shortening the talks or altering the illustrations), but not any theological variation that would undermine Alpha's 'essential character'.[78] This provoked strong reactions – 'salvation by copyright', Martyn Percy called it.[79] Some complained that the Christian gospel can never be copyrighted. Others objected to being forced to follow Alpha's narrow syllabus and wondered whether HTB was 'hell-bent on suppressing diversity'.[80] But Millar and Gumbel defended the move:

> Bearing in mind that anyone is fully entitled to write their own course with its own name, and many have, should it be permissible for some-one to remove the talk on, say, Who is Jesus? (because they do not agree that he is the Son of God); to include a different talk on aspects of healing (because, for example, they want to teach that all sickness is a result of demon possession); to do away with the day or weekend on the Holy Spirit (because they don't see the point of it) and *still call what they are doing Alpha*? We feel this would undermine people's confi-dence in recommending their friends to do the course in different parts of the country or different parts of the world . . .[81]

Like a Big Mac, the theological content of Alpha was to be identical at the point of delivery anywhere across the globe. As Gumbel remarked, it would be disappointing to visit a McDonald's in Moscow and be served a ham sandwich.[82] In practice, however, many churches did vary the material, sometimes quite considerably, and still called it 'Alpha'. There was little HTB could do to police it. Roger Arguile (vicar of St Neots, Cambridgeshire) developed his own local teaching materials, directly inspired by the Alpha model, but was warned by HTB of its overt similarities to their product. Alluding to Millar and Gumbel's background as barristers, Arguile claimed that he had been subjected to 'cross-examination' at the HTB vicarage and felt he was 'dealing with lawyers, not theologians'.[83] Likewise, when the Roman Catholic Brompton Oratory, adjacent to HTB, launched a course in 1999 called 'Alpha to Omega', they were gently but firmly asked to desist.[84] But no minister or church was ever prosecuted for breach of Alpha's copyright.

Product development and dissemination was initially funded entirely by HTB, though a 'Friends of Alpha' scheme was launched in 1996 to enable other churches to contribute financially.[85] In 1997, HTB's turnover from Alpha resources, conferences and bookshop was £521,000 – or 22 per cent of the church's total annual turnover of £2.3 million.[86] But as the work expanded there was a huge jump the following year, with turnover in 1998 of £1.8 million from Alpha resources and events, plus another £382,000 from the HTB book-shop – or 47 per cent of a total annual turnover of £4.7 million, the highest receipts of any parish in the Church of England.[87] However, HTB's budget was increasingly in danger of being swamped by Alpha, and for Alpha's growth to accelerate it needed to expand its main support base beyond one congregation. Therefore, a new charity was created – Alpha International – which came into existence on 1 January 2002. It was formally independent from HTB, though remained closely connected – the first four directors were Ken Costa (chairman), Sandy Millar, Nicky Gumbel and Tricia Neill, and HTB made a commitment to donate £1 million to Alpha International every year.[88] Alpha International's annual turnover, generated by conferences, resources, royalties, and donations via 'Alpha Partners', continued to rise steadily, from £4.1 million in 2002, to £5.1 million in 2006, to £7.7 million in 2009, to £12.5 million in 2019.[89] Meanwhile, far from shrinking when Alpha became independent, HTB's annual turnover also continued to grow, from £5.3 million in 2002, to £7.5 million in 2009, to £12 million in 2019.[90] Both HTB and Alpha International were major business operations.

Satisfied Customers

In selling Alpha products to churches, effective publicity was essential. This strategy was masterminded by HTB's head of communications, Mark Elsdon-Dew, who joined the staff team in November 1991, aged 33. He was a professional journalist, having worked for nine years at the *Sunday Express*, including as foreign editor and deputy news editor, so was well connected with the secular media. He joined the HTB congregation in 1984, shortly after becoming a Christian, but resigned from Fleet Street to serve the wider church during the Decade of Evangelism.[91] Elsdon-Dew's most important vehicle was *Alpha News*, a tabloid newspaper that disseminated 'good news' stories of Alpha's growth and impact worldwide. It was published three times a year, and ran from 1993 to 2011 (after which all Alpha communications went digital). By 1997 *Alpha News* had reached a circulation of 250,000, filled with enthusiastic reports of Alpha's global expansion, conferences, resources, commendations, and dramatic testimonies of conversion.[92] Elsdon-Dew also edited *Focus*, HTB's in-house monthly newspaper, which from 1996 included an eight-page supplement, *UK Focus*, with further Alpha testimonies and reports from sermons and addresses at HTB events. These tabloids piggybacked on other religious newspapers and thus reached readers far beyond Alpha's own mailing list. *Alpha News* was carried by the *Church Times*, and *UK Focus* by the *Church of England Newspaper*, the *Baptist Times* and the *Methodist Recorder*. In this media blitz, Christians who perhaps themselves had no interest in Alpha were nonetheless flooded with Alpha publicity whether they liked it or not. 'And please, please, stop putting this *Alpha News* rubbish in with my *Church Times*', complained one aggravated clergyman; 'I detest it.'[93]

Elsdon-Dew's editorial policy was relentlessly upbeat. Every edition of *Alpha News*, according to an atheist critic, 'contains guilt-ridden adulterers, depressed alcoholics and self-destructive hard-drug users whose lives had been transformed by Christ'.[94] Endorsements and testimonies were key to building the Alpha brand. However, this continual reportage of triumphant achievements and multiple conversions could sometimes, paradoxically, be off-putting even to Alpha's keenest supporters because it did not always match their own experience of difficulties and failures in evangelism. A *Church Times* diarist suggested that *Alpha News*'s 'relentless chronicle of mounting success' was depressing for clergy whose more modest ambition in life was simply 'to muddle through'.[95] Others were inherently suspicious of an in-house journal marking its own homework. One secular humanist believed that Alpha's 'grandiose claims' were an exercise in self-deception.[96] Nevertheless, cataloguing and celebrating the success of Alpha was essential in building brand loyalty. No one would invest in a product that paraded its own failures.

Testimonies of conversion were by far the most important endorsement of Alpha. Their potential was recognised by evangelists in every generation and testimonies were a prominent feature of Billy Graham's crusades in the second half of the twentieth century. As his biographer observed, 'Graham instinctively understood that the theology textbook was no match for the word of the satisfied customer.'[97] Gumbel adopted the same policy. One hostile Anglican clergyman reasoned that the existence of thousands of Alpha courses was 'no proof that anyone is being saved', any more than thousands of slimming courses was proof 'that people are actually losing weight'.[98] But individual testimonies, recorded in great numbers, were incontrovertible living proof that Alpha worked. Elsdon-Dew enjoyed collecting these personal stories and interviewed scores of new Christians for *Alpha News*, a remarkably rich source of first-hand accounts of conversion and renewal. Select highlights were republished in four volumes between 1995 and 2004 as *The God Who Changes Lives: Remarkable Stories of God at Work Today* – plus a special collection for the American market in 2002 – and the series sold 100,000 copies worldwide in its first decade.[99]

Testimonies are a notoriously complex genre, however. It was difficult, for example, to check the veracity of personal accounts. In 2002 Alpha published the 'uplifting story' of a young homeless drug addict on the streets of London who had been befriended by HTB and professed Christian conversion. His dramatic life story covered five full tabloid pages.[100] But when many parts of the tale later turned out to be fabricated, Sandy Millar issued a public apology for inadvertently misleading readers of *Alpha News*.[101] It was an isolated incident, but embarrassing nonetheless. Another inherent drawback was that the vast majority of published testimonies were from converts who had very recently professed faith, sometimes only a matter of weeks earlier, before that faith had matured or been tested. If the same people had been interviewed after ten or twenty years, their reflections may have been very different. In keeping with Jesus's Parable of the Sower (Matthew 13), some of those who enthusiastically professed faith at Alpha later fell away from the church. For example, a serial burglar and heroin addict attended Alpha in prison in 2002 and testified to his new faith before the congregation at Greyfriars Church in Reading, who assisted his rehabilitation. His transformation 'from drugs to God' was profiled in the *Reading Evening Post*, free publicity for Alpha.[102] Nevertheless, within months the 'born-again thief' had returned to criminality, robbing 13 churches, including Greyfriars itself.[103] These stories of deconversion, disillusionment, struggle or outright renunciation seldom made headlines. Yet Gumbel acknowledged that professions of faith could be 'spurious'.[104] He was painfully alert to the problems of converts drifting away, or crashing out, from the Christian faith. After two decades leading Alpha, he added a new emphasis to the 2010 edition of *Questions of Life*, when speaking of the spiritual fervour of the convert:

> Some people have an amazing initial experience of Christ. Some will not feel anything, and some will experience great difficulties. However, what really matters is where they are in their relationship with God in ten years' time. Similar to marriage, it's the long-term that is of the most importance. It doesn't matter whether or not you have a great honeymoon.[105]

Rival Brands

As Alpha's popularity soared, there was nonetheless a long queue of theologians and clergy eager to highlight its deficiencies as an introduction to the Christian faith. They focused often on Alpha's overt simplicities. For example, Martyn Percy warned that it was being marketed as 'a cheap package deal' without recognition of the complexities of the Christian message. Alpha, he argued, was too prescriptive – 'a package rather than a pilgrimage; a hermetically sealed hermeneutical circle which keeps out more issues than it addresses'.[106] Percy derided Alpha as 'sugar-coated, crude and narrow – "join-the-dots" Christianity', guilty of 'theological vacuity'.[107] Another Cambridge theologian, Andrew Davison, likewise accused Alpha of 'selling religion down the river'. He believed that its view of the world was too neat and tidy, offering trite and triumphant solutions to life's complexities, without sufficient room for fragility, tragedy, mystery and desolation.[108] David Jenkins (former Bishop of Durham) quipped of Alpha, 'if I was marking it, I wouldn't even give it gamma' – that is, not even a third class, a joke perhaps better suited to his earlier career marking theology examinations at Oxford in the 1960s.[109]

There was no shortage of critics. One Alpha attender claimed he had to 'leave my brains at the door',[110] while another concluded the course was a celebration of 'wilful, self-indulgent credulity'.[111] Charles

Spencer, theatre critic at the *Daily Telegraph*, attended Alpha in 1999 and found it 'insufferably smug and intellectually vacant', though he noted it was 'turning out robotic converts by the hundred'.[112] Malcolm Brown (principal of the East Anglian Ministerial Training Course, and later the Church of England's director of Faith and Public Life) asserted that Alpha was alienating people from Christianity instead of attracting them. He decried its 'insidious marketing', 'selective (and dubious) biblical literalism', 'crude emotivism', and 'patently false (and hence manipulative) dichotomies presented as knock-down arguments'.[113]

Some lamented Alpha's lack of engagement with questions of philosophy, or psychology, or biblical criticism, and viewed its old-fashioned doctrines as untenable in the modern age. One hostile Methodist chastised Alpha for 'recycling of much of the worst of conservative evangelical doctrine with which many, if not most, Methodists have no sympathy at all'.[114] Another Methodist reckoned that attending Alpha was like going back 200 years, via an 'intellectual time-warp', to a period 'when the Fall was a historical event, when umpteen prophecies were fulfilled at Christ's birth in Bethlehem and when the Gospels provided verbatim transcripts of Jesus' teachings'. He dismissed this 'Gumbelism' as 'blinkered, sectarian and archaic', and suggested it was like going back to the dinosaurs with Gumbel as 'Alphasaurus Rex'.[115] In similar vein, an Episcopalian chaplain at the University of Michigan asserted that Alpha was intellectually dishonest and warned his fellow Episcopalians against 'this invasion by protestant evangelicalism'. He rebuked Gumbel for using the Bible as a proof text, ignoring modern scholarship on the reliability of Scripture and the historicity of Jesus, and avoiding the writings of liberal theologians like Bishop John Shelby Spong, or John Dominic Cossan and Marcus Borg of the 'Jesus Seminar'. He was also troubled by Gumbel's claims that salvation is only found in Jesus Christ, and by Gumbel's conservative atonement theology.[116] Accusations that Alpha was 'fundamentalist' could cut both ways, however. Campbell Paget (rector of Chatham, Kent), a self-described 'middle-of-the-road Anglican', welcomed Alpha as a good summary of the Christian fundamentals and as an antidote to 'the speculative absolutes of much doctrinaire theological liberalism'.[117]

Alpha was the victim of what the *Financial Times* colourfully called 'the bitchier side of ecclesiology'.[118] In a pungent review, *The Herald* in Glasgow dismissed Alpha as 'too noisy, too thrusting, too intense, and too superficial', encouraging 'constant false jollity', 'instant conversion' and 'smug superiority'. Alpha churches, it complained, with their 'slickly packaged evangelical zeal', tended to undermine

> those fundamental cornerstones of Christianity: spirituality, mystery, and silence. They treat traditional, private prayer conducted discreetly as a bit of an embarrassment, tolerated as a sop for the old and the old-fashioned, both these terms being, in these 'modernising' days, a form of insult. Alpha seems, like Tony Blair, to mistake style for substance. In politics this is a pity. In religion it is a travesty.[119]

Similarly, *The Tablet* criticised Alpha's 'glossy, gung-ho, churn 'em out approach', likening it to 'a Christian motorway designed to get you to salvation as quickly as possible'. What about those people who prefer to travel with Christ by quieter paths, noticing the country fields and wildflowers *en route*? According to this analysis, Alpha risked excluding 'the contemplatives, the lonely, the marginalized, the artists, the misfits', and riding 'roughshod over the fragile beauty of the individual' by producing large numbers of 'Christian clones'.[120]

There were plenty of gaps in the market for alternative approaches to evangelism and Christian nurture. Many new initiatives emerged at the turn of the millennium, such as Emmaus (1996) and Christianity Explored (2001). Rico Tice, creator of Christianity Explored, spoke positively of Alpha and borrowed its basic methodology, though his course focused almost exclusively on Jesus Christ, with very little on the Holy Spirit, on the principle that 'Christianity is Christ, and if you get hold of him, everything follows'.[121] Tice insisted that the key message people need to hear was not 'God can change your life' but rather 'You are a sinner who needs to be rescued', and he worried that Alpha did not emphasise enough the sacrificial cost in becoming a Christian.[122] Other new initiatives also aimed to correct Alpha's weaknesses or to connect with people beyond Alpha's reach. But the fact that they often advertised themselves with reference to Alpha was itself proof of Alpha's market dominance. For example, Dave

Tomlinson, author of *The Post-Evangelical* (1995), ran a local course in Holloway, north London, called A Rough Guide to Christianity, which he advertised as suitable for 'Alpha dropouts'.[123] In 2004 academics from the Psychology and Christianity Project at Cambridge University's Faculty of Divinity launched Beta, a ten-week course to help Christians grow in their faith by addressing topics such as healthy relationships, depression, stress, grief, suffering and forgiveness, from both psychological and theological perspectives. As the name indicates, it was explicitly marketed as a follow-on to Alpha, and the Bishop of Ely claimed that 'Beta answers the questions that Alpha raises'.[124] The experiment was short-lived. In the same year, a new eight-week course called Via Media was launched by Episcopalians in the United States, developed in Southern California by All Saints Church, Pasadena, a famously 'progressive' congregation. Via Media aimed to put equal emphasis on Scripture, reason and tradition – a classic Anglican trio – and to take a 'more expansive view' of the Bible than Alpha permitted.[125]

Other evangelists believed Alpha was too inaccessible for those outside church. They therefore developed alternative brands. For example, in 2002 Methodist evangelist Rob Frost launched Essence, a six-week course aiming to connect with people interested in New Age spirituality. It drew on the teachings of Jesus and the Christian mystics, making use of meditation, music, poetry and art.[126] In 2003 the Church Pastoral Aid Society published Start!, developed by Anglican evangelist David Banbury and piloted in inner-city Bradford. It was just six sessions, compared to Alpha's fifteen, using short video clips filmed on locations such as a roller-coaster and a carousel. It was pitched as 'more tabloid than broadsheet', designed for those who found Alpha too middle class or too intellectual.[127] Likewise, the Y Course, launched in 1999, branded itself as 'The course for those not ready for Alpha':

> Thank God for Alpha. However, the gap between the Church and those outside gets ever wider. Today, many people have a long way to go before they think about prayer, healing or sharing a faith that is not yet theirs. One day. But not yet. Which is where the Y Course comes in.

Unlike Gumbel's long monologues, the Y Course DVD opted for a chat-show style, covering topics such as suffering, other religions and life after death – 'cringe-free, jargon-free, story-filled', according to *Inspire* magazine.[128] But it was a very competitive global marketplace. The *Church Times* found the Y Course 'dull' compared with the creative visuals of the popular NOOMA DVDs featuring Rob Bell (pastor of Mars Hill Bible Church, Michigan) or the 'easy informality' of Alpha.[129] Despite a proliferation of evangelistic products, Alpha's status as the brand leader proved unassailable.

Alpha Cathedral and Campus

As the headquarters of a growing global brand, the old HTB site was no longer fit for purpose. Alpha employees were crammed into make-shift offices in the Georgian crypt and the 1960s church hall, and future expansion was severely restricted. One of HTB's ambitions was therefore to transfer the entire operation to a new eye-catching venue, centred on a cathedral-like megachurch, with a purpose-built campus for Alpha and its parallel branded ministries. This in turn would provide a springboard to further worldwide advance. The idea for a dedicated campus in fact pre-dated Alpha's boom, but took several years to germinate.

In February 1993 – a month before the publication of *Questions of Life* and three months before Alpha's global launch – Ken Costa (HTB's churchwarden and deputy chairman of SBC Warburg, a large invest-ment bank in the City of London) pitched a bold vision for growth, which he hoped would 'see London won for Christ in a generation, or sooner'. London was 'a strategic capital city' and Costa longed for the day when God would act to restore the name of Jesus there. He believed HTB was called by God 'to apostolic leadership in London', and that it was no longer merely a local church but was quickly becoming a 'movement' in its own right. And yet by 1993 HTB was already near the limits of its expansion, even while planting new congregations, and needed extra space to grow. The time was ripe, Costa declared, for HTB to move from Kensington to new headquarters in central London, to allow it to operate on a larger base.[130]

Costa hoped to secure the decommissioned Battersea Power Station, which was then on the market, an iconic venue on the River Thames. His proposal included plans for a 5,000-seat auditorium, which would allow the HTB congregation to grow to 20,000 people on a Sunday (across four services). Conveniently, it could keep its established brand label – HTB, or Holy Trinity Battersea. The concept of a megachurch was familiar in South Africa, South Korea and Southern California, but not in Britain. This new venture was a departure from the norm. Costa explained:

> The evangelistic impact of this gathering is obvious. It would be new. It would be, but not look like, a church. It would be visible. It would be large and it would be filled. It could be that this act of faith helps, in a small way, to swing the tide against the downward spiral of numerical and moral decline that have marked the post-war Christian church. Above all, it becomes an actual testimony to the claim that our God reigns; that he is an awesome God to be reckoned with; and that he is not made for the fringes of social life and the City but is its very focus.[131]

Many had an image of the Church of England – as memorably pictured by Archbishop George Carey in 1991 – as an old woman 'sitting in her corner muttering ancient platitudes through toothless gums', ignored and irrelevant.[132] But HTB's central London venue would shatter that picture. It would be a 'shot in the arm of faith' for Christians in the capital, who had long been 'in retreat', and would encourage them 'to believe again in a powerful God who longs to act in mighty saving power in our nation today'. It would be a vibrant, confident, missionary congregation, building on the Alpha principle of 'attractive evangelism'. Visibility was a key criterion. Non-Christians would ask, 'A large church, what lies behind it? A huge God! is the answer.' 'To the devil, small is beautiful', Costa declared. 'The fewer believers the greater his unchallenged deception. This is a project to reverse this lie.'[133]

Costa's vision was for HTB to be 'a leading international resource centre', disseminating its brand of Christianity worldwide. 'We are endowed with talent so richly as to be an embarras de richesse', he wrote. Because of London's strategic position as a global city, the new headquarters would become an international Christian nexus. Alongside 'seeker-sensitive' Sunday services, adapted to the outsider, it would embrace the latest technologies like video and cable television. It would provide a 'school of worship', helping to train Christian worship leaders and songwriters, and a 'school of mission' for full-time and part-time theological training, since the 'failure of theology colleges to equip ordinands for their ministry is obvious to us'. It would offer training for Christian school governors, and leaders in political and public life, 'a vital part of the long-term strategy to arrest the process of secularization'. It would send mission teams across the world, with new opportunities to spread the gospel after the collapse of the Communist Bloc. Closer to home, it would be a centre of social transformation, through ministries such as debt counselling: 'Debt in this virulent strain is pandemic in the nation. The evangelistic outreach of such an initiative is obvious.' 'The project is large but we must be meek', Costa concluded. 'Any hint of triumphalism will undo the very work we are trying to do.'[134]

Audacious dreams like Costa's were typical of HTB's ethos in the 1990s, and the congregation was encouraged under Sandy Millar's leadership to pursue grand initiatives that few others would dare to attempt. Gradually over the next three years the vision took shape, with a feverish sense of excitement, alongside Alpha's explosive growth. One image was of HTB's new headquarters as 'a large bonfire' and local churches as smaller 'camp fires', fanning the flames of spiritual renewal across the land. It would be 'a modern day cathedral . . . lifting the Name of Jesus high above the nation's capital'.[135] Millar reminded his PCC in December 1995 that the HTB facilities were now overstretched and their Sunday services were overflowing. Encouraged by many prophetic words, by the recent outpouring of the Holy Spirit through the Toronto Blessing, and by 'the phenomenal growth of Alpha', the overwhelming feeling was that 'now is the time'.[136]

Britain's millennium celebrations provided the perfect opportunity. The Millennium Commission redirected over £2 billion from the National Lottery towards building projects, including notable schemes in the capital like the Millennium Dome, the Millennium

Wheel (the 'London Eye') and the Millennium Bridge. But by 1996 there were concerns among Christians that all the money was being spent on secular projects and that the birthday of Jesus Christ had been forgotten. Archbishop Carey tried to reclaim the millennium as 'a Christian party to which everyone is welcome'.[137] Prince Charles spoke of the millennium's 'spiritual importance' and its potential for 'personal and national renewal', but worried that it would become 'a giant, but essentially meaningless, party'. He found it depressing that so few of the projects submitted to the Millennium Commission transcended 'the merely material', and that Christians had not yet come forward 'with plans to erect a great religious building'.[138] Under increasing pressure, Tory MP Virginia Bottomley (chair of the Millennium Commission) asserted in the House of Commons, 'I am a Conservative and Britain is a Christian country. It is a Christian millennium.'[139] Many Anglican parishes submitted small bids for millennium finance to restore their bell towers or floodlight their church buildings. But small bids were never HTB's style. They applied instead for £50 million – the maximum grant – towards their new headquarters. The PCC wrestled over the ethics of accepting National Lottery funding, which some feared would make them complicit in gambling and would damage Alpha's public testimony. But they agreed to push ahead in the belief that, as one put it, 'we would not get the money if God closed the door'.[140] Sandy Millar publicly defended the National Lottery as generally harmless and not against Scripture.[141] Alongside Christian MPs Michael Alison and Stephen Timms, he met with Bottomley to seek her support for the HTB project and to remind her that the turn of the previous millennium had witnessed the building of some of England's greatest cathedrals, such as Canterbury, Winchester, Ely and Durham.[142]

The concept had evolved significantly from Costa's first pitch. HTB's new headquarters were now to be called the Millennium Village, on a derelict nine-acre site next to the River Thames, near Battersea Park and Chelsea Bridge. Announcing the plans, Costa declared there was a 'growing hunger' in the country for Christianity, and that the Millennium Village would contribute to Britain's 'moral regeneration'.[143] He warned that in the 1990s they were witnessing 'the unravelling of the social fabric that used to knit our nation together. The whole tapestry of inter-related community, civic responsibility, neighbourliness, is torn.' And yet, at the same time, they were experiencing 'this extraordinary new move of the Spirit of God' and a 'deep longing' in British society for satisfying answers to life's big questions. 'For too long the church has been depressed', Costa lamented. 'It has been negative; it has been small; it has been discouraged; and it has drawn into itself with an introspection unimaginable against the need that stands in our face.' But he believed the Millennium Village was the fulfilment of a prophetic vision and they must rise to action: 'Now is the moment where we say, "The gloves are off, the preparation is over. Now, by faith, we need to move forward to grasp what God is doing in our midst." . . . This is not some small little activity short of resource, short of people. It is God on the move.'[144] Millar's vision for the project chimed with these concerns for national transformation. It was high time, he suggested, 'for something to be done about the drip-feed erosion of Christian values in the nation'.[145] By building the Millennium Village they would increase the visibility and confidence of the Christian community.[146] It would 'create a blueprint for a new kind of church' and be proof that 'Christianity is very much alive and kicking in this country'.[147]

The revised proposal included a 3,500-seat auditorium, capable of expanding to 10,000 seats for special events (three times bigger capacity than St Paul's Cathedral or Westminster Abbey), a convention centre, 75 meeting rooms, a complex of Christian charities and shops, a media centre with recording studio, a cinema, restaurants and bars, a large tower with views across London, and a budget hotel with 2,500 beds.[148] It would be Alpha's international headquarters, and Sunday services would be in the usual HTB style though Mark Elsdon-Dew confirmed it would be 'far bigger and more exciting' than the HTB experience.[149] The total cost was £123 million, with £50 million pledged by a student travel company that wanted access to the hotel, another £50 million hoped for from the National Lottery, and the final £23 million from donations. The proposal forecast 13 million users a year and the creation of a thousand jobs.

Archbishop Carey, preaching at HTB in December 1996, called it 'a huge, risk-filled undertaking'. The project received enthusiastic backing from Richard Chartres, Bishop of London – even though technically it was outside his diocese, on the other side of the Thames – and from Prince Charles, who hoped it would be 'an example to the whole nation of the continuing relevance and power of faith'.[150] The *Mail on Sunday* called it 'a bold and brilliant idea' that would change the landscape of London,[151] while *The Times* agreed the plan was 'bold and imaginative', though doubted it was morally right for Anglicans to accept lottery finance.[152] Others were less impressed, deriding the proposal as 'absolutely crack-brained nonsense', and a 'religious eyesore' that would despoil the Thames when the money could be spent on better projects like schools or hospitals.[153] Local Anglican clergy in Battersea complained they had not been consulted.[154] Some were concerned that the arrival of a 'super church' in south London would undermine the old parish system.[155] In the *Evening Standard*, author A. N. Wilson protested:

> It's a free country, and if these evangelicals wish to sing their nauseous ditties or jabber with tongues, none of us would wish to prevent them. But theirs is a purely modern American religion, with little in common with the religious traditions of this country, and there is no reason why they should have the Millennium Commission's money.

Wilson predicted that if Prince Charles ever attended a service in this new Alpha cathedral, he would 'wriggle with embarrassment'.[156] Roman Catholic commentator Cristina Odone dismissed it as 'a born-again Disneyland'.[157]

The dream was soon dashed when the Millennium Commission in February 1997 rejected HTB's application outright. Costa's disappointment was palpable. 'It beggars belief', he lamented. He complained that the Millennium Commission was biased against Christians, while favouring secular or interfaith projects.[158] In Parliament, Michael Alison protested that 'the spiritual dimensions of the millennium still seem to have been missed in terms of hard cash. There is a yawning black hole where there should be a pearl of some price.' He calculated that of the £1.8 billion paid in grants by the Millennium Commission, only a tiny proportion was earmarked for Christian projects, 'a mere snowflake on the volcano of grant'.[159]

Soon after the tragic death of Princess Diana in August 1997 there were suggestions at HTB of reviving their scheme as the 'Diana Millennium Village', with the hope of attracting finance from the Diana Memorial Fund, but this idea was abandoned.[160] During these years Alpha continued to grow exponentially, but was left operating in cramped conditions, squeezed into the HTB offices. It was a global ministry, but still without proper global headquarters.

Shortly before Nicky Gumbel succeeded Sandy Millar as vicar of HTB in 2005, plans were revived for an Alpha International Campus and Costa's original 1993 'Vision for London' was recirculated.[161] However, the ambition was now much reduced in scale. The initial hope was to redevelop HTB's property, but when it became apparent that this would cause difficulties for the Roman Catholics next door at the Brompton Oratory, the focus shifted to St Paul's, Onslow Square.[162] One of the world's leading design companies, Foster and Partners (founded by architect Sir Norman Foster), was engaged to reimagine the site. Their previous work included ground-breaking designs for the Great Court at the British Museum, the Kogod Courtyard at the Smithsonian Museum in Washington DC, and renovation of the Berlin Reichstag. For Onslow Square, they proposed demolition of the 1960s vicarage, to be replaced by a four-storey glass and stone structure, with conference facilities for 1,200 people, lecture rooms, music rooms, a film broadcast studio, and a restaurant. It would be the centre for Alpha's global operations, alongside parallel ministries such as the training of church planters and worship leaders, the promotion of marriage and family life, a centre for urban mission and social transformation projects, and a theological college. The estimated cost was over £15 million.[163] HTB had no desire 'to build some empire', Gumbel insisted. These facilities were designed to enable the evangelisation of London, the nation and the world.[164]

The Alpha International Campus was backed by the Bishop of London but resisted by local residents.[165] The *Evening Standard* dubbed it 'Onslow Square's holy war'.[166] Some objected to the building's futuristic design as jarring with their plush Victorian homes. Others feared that their secluded quiet would be overcrowded on a daily basis by Alpha's busy operations. Claus von Bülow, octogenarian socialite and theatre critic, complained in February 2007: 'The happy-clappers are installing 27 lavatories and planning to serve 120,000 meals there. I mean, how many lavatories do you think Claridges or the Ritz have?' 'It's all very well to spread the word of Christ', von Bülow added, 'but not at the expense of a residential neighbourhood.'[167] Faced with the uproar, HTB withdrew the planning application.[168] Instead, in 2008, Alpha International bought a five-storey office building on the Cromwell Road for £7.8 million, opposite the Natural History Museum, equidistant between HTB and Onslow Square. It enabled about 150 Alpha and HTB staff, housed on the two church sites, to be consolidated in one location.[169] Though a pale reflection of Costa's original vision – neither a cathedral nor a campus – Alpha at last had effective headquarters from which to coordinate its global expansion.

Publishing Tensions

When Nicky Gumbel signed contracts with Kingsway in 1991 for his evangelistic booklet *Why Jesus?*, and in 1992 for *Questions of Life*, he was an unknown author on whom the publisher took a risk. But the global launch of Alpha quickly propelled him to the top of the Christian bestseller lists. Kingsway celebrated the early sales figures as 'absolutely brilliant'.[170] *Questions of Life* sold 20,000 copies in its first year.[171] Next they secured the rights to Gumbel's five other paperbacks, thus controlling Alpha's most important products. This turned out to be a publishing coup for Kingsway, as Gumbel rose from obscurity to celebrity status and his books were in constant demand across the globe in multiple translations. However, that new dynamic added severe strain to the relationship between Kingsway and Alpha. For almost 15 years, Alpha struggled to be released from the Kingsway contracts.

As early as 1995, HTB's 'frustrations and disappointments' with the publishing partnership were already apparent, especially what they considered to be Kingsway's complacency and lack of drive.[172] Gumbel entered discussions with Hodder & Stoughton to publish his fifth book, *Challenging Lifestyle*, and hoped all the previous contracts might be transferred from Kingsway to Hodder, though Kingsway naturally refused.[173] When Gumbel agreed in 1997 to give his sixth book, *The Heart of Revival*, to Kingsway it was on condition that they first relinquish the rights for *Why Jesus?*, which he then transferred to Alpha International's safe keeping.[174] HTB was particularly agitated by what they saw as an inequitable relationship – they did almost all the promotion for Gumbel's books, at considerable cost, while Kingsway pocketed the profits. Gumbel felt Kingsway's attitude was 'absolutely outrageous'.[175] Despite calls for 'an atmosphere of mutual co-operation and trust', relationships deteriorated.[176] At a crisis meeting in June 1998, Sandy Millar warned the publisher that they would have to answer for their actions on the Day of Judgement, to which John Paculabo (Kingsway managing director) replied: 'we seldom leave a meeting at HTB these days without a few bruises. Now to realise that you see us as nothing more than business journeymen or profiteers just adds to the wounds.'[177]

Under the original contracts, Gumbel received a 15 per cent royalty for his paperbacks (sometimes rising to 17.5 per cent after 15,000 copies). By 1998 this had generated £77,769 in royalties, including international rights.[178] All these monies were reinvested in Alpha's ministry and Gumbel remained on a standard Church of England stipend. HTB proposed a bold new arrangement whereby Alpha and Kingsway would divide the profits equally between them, so they would both share equally in the fruits of Alpha's growth.[179] Again the publisher declined. Kingsway defended their integrity, arguing that HTB already received preferential treatment: the royalty rate was more generous than for other authors; they facilitated frequent revisions to the text of Gumbel's books, which other publishers would not allow; and they sponsored *Alpha News* with £5,000 per issue. Moreover, they were not just a business but a ministry, investing profits in wider Christian work. 'So please support us in *our* ministry', Kingsway's publishing director wrote to HTB, 'just as we endeavour to support yours.'[180] Nevertheless, HTB continued to request 'a fair share of the revenue', which was essential to support Alpha's rapid growth, and they lamented that the publisher was 'holding up our ministry both in the UK and overseas'. In a draft letter in December 1998, HTB toyed with the idea of unilaterally terminating the contracts, reckoning that Kingsway was in fundamental breach of them: 'We are very sorry that it has come to this but your relentless pressure to look only to your own commercial interests has driven us to protect not just us but all who could benefit from the unique ministry of Alpha.'[181] Kingsway meanwhile acknowledged 'our bewilderment as we watch HTB publishing grow', and wondered whether the dynamic was 'changing from partnership to competition'.[182]

This saga rumbled on for another decade. In 2000 Alpha International offered to buy back the rights to Gumbel's books for £200,000, but this was again flatly refused.[183] In 2006 they were still longing for 'freedom from the shackles of the existing relationship'.[184] From Alpha's perspective, Kingsway was hampering their growth and raking in millions of pounds on the back of Alpha's ministry. Alpha also wanted proper control over their own products, including distribution and pricing. They were infuriated when Kingsway increased the cover price of Gumbel's paperbacks, which dented sales. In particular, Alpha wanted *Questions of Life* to be priced as low as possible to encourage Christians to buy it as a gift for their friends. They even suggested that, as the central product in Alpha's suite of resources, *Questions of Life* should be priced as 'a loss-leader', though this of course was not an attractive proposition to the publisher.[185] Ultimately, HTB felt that Kingsway was simply not committed to the Alpha vision.

On the other side of the divide, Kingsway also felt badly treated. Paculabo acknowledged in 2008 that 'our relationship is going absolutely nowhere'. He professed high admiration for Alpha's ministry, but complained bluntly: 'It has been fairly evident over the years that we as a publisher have enjoyed little respect from those in leadership within Alpha. No matter who we have talked with, national or international, the feeling has always been that we should give more, do more, etc.' He pointed to Kingsway's charitable support for churches and church leaders in the Global South, and concluded: 'As you are only too well aware ministry consumes finance, and our God-given ministry is as important to us as Alpha is to HTB.'[186] When Alpha International proposed in 2008 to push ahead and publish revised editions of *Questions of Life* and *Challenging Lifestyle* under their own imprint, as if they were new works, Kingsway warned of legal action.[187] This tug-of-war was finally settled in

December 2009 with an amicable separation, when Kingsway had a change of heart and agreed to transfer the rights for all Gumbel's paperbacks to Alpha International.

Gumbel generated excellent sales. *Why Jesus?* – and its seasonal editions, *Why Christmas?* and *Why Easter?* – was often bought by churches in bulk and given away liberally. It sold 100,000 copies by 1992, 250,000 by 1995, half a million by 1996, and 7.2 million worldwide by 2008.[188] The core Alpha text, *Questions of Life*, sold 100,000 copies by 1996, half a million by 2001 (in 28 languages), a million by 2006 (in 41 languages), and 1.5 million by 2010.[189] By the end of 2020 the cumulative global sales figures for all Gumbel's books, in all translations, were as follows:[190]

Why Jesus?	8,870,000 copies
Why Christmas?	3,137,000 copies
Why Easter?	361,000 copies
Why? series total	12,368,000 copies
Questions of Life	1,729,000 copies
Searching Issues	971,000 copies
A Life Worth Living	389,000 copies
Telling Others	266,000 copies
Challenging Lifestyle	252,000 copies (retitled *The Jesus Lifestyle*)
The Heart of Revival	25,000 copies

The Heart of Revival, which went through three printings in quick succession in 1997 and 1998, was the only Gumbel paperback not to enter a second edition. All his other five books – originally published in a frenetic three-year period between 1993 and 1996 – were constantly revised, renewed, translated and promoted, and thus continued to form the backbone of the global Alpha brand in the 2020s. Other authors were also published by Alpha International, but Nicky Gumbel's decisive contribution at the most formative period in Alpha's history meant that the names Gumbel and Alpha would always be synonymous.

4

Experiencing the Holy Spirit

ONE OF THE most significant – and controversial – aspects of Alpha is its invitation for guests to experience the power of the Holy Spirit. This is central to the Alpha brand and marks it out as distinct from other Christian evangelistic courses. The language of 'experience' pervades the Alpha materials.

Laying out his Alpha strategy in 1994, Nicky Gumbel insisted that effective evangelism must appeal 'to the whole person'. The Christian gospel involves 'both the rational and the experiential', he announced, so it impacts those from an 'Enlightenment' perspective who want explanations and those from a 'New Age' perspective who want experiences. Those in the second category – often younger people – were left cold by intellectual and historical arguments but were 'on more familiar territory in experiencing the Spirit'.[1] Because of Alpha's relentless pursuit of a younger demographic, the invitation to experience God was a high priority.[2] 'God is not meant only to be understood in our minds', Gumbel reiterated, 'but also experienced in our hearts and lives.'[3] Sometimes Alpha guests were already Christians, but 'without any real experience of God'.[4] They were missing an essential component. According to *Questions of Life*, it was the Holy Spirit who led people into 'the deepest possible experience of God'.[5] Experiential Christianity, mediated by the Spirit, was Alpha's chief selling-point.

More Holy Spirit, More of Jesus

For much of the late twentieth century the most popular evangelistic tract was *Journey Into Life*, written by Anglican clergyman Norman Warren (1934–2019). It was first published in 1963 and went through multiple editions into the early 1990s, selling over 30 million copies.[6] But its market share declined rapidly with the arrival of Nicky Gumbel's *Why Jesus?* in 1991, the same year as Warren's final revision, both published by Kingsway. Comparison between the two tracts is illuminating. Both were very succinct explanations of the Christian message – *Journey Into Life* was 2,100 words in 13 pages, priced at 35 pence; *Why Jesus?* was 3,300 words in 21 pages, priced at 50 pence. Both were illustrated with cartoons. Both were strongly Christocentric and crucicentric. Jesus Christ was named by Warren 32 times and by Gumbel 38 times (including the title), while the cross of Christ and its benefits for humanity were the central focus for both authors. Both urged readers to repent and turn to God without delay. In other ways, however, their presentations struck a different chord. Warren used the word 'sin' (and its cognates) 39 times, averaging three times per page, a dominant feature of his presentation. Gumbel, by contrast, used the word 'sin' only five times in total, though he expressed a similar idea in less religious language as 'the things we do wrong' and spoke of humanity's 'guilt' before God. Gumbel's dominant motifs instead were the divine offer of relationship, forgiveness, and freedom.

There was another striking contrast between the two evangelistic tracts. The Holy Spirit was almost entirely absent from *Journey Into Life* – mentioned just once on the penultimate page, almost as an afterthought, assuring the new convert that Jesus Christ 'now lives in your heart by his Holy Spirit'.[7] *Why Jesus?* named the Holy Spirit 13 times, as a core aspect of the blessings of Christianity. 'As we look at the cross we understand God's love for us', Gumbel declared. 'When the Spirit of God comes to live within us we experience that love.'[8] Gumbel linked freedom, forgiveness and the Holy Spirit very closely together. This contrasting emphasis is seen clearly in the model conversion prayer that each booklet recommended. Warren's classic prayer (115 words) ran as follows:

Lord Jesus Christ,

I know I have sinned in my thoughts, words and actions.

There are so many good things I have not done.

There are so many sinful things I have done.

I am sorry for my sins and turn from everything I know to be wrong.

You gave your life upon the cross for me.
Gratefully I give my life back to you.
Now I ask you to come into my life.
Come in as my Saviour to cleanse me.
Come in as my Lord to control me.
Come in as my Friend to be with me.
And I will serve you all the remaining years of my life in complete
   obedience.
Amen.[9]

Gumbel's prayer (87 words) followed similar lines, with some direct word-for-word parallels – it was also addressed to Jesus Christ, expressed sorrow and renunciation of wrong, and celebrated the cross. But Gumbel's prayer specially emphasised the gift of the Holy Spirit:

Lord Jesus Christ,
I am sorry for the things I have done wrong in my life.
Please forgive me.
I now turn from everything which I know is wrong.
Thank you that you died on the cross for me so that I could be
   forgiven and set free.
Thank you that you now offer me this gift of forgiveness and your
   Spirit.
I now receive that gift.
Please come into my life by your Holy Spirit to be with me for ever.
Thank you, Lord Jesus.
Amen.[10]

Here in briefest form was Gumbel's model of conversion. The *Why Jesus?* prayer was regularly used during Alpha, and Alpha team members were taught how to lead people to Christ with the booklet. When anyone prayed this conversion prayer, Gumbel usually followed it with another of his own, asking again for the Holy Spirit to 'come and fill them'.[11] In Alpha's theology, repentance and faith in Jesus Christ were not in tension with receiving the Holy Spirit, but integral parts of the same transformative process. The central message of Spirit-initiated revival, Gumbel insisted, is Jesus Christ. He quoted with approval the

Roman Catholic theologian Raniero Cantalamessa (an Italian Capuchin friar and Preacher to the Papal Household): 'The point is Jesus Christ. Whenever the Holy Spirit comes in a new and fresh way upon the church, Jesus Christ comes alive. Jesus Christ is set at the centre.'[12] The same idea was expressed epigrammatically by Sandy Millar for the HTB congregation: 'More Holy Spirit – More of Jesus.'[13]

Alpha converts often spoke of the impact of *Why Jesus?* For example, Andy Green, manager for an insurance company in Brighton, was overwhelmed by grief at the death of Princess Diana in August 1997 and found himself often in tears. Although he was a 'confirmed atheist', he expressed interest in attending church and a Christian colleague at work gave him *Why Jesus?* Gumbel's gospel summary rang true, but when Green reached the prayer of commitment he could not get beyond the first six words, 'Lord Jesus Christ, I am sorry . . .' He broke down in floods of tears, shaking, and kept repeating, 'I am so sorry. I am so sorry.' As Green continued to read the prayer, he felt a pulling sensation, 'as if everything I had ever done wrong was being pulled and all of a sudden I was filled with the most incredible sense of joy'. He joined a Salvation Army community church, was baptised in January 1998, and said in his baptismal testimony that *Why Jesus?* was without doubt 'the best earthly gift that I have ever been given'.[14]

Gumbel's tract also featured prominently in the testimony of stage actor Jamie Hinde. His career began with the Royal Shakespeare Company in the late 1980s, followed by roles in plays like Alan Bennett's *The Madness of George III* at the National Theatre and J. B. Priestley's *An Inspector Calls* in the West End. He enjoyed global travel on tour, including lavish parties in Los Angeles and mingling with famous faces. Yet despite his success, Hinde remained dissatisfied and began 'a spiritual search'. He investigated Buddhism and Taoism, and read books by the New Age guru Deepak Chopra. In 2003, Hinde won a major part in *The Lion King* at London's Lyceum Theatre, with a good salary from Disney and the applause of 2,500 people every night, but he no longer felt the same 'buzz' that he had before. When his Roman Catholic fiancée took him to a service at HTB in late 2004, he burst into tears within moments of arriving, without knowing why. He signed up for Alpha, aged 35, but recalled:

'I was in a bad way. I was drifting, with no real zest for anything. It was like, "Why am I here? Do I want to be an actor?" I felt numb.'

Hinde's initial cynicism about Alpha soon melted away. Only two weeks into the course, on Saturday 29 January 2005 – 'the day that changed my life' – he read Why Jesus? while travelling by train to Cardiff. Alone in the carriage, he prayed out loud Gumbel's recommended prayer, repenting of his sins and inviting Jesus into his life by the Holy Spirit. Hinde recalled:

> I can't explain what happened, but it was the most amazing, profound experience. I expected nothing – I was just saying the prayer. But I said it with integrity, with force and with absolute meaning. I was at peace, serene, joyful and blissful. I felt incredible. The Spirit was just coming into me and saying, 'Jamie, it's true. Let's go for it.' And I remember having an image of Jesus in me. I could see him – not looking at me, but it was like he was in me. It was a really overwhelming experience and it went on for about 20 minutes.

Hinde's outlook on life was transformed. He began to read the Bible, likening it to watching The Matrix: 'you open up a little thing and start delving into this new world'. At the Alpha weekend he enjoyed 'an incredible, overwhelming, unbelievable experience of the Holy Spirit. I was absolutely euphoric – high as a kite. I was beaming.' Hinde's ambition was now 'to glorify God in every way I can'.[15] This sort of spiritual experience – mediated here by Why Jesus? and expressed in terms of serenity, joy and euphoria – was typical of Alpha testimonies.

Firing on All Cylinders

'We should be completely overwhelmed by, immersed in and plunged into the Spirit of God', Gumbel proclaimed in Questions of Life.[16] He was careful to adopt Trinitarian language – 'what I am talking about is experiencing God as Trinity: Father, Son and Holy Spirit' – but he connected this experience directly to being filled and refilled with the Holy Spirit.[17] Every Christian was 'indwelt' by the Spirit from the moment of conversion, he taught, but not every Christian was 'filled'.

It was like the difference in a gas boiler between having the pilot light on or firing 'on all cylinders'.[18]

The climax of the Alpha weekend – and for many guests, the climax of their whole Alpha experience – was the session, 'How can I be filled with the Spirit?' It was the moment when 'experience' of God was emphasised most strongly. After teaching on the subject, Gumbel usually asked everyone to stand, close their eyes, and hold out their hands ready to receive. He then led guests in the *Why Jesus?* prayer of repentance and faith in Jesus Christ, and invoked the Holy Spirit.[19] This sequence was important, aiming to follow the pattern of the Day of Pentecost in the Acts of the Apostles – first repentance and faith, then filling with the Spirit, not an experience of the Spirit separate from Jesus. Nevertheless, sometimes the paradigmatic Pentecost sequence was disrupted, and a prior experience of the Spirit led Alpha guests to put their faith in Jesus.[20]

At the Alpha weekend Gumbel prepared the ground, heightening expectations by teaching that although filling with the Spirit was 'different for everyone', it 'rarely happens imperceptibly'.[21] Participants could expect 'physical manifestations', parallel to the wind and fire experienced at the first Pentecost:

> Sometimes, when people are filled, they shake like a leaf in the wind. Others find themselves breathing deeply as if almost physically breathing in the Spirit . . . Physical heat sometimes accompanies the filling of the Spirit and people experience it in their hands or some other part of their bodies. One person described a feeling of 'glowing all over'. Another said she experienced 'liquid heat'. Still another described 'burning in my arms when I was not hot'.[22]

These phenomena were a major feature of some Alpha testimonies, often interpreted as confirmatory of conversion. For example, when postman Derek Fox delivered letters to the HTB vicarage on his daily rounds, and shared his life's story with Annette Millar, she gave him a Bible, *Why Jesus?* and *Questions of Life*. He prayed the prayer of repentance and faith in Christ, as outlined in *Why Jesus?*, but was disappointed when 'Nothing seemed to happen.' It was not until the Alpha weekend, when Gumbel invoked the Holy Spirit, that Fox experienced a tingling sensation down his left arm, 'like little electric shocks', and began to shake. He wept as Alpha leaders laid hands on him in prayer, 'sobbing like a child with tears pouring down', but felt like 'a new person', more joyful and with renewed confidence.[23] When Carolanne Minashi, director of management training for Citibank, attended an Alpha weekend at Chichester in 1997, she responded to Gumbel's invitation to say the *Why Jesus?* prayer, welcoming Jesus into her life, during which she experienced 'this feeling like a gold Catherine wheel hitting me in the chest and then shooting all down my arms and legs'. 'I now have a living relationship with Jesus', she celebrated, 'and I know that he loves me for what I am.'[24] The Alpha weekend was similarly life changing for Minashi's husband, Mark, a year later. He repeated the *Why Jesus?* prayer and then invited the Holy Spirit: 'I felt a physical force like I was being inflated. My mouth, my lungs, my chest, seemed to be being inflated continually and very powerfully . . . It didn't feel as if I was breathing. But I was strongly aware of God's presence with me.' He likened it to an 'eternal kiss of life'.[25]

For other Alpha guests, the primary physical response was weeping, often combined with joyful exuberance. For example, Philippa Deane had been raised as a Christian but drifted away from the church for several decades. In 1996, her aunt recommended Alpha and when Deane attended the course at St Barnabas, Kensington, in her mid-40s, she found her life was soon turned around. On the Holy Spirit weekend, she was 'filled with the most overpowering love and comfort. Tears poured down and yet I couldn't stop smiling.' She likened her experience to the parable of the prodigal son: 'I was lost and then I was found. I've been welcomed back home by Jesus with such grace and it's stunning how much he has forgiven me.'[26] Likewise, Sandy Meaney began to attend HTB at the invitation of her son, Ashley, who had recently become a Christian while working for a modelling agency in Paris. She recalled that the Alpha weekend in Northampton in 1992 was 'the big turning point in my relationship with God'. When Gumbel invited the Holy Spirit, 'I was just totally overcome. I couldn't control what was happening to me.'[27] She wept copious tears, combined with a 'wonderful feeling of elation – and I knew it was God'.[28]

In contrast, 21-year-old American Keith Prestridge described the Alpha weekend in pugilist terms. He modelled his life on the ultra-violent teenage protagonist in Anthony Burgess's dystopian novel, *A Clockwork Orange* (1962), and acknowledged that he had done 'very many evil things', before he was invited to Alpha by the Vineyard Church in Kansas City. He described his encounter with the Holy Spirit as 'like being in a really good fight, and then getting blacked out. It was good! But, uh . . . it was cool.' After experiencing God's 'unconditional love', Prestridge reported that he was now calmer and less angry, and although he still felt that the devil 'has many hooks on my flesh', his new battle cry was 'All for Jesus! All for Jesus! All for Jesus!'[29]

One of the most widely discussed Alpha testimonies was Nigel Skelsey's 1994 account, which was promoted strongly in Alpha's publicity and selected for inclusion in Gumbel's *Telling Others*. Skelsey had committed his life to Christ in September 1971, aged 17, at a Nationwide Festival of Light rally in London's Hyde Park, in response to the preaching of American evangelist Arthur Blessitt (part of the Jesus People movement and famous for travelling the world carrying a giant wooden cross). Skelsey had an immediate passion to share his new faith and studied at London Bible College hoping to be an evangelist and pastor, but failed academically and felt he was viewed as a failure by his parents and by God.[30] For 15 years his Christianity went 'on the back burner' and was replaced by 'a faithless and obsessive pursuit of success for its own sake'. He became picture editor at the *Sunday Telegraph* and had 'everything I ever wanted in life', including a beautiful wife and a Porsche 911, though 'deep down I hated myself'. When Skelsey turned 40, he began to reflect on his achievements, troubled by the words of Jesus, 'What good will it be for a man if he gains the whole world, yet forfeits his soul?' (Matthew 16:26). After reading about Alpha in a magazine, he signed up for the course at HTB, fixated upon the Holy Spirit weekend. Skelsey recalled: 'I felt like a dying man waiting for a life-saving operation. Never mind the weeks of pre-med, I just had to get into the operating theatre.' His focus was particularly the Saturday afternoon session, on how to be filled with the Spirit, as he wrote in a letter to Gumbel:

I looked at the order of play, saw that session three was at 4.30 pm and simply hung on like a marathon runner weaving his way up the finishing straight with nothing but the finishing tape as the focus of his attention. I'll never forget that final session. I felt as though I was being torn in two. Half way through I just couldn't stand it any more. The prize was so near and you were getting there so slowly! I literally wanted to scream out, 'Do it now! Do it now! I can't hold out any longer.' I'm not exaggerating when I say I was in agony. Then He came and, oh, the relief.[31]

This sense of spiritual and psychological struggle, and desperation to be filled with the Holy Spirit, was a recurrent theme in Alpha testimonies. It often resulted in increased hunger for intimacy with God. 'Now all I want to do is pray and read my Bible', Skelsey testified at an Alpha conference in Edinburgh a few days later.[32] Elsewhere he described his experience in more Christocentric terms. He recalled sitting at Alpha 'week after week in a self-imposed pit of hate and self-loathing, feeling I was on the very brink of destruction. But at my lowest point Jesus came marching in, grabbed me by the throat and said "You're coming with me." I did not decide for him. He mugged me.'[33] Many attenders at Alpha, like Skelsey, had a church background and yet the rekindling of latent faith brought such a dramatic change to their experience of Christianity that it seemed like brand new faith, as if they had been converted for the very first time.

These reports provoked the hostility of conservative Christian commentators. Although Australian evangelist John Chapman agreed that Gumbel was a 'first-class communicator', he complained that the Alpha syllabus was unbalanced with too little about Jesus and too much about the Holy Spirit, so it should be avoided 'by anyone who takes the Bible seriously'.[34] *Prophecy Today* was likewise concerned that the first two Alpha sessions on Jesus seemed merely 'preparatory to the real business of an experiential encounter with God through his Spirit'.[35] Baptist pastor Chris Hand, co-founder of the Christian Research Network and author of *Falling Short? The Alpha Course Examined* (1998), rebuked Gumbel's 'hard-sell' technique at the weekend away, which left people 'boxed into a corner so that unless they co-operate they are "missing" out on what the Holy Spirit wants to

do'.[36] Hand complained that Alpha pushed 'experience' above repentance and faith: 'For many it is simply an emotional experience or
bodily sensation devoid of anything meaningful. There is no conviction of sin, no grasp of one's spiritual state, no comprehension of the
holiness of God or of our desperate need to be reconciled to Him.'[37]
However, Gumbel insisted that Alpha's teaching on the Holy Spirit
was an essential component of the course, and to remove it would be
like attempting to drive a car without an engine.[38] Some churches
dropped the material from their Alpha programmes, but Tricia Neill
warned that they would therefore be disappointed in Alpha's results.[39]
A high proportion of Alpha conversion testimonies referenced the
Holy Spirit weekend as a crucial, often life-changing, experience.

Tongues of Praise

Of all ecstatic phenomena, Gumbel especially emphasised that filling
with the Spirit was often accompanied with 'speaking in tongues'.[40]
This was a regular occurrence at HTB. For example, in 2003 Sandy
Millar urged the congregation to speak more often in tongues: 'We
need to see everybody equipped and launched and filled with the
Spirit, fizzing and humming.' He described HTB as 'a pentecostal
church with a small "p"', and suggested that praying in tongues was
often 'the gateway to other spiritual gifts' such as healing, words of
knowledge, and 'movement in the supernatural'.[41]

Gumbel distilled the reception process into six simple steps, but his
first attempt in *Questions of Life* merged filling with the Spirit and
speaking in tongues, as if they were synonymous and simultaneous:
'Ask God to fill you with his Spirit and to give you the gift of
tongues.'[42] The next edition more carefully distinguished them as
separate steps: 'Ask God to fill you with his Spirit . . . If you would
like to receive the gift of tongues, ask.'[43] But tongues were the hoped-
for result for every Alpha participant. 'You don't need to speak in
tongues. It is not the most important gift', Gumbel told one Alpha
weekend, but 'it would be wonderful if you tried'.[44] He reckoned the
greatest barrier to receiving the gift was self-consciousness, so he
encouraged Alpha guests to copy the vocal sounds made by others

until they found a supernatural prayer language of their own.[45] The Alpha youth manual gave similar advice to teenagers: 'Go with the flow! Open your mouth and begin to speak. Try on your own in your room. Believe that God wants to give it to you.'[46] Corporate singing in tongues on the Alpha weekend was celebrated by Gumbel as 'one of the most beautiful and almost angelic sounds I have ever heard'.[47]

Published Alpha testimonies often highlighted tongues. However, without the theological vocabulary to express their new spiritual experiences, some guests borrowed concepts closer to home. One American convert, for example, concluded that the gift of tongues was more powerful than any drugs trip. He had been an addict for 21 years when he attended Alpha in 1997 at the Church of the Good Shepherd, an Episcopalian congregation in Springfield, Missouri. At the Holy Spirit weekend at Cliff Springs camp, he lay in the back of his pick-up truck in the evening and asked God 'to stir me and fill me to the full with the Holy Spirit'. Late that night, 'I was awakened by God and he did some powerful ministering to me. I felt as though God opened my heart and poured all the stars in the universe in me. And then they were all released.' This ecstatic experience lasted about three hours, during which he received the gift of tongues:

> I never shook so much in my life. I didn't know you could laugh and cry at the same time. And then I couldn't walk. It was the most power-ful thing that I have ever felt – and I've done every kind of drug that you can imagine. That feeling that I felt that night was the feeling that I'd been looking for.[48]

Donna Matthews found fame in the mid-1990s as lead guitarist with the Britpop band Elastica, though her career was ruined by heroin addiction. Plagued by paranoia, she found it impossible to break her drugs habit: 'It was stealing my soul.' In deep distress and terror one night, at a treatment centre in Bristol in 1999, she turned to prayer as a last resort: 'If there is a God and you can hear me, then please help me.' Matthews felt that something changed in her that night, the beginning of a long road to recovery, and she resolved to find out more about God. In 2002, aged 30, she attended Alpha at HTB, and was particu-larly impacted by the weekend away at Pakefield in Suffolk. Though initially cynical, as she held out her hands in prayer to receive the Holy Spirit, 'suddenly I started singing in tongues. I felt like a bird. I felt like this music was coming out of my mouth . . . this beautiful voice came out – and I haven't got a beautiful voice.' She felt 'flooded with warmth' and 'completely, completely at home', as if 'clear water was coming through me, pushing everything out of me'. Matthews started sobbing and shaking, and the next day she prayed a prayer of repentance, offering her life to Jesus. She was baptised at HTB in January 2003.[49]

Damian McGuinness's reception of tongues took place not on the Alpha Holy Spirit day, but unexpectedly 24 hours later. He had served three years in prison (in Lancashire and Northumberland) for his part in an armed robbery in July 1998, aged 18, of a takeaway restaurant using an imitation firearm. While incarcerated he attended prison chapel classes and read in his Gideon's Bible that 'if you confess with your mouth, "Jesus is Lord", and believe in your heart that God raised him from the dead, you will be saved' (Romans 10:9).

> So I said, 'OK, Jesus is Lord.' At once I was filled with a rush from the soles of my feet, up my back and into my head. Within a short time, I was dancing around my cell. I'd been touched by God. It was the most amazing experience ever. Nobody could tell me after that that God wasn't real.

In the prison library McGuinness found a copy of Mark Elsdon-Dew's *The God Who Changes Lives*, which gave him a hunger for the transforming power of the Holy Spirit. However, on his release from prison, he drifted back into his old circle of friends, often high on drink and drugs. McGuinness attended Alpha in 2002 at North Manchester Family Church and gave his life to Jesus after hearing the parable of the prodigal son, but when he went forward for prayer on the Alpha Holy Spirit day, he remained resistant, saying, 'No, no, no' and refusing to mimic praying in tongues. He resolved never to return to church and the following day 'got hammered' on alcohol and cannabis with his friends. On their way home, parked outside a fish and chip shop, McGuinness suddenly felt 'as if God had removed the front window screen of the car and just imparted the Holy Spirit on me'. He began to speak in tongues, and later reasoned:

God was in the car with me and no one can tell me any different. Satan might tell me it was the drugs or drink. But I know I received the Holy Spirit that night. When God or the Holy Spirit touches you, there's no messing about, you just know it. It's not mistakable for any other feeling in the world. When God entered that car, I felt a physical presence upon me. I felt absolute joy and peace well up inside and come out of my mouth in a tongue that I'd never spoken before. I started giggling to myself, thinking, 'This is amazing.'

Over the next nine days, McGuinness continued to get drunk with his friends, and on one occasion was involved in a fight, until he decisively cut links with them. He began to read the Bible and Christian paperbacks like Nicky Cruz's *Run Baby Run*, and prayed in tongues every night before bed. His mother, sister and brother all became Christians shortly afterwards.[50] *Alpha News* profiled his story.

These sorts of experiences were common and journalists who attended the Holy Spirit weekend were often at a loss to know how to interpret what they were witnessing. Dominic Kennedy, a self-styled 'lapsed Catholic', attended Alpha at HTB in autumn 1996, with a weekend away at Chichester. He watched, bemused, as 'healthy young adults degenerate into a helpless mass of quivers, jerks, babbles and moans befitting a victim of a cruel degenerative illness'. Kennedy's evocative description for *The Times* of the session on 'How can I be filled with the Spirit?' was typical of newspaper accounts:

Mr Gumbel asked us to put our hands out. He prayed: 'Fill us with your Spirit', then described aloud what he saw. 'The Spirit of God has come and is filling people all around the room. Some people are shaking. Some of you feel a great weight on your hands. Others, tears are rolling down your face and you are thinking, "Why am I crying?" That is the Spirit of God, don't be embarrassed. Don't resist the Spirit. Some of you feel waves coming over you. Waves and waves of liquid love . . .' We were invited to sing in tongues. What should have been a cacophonous babble sounded strangely melodic and beautiful, the men's deep voices washed over by the rising spontaneous harmonies of the women, the words meaningless. Like a Turkish ballad, exotic but not completely alien. Around the room, people were crying. One woman was gripped by a violent seizure which rocked her body back and forth.[51]

Likewise, journalist Julia Llewellyn Smith, a 'confirmed atheist' who attended Alpha in 1998 for *The Express*, was increasingly disconcerted as the course shifted approach from its appeal to logic and rational argument in the early weeks, to then 'targeting our emotions'. She was alarmed at the weekend away as 'All around the room, grown men and women began to shake and weep and sing "in tongues"', and reckoned she had 'witnessed a scene of mass hysteria'.[52] When Victoria Moore attended the course for the *Daily Mail*, she found the Holy Spirit weekend 'very disturbing' and concluded that Alpha was 'no different from any New Age quackery', with Gumbel as 'a charming Svengali figure' preying upon the emotional anxieties of young professionals.[53] *Time Out* similarly derided Alpha as 'a cult for the emotionally incontinent', offering 'a hysterical hotch-potch of Bible belt-cum-hippy talk'.[54]

There were strong denunciations from Christians also. *The Banner of Truth*, a Calvinistic magazine, argued that the Alpha weekend was guilty of using 'auto-suggestion, mimicking and emotional pressures' to create tongues speaking.[55] From a liberal perspective, a Methodist superintendent in Manchester complained that whereas the early church 'stressed the universality of love', Alpha reduced Christianity 'to those who can babble hysterically'.[56] But the HTB model was not necessarily followed in all Alpha churches. Even among those who enthusiastically embraced the course, tongues were often absent from their Holy Spirit weekends. For example, a Baptist minister in Essex testified in 1998 that his congregation had seen 37 people make 'commitments to Christ' during six Alphas, and that their Holy Spirit day 'took place in an atmosphere of quiet dignity':

No one spoke in tongues, no one fell over, no one found themselves laughing hysterically, some shed tears, but everyone spoke of how they had a powerful sense of the presence of God, some found difficult issues being resolved, others were encouraged in various ways, and one person trusted Christ as Saviour for the first time.[57]

Despite strong pressure upon Gumbel to delete his teaching on tongues from the Alpha syllabus, he refused to do so on the grounds that it was one of the key reasons for Alpha's effectiveness. He calculated that, in any case, it was only one-third of one talk, or 2.2 per cent of the whole course – though by far the most controversial component.[58] Gumbel justified its inclusion on the grounds that Alpha is 'a beginner's course' and tongues is 'a beginner's gift'.[59]

The Revelations

Negative reactions to the Holy Spirit weekend went unrecorded by *Alpha News*, of course. To some participants the weekend seemed pressurised, weird and disturbing – excellent source material for psychological fiction. Oxford graduate Alex Preston attended Alpha at HTB in 2005 while working for a finance company in Mayfair, and used it as the basis for his novel, *The Revelations* (2012), with the Holy Spirit weekend away as the plot's climactic focal point.[60] The story portrayed a fictional six-week evangelistic programme called 'The Course', pioneered by a trendy Anglican congregation in Chelsea and copied by hundreds of churches across Britain. It attracted young, wealthy, successful people and was led by a middle-aged clergyman, David Nightingale, a keep-fit fanatic and former merchant banker. It had global ambitions, sold branded merchandise, and placed advertisements on London buses with the slogan, 'Shouldn't there be more to life than this?' (a direct parody of a real-life Alpha slogan, 'Is there more to life than this?'). 'We need to make sure that nothing stalls the growth of the Course,' Nightingale declared. 'Momentum is everything; keeping Course membership growing is all-important. Even those who try to do us down can't argue with the fact that the Course is attracting people back to Christianity.' His scheme was bankrolled by millionaire hedge fund entrepreneurs, with money siphoned through trusts in the Cayman Islands.

Preston's plot centred upon the relational angst of four young friends, a *ménage à quatre,* part of Nightingale's inner circle as deputy leaders on the Course. All of them found it impossible to keep the rule of celibacy outside marriage. One was not sure he believed in God at all, though he could parrot the language. He 'found it disconcerting that the Course insisted on marketing itself as a forum for philosophical enquiry when it was so clearly focused on pushing a fairly narrow form of evangelical Christianity'. The narrative's heart was 'The Retreat', a weekend away in the Cotswolds, where music and lighting were used to manipulate guests into discarding their inhibitions and speaking in tongues – described by Preston at length. 'Don't be afraid of letting yourself go,' Nightingale purred. 'Let the Holy Spirit into your hearts, lose yourself in the love of Jesus.' 'Half of us fake it anyway,' confessed one of the leaders. 'It's all just part of the game.' But amid the tongues speaking and spiritual deception, the weekend away was dominated by heavy drinking, illicit sex, and the mysterious disappearance of one of the young women who was later found dead. Preston's dramatic fiction was widely reviewed, demonstrating Alpha's ability to capture the public imagination, even among a hostile audience suspicious of Alpha's motives but intrigued by its popularity.[61]

Liquid Love

At heart, Nicky Gumbel is a theologian of the love of God. Love runs through Alpha from beginning to end like a golden seam. 'God loves us and wants the very best for our lives', rejoiced *Questions of Life* in a repeated refrain.[62] 'It all starts with God's love for us', Gumbel declared.[63] 'The good news of Christianity is that God loves us and he did not leave us in the mess that we make of our own lives.'[64] A similar emphasis is found in Gumbel's other paperbacks. In *A Life Worth Living*, for example, he argued that God's love, seen supremely in the cross of Christ, is the central theme of the New Testament and indeed of the whole Bible.[65]

This priority was directly shaped by Gumbel's own history. As a young Christian in 1974, when friends prayed for him to be filled with the Holy Spirit, he received not only the gift of tongues but also a deep sense of God's love.[66] It was one of the reasons he became an evangelist, 'because I long for other people to experience that same love in their own lives'.[67] Therefore, at the climax of the Holy Spirit weekend, Gumbel taught that for many Alpha guests 'the experience of the Spirit may be an overwhelming experience of the love of God . . . It is not enough to understand his love; we need to experience his love.'[68] Once again, the Holy Spirit and personal experience were inseparably linked – key Alpha themes – but now with the love of God as the third vital constituent of that spiritual nexus. In support of his doctrine, Gumbel pointed to earlier exponents across the English-speaking world. For example, American revivalist Charles Finney likened his experience of the Holy Spirit to 'a wave of electricity . . . it seemed to come in waves and waves of liquid love'. D. L. Moody prayed earnestly to be filled with God's Spirit, but when it happened, he had 'such an experience of His love that I had to ask Him to stay His hand'.[69] South African renewal leader Bill Burnett (Archbishop of Cape Town) likewise described his encounter with the Holy Spirit as 'electric shocks of love'.[70]

Evangelical critics often homed in upon this part of Alpha's teaching. For example, Chris Hand dismissed Alpha as 'a toothless and sentimental gospel that fails to ground the love of God in His justice'.[71] He complained:

> Yet again, it is all about love. This is the heart of the appeal that is made. God is 'longing' for a relationship with us and is waiting for us to wake up to this. In the language that Alpha uses, we are already His children. It sounds very intimate and close. We are not made remotely aware that we are sinners far away from God and far removed from His love. We are not told that we need mercy if we are ever going to enter the kingdom of God.[72]

Again, Hand protested that in Alpha there was 'no listing of sins . . . no full description of man's hopelessly sinful ways and of his irretrievably sinful nature':

> Instead of appearing sinful, man comes across as being rather sad. The portrait of ourselves that we are presented with is one of pathos rather than obstinate sinfulness. We are creatures in a lost, dark and confused world, making a mess of our lives, and tragically ignorant that God really does love us. Our sins are taken as evidence merely that life is not what it could or should be. We are missing out. This is Alpha's message

to us. There is no bite, there is no confrontation of ourselves as sinners. We feel sorry for ourselves rather than ashamed of ourselves.[73]

Alpha focused on the consequences of human sin, but not the fundamental nature of sin as offence against God. Gumbel was alert to these critiques and responded by revising his text. Where the first edition of *Questions of Life* had 'The root cause of sin is a broken relationship with God', this was changed in 1995 to 'The essence of sin is a rebellion against God.'[74]

A parallel complaint was that Alpha was silent about God's wrath and the reality of hell. The theme was, in fact, mentioned briefly in *Questions of Life*. For example, citing the parable of the sheep and the goats (Matthew 25), Gumbel explained that 'What happens to us on the Day of Judgement depends on how we respond to Jesus in this life.'[75] Likewise, he taught that all sin deserved punishment, that one day all humanity would face divine judgement, and that for some the result would be 'eternal isolation from God'.[76] Judgement Day, he reiterated, would be 'a day of destruction' for all who rejected the gospel of Jesus Christ.[77] Despite these affirmations, evangelical critics thought them too indirect and complained that Alpha tiptoed through the subject *sotto voce*.[78] In his other books Gumbel spoke more fully. When addressing 'righteous anger' in *Challenging Lifestyle*, he observed that there were 20 different words for 'wrath' in the Old Testament, used in total 580 times. God's anger, he explained, 'is part of his holy love, a flame that sears and purifies. There is no moral flabbiness in God. Anger is God's personal reaction to sin.'[79] Likewise in *The Heart of Revival*, Gumbel expressed the urgency of evangelism: 'Our task as God's servants today is to tell others now so that they will rejoice and reign with him, rather than face his terrifying judgement against them. We need to tell people the good news and warn them of the dangers of rejecting God.'[80] He emphasised that according to the New Testament the basis of God's judgement was whether or not an individual had responded to the gospel by putting their faith in Jesus:

> Again, there is no middle ground, no hybrid, no category of those who are unsure, undecided or don't know ... We deserve hell and cannot save ourselves, but Jesus died for us, to enable us to be his

servants and to make heaven a reality . . . For those who accept the authority of the Bible, there may be some debate about the nature of hell (for example, whether it means eternal punishment or judgement and annihilation), but there is no doubt about its reality.[81]

Nevertheless, in the face of complaints that Gumbel overstressed God's love, he refused to back down. Indeed, when revising *Questions of Life*, he accentuated the theme even more. Why did Jesus die? 'The answer in a nutshell', Gumbel explained in 2001, 'is because God loves you.' He quoted from Augustine of Hippo, 'The whole Bible does nothing but tell of God's love'; and from Cantalamessa, 'The love of God is the answer to all the "whys" in the Bible.'[82] In 2003 he added: 'God accepts us and loves us simply because he loves us', an apparent tautology.[83] In 2010 he added further: 'If you are ever in any doubt that God loves us, look at the cross.'[84] Some Christians, Gumbel observed in *The Jesus Lifestyle*, were prone to exaggerating God's anger as if it was an essential part of the divine character. The Bible says 'God is love' (1 John 4:16), but never 'God is wrath', he replied.[85] The extravagant love of God remained Alpha's persistent keynote.

Some Alpha guests needed no reminder that they were sinners – it was already painfully obvious to them. What they needed to hear most of all, in Gumbel's opinion, was of God's love for the unlovely. For example, when a former prostitute and drug addict attended Alpha at HTB, she was deeply impacted by hearing the proclamation, 'Jesus loves you, and if you had been the only person in the world, Jesus would have died for you.' She felt as if she had previously been imprisoned in a 'kind of concrete underground bunker', but the declaration of love broke through:

> Nothing could penetrate me, but those words completely and utterly destroyed me. It completely broke down all that anger, all that rage, that sort of self-disgust and everything. I prayed: 'Jesus, this is who I am. This is who I've been. And I now turn away from this.' And I asked Jesus to come in.

She rejoiced that her life had been 'completely transformed': 'Christ did come into the most polluted, most toxic, most self-serving person and he's filled me with love, and he's forgiven me . . . I feel so cleansed! I am truly, truly restored.'[86]

Alpha News published many similar testimonies in which an experience of the Holy Spirit, often with physical manifestations, was simultaneous with the language of love. Michaela Flanagan, in her mid-20s, from Cheshire, had been through a series of unhealthy relationships, suffered from panic attacks and was growing addicted to cannabis. 'I hated myself', she recalled; 'I hated the mirror and I was devastated with how my life had turned out. There didn't seem to be a way out of it.' When one of her friends committed suicide, she was increasingly troubled about questions of life and death, so approached the local Methodist minister, Andrew Baguley, in the street, and he invited her to Alpha. Flanagan dropped out of the course after a few weeks, but Baguley reassured her: 'God loves you. Just ask him for forgiveness and he'll sort you out.' When Anne Watson (widow of evangelist David Watson) led a teaching seminar at the church, Flanagan went forward for prayer:

> Anne put her hand on me and said, 'Come, Holy Spirit' and the most incredible thing happened. I felt as if someone took two torches and put them into my eyes. I saw this incredible white light and my whole body, from my head to my toes, was bathed with bright white light. Liquid love was flooding into me and I kept saying over and over again, 'I've met Jesus, I've met Jesus.'

She committed her life to Christ and 'knew without a shadow of a doubt that the old Michaela was dead and I was a brand new person. I didn't feel any shame or guilt, self-hatred or addictions.' The experience was 'ecstasy', she told *Alpha News*. 'I was bursting with Jesus and I wanted to spend all my time on my knees praising God.'[87] Yet Flanagan's description of being flooded with 'liquid love' was unknowingly borrowed from Charles Finney's recollection of his own conversion and 'mighty baptism of the Holy Ghost' in Jefferson County, New York, in 1821, now mediated to a new generation of converts on the other side of the globe via Gumbel and Alpha.[88]

Resisting the Occult

Gumbel delineated Christian conversion as a decisive transfer from the 'dominion of darkness' to the 'kingdom of light'. Although Christ had defeated 'Satan and all his minions' on the cross, new converts should not be surprised to find themselves caught in 'spiritual warfare' and 'under a powerful assault from the enemy'.[89] Therefore Gumbel recommended that the Holy Spirit weekend should always be followed by the Alpha session on 'How can I resist evil?'[90]

Many testimonies in *Alpha News* drew attention to this spiritual dynamic. For example, in Whitby, North Yorkshire, there was controversy in 1997 surrounding the centenary celebrations of Bram Stoker's *Dracula*, which was expected to draw crowds of thousands from all over Europe. The local Whitby Dracula Society planned a Gothic parade through the town, culminating in a midnight finale in the graveyard of St Mary's church, where the Transylvanian Count famously sucked the blood of his first English victim and turned her into a vampire. But the church council threatened the Dracula enthusiasts with a court injunction to prevent this desecration of consecrated ground. They believed that far from being 'a harmless bit of fun', these activities were 'deeply unchristian' and had 'a very sinister link with the occult'. Vanda Lee, president of the Whitby Dracula Society, protested that vampires and Christians had a lot in common – they both believed in the resurrection of the dead![91] She found it insulting to be accused of devil-worship and told the Anglican curate, Graham Taylor, 'Vampirism offers me eternal life without having to believe in your Jesus!' However, Taylor gave her a copy of Gumbel's *Questions of Life*, which she read in a single evening, and invited her to an evangelistic event in Scarborough on the occult and New Age. Lee went forward to give her life to Christ, praying the conversion prayer in *Why Jesus?*[92]

Five years later, Taylor transitioned from evangelist to children's novelist, and like Bram Stoker chose Whitby as the setting for his Gothic fantasy, *Shadowmancer* (2002). Capitalising on the huge commercial success of J. K. Rowling's *Harry Potter* and Philip Pullman's *His Dark Materials*, Taylor created a world of sorcery, ancient secrets, and the cosmic struggle between good and evil, which was quickly picked up by Faber and Faber and became a runaway bestseller. The novel's chief antagonist, sadistic clergyman Reverend Obadiah Demurral, made a pact with the devil for global dominion, beginning in Scarborough, until defeated by a group of children. Taylor was concerned that many children's books 'glorified the occult' and wanted instead to write a novel with 'a strong influence of the Holy Spirit running throughout'. He testified to the impact of Alpha upon his ministry and was trumpeted by *Alpha News*.[93]

Gumbel warned explicitly against the dangers of the occult and 'the demonic'. He urged that anyone involved in spiritualism, Ouija boards, palm-reading, fortune-telling, astrology, horoscopes or witchcraft must not only repent of such activities but destroy anything associated with them, such as books, charms, videos, DVDs and magazines.[94] In his analysis of the 'New Age', he extended the catalogue of spiritual dangers to fantasy games like *Dungeons and Dragons* and its television spinoff, *The Crystal Maze* (first broadcast between 1990 and 1995).[95]

Alpha News again picked up these themes in accounts of new converts. For example, telecommunications engineer Lee Duckett 'dabbled in magic', tried Ouija boards several times, and visited a medium. When he was sent to HTB in May 1993 to install new telephone equipment, the receptionist gave him a copy of *Why Jesus?* and invited him to Alpha. Duckett began to read the New Testament and Christian books like *Run Baby Run* and Benny Hinn's *Good Morning, Holy Spirit* (1990). One night in bed, after reading the Bible, he prayed for the Holy Spirit to baptise him, but began to feel that there was 'a battle going on over me', which left him 'really frightened'. His Alpha group leader urged him to throw away the occult books and pictures in his room, and to read Psalm 23 and Ephesians 6, and at the Alpha session on evil a few days later Duckett felt nauseous and wanted to run away. At the Alpha weekend, when Gumbel called down the Holy Spirit, Duckett heard and felt blowing in his left ear and his knees began to buckle. He collapsed into a chair and received the gift of tongues. The next evening, when he was prayed for at HTB, he 'felt the Spirit start from my feet and "wash" through my body ... When it was all over I just felt completely reborn.'[96] He was later ordained as an Anglican clergyman.

There were many similar testimonies. Business couple Fatimah and Iain Murray, in their late 40s, both became Christians through Alpha at HTB in 1994. As part of renunciation of their former beliefs, she burned her tarot cards and astrology books, worth over £3,000, and he burned all his freemasonry regalia in an incinerator.[97] Christine Woodall was raised within Roman Catholicism on the island of Guernsey, but drifted into New Age spirituality, fascinated by astrology, energy healing, mediums and 'spirit guides'. She returned enthusiastically to her Catholic roots after she became a Christian in 1999 through Alpha, run by a local community church, testifying that Alpha had 'brought me back to Mass'.[98] School teacher Claire Jerath was obsessed with tarot cards, angel cards, wish sticks, numerology, astrology, crystal balls, and reading palms and tea leaves. 'It was completely controlling me', she testified. She placed every decision in the cards and began to have frightening experiences: 'It seemed like some outside power was trying to control me.' She attended Alpha at HTB in 2006, repenting of her sins and asking Jesus into her life during the weekend away. She threw out all her occultic paraphernalia, began to read the Bible and books by Pentecostal pioneer Smith Wigglesworth, and renounced her former way of life as 'counterfeit and dangerous. I had a very lucky escape.'[99] Alpha took the spiritual realm very seriously.

Power Evangelism

Alpha's favourite methodology was 'power evangelism' – that is, Gumbel explained, 'the supernatural display of the power of the Holy Spirit' in 'signs, wonders and miracles', alongside spoken proclamation of the Christian message. Throughout the New Testament, he observed, church growth was accompanied by 'conversions, miraculous signs, healings, visions, tongues, prophecy, raising the dead and casting out evil spirits. The same God is at work today among us.'[100] Vineyard pioneer John Wimber advocated this approach in his bestselling *Power Evangelism* (1985), which deeply shaped Gumbel's understanding. In direct imitation of Wimber – as modelled, for example, during the Californian's first memorable visit to HTB in

1982 – the Alpha session on supernatural healing suspended the usual post-talk discussion groups and replaced them with a practical demonstration.[101] Alpha was a major conduit for the propagation of Wimberite theology and praxis across the globe.

Alpha News and *HTB in Focus* published many testimonies of supernatural healing at Alpha, often linked directly to conversions or to fresh experiences of God's reality. For example, while worshipping in the HTB wives' group in early summer 1992, led by Pippa Gumbel, Francie Lygo received an unusually detailed word of knowledge, 'like a photographic print', of the right arm of a young woman who was dressed in bottle green, had blondish hair, and wore a gold chain bracelet on her wrist. At the same time Lygo had a physical sensation, 'like a thousand volts going through me', and felt she must say something but instead kept silent. Over the next three weeks the picture returned about eight times, while she was walking the dog or doing the washing up. Then, at the Alpha evening on healing she experienced the same sensation of 'power' coming through her and felt compelled to speak when Nicky Gumbel invited words of knowledge. Lygo looked in vain around the crowded room for a blonde woman wearing green, until Seonaid Fresson put up her hand and announced, 'That's me!'[102] Two years earlier, Fresson had slipped on the platform at Liverpool Street Station, torn a ligament in her foot, broken her left hand, and smashed her right elbow. Her elbow still caused pain, despite surgery and physiotherapy, but as she received prayer at Alpha she experienced a 'very hot sensation around my whole arm' and the pain disappeared. Fresson was already a Christian, but it confirmed for her God's reality: 'My faith was strong anyway, but I think God was just proving to me that he was really there.'[103]

Similarly, businesswoman Judy Cahusac, in her mid-40s, had injured her right shoulder while skiing, but it was healed during Alpha at HTB in 1990 when she went forward for prayer in response to a word of knowledge. 'That was the moment that Jesus became real to me', she recalled, 'and I asked him into my life.'[104] 'God is real' was also the reaction of Quincy Bellot, a Royal Marine, who decided in 2009 'to try God and try Alpha' after suffering for 12 years from severe cartilage damage to his knee. The pain disappeared after he received prayer and he was soon able to start running again. 'God just completely healed me,' he testified. 'It's absolutely miraculous!' Another Alpha attender who had been walking with crutches because of a badly damaged knee was also 'totally healed' on the Holy Spirit weekend at the moment when he prayed 'to give his life to Christ'.[105]

Jean Smith, in her 60s, had been registered blind for 16 years and was told by the hospital specialist she would never see again after an infection damaged her retinas and left her in constant pain. In 1997 she attended Alpha at her local church in Cwmbran near Newport, South Wales, though somewhat reluctantly because she could not see the videos. On the Holy Spirit day she experienced an unusual sensation during prayer: 'it was as if someone had plucked the sun out of the sky and laced it in my head. My head was full of a brilliant light.' By the end of the day, the pain in her eyes had completely disappeared. After Alpha, she was prayed for at a healing service and 'became hotter and hotter to such a degree my clothes were wringing wet. My thoughts were, "Please hurry up and finish. I cannot take any more."' She was anointed with oil (which had been brought back from Galilee) and was led back to her seat. As she continued in prayer, and wiped the perspiration from her forehead, she accidentally rubbed the oil into her eyes and then realised she could see the cross on the communion table and her sight returned. There were tears of joy as the church praised God for a miracle.[106] There were similar reports from Zimbabwe, where pre-school teacher Sally van Wyk was diagnosed with optic neuritis after contracting measles. She was increasingly blind, but after receiving prayer during the Alpha Holy Spirit weekend in 1997 at Marondera, Mashonaland, her sight was restored, to the amazement of her eye surgeon.[107]

At Cromer in Norfolk in autumn 1998, atheist Steve Downes (a 24-year-old journalist with the *Eastern Daily Press*) agreed to attend Alpha only because his wife, Yolande, insisted on going and he wanted to protect her from 'brainwashing'. It was a small course, run jointly by the local Anglicans and Methodists – just seven participants, meeting in a home to watch Gumbel on video. Yolande was pregnant with their first child, but the 20-week scan revealed the baby had cystic fibrosis, so they went for an abortion, only changing their minds at the last minute. Steve had a dream about calling the baby 'Ezekiel', a name he had never heard before but later discovered meant 'God is strong'. On the Alpha evening dedicated to healing, Yolande was invited to stand in the middle of the group, gathered in a circle, while the Anglican curate prayed that God would protect her and the baby. She began to cry and 'felt heat going through her womb'. Soon afterwards, another scan at the hospital showed no signs of cystic fibrosis, which the doctors were at a loss to explain. 'We were confused,' Steve testified. 'We had no faith in a God of healing power, but had witnessed something out of the ordinary and mind-blowing.' The couple both 'gave our lives to Jesus', and two months later their healthy son was born. *Alpha News* profiled the story, as did *Christianity* magazine under the title 'Miracle Child'.[108]

Despite these celebratory testimonies of healing, Gumbel's teaching was tempered by recognition that God does not always heal. Interwoven with the theology of divine blessing, there was also a theology of suffering, which grew more prominent in later editions of Alpha as the course matured. 'Our bodies are decaying', Gumbel wrote in *Questions of Life*. 'At some point it may be right to prepare a person for death rather than praying for their healing.'[109] In the second edition he praised the hospice movement and its care for the terminally ill, as another good way to express Jesus's compassion for the sick.[110] The 2010 edition went further, acknowledging that although miraculous healing was a sign of God's kingdom breaking into the present age, yet there was always 'an element of waiting' and of 'groaning inwardly as we wait eagerly for . . . the redemption of our bodies' (Romans 8:23).[111] Gumbel offered the example of his friend Patrick Pearson Miles – whose wife, Philippa, was Gumbel's secretary and PA from 1992 and typed many of his Alpha paperbacks. After developing nephrotic syndrome, Pearson Miles underwent a kidney transplant in November 1993, aged 28, but the transplant failed and he began an exhausting long-term pattern of dialysis. On many occasions he received prayer for healing, including from John Wimber, with no apparent results. Ten years after the transplant, Pearson Miles exclaimed: 'I might not have been miraculously healed yet, but I do believe I have been miraculously sustained.'[112]

One of the experiences that most deeply shaped Gumbel's theology of suffering was the sudden death of one of his closest friends, Mick Hawkins, in July 1996. At the very point when Alpha was beginning to grow exponentially across the globe, and HTB was delighting in success upon success in its expanding sphere of influence and testimonies of God's supernatural power, here was personal tragedy that shook the whole congregation. Hawkins, aged 42, was a Lloyds insurance broker, HTB churchwarden, and chairman of the church's Focus summer holiday in Suffolk. On the first Monday afternoon of the Focus week, Gumbel and Hawkins were playing squash together in a local gym. Hawkins was two games up, when he suddenly collapsed and died on the court from a heart attack, leaving a widow and six young children.[113] Gumbel was in shock and 'in floods of tears'.[114] In *Questions of Life*, he recalled: 'I have never cried out to God more than I did on that occasion; asking him to heal him, restore him, praying that the heart attack would not be fatal. I do not know why he died.' Unable to sleep that night, Gumbel went walking at 5am, pouring out his heart to God, and realised he faced a choice: 'I could say, "I am going to stop believing." The alternative was to say, "I am going to go on believing in spite of the fact that I don't understand and I am going to trust you, Lord, even though I don't think I will ever understand – in this life – why it happened."'[115] This sudden, traumatic bereavement forced Gumbel to question the biblical certainties he so confidently proclaimed. 'It's a constant battle', he admitted. 'Faith and doubt are two sides of the same coin, they are not opposed to each other.'[116] 'In my experience', he wrote in *Questions of Life*, 'it sometimes seems almost as if God has hidden his face from us.'[117] There was similar trauma in later years. In August 2000, three members of HTB were involved in a serious car accident, heading for their summer holidays – Dave McGavin, aged 28, was killed, and Sue Arundale (HTB's Alpha administrator) was left with life-changing injuries.[118] Alpha's persistent emphasis on experiencing God through the power of the Holy Spirit, with miraculous tongues of praise and gifts of healing, was not mere naive Christian triumphalism. Alpha's theology continued to mature and evolve in the crucible of painful lived experience.

5

Marketing the Gospel

ONE OF ALPHA'S primary ambitions is to reach young people with the Christian message. This has long been a major focus of HTB's mission. Under Sandy Millar's leadership, the church embraced a contemporary, informal style, a model he brought back to London from California. In 1990, HTB's professional robed choir was finally disbanded after many decades of service and replaced with a worship band, led by 25-year-old Ric Thorpe (later Bishop of Islington), to outcries in the local press.[1] The HTB clergy stopped wearing robes and sat more lightly to the inherited Anglican liturgies. 'I don't dislike robes', Millar explained, 'but young people cannot understand why a perfectly ordinary man needs to dress up.' He rejected suggestions that informality was somehow un-Anglican. 'Anglicanism would never have been born if people had not wanted change', he reasoned.[2]

This drive to embrace contemporary youth culture was energetically pursued by Alpha. Tricia Neill argued in *Alpha News* that churches that attracted young people to Alpha were likely to experience the greatest growth. She therefore recommended that everything should be tailored towards younger guests, including the music, lighting, testimonies and choice of venue – pubs, clubs, restaurants and sports centres were preferable to church halls. Neill encouraged:

> make the food attractive to the young, provide young leadership, and publicise the course with young people in mind. Many of the official Alpha posters and promotional material are specifically positioned towards attracting young people. Our experience is that the older age groups will continue to come if there is 'young' promotion – but not vice versa.[3]

Nicky Gumbel also emphasised the importance of reaching this demographic: 'In ten or 15 years, these people will be running the country – they will be the headmasters, the magistrates and so on.'[4] There were echoes at Alpha of the Bash-camp strategy (which Gumbel experienced as an undergraduate) of seeking to influence the influencers of the future, in order to transform the nation at large. Alpha invested considerable resources in marketing itself to successful young people.

Wealth and Beauty

Despite its radically changed theological ethos, HTB remained as much a 'society' church in the 1990s and early 2000s as it had been in the 1960s. *Harpers & Queen* fashion magazine ranked it prominently in the 'A-list' of churches to be seen in at Christmas.[5] The *Mail on Sunday*'s *You Magazine* called Alpha 'the hottest social ticket in town', and was impressed to see HTB's carpark 'crammed with Porches and Mercedes'.[6] It attracted thousands of successful young men and women, including celebrities, City workers, and the monied classes of Kensington. The first Alpha promotional video in 1994 was likened by a critic to watching an episode of *Baywatch* or *Beverly Hills, 90210*, where only beautiful people were allowed on camera.[7] When Julia Llewellyn Smith attended HTB, she was seized with envy 'as I gazed at the Prada bags and Voyage cardigans . . . This was more like a posh cocktail party than a church service.'[8] Gyles Brandreth dubbed HTB 'the Fortnum & Mason of evangelism', associated with luxury.[9]

Journalists enjoyed constructing these sorts of caricatures. According to Alex Preston, Alpha at HTB was 'a heady mix of Gieves & Hawkes-attired bankers, hedge funders in chinos and button-down collars, and horsey young women in pink pashminas and quilted gilets. Cut-glass accents rose into the church's airy heights.'[10] Likewise the *Sunday Times* depicted the stereotypical Alpha guest:

> The shoes could be by Jimmy Choo or Manolo Blahnik – pricey either way. The tight, slinky summer clothes could have come from any of the shops in the Golden Triangle of SW1 – Joseph, Armani,

Gucci, whatever. The blonde hair could be Toni & Guy. This, triumphantly, is a material girl, living happily in a material world. Except that she isn't. She's finding God. And she's finding Him where she found her clothes – in Knightsbridge.[11]

Fashion magazine *New Woman* praised Alpha and announced, 'It's official: God just got cool.'[12] Similarly, *Elle*'s profile of 'fashionistas who are keeping the faith' lauded HTB as 'über trendy'.[13] Alpha not only welcomed the publicity, but deliberately aimed to attract that audience. When a professional model agreed to help market the course in 2006, a full-page photograph of her gazing into the camera at a fashion show was published by Alpha in *Cosmopolitan* magazine, with the strapline, 'Is there more to life than this?'[14]

HTB provided a startling contrast to the public perception of church as filled with old and uninteresting people. A church packed with young adults puzzled the secular media and grabbed their attention. Sue Arnold from *The Observer* attended an Alpha session at HTB in 2000, where many of the guests had come straight from work, 'young men still making deals on their mobiles . . . girls in sleek designer suits and high heels carrying briefcases'. Alpha, she suggested, was 'a new, improved – dare one say cool – way to salvation', successfully rebranding the gospel for attractive young people who 'would rather be crucified than wear sandals'. Muscular Christianity in the twenty-first century, she quipped, meant gym membership.[15] 'I've worked with models', observed another visitor to HTB, 'but it has been a long time since I've seen so much beauty under one roof.'[16] *The Scotsman* likewise focused on the target market:

> Welcome to Chardonnay-and-croissant Christianity, where beautiful people are born again over pasta and chilled, unoaked white wine. Watch perfectly groomed young preachers in rimless hexagonal spectacles flash their Tony Blair grins; listen as their radio microphones relay slick soundbite sermons.

It mocked Alpha as 'one of the most effective forms of Christian instruction since the Inquisition', which had 'brought tens of thousands of power-suited bourgeoisie to Christ'. 'Alpha teaches an essentially experiential Christianity', *The Scotsman* concluded, 'short on intellectual rigour, long on emotional uplift. It is perfectly tuned into new-age yearnings of a moneyed middle class bereft of spirituality.'[17] *Time Out* likewise dismissed Alpha as 'white professionals seeking a spurious instant karma'.[18] *The Guardian* called it 'salvation tailored for the Me, Me, Me generation', offering an 'instant fix' with its simplistic message that 'Jesus loves you'.[19]

The contemporary style of band-led worship propagated by HTB and its network of church plants was an important part of its appeal to youth culture, at a period when 'Cool Britannia' was at its height and rock stars were fêted by New Labour in Downing Street. Journalist Pete May described Christianity in 1997 as 'the new rock'n'roll' and HTB's Sunday evening worship as 'more like a U2 concert than a service':

> TV monitors relayed video images of the packed congregation and lyrics from the Bible were sung over a rock / soul backing; more early Dexys than Songs of Praise, with punters in the pews punching the air. Prayers were kept to a minimum and in a startling concession to modernity the church was even warm . . . There was plenty of incentive for male Christians too – around eight out of ten members are young wealthy women clearly too sexy for their church.[20]

When actor Imogen Stubbs attended an HTB evening service in 2000, she thought the worship band would have looked equally at home supporting The Corrs, and 'kept expecting one of them to shout, "Hello, Knightsbridge!" and for everyone to hold up their lighters'.[21] The HTB church plant at St Mary's, Bryanston Square, was portrayed by *Elle* magazine in similar fashion:

> It's half past six on a Sunday at a hip London venue. A blond, Kurt Cobain-cute bloke ruffles his hair and begins to strum a guitar. As the rest of his band joins in, a gathering crowd files into their seats and sways to the sound. A scruffy student in cords and a vintage lumberjack shirt throws off his trainers and dances in his socks. Next to him a junior fashion PR closes her eyes, letting the music pulse through her body. I'm not at a free indie gig, although you'd be forgiven for

thinking so. This is the first five minutes of evening worship at St Mary's church in Marylebone, where a number of London's most fashionable go to worship. Forget fire and brimstone, these people are just as likely to enthuse about Dolce & Gabbana.[22]

One member of St Mary's, Danny Kruger (a policy adviser for the Conservative Party and later MP for Devizes), described HTB in *The Spectator* as 'the mother-church of the evangelical revival' and his own congregation as packed 600-strong with 'young metropolitan trendies'. But it had not achieved this status 'by diluting the Christian message', he explained: 'On the contrary, St Mary's preaches a firmly orthodox doctrine. But it is entirely relaxed about questions of ritual (there isn't any), hierarchy (there isn't any) and dress (on a lot of the girls, there isn't much). It has kept the substance of the faith and modernized the style.'[23]

'It is easy to see how people – especially those who might otherwise have spent a lifetime and a fortune in therapy – could get addicted to this world', Stubbs reflected.[24] Mary Wakefield, a 23-year-old columnist (and later commissioning editor) at *The Spectator*, visited HTB in 1999 to 'test the holy waters at London's most famous born-again church'. But she derided it as a 'complacent theological vacuum', 'just a club for people who deify niceness and miss the solidarity of the lacrosse team'. She found the experience 'nauseating and claustrophobic' and feared she might have 'stumbled across the *Brave New World* factory floor'.[25] Celia Walden, a 28-year-old columnist and MP's daughter, was alarmed when several of her friends were 'bitten by the Alpha bug', but she concluded that they were simply facing the 'late-twenties blues' and wrestling with 'existential disgruntlement', the so-called quarter-life crisis. 'Once you've got the dream job and the most desirable handbag, or your Prada shoes and your City bonus, what do you do with them? Especially if you are momentarily lacking an ideal partner to match?' For these restless young professionals, Walden argued, Alpha offered the quick fix of group therapy with no long-term commitment. It acted as 'a posh counselling and dating agency, minus the shame of both'.[26]

The possibilities of romance were an obvious attraction. A *Sunday Express* guide in 1994 to the best London venues 'to pick up a perfect partner' – from nightclubs to art galleries – recommended Alpha at HTB as the place where matches were 'literally made in Heaven'. Alpha, it averred, was quickly gaining a reputation as a Christian version of Dateline, the computer dating service.[27] Likewise, the *Evening Standard* proclaimed that 'God is working in league with Cupid' at HTB, and that its Sunday services were a 'devout version of blind date'.[28] The acronym HTB was known among younger members of the congregation as 'Hunt The Bride'.[29] Alpha testimonies often referred to this sex appeal. When Vanessa Rayne, a businesswoman in her early 30s, attended Alpha at HTB in 2005, 'I walked in and my first impression was, "Gosh this is better than speed dating." I had never seen so many good-looking men in my life!'[30] Natalie Joannou, in her mid-20s, was persuaded to attend Alpha at HTB in 2009 because her mother told her there were 'lots of hot guys' there.[31] Likewise, Pete Greig (founder of the 24/7 prayer movement) joked that 'Too many Christian guys are waiting for Claudia Schiffer to come through the Alpha Course!'[32]

Billboard Advertising

During the late 1990s the Churches Advertising Network (CAN), coordinated largely by Anglican clergy, ran a series of provocative poster campaigns aiming to attract the attention of young people outside the church. Their Christmas 1996 design was a zany picture of three kings, with the caption, 'Bad Hair Day?! You're a virgin, you've just given birth and now three kings have shown up.' It was reproduced on posters, T-shirts, Christmas wrapping paper and car stickers, but left the Archbishop of York 'incandescent' with anger at this shallow trivialising of the birth of Jesus Christ.[33] The CAN poster for Easter 1999, plastered across billboards, caused similar levels of outrage. It showed Jesus in the style of Marxist revolutionary Che Guevara, with the caption, 'Meek, Mild, As If' – what has been termed the 'Cheification' of Christ – but offended many as sacrilegious.[34] At Christmas 1999, the poster was a modern representation of Leonardo da Vinci's *The Last Supper*, reconceived as a boardroom meeting of multinational companies, with Microsoft in the role of

Judas Iscariot.[35] The CAN campaigns generated vociferous debate within the church, which spilled over into the secular press, but many bishops and parishes refused to countenance them.

At the same period Alpha took to the billboards in an annual national advertising initiative. The immediate inspiration was 23 churches in Ramsgate and Margate, east Kent, who combined their resources in September 1997 to take out a full-page advertisement for their Alpha courses in their local free newspaper, *Adscene*, with a circulation of 91,000.[36] It was a successful experiment and gave HTB the idea for a similar campaign the following autumn on a much grander scale. In September 1998, Alpha posters were placed on 1,700 billboards nationwide. The creative professionals, who donated their services free of charge, had experience of CAN's 'Bad Hair Day' and recommended Alpha adopt provocative slogans such as 'If Diana's in heaven, where's Dodi?' This was certain to incite press coverage, but Gumbel insisted that Alpha posters must always avoid offence.[37] Therefore the billboards carried less shocking questions: 'You're born. You live. You die. End of story?' and '9 to 5 for the next 30 years. Surely there's more to life?' Another was aimed particularly at young men: 'Job. Flat. Girlfriend. Car. Season ticket to United. Still not satisfied?'[38]

Over 4,000 local churches joined the initiative, distributing 4.5 million Alpha invitations. There were also large advertisements in regional newspapers, including three full pages in the *Evening Standard*, with details of the 500 Alpha churches within the M25.[39] An Alpha-themed edition of *Songs of Praise*, watched by 5 million people, further boosted publicity.[40] In Wokingham, Berkshire, actor Wendy Craig released 1,000 helium balloons to promote the initiative. In Devon, local clergyman Alex Welby hired a poster-van and drove with two of the billboard posters through ten towns in the West Country. In Derbyshire, a grandmother decorated her motorbike with Alpha regalia and took to the road distributing invitations. At HTB itself, more than 900 people (including hosts and helpers) attended the first night of the autumn course – the largest number ever seen – and more than 150 guests turned up without warning in response to the publicity.[41] The number of guests at other Alpha churches was minuscule by comparison, but also showed a significant increase – from an average of 11 guests in summer 1998 to 18 guests in October, a rise of 64 per cent – while the number of 'unchurched' guests doubled.[42] The whole promotion cost £682,000, of which £515,000 was raised from participating churches and other supporters.[43]

The campaign brought Alpha sustained national media attention for the first time. The *Evening Standard* called it 'the biggest evangelical crusade mounted since the crusades'.[44] *The Economist* praised Alpha as 'powerful medicine for a sickly old church'.[45] *The Independent* dubbed Gumbel 'God's own spin doctor', attempting

> to do for the Church of England what Peter Mandelson did for the Labour Party – drag it into the modern world and, through sheer force of presentational skill, restore it to its former power and glory . . . The man behind this revolution, you might think, must be a spiritual tiger; a roaring prophet in the cast of Ian Paisley. Yet Gumbel, as befits a man of God in the New Labour age, is an altogether svelter creature, as smooth-edged as a breakfast television presenter.

Alpha was 'an ideological machine of stunning power', the profile continued, but was a 'fundamentalist' and 'charismatic' version of Christianity that would go down in many Anglican parishes 'like guacamole at a Rotherham working men's club'. Nevertheless, the newspaper prophesied, if Gumbel had discovered 'the secret of putting bums back on pews – as his detractors most certainly have not – then tomorrow's C of E may well belong to him'.[46] Particularly effusive was a profile in the *Daily Telegraph* from Clifford Longley who described the Alpha advertising initiative as 'not unlike the commercial launch of a new product by a slick PR firm . . . They make the Church seem professional, competent, self-confident and up-to-date.' 'Alpha is an unqualified triumph', Longley purred. 'The reconversion of England, so oversold by Evangelicals so often, is suddenly almost believable.'[47]

Other commentators were more hostile. Political satirist Steve Bell used his long-running 'If . . .' comic strip in *The Guardian* to lampoon Alpha. It showed his familiar penguin passing a billboard with the words:

You're born
You live
You join a rich anti-abortion sect
You buy up poster sites . . .
Is that all there is? AFRAID SO . . .[48]

The satirical magazine *Private Eye* likewise joked about the launch of the new Alphayed Course – a play on the surname of Egyptian millionaire Mohamed Al-Fayed, owner of Harrods, conspiracy theorist, and father of Dodi Al-Fayed. The Alphayed Course aimed to answer life's major questions such as 'Who killed Diana?' and 'Why can't the owner of Harrods get a British passport?'[49] These responses, though scornful, were nonetheless evidence of Alpha's increasing public recognition.

Alpha advertising initiatives continued every autumn on an annual cycle, becoming increasingly sophisticated. 'Although Holy Trinity Brompton might put all their success down to the action of the Holy Spirit', observed *The Tablet*, 'they do give him a lot of help.'[50] In September 1999 the world was in feverish excitement about the turn of the millennium, dominated by controversy over the Millennium Dome and anxiety over the Millennium Bug. Alpha made the most of the opportunity. At the advertising launch party in Covent Garden, a jazz band played, an entertainer juggled with knives and lay on a bed of nails, and Sandy Millar unveiled the latest poster, to a trumpet fanfare, in front of a cheering crowd of over a thousand people. The poster read simply, 'Dome. Bug. Party. Is there more to the Millennium?' A team of helpers in Alpha sweatshirts distributed hundreds of 'millennium survival kits', containing a party hat, party popper, balloon, party blower, corkscrew, Alka-Seltzer tablet to cure the hangover, and an Alpha invitation.[51] This was typical of the Alpha brand – contemporary, humorous, celebratory, relaxed, and definitely not prudish. Survival kits were sent to all MPs and distributed at 13 further 'regional roadshows' in cities such as Belfast, Brighton, Cardiff, Edinburgh, Glasgow, Leeds, Newcastle, Nottingham and Plymouth, with helium balloons and banners to create 'a festival atmosphere'.[52] The campaign again generated considerable publicity in the national media. At the launch in Birmingham, local MP Caroline Spelman announced that Alpha was now 'more popular than Weightwatchers'.[53]

The Alpha campaign in September 2000 aimed for a more personal approach than the previous slogans. To capture something of the vivacity and excitement of Alpha, the design agency arranged a photoshoot with HTB members and the image chosen for the billboards was a close-up of Greta Greenwood (HTB's children's worker), a 25-year-old New Zealander, laughing, with a broad, friendly smile.[54] She seemed to embody the typical Alpha guest – young, happy, attractive, carefree – or perhaps was herself meant to be an attraction of Alpha. *The Observer* called her Alpha's 'pin-up girl' and criticised the course for stressing its social, even sexual, advantages.[55] With Greenwood's perfect complexion and gleaming white teeth, the *Financial Times* suggested, the Alpha billboards might 'easily be mistaken for health food advertisements . . . The message is one of health, psychological wholesomeness and the discovery of the Holy Grail of human joy. "Come," it says. "Be like me."'[56] When the *Financial Times* journalist attended the opening Alpha evening at HTB, surrounded by young professionals, he lamented: 'They look like the new master race. The women have shiny hair, peachy skin and little bottles of mineral water; the men are gym-fresh and wear suits that say they are going places.'[57]

The wider set of Alpha posters designed for the 2000 campaign were equally problematic. One showed eight young people sitting around a supper table, and another was an assortment of nine faces, but all except one were white, and none were Asian. This was surprising, given Alpha's desire to reach the whole nation, but in response to criticism HTB defended the posters as merely reflecting their local membership, and said that although there were some Asians in the congregation, none was available when they were selecting models for the photoshoot.[58] This was an unsatisfactory answer and there was greater racial diversity the following year. The face chosen for the 2001 billboard campaign was Ade Adebajo, a 33-year-old Nigerian investment banker and HTB member who, like Greenwood, was shown laughing. Although the photoshoot took place in Fulham in the depths of winter, Adebajo was told to pretend he was 'on a beach in Barbados, lying back and enjoying the sun'.[59] Again, this sense of relaxed fun and youthful friendship pervaded the Alpha ethos. Some of the posters in 2001 carried the slogan, 'The Alpha Course: The one where you explore the meaning of life', a nod towards 'The one where . . .' titles of the *Friends* sitcom, then at the height of its popularity among younger viewers.[60] In 2002 the Alpha campaign posters were again colourful and contemporary, but the photographs were deliberately blurred so that no one felt excluded whatever their age, race or social class.[61]

Inviting the Nation to Supper

The primary purpose of Alpha's annual advertising campaign was to raise public levels of awareness and thus make it easier for Christians to invite their friends and neighbours to a local course. Alpha posters were a familiar sight each autumn on billboards, buses, taxis, bus stops, railway station platforms and the London Underground. Yet *Alpha News* emphasised that this marketing was not intended as a substitute for a personal invitation – the multiplication strategy was still 'friends bringing friends'.[62] Nonetheless, some guests signed up for Alpha simply after seeing the advertisements.[63] For example, Ann Hughes, a primary school headteacher in her 50s, stumbled across an Alpha advertisement in 1999 while leafing through her local parish magazine in the village of Lilleshall, Shropshire. She then spotted two Alpha posters, on the church notice board and on a garden fence, which read: 'If you don't look, you can't find.' Every day driving to work she faced the poster at a T-junction in the village 'and it really niggled me', so she signed up for the course.[64] Chris Green, a chartered building surveyor in Birmingham, first heard Alpha advertised at the baptism of his nephew at St Barnabas, Kensington, in 2000. The next week, driving to work, he saw a billboard announcing that Alpha was 'starting soon at a church near you', with a website address. So he went online, typed in his postcode, and was directed to a local course, a mile and a half from his house. It took place in a church hall with about a dozen people, watching Gumbel on video, and Green read voraciously through *Searching Issues* and *Questions of Life*. 'Everything just seemed to fall into place', so he prayed the *Why Jesus?* prayer and 'invited Jesus into my life'.[65]

By raising the profile of Alpha throughout the United Kingdom, the annual campaign was a stimulus to local churches in their own evangelism. Some congregations leafleted their entire town. Christ Church, Anerley, in south London, distributed breakfast packs to busy commuters at their local station in the rush hour, containing a Danish pastry or chocolate croissant, fruit juice, and an Alpha invitation.[66] One over-enthusiastic Anglican curate in Carlisle, Ben King, fell foul of the law when he plastered his parish with Alpha posters, and was warned by the city council that he faced a possible fine of £50 for each one. But when his mistake made the front page of the *Cumberland News*, it simply increased Alpha's local profile still further.[67]

From 2000 the national advertising was combined with an initiative each September to 'invite the nation to supper', with thousands of Alpha supper parties organised by local churches.[68] Usually these events included Alpha testimonies and the introductory talk, 'Christianity: boring, untrue, and irrelevant?', in an attempt to persuade guests to sign up for the autumn courses. Some were major 'beacon' suppers for hundreds of people in grand venues like cathedrals and city halls, preceded by a reception for local dignitaries. But the vast majority were smaller events in a multitude of venues, not only in churches and church halls, but in nightclubs, hotels, bars, pubs, curry houses, pizza restaurants, coffee shops, theatres, cinemas, golf courses, and on cruise boats or paddle steamers. Many were buffets but some were black-tie dinners, or barbeques, or medieval banquets. In Edinburgh, there was an Alpha Ceilidh, with bagpipes and traditional Gaelic singing. In Reading, there was an Alpha Elvis Presley evening, with an evangelistic talk entitled, 'Is the King still alive?'

Unusual venues were an added incentive. Supper parties were held at the Whitley Bay lighthouse in Tyne and Wear, the Helicopter Museum at Weston-super-Mare in Somerset, the Royal Military Academy at Sandhurst, and on a Blue Funnel cruise ship in port at Southampton. There were 550 at supper at the Royal Air Force Museum at Cosford in Shropshire, where Sandy Millar gave the address standing underneath the fuselage of a Second World War bomber. At an Alpha supper at the Porsche Centre in Leicester, guests were given a special tour of the cars. At Dreamland amusement park in Margate, the Alpha supper was followed by free rides on some of the attractions. Sports venues were particularly popular, with Alpha suppers held at Nottinghamshire county cricket ground, the National Hockey Stadium at Milton Keynes, the Greyhound Stadium at Chester-le-Street, and at football grounds including Pittodrie in Aberdeen, Old Trafford in Manchester, Fratton Park in Portsmouth, and Molineux in Wolverhampton.

At some events, local celebrities were invited to share their Christian faith. From the world of professional sport, these included footballers Cyrille Regis, Tim Howard, Adriano Basso and Willie Bell, golfer Luther Blacklock, and New Zealand rugby league international Ali Lauiti'iti. In York there was an Alpha-sponsored football match between York City and Salisbury City, in front of 2,200 fans, and the York City chaplain interviewed former player Gordon Staniforth on the pitch at half time, about football, faith and Alpha. Alpha provided the man-of-the-match bottle of champagne. Other local speakers at Alpha suppers across the United Kingdom came from the world of television or entertainment, including *Blue Peter* presenters Diane Louise Jordan and Simon Thomas, *Big Brother* winner Cameron Stout, *Pop Idol* finalist Susanne Manning, actors Russell Boulter and Jamie Hinde, ballerina Jane Rosier, and comedians Syd Little from *Little and Large* and Bobby Ball from *Cannon and Ball*.[69] Popstar Shane Lynch, who won global fame with Irish boy band Boyzone, also helped to promote Alpha. After becoming entangled in the occult, and experiencing a series of terrifying 'demonic visitations', he had turned to Christianity in 2003.[70] At an Alpha supper in a Worcester hotel, Lynch declared, 'I'm not a preacher, but I am a witness. I can tell you the difference Jesus has made in my life', before urging his audience to attend Alpha.[71]

The Topless Model and the Disgraced Politician

Alpha attracted not only celebrity endorsers but also celebrity guests, from the worlds of music, sport, politics, stage and screen, some of whom professed Christian faith after attending the course. Their association with Alpha boosted its profile to new heights. The first famous convert joined just a few months after Alpha's global launch. Samantha Fox became a household name modelling topless, from age 16, for Page Three of *The Sun*, before launching a pop music career with steamy hits like 'Touch Me' (1986) and 'Naughty Girls' (1988). In 1993, aged 27, she met a Christian make-up artist, Fiona Corrigan, who invited her to HTB, very different from her Roman Catholic upbringing.[72] 'The church I used to frequent was dull and dreary', Fox recalled. 'The songs and people needed lifting. I walked into Holy Trinity and it was just alive, I couldn't believe it!' She attended Alpha in early 1994, on the cusp of the Toronto Blessing, and made a profession of Christian faith. She witnessed healings and had a personal experience of the Holy Spirit 'from the bottom of my feet to the top of my head. It felt like my feet were a dead weight. My body was just so light.' Fox observed:

> You think about everything when you've been touched by the Holy Spirit. Every opportunity you have to think about God, you do. He's on your mind all the time. I've just been doing a big concert in the Ukraine. Every opportunity I got, I was talking to people about the word of the Lord.[73]

The tabloid press delighted in the story, with headlines like 'Sexy Sam has found religion' and 'My heavenly bod is just for God'.[74] It was front-page news in *The Sun*, though Gumbel insisted: 'It doesn't make any difference whether it's Sam Fox or Joe Bloggs who joins our church. We're concerned about people not personalities.'[75] In August 1994, Fox played the Greenbelt Christian music festival and spoke of 'my new-found faith'. *Cross Rhythms*, a Christian pop music magazine, excitedly declared that she was 'solidly saved'.[76]

However, Fox soon drifted away. In later media interviews, she distanced herself from reports of a 'born-again' conversion, suggesting that she had attended Alpha because she had been confused by her very difficult relationship with her abusive father and wanted to know why people suffer.[77] She agreed that Alpha had 'helped me find myself a bit', but was ultimately dismissive of the experience.[78] In her 2017 autobiography, Fox spoke more fondly of her HTB experience, recalling a church 'full of young, trendy people', modern music with important lyrics, and clergy in contemporary dress who talked about real issues. 'No matter how much or how little I believed in God, just being there made me feel good', she recalled. 'Sadly, however, the press caught wind of it and wrote that I had become a bible basher, and suddenly there would be paparazzi waiting for me every time I left the church. It assumed such absurd proportions that eventually, I no longer had the energy to keep going.'[79] Despite cutting her ties after just a few months, in popular press coverage of Alpha and HTB the name Samantha Fox was forever linked.

Another famous face at Alpha was the disgraced politician Jonathan Aitken, who was embroiled in scandal. A member of John Major's cabinet as Chief Secretary to the Treasury, Aitken was tipped as a future prime minister, but when *The Guardian* accused him of shady arms deals and pimping prostitutes for Saudi princes, he launched a libel suit, proclaiming his intention 'to cut out the cancer of bent and twisted journalism in our country with the simple sword of truth and the trusty shield of British fair play'.[80] However, in June 1997 – a month after Aitken lost his seat in Parliament in the New Labour landslide – his case sensationally collapsed when it was discovered he had lied about the payment of a bill at the Ritz Hotel in Paris, and had involved his wife and daughter in his deceit. Aitken was left a public pariah, facing what he called 'those four apocalyptic horsemen of disgrace, divorce, financial disaster and jail'.[81] In the midst of his political downfall and ritual humiliation, Aitken underwent a spiritual reawakening. He had long been a practising Anglican, attending church almost every Sunday, but looking back he described himself as 'one of those people who call themselves a Christian without actually being one'.[82] During Lent 1997 he took part in the annual Parliamentary Prayer Retreat, working through some of Ignatius Loyola's spiritual exercises with the Jesuit theologian Gerard W. Hughes, and when Aitken was hiding from the paparazzi that summer in a log cabin in California, he took solace in the penitential psalms.

Aitken sought guidance from many different Christian mentors, including Richard Nixon's former adviser Chuck Colson, who was famously 'born again' shortly before his incarceration in 1974 for his part in the Watergate scandal. Aitken also joined a small weekly prayer breakfast coordinated by his fellow parliamentarian Michael Alison (a former HTB churchwarden and Margaret Thatcher's parliamentary private secretary in the 1980s). Sandy Millar persuaded Aitken to attend Alpha at HTB in autumn 1997, at the height of his notoriety, though Aitken was 'an extremely reluctant Alpha joiner. I really only began it out of good manners to old friends.'[83] He attended every session, including the Holy Spirit weekend at the Chatsworth Hotel in Worthing, West Sussex, though he was initially 'a Holy Spirit sceptic'.[84] The talk on being filled with the Holy Spirit was delivered by HTB member Bruce Streather, a solicitor who later acted for Aitken during his perjury trial. But Aitken was deeply unimpressed by Streather's religious 'mumblings':

> His talk was as far removed from Bible-thumping or hot-gospelling as the Chatsworth Hotel is from Claridges. When he brought his preaching of Scripture to the climax of an appeal to the Almighty with the words, 'Come Holy Spirit, come', his tones sounded so monotonous that he might as well have been reading out the small print of some dry-as-dust contract in a commercial court.

Nothing unusual happened until another Alpha guest, a young tax barrister, laid his hands on Aitken's shoulder and prayed again for God to send down the Holy Spirit. Aitken recalled:

> At this point my palms suddenly began to tingle with a strange physical sensation which strengthened until my hands and wrists became hot and uncomfortable, as though they were charged with an electric current. Then I began to cry. This should have been deeply embarrassing, for shedding tears in public is anathema to me . . . Yet here I was in a room full of people in the lounge of a seaside hotel, letting out not just a trickle but a torrent of tears. To my surprise I felt amazingly warm and good about those tears. The more they flowed, the more I recognized that they were tears of happiness. I smiled, beamed and physically shook with silent laughter. Something extraordinary and uncontrollable was going on inside me.

After this 'high emotion', Aitken 'calmed down, cooled down and reverted to normal', but was left 'bemused' by the experience.[85] He later described the Alpha weekend as 'a major turning point towards repentance and a commitment to a new life'.[86] He did not become an HTB recruit, but continued to draw inspiration from a wide variety of traditional Christian authors and mentors. He spent an hour in prayer each morning at Westminster Abbey, and made his confession to a Roman Catholic priest at Westminster Cathedral, receiving sacramental absolution.[87] At Christmas 1997, Aitken announced his new-found faith to the world via *The Spectator*, positioning himself as a member of 'the Church reticent wing of Anglicanism' who was suspicious of 'foxhole conversions'. But he wrote enthusiastically of Alpha's 'astonishing' growth and its helpful impact on his own life, defending the course against rumours that it was 'the socially exclusive preserve of a demented handful of HTB Hooray Henrys with double-barrelled names from SW7'.[88] Aitken's spiritual awakening was derided by the secular media.[89] *Time Out* later mocked that in transferring from Thatcherism to Alpha, he was 'exchanging a joyless right-wing ideology for something remarkably similar'.[90]

In the continuing fallout from the libel trial, Aitken was charged in May 1998 with perjury and attempting to pervert the course of justice. He pleaded guilty and was sentenced at the Old Bailey in June 1999 to 18 months' imprisonment – eventually serving seven months behind bars. Nicky Gumbel visited him in Belmarsh Prison and encouraged him to pursue his new vocation as a Christian author and speaker, because he could have 'a powerful impact as a witness for Christ'.[91] On his release, Aitken studied theology for two years at Wycliffe Hall, Oxford, and then began an energetic round of Christian outreach. Each autumn, during the national Alpha advertising campaign, he was a regular on the Alpha circuit speaking at launch events – beginning in 2002 with the HTB supper party, followed in 2003 by 18 supper parties across the country (including at Norwich and Bradford cathedrals), a pattern repeated for several subsequent years.[92]

The Bible meets Big Brother

Alpha's profile received a major boost with its first appearance on national television in 2001. The reality genre was at the peak of its popularity, with the emergence of global franchises such as *Survivor* from 1997 and *Big Brother* from 1999, and production companies were hungry for similar 'fly-on-the-wall' material. ITV agreed to broadcast the entire Alpha course, focused upon the experiences of ten participants (or 'contestants'). All, bar one, were regular applicants among the 700 guests on the HTB course, but they were hand-picked by the television producers to take part in the programme, filmed between May and July 2000. They included an accountant, a lawyer, a property dealer, a recruitment consultant, a teacher, and a Pizza Hut restaurant manager, and were aged between 24 and 37. *Alpha: Will It Change Their Lives?* was fronted by Sir David Frost, best known for his heavyweight political interviews with prime ministers and presidents (including, famously, the disgraced Richard Nixon).[93] He christened the programme, 'The Bible meets Big Brother'.[94]

The cameras were given full access, except to the prayer time on the weekend away when Nicky Gumbel called down the Holy Spirit and people began to speak in tongues, which was behind closed doors. One of the participants, Harry Powell, an investment banker, felt deeply uncomfortable during that session and dismissed it as 'a complete load of mumbo jumbo'.[95] James Bann, a publisher, was so 'freaked out' that he left the room in a hurry – that evening he went with two others from the group to the local pub, to watch England beat Germany in Euro 2000, and got 'completely and utterly plastered'.[96] But for Tony Bolt, a painter and decorator from Battersea, it was a life-changing moment. He was increasingly attracted to Christianity and had begun to read about Jesus in Mark's Gospel, after being given Eugene Peterson's *The Message* (1993), a dynamic translation of the New Testament. After Gumbel prayed for Bolt at the weekend away, 'my legs just "went" and I fell, wallop, crash on the floor'. Lying there for 'what seemed like an hour', he repented of his sins and committed his life to Christ. The rest of the group thought he had 'gone mad'.[97] Asked later whether Alpha had in fact changed his life, Bolt replied: 'Jesus changed my life. Alpha was the tool, the vehicle, that got me on the road to finding Jesus.'[98] Another participant also became a Christian on the weekend away, while a third had her existing faith strengthened.

In the mainstream press, television critics were unanimously, and sometimes pungently, negative. The Independent lambasted Alpha: Will It Change Their Lives? as a 'shamefully partial and brainless farrago', consisting of 'bright-eyed, smiling converts gazing at the camera and explaining how the Alpha movement had saved them from unhappiness, negative relationships, sin and moral confusion, to a background of gloopy, sentimental music'.[99] The Spectator called it 'truly awful' and 'fantastically dreadful', while the New Statesman reckoned it 'contender for worst programme of the year'.[100] The Observer watched 'in disbelief', wondering if it was a spoof.[101] A consistent complaint was the programme's lack of objectivity, devoid of critical voices, which made it seem like a ten-week advertisement for Alpha, better suited to the God Channel than to ITV. The Evening Standard likened it to a promotional video, marketing a form of Christianity 'from which all the tricky and difficult bits had been carefully trimmed away'.[102] The series was dismissed as a 'laughably inept and thinly veiled recruitment drive'.[103] Even the Church of England Newspaper, generally supportive of Alpha, was startled at the absence of critical analysis – there were no 'embittered drop-outs, or mad machete-whirling Liberal Catholic detractors' to offer an alternative viewpoint, observed Catherine Fox.[104] The sexagenarian Frost came in for particular chastisement for his genial style, more typical of Through the Keyhole than the biting satire and robust political interviews with which he had built his early reputation. 'I have seen more rigorous interviewing in Daz commercials', one reviewer protested.[105] Keith Porteous Wood, executive director of the National Secular Society (NSS), called it 'Alpha's greatest promotional coup yet'.[106] The NSS lodged a formal complaint with the Independent Television Commission, arguing unsuccessfully that ITV was in breach of its code of conduct by allowing proselytism.

The ten-week series was originally scheduled for broadcast during summer 2001, a perfect boost to the Alpha advertising initiative that autumn. However, ITV perhaps got cold feet after reading the early reviews. It was shown very late on Sunday nights and the schedule was highly erratic, ultimately drawn out over four months, which dented viewing figures. The first episode, broadcast at 10.45pm at the end of July, peaked at a respectable 2.3 million viewers and averaged 1.7 million (a 16 per cent share of the late-night audience). The second episode reached less than half that number. It was broadcast at midnight in England and Wales, and at 1.30am in Scotland, averaging 700,000 viewers (1.1 million at its peak), a 14 per cent share. Clearly the programme was not a priority for ITV after all. It was knocked off the schedules for two weeks in mid-August, replaced by highlights of the Hungarian Grand Prix, and then suspended for a further five weeks in September and October in the wake of the disruption caused by the 9/11 terrorist attacks on New York and Washington. At its lowest point, the seventh Alpha episode reached 300,000 viewers. The last in the series was not broadcast until mid-November.[107] Some Christians complained that this unfavourable scheduling was the result of prejudice in the secular media and lobbied ITV with letters and phone calls.[108] One Methodist viewer, for example, rebuked the broadcaster for their 'grossly unfair bias'.[109] Likewise, a Baptist viewer felt that the television executives were treating the Christian community with 'contempt'.[110]

Despite the widespread hostility, *Alpha: Will It Change Their Lives?* elevated Alpha's profile to new levels. Gumbel's *Questions of Life* was republished with a new cover to link it to the television series, marketed as an 'international bestseller', and was stocked for the first time by mainstream retailers like Waterstones and WH Smith – a rare example of a Christian product that had the potential to cross over into the secular high street.[111] HTB's own Alpha courses in autumn 2001 reaped immediate benefits, with 978 guests, the highest ever, a steep rise compared with 660 guests the previous autumn. Administering such a large enterprise was a logistical headache, run three times a week, with 180 small-group leaders, 286 helpers, and another 160 volunteers, a combined attendance of over 1,600 people.[112] During 2002, across all its nine Alpha courses, HTB welcomed 2,186 guests, with nine Holy Spirit weekends and seven Holy Spirit days.[113] After this peak, numbers fluctuated downwards, with 1,608 guests in 2003 and 1,297 guests in 2005, but Alpha at HTB remained by far the largest in the world with numbers beyond the dreams of most parishes.[114]

Name recognition was a major incentive for other churches to adopt the brand. Annual MORI polls commissioned by Alpha International into brand awareness found in 2001 that 16 per cent of British adults recognised Alpha as a Christian course, rising to 23 per cent by 2006.[115] 'Whatever we think of Alpha it is the only evangelistic effort which at present commands the attention of the nation and the media', observed *Evangelicals Now*. 'Many churches will get involved with Alpha as simply the best boat to fish from. Who can blame them?'[116] Less hesitantly, Andrew Burnham (Bishop of Ebbsfleet) gave Alpha his enthusiastic backing, reasoning that if he was selling gravy granules he would sell Bisto because it was a household name, and in the same way Alpha was the only evangelism brand with serious market penetration.[117]

Celebrity Converts

In the early 2000s the number of celebrity attenders at Alpha multiplied. Pop superstars followed in Samantha Fox's footsteps, though learning from her experience they kept a low profile. HTB was careful never to release their names, but the tabloid press discovered them nonetheless. Geri Halliwell, formerly of the Spice Girls, attended Alpha at HTB in autumn 2001, aged 29, and told Channel 4's *Richard & Judy* chat show that Alpha was 'amazing': 'we're all on a spiritual journey. I'm always looking for faith of some sort.'[118] Her interest in Alpha was covered by media as varied as *The Sun*, the *Daily Mail*, the *Daily Telegraph*, and gossip magazine *Heat*.[119] Will Young also attended Alpha at St Paul's, Onslow Square, in 2002, aged 23, soon after being catapulted to fame as winner of *Pop Idol*.[120] Actor Sally Phillips – best known for her comic roles in *Smack the Pony*, *Bridget Jones's Diary* and *Miranda* – attended Alpha in 2002 at St Barnabas, Kensington, and was married the following year to Andrew Bermejo, one of her Alpha group leaders.[121] Radio DJ Johnnie Walker attended Alpha at HTB in 2007, as did film director Guy Ritchie.[122]

Although Alpha had a strict policy of confidentiality for participants, *Alpha News* carried the testimonies of several celebrities who publicly professed faith in Christ after attending Alpha. These narratives were a key part of Alpha's marketing strategy. For example, actor Laura Michelle Kelly made her name as a leading lady in West End musicals like *My Fair Lady* and *Mary Poppins*. She was raised in a Christian family, members of Sandown Baptist Church on the Isle of Wight, but when she moved to London in 1998, aged 17, for her first big role – Belle in *Beauty and the Beast* at the Dominion Theatre – she stopped going to church. However, she met another young actor, Matthew Rutherford, who had also just launched his career in a West End musical, *The Buddy Holly Story*. Rutherford was a Christian and invited Kelly to an Alpha he was running in the West End, specially scheduled in the afternoon for people in the entertainment industry, but she refused and forgot about it. Soon afterwards, she was sitting one afternoon in a café near Covent Garden when someone asked, 'Oh, are you here for the Alpha course? It's on in five minutes next door.' Startled by the coincidence, Kelly decided to attend, and went back every week. Through Alpha, the Christian message she had often heard as a child began at last to make sense, and she testified to 'a whole new relationship with God'. She began to attend HTB, where she was baptised in May 2000, aged 19.[123]

Rugby union winger Ugo Monye (later a familiar face on television's *Question of Sport*) made his debut for Harlequins in 2002, aged 19, and toured the world with England Sevens, playing in packed stadiums of 60,000 people. He had been brought up in a Christian family, members of a Pentecostal church in north London, but he stopped attending when he left home and it quickly became 'a distant memory'. This was initially a happy period of independence, dominated by rugby and nightclubbing, but Monye admitted, 'it was all me, me, me'. After being plagued by injury – including, in quick succession, a broken ankle, a broken sternum, and a damaged back that left him in agony, lying for four days on the floor unable to move – he decided that 'something had really got to change'. In October 2007 a Harlequins masseuse (a member of HTB) encouraged Monye to attend Alpha, where he committed his life to God. A natural evangelist, he soon invited friends to the course and became an HTB Alpha small-group leader. After scoring a remarkable try against rivals Wasps, he lifted up his rugby jersey in front of the crowd to reveal a T-shirt with the message, 'I love Jesus'.[124] Among his tattoos was a large cross inked on his right forearm, with the words, 'Do not be overcome by the flesh, but live life by the Spirit', expressive of his renewed faith.[125] Monye made his England international debut in 2008, and became an 'ambassador' for Youth Alpha and Student Alpha in 2010.[126]

Rock star Charlie Simpson found global fame as a teenager as lead guitarist with the pop sensation Busted, who had four No. 1 hits, sold 5 million records, and won two Brit awards, between 2002 and 2005. The band split at the height of their fame and he signed instead for Fightstar. His older brother and fellow musician, Edd Simpson, had become a Christian in the late 1990s as a pupil at Uppingham School and in 2007 Charlie attended Alpha, run by Edd at a friend's home in north London, watching Gumbel on DVD. Although 'still on a journey', Charlie spoke publicly in interviews of his Christian faith and praised Alpha as 'brilliant'.[127]

Welsh baritone Rhydian Roberts became a Christian as a drama student. While preparing for the part of Pontius Pilate in the musical *Jesus Christ Superstar*, he was overcome with emotion when watching a video of Christ on the cross and listening to Andrew Lloyd Webber's song 'Gethsemane'. Soon after graduating from the Birmingham Conservatoire in 2007, Roberts was runner-up on *The X Factor*, mentored by Dannii Minogue. He signed for Simon Cowell's record label and his debut album sold over 600,000 copies. Although Roberts was already a Christian, he attended Alpha at HTB in 2009, aged 26, and became another celebrity endorser.[128]

Is There More to Life?

Alpha's annual campaign aimed to break new ground each year. In 2002 it advertised on commercial radio for the first time.[129] Then, in 2005, it hit cinema screens, with a 60-second promotion featuring adventurer Bear Grylls, Premier League footballer Linvoy Primus and model Kim Johnson – all Alpha graduates. Primus had attended Alpha in Portsmouth in 2002, shortly after his conversion to Christianity.[130] Johnson had attended Alpha at HTB in 2004 after her boyfriend searched the internet for a 'cool church'.[131] The commercial, created by leading production company The Mob, showed Johnson sashaying down a catwalk, Primus scoring a goal and Grylls on top of a mountain, before each turned to camera and asked, 'Is there more to life than this?' It was watched by more than 3 million cinema-goers and received significant press publicity. 'God gets glitzy', declared *The Guardian*. It would have cost £500,000 as a business venture, but the three stars gave their services *gratis*. Grylls agreed as a favour for Gumbel, and joked that during the filming in Snowdonia, 'I spent quite a lot of time clinging on by my fingernails over a 200-foot overhang, shouting to the Alpha people down below, "You'd better bloody be grateful for this!"'[132] The advertisement, like all Alpha productions, was aimed at young people and was notably unreligious, seeking to attract attention without preaching. 'It perhaps says something about the church's image, or self-image', mused Stephen Tomkins, 'that it advertises the faith without any mention of God, religion, or church.'[133] The 2006 campaign experimented with a viral internet advertisement, designed by 23-year-old Alastair Duckworth for which he won a £2,000 prize from Alpha. His 60-second animation depicted human life as a conveyor belt from birth to death, mixing humour with pathos.[134] It became the centrepiece of the tenth Alpha campaign, in 2007, broadcast for two weeks on 2,000 cinema screens, in 250 gyms and health clubs, and on digital television channel E4, popular with the 18 to 35 age group.[135]

Alpha's marketing initiatives sometimes provoked strong negative reactions. Its 2008 campaign centred on the question, 'If God did exist, what would you ask?' Billboards and beer mats carried questions like, 'Is this it?', 'Who cares?', 'What am I doing here?' and 'Why's it so messed up?'[136] A few months later, in January 2009, the British Humanist Association launched the world's first 'atheist bus campaign', which was imitated worldwide and grew into a global phenomenon. It was supported by New Atheists such as Richard Dawkins, author of *The God Delusion* (2006), and adopted the slogan 'There's probably no God. Now stop worrying and enjoy your life.'[137] This atheist activism was originally conceived as a riposte to bus advertisements from a small evangelical group called 'Proclaiming Truth in London', but it was widely interpreted as a swipe at Alpha. 'It's about time we stood up to the people at Alpha and their mindless advertising', wrote one atheist.[138] Some Christians denounced the initiative, and the Trinitarian

Bible Society replied by placing a verse from the Bible upon 100 buses: 'The fool hath said in his heart, there is no God' (Psalm 53:1). But many Christians viewed the atheist campaign with amusement, especially its surprising caveat 'probably', and welcomed the publicity it gave to debates about God's existence. Alpha capitalised in its own 2009 national initiative, with posters on 900 billboards, 2,200 buses, 200 London Underground stations, and 1,100 railway stations, which asked 'Does God exist?' and 'Is this it?', offering three possible answers, 'Yes', 'No', or 'Probably'.[139] It conducted the same survey online, but when a massive 96 per cent of 88,000 respondents answered 'No' to God's existence, the results were quietly buried. The survey was not a fair representation of British religious opinion, Alpha complained, because it had been hijacked by atheists.[140]

Bear Grylls's Greatest Adventure

From the mid-2000s, Bear Grylls became synonymous with Alpha, as one of its most important celebrity endorsers, especially helping Alpha to reach young people. Son of Tory MP Sir Michael Grylls, he was educated at Eton College where, aged 16, he developed a 'quiet, but strong Christian faith' after the sudden death of his godfather. Relationship with Jesus Christ, he testified, became 'the great empowering presence in my life' and 'the secret strength to so many great adventures', though he had no patience with boring religiosity.[141] One of Grylls's closest friends was Alpha cartoonist Charlie Mackesy, with whom he enjoyed many youthful escapades.[142] They shared an unconventional, free-spirited, fun-loving approach to life, which was harnessed by the Alpha brand. Grylls served as an army reservist with the SAS, training as a survival instructor, and first sprang to fame in 1998, aged 23, as the youngest Briton to reach the summit of Mount Everest. With a taste for high-risk adventure, in 2003 he made the first unassisted crossing of the North Atlantic Ocean in an inflatable boat. Global superstardom came with the huge ratings success of his television survival series *Man vs. Wild* (also known as *Born Survivor*), which ran for seven seasons from 2006 to 2011, reaching 1.2 billion people in 180 countries.[143] In 2009, aged 35, Grylls was appointed the youngest ever Chief Scout, and enjoyed a steady flow of television and book deals. He wrote of his Christian faith in narratives of his record-breaking feats, like *Facing Up* (2000) and *Facing the Frozen Ocean* (2004), especially his reliance on God in moments of danger and desperation.

Soon after marriage in 2000, Grylls and his wife Shara attended Alpha. He explained how it helped him to appreciate better the daily relevance of Christian faith, in contrast to the cassocks and liturgies of school chapel:

> I have always struggled with the religious side of Christianity and I think I still do to quite a large extent. I find church often quite daunting and people smiling too much. That has always put me off faith. Alpha was a real relief . . . I found that you didn't have to be together, you didn't have to be sorted, you didn't have to be perfect. It was OK if you swore or needed a cigarette suddenly.[144]

Likewise, on the Sky News breakfast show, he announced, 'I've never been very religious and not very good at going to church', but Alpha showed him that the core of Christian faith was 'about being held, about being understood, forgiven and loved – and I think we all need a bit of that in our lives'.[145] As he expressed it elsewhere, Alpha helped him to 'distinguish real, living faith from dry religion'.[146]

Grylls and Gumbel became good friends, and at one stage in the mid-2000s they played squash together four times a week.[147] Following the 2005 cinema promotion, Grylls was again the face of the 2006 Alpha campaign. Buses, billboards and car stickers carried an image of him standing on the summit of Mount Snowdon, with the caption, 'Is there more to life than this?'[148] He also fronted the Alpha campaign in 2009, in a 60-second internet commercial filmed in the Malaysian jungle. It showed the adventurer leaping from a tree, scrambling down an escarpment, diving off a cliff into the sea, and trying to attract the attention of a helicopter from a deserted beach, before the punchline revealed Grylls writing in the sand, 'I did Alpha'.[149] He was also the face of Alpha's first global advertising initiative, which ran for 16 months during 2016–17 in 68 countries and 32 languages, with the motto 'My greatest adventure'.[150]

Although Grylls's global fame was significant in marketing Alpha, it was not his macho image that was played upon the most – indeed, in Alpha interviews he often spoke of his personal fears and struggles, and of Christian faith as a much-needed 'crutch'. Instead, it was Grylls's laid-back unchurchy persona that chimed most closely with Alpha's brand. For several autumns in a row, he was the star attraction at 'An Evening with Bear Grylls', attended by over a thousand people, to help launch HTB's own course. After jazz music and canapés, he was interviewed by Gumbel on life, faith and passion for extreme adventure, interspersed with clips from *Man vs. Wild*. In 2009, for example, guests were treated to footage of Grylls diving under the Arctic ice, killing an African porcupine, chewing the flesh of a venomous snake, and eating the eyeball of a South American yak, before he encouraged them to attend Alpha and embrace 'life to the full'.[151] Afterwards he signed autographs and posed for photographs with fans.[152] On one occasion the transcript of Grylls's HTB interview in *Alpha News* needed asterisks to cover his swearing, an intentional breaking of religious taboos.[153] In his autobiography he confessed that he often enjoyed telling Gumbel 'irreverent jokes, with the suggestion he uses them in his next sermon. Thank God he never does.'[154] Grylls's relaxed, down-to-earth style helped to make Alpha attractive to a younger demographic. He was happy to recommend the course because 'no one is ever judged or bible-bashed'.[155] He repeatedly praised Alpha as 'super laid back', and as 'very low pressure, very cool, very mellow'.[156]

Although Grylls sold millions of copies of his survival books, Alpha encouraged him also towards the Christian market. Alpha International co-published Grylls's collection of fatherly advice for his sons – including encouragements like, 'Bet your life on Jesus. Ultimately that's the big one!' – with a parallel volume from Shara Grylls with wise aphorisms for married couples. Both were illustrated with humorous Mackesy cartoons.[157] Gumbel also helped Grylls with his book *Soul Fuel* (2019), a collection of daily Christian devotions.[158]

Pray, Pray, Pray!

Sandy Millar quipped that every church should invest in excellent PR – by which he meant not public relations but 'Prayer for Revival'.[159]

Although HTB and Alpha spent huge sums on the best modern marketing techniques, guided by the latest professional branding experts, they also invested heavily in the ancient spiritual discipline of prayer. *Questions of Life* described prayer as 'the most important activity of our lives'.[160] The three keys to revival according to Nicky Gumbel – echoing Billy Graham – were 'prayer, prayer, and prayer'.[161] In similar fashion Millar urged his congregation, 'Pray, pray, pray!'[162]

The rise of Alpha during the 1990s coincided with 'unprecedented growth' in HTB's prayer life.[163] Corporate prayer was overseen by Jeremy Jennings, a senior member of the HTB staff, who believed that God was 'screaming at us to pray for the spiritual rains to end the spiritual drought', and that these rains would bring 'cleansing, judgement, refreshment, life, destruction (of that which opposes God), joy and above all else millions to Christ'. But spiritual renewal, and mass conversions, would not take place without 'persistent, united, constant and deep corporate intercessory prayer'.[164] The Christian church was 'the only army on earth that finds victory on its knees', Jennings exclaimed.[165] HTB held its first 'prayer weekend' in Kidderminster in March 1994 – a few months after Alpha's global launch – devoted to praying for the church and nation, with 'the hope that a period of revival will be triggered'.[166] It was promoted with the motto, 'Let's change the news', and Jennings reckoned it was no coincidence that the Toronto Blessing arrived soon afterwards, sparking long queues to get into church and wide media attention.[167]

HTB's other regular prayer initiatives included prayer celebrations, all-night prayer, and an annual 'prayer party' on 31 December to welcome in the New Year, sometimes attended by over 900 people.[168] On several occasions they hired a boat and cruised down the River Thames, with a live worship band, praying for the government, the royal family, the media, the City, the homeless, the national church, and HTB's visionary Millennium Village, while passing the Houses of Parliament, the Tower of London, Waterloo Bridge, St Paul's Cathedral, Battersea Power Station and other iconic buildings. 'So *from* the heart of London we were able to pray *for* the heart of London', Jennings recalled. Those keen to pray for physical healing did so as the boat passed St Thomas' Hospital.[169] HTB's prayer ethos exuded joyful excitement and the thrill of anticipation at what God might do next.

Theologian Michael Lloyd struck an altogether different note at Focus in 2003 in his address 'In praise of boredom', when he announced 'Prayer can be boring . . . It can be a plain, old-fashioned, chore.'[170] More typical was the HTB prayer weekend at Chichester a few months later, for 230 people, when a spontaneous conga dance broke out around the Pontins ballroom.[171]

Alpha's advertising campaigns were always the focus of intense prayer. Tricia Neill named prayer as Alpha's top strategic priority and 'the foundation for all our plans'.[172] Jennings coordinated the annual Alpha prayer initiatives. His book, *The Church on Its Knees* (1998), distilled practical lessons from HTB for a wider audience, and he ran regional 'Dynamic Prayer in the Local Church' conferences to train prayer leaders. Before the first major Alpha campaign in September 1998, there were 158 prayer meetings across Britain, involving 10,000 people.[173] In September 2001 there were over 600 Alpha prayer meetings, all following the same programme, involving 18,700 people.[174] Two years later, cathedrals joined the initiative for the first time, holding supper parties and prayer meetings. There were major 'beacon' prayer events, for example, in the Anglican cathedrals in Coventry, London, Manchester, Oxford, St Albans and York.[175] The Alpha prayer meeting at St Paul's Cathedral was packed by 2,400 people, exhorted by Bishop Chartres to be united in prayer 'for the soul of this city – for the future of London'.[176] Before the 2004 campaign, London's main Alpha prayer event took place in a giant tent on Clapham Common with a crowd of 4,000 people.[177] Jennings was succeeded as HTB's director of prayer in 2009 by Pete Greig, who noted the close resonance between Alpha and his own 24/7 prayer initiative – both movements were passionate about the evangelisation of the world and the transformation of society, with prayer as the key.[178] Although Alpha invested millions of pounds in sophisticated marketing and in establishing brand recognition, they looked for ultimate success not to the skills of advertising executives or the endorsements of global celebrities, but to the blessings of Almighty God.

6

Embracing Rome

ONE OF THE most prominent features of Alpha is its emphasis upon Christian unity, in striking contrast to media commentary on church affairs, which prefers to focus upon disputes and divisions. Alpha instead speaks always of harmony between Christian believers. This core dimension of the Alpha brand enabled it to woo new markets, navigating nimbly between divergent denominations, even as far as the Vatican. Yet Alpha's ecumenical embrace also provoked fierce backlash in some quarters.

This ecumenical ethos pervaded HTB's public statements during the incumbencies of Sandy Millar and Nicky Gumbel. For example, in October 1994, HTB co-hosted a major prayer event in the Royal Albert Hall called 'London for Jesus', with an attendance of 4,300 Christians from a wide spectrum of denominations, ranging from Pentecostals to Roman Catholics. In his address from Psalm 133 ('How good and pleasant it is when brothers live together in unity'), Millar exhorted the gathered crowd: 'God is destroying the barriers between us . . . Doctrine matters but love is the best way.' He proclaimed that when Christians lived together in harmony, then God would bestow blessings upon their endeavours.[1] Millar pledged himself 'to work with anybody of good will who knows and loves the Lord', regardless of denomination.[2] 'We are brothers and sisters', he declared. 'We may look different, sound different, smell different, but we are the body of Christ.'[3] Gumbel often struck a similar note. Christian unity was an imperative, he insisted, flowing from the ministry of the Holy Spirit and enabling effective mission. Preaching at HTB in 2003, for instance, Gumbel explained from the Book of Ephesians how the Christian gospel breaks down barriers:

Every Christian – every Catholic, every Protestant – who puts their faith in Jesus has the Holy Spirit living within them. That unites us. Our doctrine does not unite us . . . But our relationships unite us because we are all sons and daughters of God the Father; we are all lovers of Jesus; and we all have the Holy Spirit living within us. This is the gospel.

Christian concord, Gumbel suggested, was a visible demonstration of the gospel and if the church was not united then it had little to say to a watching world. As an example, he pointed to the Alpha prayer initiative when 2,400 people of many denominations packed St Paul's Cathedral – an expression of unity at which, in Gumbel's words, 'the demons scream and the angels rejoice'.[4] This was central to Gumbel's priorities. When he was installed as vicar at HTB in 2005, a service attended by a thousand people, the prayers were led by representatives of the Roman Catholic Church, the Russian Orthodox Church and Glory House (one of London's largest black-majority Pentecostal congregations).[5]

In *Questions of Life*, Gumbel taught that one of the most joyful and important works of the Holy Spirit was to bring unity to the Christian family as a supernatural testimony in 'a troubled and divided world'. Because the Holy Spirit lives in every Christian, no matter their culture or denomination, it was 'a nonsense' and 'a tragedy' for the church to be fractured into competing groups.[6] 'We need to follow the words of Jesus and cut out our petty squabbles and our judgementalism,' Gumbel wrote in *Challenging Lifestyle*. 'We need to forget the past, drop the labels and unite around the person of Jesus Christ.'[7] One of Alpha's golden rules was therefore 'never to criticise another denomination, another Christian church or a Christian leader'.[8]

Millar sometimes broke this ban on criticism, if he felt sufficiently provoked by bishops within his own denomination. For example, a few days before Christmas 1993, David Jenkins (Bishop of Durham) – no stranger to controversy – kicked up a storm by announcing on television that familiar parts of the Christmas nativity (like the star, the wise men and the virgin birth) were 'splendidly symbolic' but not factually true. He was rebuked by the Archbishop of Canterbury, MPs and the tabloid press. One parliamentarian accused Jenkins of 'destroying the faith of millions of believers'.[9] Millar joined the protests, publicly defending the historicity of the Christmas narrative in television, radio and newspaper interviews.[10] To his congregation, he expressed frustration that 'the very people who ought to be proclaiming the excitement and joy of the risen Christ (the Bishops – and one in particular!) seem hell-bent on destroying the very ground on which the faith of the true Christian rests'. He longed for a return to episcopacy as laid down in the New Testament, with church leaders who 'hold firmly to the trustworthy message as it has been received' rather than 'ruining whole households by teaching things they ought not to teach' (Titus 1:9–10). 'Do not let us be fooled by all this!' Millar continued. 'Modern liberalism is as old as the devil himself' and a revival of 'ancient heresy'.[11] Ten years later, in 2003, Millar was again loudly critical when the Episcopal Church in the United States consecrated a gay bishop.[12]

Nevertheless, the Alpha rule of never criticising other church leaders was usually obeyed, and Gumbel, in particular, was highly diligent in his refusal to permit any public censure of another Christian. This was partly a matter of theological conviction, but also ensured that Alpha was not mired in divisive controversies and maintained its appeal to churches of all theologies and all denominations. Gumbel told Focus in 2010 that to speak negatively about another Christian or church was to grieve the Holy Spirit and to undermine their corporate public witness. Churches in harmony were attractive, whereas 'there's nothing more off-putting to the world than disunity . . . When churches fight each other, people are not interested.'[13] A refusal to criticise other Christians was therefore an essential marketing strategy, if Alpha was to continue attracting people to the Christian faith.

Christianity without Labels

Although Alpha was born within one Anglican congregation, it marketed itself as a course in the core truths of Christianity as held in common by all churches. C. S. Lewis's popular classic, *Mere Christianity* (1952), aimed to expound 'an agreed, or common, or central, or "mere" Christianity' as held by 'nearly all Christians at all times'. Lewis therefore kept silence on disputed points, avoiding theological polemics or denominational distinctives. It was an attractive project that won a worldwide fan-club.[14] Alpha wanted to occupy the same centre-ground. It aimed to swim in the Christian mainstream, while Gumbel suggested that Alpha's critics came mainly 'from the fringes' – 'from extreme fundamentalists, extreme liberals, extreme catholics'.[15] Lewis was quoted far more often in *Questions of Life* than any other thinker. Among the other theologians and preachers referenced by Gumbel in this core Alpha text, he placed famous evangelicals (such as Billy Graham, Martyn Lloyd-Jones, D. L. Moody, J. C. Ryle, C. H. Spurgeon, John Stott, David Watson, John Wesley and John Wimber) side by side with Catholics, liberals and Orthodox (such as Raniero Cantalamessa, Tom Forrest, Søren Kierkegaard, Jürgen Moltmann, Malcolm Muggeridge, Aleksandr Solzhenitsyn, Mother Teresa and Paul Tillich). This ecumenical breadth was central to Alpha's appeal, but it also formed a target for detractors. Alpha critic Chris Hand complained that some of the theologians in *Questions of Life* taught doctrines 'diametrically opposed to the gospel', and yet they were quoted uncritically, without 'a murmur of reservation' or 'a hint of a doctrinal quibble'. Since Alpha was designed for new Christians, not yet able to discriminate theologically, Hand believed Gumbel's approach was 'nothing short of irresponsible'.[16]

Alpha avoided disputed topics like the sacraments. This was not a deliberate dodge – it had never been part of the syllabus, which Gumbel celebrated in retrospect as 'God's providence' because it enabled all denominations to run the course, from Roman Catholics to the Salvation Army.[17] Alpha focused on what it saw as the Christian basics and left others to provide supplementary material if they wished. For example, in 2001 the Baptist Union of Great Britain published *Baptism and Belonging*, a short course on believers' baptism and church membership, designed as an Alpha 'add-on' to help integrate Alpha more fully in Baptist circles.[18] However, *Evangelicals Now* was worried by Alpha's ecumenical policy:

> Why is the course so gladly accepted right across the denominations, from the Baptist Union, through Anglicanism to the Roman Catholics?

Is it that the denominations are changing under the desperate decline in church numbers? Or is it that Alpha has cut and presented its biblical content in a way that suits everyone?

The idea that Alpha taught core truths, to which denominations were then free to add their own distinctive doctrines, 'sounds fine in the ears of non-Christians who have seen too much church squabbling, but rings alarm bells for conservative evangelicals'.[19] Alan Howe, one of Hand's collaborators in the Christian Research Network, asserted that Alpha was able to appeal to an ecumenical audience only because it had 'fatally watered down' the gospel. It was thus guilty of accelerating 'the slide away from sound biblical doctrine' and was in danger of 'deceiving more people than it is saving'.[20] 'Could there be anything more tragic than filling our churches with "converts" who in reality have been sold short?' complained another.[21] But Alpha supporters dismissed these sorts of criticisms as 'utter tosh' and pointed to evidence of Alpha's widespread fruitfulness.[22]

A strong ecumenical spirit also pervaded other Alpha products, such as Michael Lloyd's *Café Theology: Exploring Love, the Universe and Everything* (2005), based on his theology seminars at Focus. An accessible and humorous overview of Christian doctrine, it was marketed as 'a mind-stretching journey from Creation to New Creation'.[23] Lloyd 'makes theology hot stuff', glowed one reviewer. 'This isn't just café theology – it's Cordon Bleu Christianity.'[24] He considered calling the volume *Mere Theology* – a play on Lewis's *Mere Christianity* – because it aimed to present 'an understanding of the faith that is common to Christians of all types and stripes'. Lloyd wanted to demonstrate 'the complementary richness' of the different Christian traditions.[25] His vast fund of quotations encompassed twentieth-century theologians as diverse as Metropolitan Anthony Bloom, P. T. Forsyth, Hans Küng, Henri Nouwen, J. I. Packer, Michael Ramsey, Desmond Tutu and Rowan Williams, among many others. All were quoted with approval, as if in broad agreement with each other. This was typical of the Alpha policy to emphasise Christian consensus and to draw a veil over contentious topics. Steven Croft (leader of Fresh Expressions and later Bishop of Oxford) welcomed *Café Theology* as proof that Alpha took theology seriously, but wished that the reality of doctrinal disagreements and controversies in the church was frankly acknowledged.[26]

At Focus in 2003, Bishop Chartres praised the HTB network for its ability to build new alliances, and to move beyond the theological and liturgical 'punch-ups' and 'argy-bargy' that too often character- ised wider church life. In place of the old 'sterile and boring confrontations', he urged them to pursue 'deep church' (C. S. Lewis's synonym for 'mere Christians'). 'Some of us like Mozart masses,' the bishop quipped, 'some of us like Yawoo-doo-diddy-ba-ba-ba. But the truth is beyond all these differences of style and temperament which make for high church and low church and broad church and all that, there lies deep church. That's what the Spirit is doing among us.'[27] Chartres was therefore a strong supporter of Gumbel's vision for a new Alpha theological college. Not one for small dreams, Gumbel wrote of his intention that it should be nothing less than 'the best (non-residential) theological college in the world'. It would train students in 'models of excellence', including Alpha, and expose them to a wide range of perspectives from leading Roman Catholic, Orthodox, Pentecostal and Anglican theologians.[28] Launched in 2005 under Graham Tomlin's leadership as St Paul's Theological Centre, it formed part in 2007 of St Mellitus College, soon the largest theologic- al college in the Church of England.[29] Chartres welcomed this collaborative enterprise for embodying 'a new spirit of openness . . . a charismatic, catholic, orthodoxy ancient but fresh'.[30] Instead of 'mere Christianity', St Mellitus College adopted the language of 'generous orthodoxy', a parallel concept first coined in the 1980s by American 'post-liberal' theologian Hans Frei and popularised in the 2000s by 'emerging church' leader Brian McLaren, as a way of holding together the Church's different theological traditions and embracing the best in each of them.[31]

Gumbel sought to distance himself from theological partisanship, and especially from the popular epithets used to categorise Christians into separate groupings. Party labels were a hindrance in crossing boundaries and were much too easily misunderstood, both inside and outside the Church. Sometimes Gumbel expressed his willingness to embrace every designation, such as in an interview with *Christianity* magazine in 2000:

I am very happy with the labels providing we have them all. I am very happy to be called catholic, or evangelical, and charismatic and a liberal because I see the value in the Catholic view of the Church, the evangelical emphasis on the Bible, and the liberal emphasis on using our minds in a critical method of study of the Bible. Providing we have all those I am happy with it but I am not happy with having just one.[32]

More frequently, however, Gumbel vociferously rejected theological labels altogether. He asserted that such partisan categorisations were 'thoroughly unbiblical – they're a thing of the past'. Most Alpha guests had no interest in these multiple codifications that absorbed polemicists and ecclesial taxonomists. Deep divisions existed among Christians, Gumbel admitted, but 'labelling each other and name-calling is not the way forward'. Concerning the title 'evangelical' – often attached to HTB and Alpha by both its friends and foes – he insisted: 'I would never, ever use that term. It's unbiblical.'[33] The two titles Gumbel preferred to claim were 'Christian' and 'Anglican'. He celebrated the broad comprehensiveness of modern Anglicanism, which encompassed a remarkably wide range of basic theologies from Pentecostal to Catholic. Alpha's Anglican roots were a great blessing, in the providence of God, Gumbel argued, because the course there-fore posed 'less of a threat' to other denominations and was able to embrace them all.[34]

Ironically, however, the 'Alpha' label itself soon became a short-hand method of categorising churches, encouraged by the HTB leadership. In place of the old nomenclature of 'evangelical', 'charis-matic', 'catholic' or 'liberal' Christians, there were now 'Alpha' Christians. Millar suggested in 1998 that 'Alpha is the single most significant influence for unity in the church today.'[35] 'Alpha is much bigger than HTB', he celebrated. 'It is much bigger than the Church of England, thank God.' Growing numbers of congregations branded themselves as an 'Alpha church', seeing this as central to their ecclesial identity, which Millar welcomed as proof of the Holy Spirit's unifying ministry: 'It is not now any longer just an Anglican church or a Methodist church or a Salvation Army church or a Roman Catholic church, it's an Alpha church.'[36]

Alpha for Catholics

Alpha's remarkable breadth of appeal was shown most clearly in its warm embrace of Roman Catholicism. During the last quarter of the twentieth century the evangelical movement in the Church of England had grown much more friendly towards Rome, putting aside historic animosities. For example, the National Evangelical Anglican Congress in Nottingham in 1977 declared: 'Seeing ourselves and Roman Catholics as fellows Christians, we repent of attitudes that have seemed to deny it.'[37] Renewalist leaders like David Watson and George Carey frequently lamented the divisions caused by the Reformation.[38] John Wimber brought a similar ecumenical emphasis, insisting always that Protestants and Catholics must work together, united by the Holy Spirit.[39] HTB was swept along by this wave of ecumenical rapprochement.

HTB's reputation among English Catholics in the early 1990s was mixed. There seemed to be a vast theological and cultural gulf between them. In the *Catholic Herald*, the congregation was mocked in a scathing review by Adam Zamoyski, a traditionalist European Catholic. He likened the Sunday service to a Dire Straits concert, dismissing it as 'grotesque', 'superficial' and 'utterly meaningless'.[40] Yet this was met with a riposte from Catholics who enjoyed attending HTB on a regular basis, in tandem with Catholic Mass in their own parishes, and viewed them as complementary.[41] Francis Holford, a Catholic businessman, attended the first Alpha conference in 1993 because several of his children had been 'radically changed' by the course, and he praised it highly to the *Catholic Herald*:

> At a time when our church congregations are falling and our young people are voting with their feet in droves, I suggest that we should have the humility to learn from our Anglican brothers and sisters. I have not heard anything like this in the Catholic Church. Viva HTB! Viva el Spirito Santo![42]

Alpha was eagerly picked up by members of the Catholic Charismatic Renewal (CCR), a renewalist movement that began among university students in the United States of America in the 1960s and soon swept the world.[43] There were strong parallels between the ethos of Alpha and the CCR, both of which promoted evangelism and renewal by the Holy Spirit. Michael and Joan Le Morvan at the Catholic Bible School in Chichester had taught the CCR's Life in the Spirit seminars over 100 times in 15 years since the late 1970s, but they soon embraced Alpha, noting that 'the Holy Spirit is always on the move'.[44]

The first official promoter of Alpha among English Catholics was David Payne, director from 1996 of Catholic Evangelisation Services, one of the CCR's service agencies. Payne had been raised in a Catholic family in Hertfordshire but by his mid-20s was an unemployed drug addict, hooked on speed and LSD, living in squalor, filled with anger and self-loathing. He found himself 'on the verge of an early grave, psychiatric hospital or prison', and tried to commit suicide by overdosing on sleeping pills, but felt 'utterly trapped . . . more drugs, more parties and more darkness'. After listening to a former Hells Angel at a meeting of the Full Gospel Business Men's Fellowship, Payne prayed a prayer of repentance and faith in Christ, though his addictions continued. Shortly afterwards, in February 1985, at a Life in the Spirit seminar, he experienced a 'personal Pentecost', was filled with the Spirit and began to speak in tongues. He threw away his drugs, without withdrawal symptoms, and celebrated: 'It truly was a miracle. It was as if I'd been given a brand new start in life, like I'd been "born again".' With other young renewalist Catholics, Payne founded the Upper Room community in St Albans, which within three years had grown to 100 people. Within this vibrant youth network, many were 'zapped in the Spirit', witnessed miracles, and began evangelising in schools, prisons and on street corners.[45]

When Payne joined Catholic Evangelisation Services, he quickly identified Alpha as a good vehicle for promoting Catholic renewal and began marketing it among Roman Catholic parishes with the support of Gumbel and Millar.[46] In May 1997 the first major 'Alpha for Catholics' promotional event took place at the Westminster Cathedral complex, the institutional heart of British Catholicism – not in the cathedral itself, but in the hall next door. There were 400

Catholics in attendance, including 80 priests.[47] Delegates were treated to 'a snowstorm of quotations' from Pope John Paul II about the need for Catholics to engage in a 'new evangelisation', and Alpha was sold as part of the answer to that papal appeal.[48] Ambrose Griffiths (Roman Catholic Bishop of Hexham and Newcastle), a CCR supporter, urged that although Alpha was 'not a complete exposition of Catholic doctrine', it did provide 'the basis of Christian belief which many Catholics have never cottoned on to. They have been sacramentalised, but have never been evangelised.'[49] Not all were pleased, however. One dismayed Catholic critic rebuked Cardinal Basil Hume (Archbishop of Westminster) for granting a platform at the cathedral for 'the operatives of Holy Trinity Brompton' to expound their 'extremely questionable theories'. He decried this 'disastrous experiment' and warned that through Alpha the faith of many Catholics was being 'dissipated and weakened'.[50]

Payne joined in transatlantic partnership with Dave Nodar in Baltimore, Maryland, a fellow member of the CCR and founder in 1995 of ChristLife, which promoted the 'new evangelisation' in the United States. Nodar took charge of Alpha for Catholics in North America, and the two men travelled to Rome in 1998 and 1999 to advocate for Alpha at the Vatican.[51] The course began to attract enthusiastic write-ups not only in *Goodnews* (the CCR's in-house journal), but in mainstream Catholic media like *The Tablet*, which spoke effusively of 'The magnet of Alpha'. For the Church of England, *The Tablet* observed, Alpha had 'fallen out of the blue like manna from heaven after 40 years in a post-war wilderness of declining congregations, failing organs and leaking roofs'. But it was also being adopted by Roman Catholics and other denominations, throughout Britain and the globe,

> who after years of struggling against the odds have tried Alpha and experienced a phenomenal burst of growth. Of course it has not worked for everyone, but the stories of success are extraordinary in religious institutions that only a decade ago seemed doomed to post-millennial extinction. No one seems able to say just what it is that lies behind this resurgence in Christianity. Some fear a spiritual South Sea Bubble or a religious equivalent of the Wall Street crash, destined to

collapse around everyone's ears. Others insist it is simply the Holy Spirit . . .[52]

The Universe, a Roman Catholic newspaper, noted that English Catholics had 'climbed cautiously onto the bandwagon'. It sought to allay Catholic anxieties about these new ecumenical friendships: 'Some have expressed concern that Alpha will make the Catholic Church more Anglican. But the reverse seems at least as likely: that Alpha will make the Anglican Church more Catholic.'[53] By 2000, about 600 of the 3,100 Catholic parishes in the United Kingdom had run Alpha at least once. Some ran it regularly, like the working-class parish of the English Martyrs in Wakefield, West Yorkshire, who were on their twelfth course and found that their church was visibly growing. The parish priest, Father Tom Kenny, encouraged his fellow Catholics that through Alpha he had seen lives 'truly transformed, which is ultimately what it is all about. Alpha is just a basic Christian tool to bring people to a point of decision about Jesus Christ and then you can start incorporating them more into structures of parish life.'[54]

Catholic adopters of Alpha were troubled, however, by how to lead converts from Alpha's simplicities towards the full teachings of the Roman Church. The *Catholic Herald*, for example, agreed that evangelicalism could be 'a helpful base camp in the assault on the high peaks of classical Christianity', as it had proved for John Henry Newman in the early nineteenth century before his conversion to Rome, because it introduced enquirers to fundamental truths such as atonement, resurrection and personal salvation. But Scripture and Tradition were 'the two lungs of the Church', so if converts were introduced to one without the other, they would suffer from 'serious altitude sickness' when they tried to move beyond 'the limitations of base camp Alpha' to the full heights of Catholicism.[55] The Rite of Christian Initiation for Adults (RCIA) was the established programme for Catholic catechesis worldwide, so Alpha tried to position itself not as a rival, but as a useful prelude to the RCIA process.

Even as a basic introduction to the Christian faith, Alpha was deficient from a Catholic perspective because it had very little teaching about the Church or the sacraments, and nothing about the Virgin Mary. David Payne asked HTB for permission to produce a new version of Alpha, specially adapted for Catholics, but Gumbel refused on the basis that Alpha must remain a single global product, not different versions for different audiences.[56] Nevertheless, anyone was free to produce supplementary materials. Payne therefore filmed two sessions of Post Alpha Catholic Teaching (PACT) in 1997, designed as 'a pointer to the further riches of the Catholic faith', entitled 'Why should I listen to the Church?' and 'Why should I go to Mass?'[57] They tried to imitate Alpha's glossy style, but were filmed on a very small budget and looked embarrassing alongside the high professionalism of Alpha. The strategy backfired; as one Catholic traditionalist complained, 'It makes the "Catholic" case seem even weaker.'[58]

Catholic Evangelisation Services and ChristLife produced extra teaching resources called Catholic Faith Exploration (CaFE), beginning with *Drink from the Wells of the Church* (1999), a seven-week course by Raniero Cantalamessa on topics such as Bible reading, prayer, obedience to the Holy Spirit, the sacraments and the Virgin Mary.[59] Next came Marcellino D'Ambrosio's *Exploring the Catholic Church* (2000), with advice on 'getting more out of the Mass', and Mark Coleridge's *Catholics Listening to God* (2001) on Scripture, tradition and the Catholic magisterium.[60] These were initially marketed by *Alpha News* as Catholic follow-ups to Alpha, but were soon selling faster to Catholics than Alpha itself. They were shorter, less charismatic in content, and most importantly were presented not by Gumbel but by *bona fide* Catholics. Although the Catholic bishops remained circumspect about Alpha, they embraced CaFE, which soon found a global market. This became Payne's primary focus and in 2001 he and Alpha parted company.[61] Alpha International decided to absorb Alpha for Catholics back within their own structures, rather than delegating its promotion to the Catholic Charismatic Renewal, and employed 23-year-old Oxford graduate Kitty Arbuthnott (later Kitty Kay-Shuttleworth) to lead the work.

Protestant Polemics

Alpha's overtures to Rome provoked strong reactions on both sides of the historic Catholic/Protestant divide. For example, the *Evangelical*

Times (a conservative Protestant newspaper) predicted that Alpha would mislead thousands by its 'manifest distortions of the gospel' and asserted that the renewal movement opened the door to Roman Catholic doctrine by exalting spiritual experience as the final arbiter of Scripture. It warned that Alpha 'fever' was carrying adherents 'inexorably closer' to Rome, which 'waits with consummate patience to embrace those who wander from the path of Scripture'.[62] *Vanguard* magazine, associated with Christian Witness Ministries (a conservative Pentecostal organisation), likewise published an exposé of Nicky Gumbel 'unmasked'. It suggested he was guilty not only of ecumenism, but of syncretism, because he considered Roman Catholics to be Christians.[63] Another critic reckoned that Alpha's ultimate agenda was the unity of all churches under papal authority, and warned friends of the true gospel to 'avoid Alpha like the plague'.[64]

Objections from Protestants in Northern Ireland were particularly vociferous. In May 1996 more than 200 people packed into Omagh town hall, County Tyrone, to hear a vivid presentation from Cecil Andrews of Take Heed Ministries. He denounced the Toronto Blessing as 'blasphemous and heretical' and was equally scathing of Alpha, which had been started by some local churches, likening it to 'rat poison'.[65] When five congregations in Belfast – Anglican, Roman Catholic and Presbyterian – combined to run Alpha in 1998, it was condemned as 'dangerous and devious', and as a camouflage for the Toronto Blessing.[66] Likewise when churches in County Fermanagh advertised Alpha in the local press, three ministers from the Free Presbyterian Church of Ulster (founded by Ian Paisley) castigated it as 'the worst form of evil' and warned Christians to 'beware of this latest attempt to beguile the people of God'. They held a special anti-Alpha rally in Enniskillen to alert the local populace.[67] Paisley's journal, *The Battle Standard*, carried an analysis by Paul Fitton (minister of Bridlington Free Presbyterian Church, Yorkshire), who asserted that Alpha was disseminating 'the poison of false doctrine', especially the errors of Arminianism, ecumenism, humanism and charismaticism. He was particularly alarmed at Alpha's origins, noting that the Toronto Blessing in Britain 'first showed its ugly and ungodly head' at HTB, and that Anglicanism was a morally and doctrinally corrupt denomination. If Gumbel really was a spiritual person, Fitton reasoned, 'he would not be a curate in the Church of England. God calls men out of apostasy, not into it.' Alpha, he concluded, was nothing less than 'Hell-inspired' and should be avoided at all costs.[68]

It was Alpha's links to Catholicism, as much as Toronto, that offended conservative Protestants. A local Free Presbyterian newspaper, *The Burning Bush: A Protestant Witness in a Day of Apostasy*, denounced Alpha as 'a counterfeit and a fraud that will only undermine the true gospel of Christ and work havoc amongst those who submit to its instruction'. It called on all true Christians to separate, as a matter of biblical obedience, from churches that promoted the course. Pointing to Alpha's own publicity materials, which emphasised its compatibility with Catholic teaching, *The Burning Bush* saw this as proof that Alpha was 'helping to build the Roman Catholic Church . . . God is calling people out of Rome but the Alpha Course is bringing people back to her evil embrace.' It rebuked Alpha as 'a rehash of the old charismatic fables and fancies mixed in with new ageism and plain old-fashioned baloney', its evangelists for grinning like popstars, and its converts as duped by high-pressure salesmanship. But the capstone of the assault, once again, was Alpha's origins within Anglicanism: 'Can any good thing come out of the most apostate denomination in the United Kingdom? . . . Who ever heard of revival emanating out of Sodom or Gomorrah?'[69]

These sectarian tensions continued to simmer. An 'Alpha Ireland' board was formed in 2005 to promote Alpha ecumenically, with Roman Catholic businessman Paddy Monaghan as national coordinator. Monaghan had been simultaneously 'born again' and 'baptised in the Spirit' after attending a renewalist prayer group as a Dublin student, and personally identified as an 'Evangelical Catholic'.[70] He worked energetically for reconciliation between Catholics and Protestants, and had chaired the organising committee for John Wimber's first Vineyard conference in Dublin in the 1980s.[71] Alpha shared Wimber's ethos and Monaghan spoke of his excitement, as a Catholic, at Alpha's potential 'to change the face of Ireland'.[72] However, when seven churches across Bangor, County Down, combined to coordinate Alpha in 2007, it was again assailed by the local Free Presbyterian minister with eschatological fervour as 'part of the ecumenical and charismatic delusion of the last days'.[73]

Catholic Traditionalists

From the other side of the Reformation divide, there was similar heightened rhetoric among Roman Catholic critics of Alpha, especially within the traditionalist wing of the church. Some were especially concerned that Alpha was subtly sowing the seeds of Protestantism among Catholics. For example, Caroline Farey of the Maryvale Institute in Birmingham argued that Gumbel's Alpha talks tended, whether explicitly or implicitly, to promote

> a lay Church with no need for priests or hierarchy, no source of revelation other than the Scriptures, no magisterium other than his own through the power of the Spirit, a common meal with no Eucharistic sacrifice, a Protestant understanding of atonement, redemption, the human condition and prayer, and no real denominational differences.

Were doctrinal disagreements between Protestants and Catholics only a matter of 'packaging', rather than 'the one unchanging message of salvation', she asked. If so, then for what purpose did the Roman Catholic martyrs of the English Reformation give their lives at the gallows?[74]

Christian Order magazine – which marketed itself as 'devoted to the defence and propagation of the One True Faith: Catholic, Apostolic and Roman' – lambasted the rest of the English Catholic media, like *The Tablet* and *The Universe*, for being 'lukewarm appeasers' by welcoming Alpha and its advertising revenues into the fold. *Christian Order* believed its duty was instead to expose 'the enemies of Catholicism', and it vilified Alpha as 'the latest in the long line of New Age/Protestant trojan horses to be wheeled into Catholic parishes with episcopal blessing'.[75] One of the magazine's contributors, Gillian van der Lande, worried that 'the Alpha "magisterium"' was being absorbed into Catholicism.[76] She circulated her complaints not only to Cardinal Hume, but also to the pope and to several influential cardinals in the Roman curia.[77] A hostile profile in the *Catholic Herald* likewise suggested that Alpha was 'fundamentally Protestant' and that Catholic Alpha was merely 'Protestantism with optional

extras'.[78] *Pro Ecclesia et Pontifice* (For Church and Pope), another traditionalist Catholic pressure group dedicated to fighting against liberalism within the Roman Catholic Church, issued a stern warning
against Alpha as '*diametrically* opposed to Catholic teaching' and
indeed 'a different religion'.[79]

Unsurprisingly, some Protestant converts to Rome were particularly hostile to Alpha as representing a former way of life that they
had renounced. Robert Williams, an Anglican evangelical before
his conversion, suggested that evangelicalism and Catholicism were
'two different systems that disagree on grace, on the sacraments, on
the Church. The whole Alpha course is theologically flawed.' He
warned that for Catholics to attend Alpha was like entering 'a lion's
den . . . To my mind, it's selling your birthright for some pottage.'
Alpha, Williams declared, trained Catholics 'to think in a Protestant
way'. He was particularly insulted by comments he had overheard
in some evangelical circles that Alpha was a good way 'to share the
gospel with the Catholics', and was alarmed that the Catholic hierarchy seemed unable to recognise this proselytising agenda.[80] One
mother grieved that she had 'lost a daughter to Protestantism'
through Alpha.[81]

The letters pages of the Catholic press were filled with similar
objections. A traditionalist complained that 'Alpha promotes heresy!',
principally the Protestant doctrine of *sola scriptura*.[82] He criticised the
lack of teaching on 'essential Catholic beliefs' such as sanctifying
grace, the Virgin Mary, the communion of saints, papal infallibility
and the sacrifice of the Mass, asserting that Catholic Alpha was a
'catechetical dog's dinner' favoured by 'woolly minded priests'.[83] An
attender at an 'Alpha for Catholics' weekend complained that there
was no mention of the one holy catholic apostolic church as understood by the great patristic theologians or ecumenical councils.
Indeed, she was left with the sad impression that the Roman Catholic
Church could be 'confined to the dustbin of history' and that all one
needed was to become 'a Gumbel-inspired Bible-based Christian'.[84]
When the Catholic diocese of Brentwood, in Essex, joined forces in
2003 with the Anglican diocese of Chelmsford to run Alpha in the
Catholic cathedral, some parishioners were upset at the prospect of
Nicky Gumbel taking over their cathedral pulpit. 'What a

desecration, and a travesty', wrote one. 'God help Brentwood! Our Blessed Mother Mary protect her poor children!'[85]

A much more positive theological assessment was offered by Father Peter Hocken (1932–2017), chaplain to the Roman Catholic Bishop of Northampton. Hocken was an ecumenist, scholar, author, and leader within the Catholic Charismatic Renewal. He published widely on the renewalist movement within both Catholic and Protestant contexts, including *Streams of Renewal* (1986), *The Strategy of the Spirit?* (1996), and *Blazing the Trail: Where is the Holy Spirit Leading the Church?* (2001).[86] Hocken became one of Alpha's key theological advisers, regularly approached by Gumbel for guidance on adapting the course for Catholics. Catholic critics, Hocken argued, were addressing Alpha with the wrong question. If they asked, 'Is Alpha fully Catholic?', the answer was obviously negative and they would therefore have nothing more to do with it. But if instead they asked, 'Is Alpha a work of the Holy Spirit?', then a positive answer would open new possibilities of viewing Alpha as an ecumenical gift, to be used 'in a way that serves the Catholic fullness that we cherish'.[87]

In response to critics, other Catholics simply pointed to the fruit of Alpha in their own lives and parishes. 'There are many cradle Catholics, like myself, who have had their faith come alive on Alpha', testified one.[88] Another explained that, like many of his contemporaries, he had for many years been a 'semi-lapsed Catholic' and occasionally went to Mass but it seemed to make no difference to his life. Attending Alpha was 'like coming home to my early rock-like faith', with its intellectual certainty about the Christian message, and he had been a committed Catholic ever since.[89] Another agreed that Alpha had helped to 'revive and refresh my Catholic faith', and recommended that Catholics should welcome it as 'a marvellous vehicle for revitalising and evangelising' rather than 'moaning that Alpha was not invented by Catholics'.[90] Still another defended Alpha as 'the most exciting Christian initiative of our age'.[91]

Alpha News regularly carried reports of Catholic parishes that had embraced Alpha, or testimonies from those who had become Christians through Alpha at their local Catholic church. For example, at the Convent of Jesus and Mary Language College, a girls' Catholic secondary school in north-west London, two teachers who had attended Alpha at HTB began running the course for pupils in 1997. The RE teacher, a regular attender at a Catholic church, said of Alpha: 'It has given my Catholicism a new meaning. I am more of a Catholic than I was before.'[92] At the same period, on the other side of the Atlantic, Alpha was significant in the religious development of Justin Trudeau (later Prime Minister of Canada), who had been raised a Catholic but lapsed in his teens. In his late 20s, he went through a period of 'spiritual crisis' in the wake of family tragedy. His younger brother, Michel, drowned in November 1998, aged 23, when he was swept into Kokanee Lake, British Columbia, by an avalanche while skiing. Through the 'searing emotional pain' of sudden bereavement, Justin came to realise that 'my life, like everyone else's, is in God's hands'. He was invited to Alpha by a friend, Mariam Matossian (later a successful Armenian folk musician), with whom he often talked about questions of faith, and testified in his autobiography that Alpha 'helped me welcome God's presence into my life'.[93]

A Perfect Wife

One of the most acerbic Catholic critics of Alpha was Cristina Odone, editor of the *Catholic Herald* between 1991 and 1995. Her novel *A Perfect Wife* (1997) centred upon the web of deceit around the fictitious Alexander Connaught, a young, elegant, athletic Old Etonian and founder of the Renewal Movement. He was vicar of a well-heeled evangelical church in Chelsea, a galleried Victorian building with TV screens, a worship band, mesmerising preaching, prayers for healing, and full congregations. A strict disciplinarian and 'puppet master', the charismatic Connaught held many adoring acolytes under his spell as their mentor and spiritual adviser. In recruiting new disciples he kept his eye 'on pedigrees as well as piety, and on Debrett's as well as the Day of Judgement', successfully raising millions of pounds for his ministry. The Renewal Movement's political arm, the Christian Coalition, was led by a closeted gay MP who preached conservative family values, leading a moralistic campaign against divorce, abortion, pornography, homosexuality and a corrupt left-wing media. With the new millennium looming, the Renewal Movement saw its mission to purify society in apocalyptic terms as a titanic battle between good and evil, with the ultimate aim to destroy the liberal establishment. Connaught tried to harness the newspapers to spread his puritanical message and established a network of weekly meetings across London, called 'The Circle', where teenagers and young adults confessed their sins and were given spiritual instruction. As these Circles multiplied throughout England, some turned to flagellation, publicly admitting their fornication before beating themselves with rods. Other Renewal Movement fanatics became terrorists and bombed an abortion clinic. It was a sordid tale of secrets, hypocrisy, manipulation, abuse, adultery, suicide and a lust for power.[94]

Although Odone insisted *The Perfect Wife* was not a *roman à clef*, the allusions to HTB were unmistakable. The *Evening Standard* called it 'a devastating satire on Knightsbridge's trendiest church'.[95] Her villain, Alexander Connaught, shared a first name with Sandy Millar. 'I want to alert Britain to the danger of Christian fundamentalism', Odone proclaimed: 'While it is cloaked in a squeaky-clean presentation it is actually promoting a narrow moral policy – both anti-gay and anti-feminist.'[96] In order to promote her novel, she launched a swingeing attack upon HTB in *The Spectator*, mocking them as Barbour-clad fundamentalists with double-barrelled surnames, 'whose stiff upper lip melts into a Teletubby's gormless smile as they pray for Jesus, shout for Jesus and weep for Jesus'. In a hit at the Toronto Blessing, she claimed that the youthful congregation 'throw themselves to the ground, shaking, laughing and issuing the inbred bark of the beagle that accompanies their shooting parties'. Recruitment for Alpha, Odone suggested, took place

> at drinks parties where, armed with a champagne glass and a cocktail sausage, dewy-eyed converts enthuse about Jesus Christ as if He were a particularly glamorous guest on the party circuit, and praise the Holy Spirit as if It were a fabulous, no-nonsense nanny who has taken charge of their spiritual upbringing.

The social framework built around Alpha was bolstered by weekly Bible studies with 'well-heeled hostesses from Chelsea and

Kensington', seeking to reconcile 'Jacob's ladder and the social ladder' while propagating 'black-and-white morality' and prurient attitudes to sex. While Jesus Christ cast his net wide, to Odone HTB seemed (like her character Alexander Connaught) 'more interested in trawling through Debrett's for their disciples'.[97] HTB complained to *The Spectator* that these portrayals were malicious and largely fabricated, but Odone was unrelenting.[98] In a follow-up article, she accused them of 'unscrupulous emotional manipulation' and of importing 'Bible Belt fundamentalism' from America: 'Behind their clean and glossy façade and under the misleading label "Church of England", HTB and its ever-expanding network of satellite churches are touting a sinister theology rooted in a literal interpretation of the Bible and obsessed with Satan.'[99] The *Church of England Newspaper* concluded, however, that Odone's antipathy was motivated by naked 'commercialism' – by a desire to sell as many copies of her novel as possible by kicking up a storm.[100] The trick about publicising a book, explained Andrew Brown in the *Church Times*, was to get it off the book pages and into the news.[101]

In subsequent years, Odone continued to criticise Alpha in dismissive tones, suggesting that it was staffed by 'cheery, clappy Sloanes'.[102] Similar hostility was evident from another Roman Catholic novelist and regular *Catholic Herald* columnist, septuagenarian Alice Thomas Ellis. She stumbled across Alpha on television but recoiled from the '*schmaltz*' in Gumbel's polished presentation: 'the audience sat there with smiles on their faces lapping it all up as he read snippets of scripture and told little jokes. I stared in horrified disbelief. They were *enjoying* it.' Ellis, a staunch traditionalist, mourned the growing dominance of Alpha's brand of Christianity, which she found 'nauseous', 'oleaginous, saccharine and feeble'.[103]

French Catholic Scrutiny

The adoption of Alpha by Roman Catholics in France was a breakthrough moment for Alpha's penetration of the global Catholic market. A young French Catholic couple living in London – Marc de Leyritz, an investment banker, and his wife Florence – attended Alpha at HTB in 1997 and found it a transformative experience. At the Holy Spirit weekend, as Marc began speaking in tongues, he was reminded of the words of St Paul: 'Announcing the gospel is for me a necessity. I shall be cursed if I don't announce it' (1 Corinthians 9:16). His immediate desire was to resign his job and commit the rest of his life to evangelism, but Gumbel cautioned him not to rush into any precipitate action. To test the water, the De Leyritzes began running Alpha for the French diaspora in London, first at the French Lycée, an independent school in Kensington, and then at their church, Notre Dame de Paris, near Leicester Square. Increasingly they felt a burden to reach their homeland. A few churches in France had embraced Alpha, yet all except one were Protestant. As the De Leyritzes explained in their pitch to Gumbel, revival in France would never be possible without the Catholics – in a population of 60 million, 80 per cent were professing Catholics, 5 per cent Muslims, and less than 2 per cent Protestants. Yet only 5 per cent of French Catholics attended church on Sundays and many young people were looking elsewhere to meet their spiritual hunger. Therefore, with Gumbel's encouragement, the De Leyritzes returned to Paris in 1999 to launch an Alpha office.[104]

French monastic communities, linked to the Catholic Charismatic Renewal, were early adopters of Alpha. The first Catholic parish to run the course was Saint-Denys de la Chapelle in Paris, under the auspices of Chemin Neuf, a community founded in 1973 by charismatic Jesuit Laurent Fabre. The entire Chemin Neuf community of 800 members was trained in Alpha by the De Leyritzes in 1999 and began running the course throughout France. It was also taken up by the Emmanuel Community (founded in 1976) and the Community of Saint John (founded in 1975), who ran Alpha in their parishes and monasteries.[105] Anglican minister Charlie Cleverly, a church planter in Paris, wrote excitedly of Alpha's potential in France to bring the 'huge Catholic fringe to saving faith in Christ'. Meanwhile, Argentinian evangelist Carlos Annacondia, known for his 'ruggedly Pentecostal and anti-Catholic ethos', chose Alpha as the follow-up to his 10-day Paris mission at Easter 2000.[106] Soon the French Catholic bishops began to investigate, troubled by whether Alpha was compatible with Catholic Christianity. Their scrutiny committee was headed by Bishop Michel Dubost (president of the French Episcopal Commission for Catechesis and the Catechumenate), alongside Pierre d'Ornellas (later Archbishop of Rennes) and Gérard Daucourt (Bishop of Orléans).[107] With the assistance of two theologians from the Institut Catholique de Paris, the bishops identified several doctrinal shortcomings with Alpha. The De Leyritzes urged Gumbel that there could be no official endorsement of Alpha in France, and little possibility of further Alpha growth, until these objections were met.[108]

Les Questions de la Vie, the first French translation of *Questions of Life*, was published in Switzerland in 1998 by Jeunesse en Mission, the French branch of the Protestant mission agency Youth With A Mission (YWAM). But a new version was needed, better suited to Catholic readers. However, one of Alpha's fundamental principles was that there should be no special versions of Alpha for particular nations or denominations. There was one global, uniform product, which could be translated but never locally adapted. Therefore, no breakthrough in Catholic France was possible unless Gumbel agreed to revise his core English text, with ramifications for Alpha worldwide. Faced by the demands of the French episcopate, he sought advice from Peter Hocken, who counselled him to give ground in some areas but to remain unmoved in others.[109] These revisions were seen in the new 2001 English edition of *Questions of Life*, a significant attempt to conciliate French Catholic opinion.

Some changes involved tweaking a single phrase here or there, but were theologically significant. For example, in the chapter 'How and why should I read the Bible?', Gumbel explained that Scripture was inspired by God and must be the Christian's 'supreme authority', above the opinion of church leaders. He acknowledged that 'due weight' must be given to church teaching, but then added a typically Protestant caveat, 'provided it does not conflict with the revealed word of God'.[110] This phrase worried the French bishops because it raised the question of the church's authority (and perhaps conjured the image of individual Christians reading their Bibles and then censuring their clergy), so Gumbel agreed to delete it. In the chapter 'What about the Church?', Gumbel originally listed Roman Catholicism as a 'denomination', alongside Anglicans, Baptists and Methodists.[111] However, some Catholic readers took offence at the implication that their church was equivalent to these Protestant groupings, rather than the one true church of God, so he deleted the reference.[112] A few pages later, Gumbel taught that in the Old Testament access to God was via a priest who made sacrifices at the Temple on behalf of the people, whereas in the New Testament 'Jesus, our great high priest, has made the supreme sacrifice of his own life on our behalf'. This led naturally to a summary of the Reformation doctrine of the 'priesthood of all believers':

> No further sacrifices are necessary and no further priests are neces-
> sary . . . All Christians are priests in the sense that we all have access to
> God, we can all represent men to God as we pray for others, and we
> all represent God to men as we go out into the world . . . There is no
> need for sacrificing priests today because there is no need for further
> sacrifices.[113]

The French bishops objected strongly, so Gumbel deleted all this Reformation material from the new edition of *Questions of Life*.

On other subjects, however, Gumbel refused to budge. His original Alpha text taught that at Holy Communion the bread and wine 'represent' the body and blood of Jesus – translated in *Les Questions de la Vie* as *représentent* – which seemed like a denial of the Roman Catholic doctrine of transubstantiation.[114] The French bishops wanted this changed to 'signify' (*signifient*), a more ambiguous term that could encompass both Protestant and Catholic interpretations of the sacrament, but Gumbel refused. He had previously consulted on this point with Rowan Williams, who said that if he could solve the historic conundrum he deserved the Nobel Peace Prize, so Gumbel retained his original wording.[115]

The most intense negotiation concerned Gumbel's chapter 'Why did Jesus die?', which emphasised penal substitutionary atonement, an unpopular doctrine in Catholic circles. Gumbel taught that Jesus died 'instead of us' – a classic Reformation formula – but the French bishops wanted him to teach that Jesus died 'for us', a broader concept that they argued was closer to the original phraseology of the New Testament. They also called upon Gumbel to strike out his reference to the 'self-substitution of God', a quotation from John Stott's *The*

Cross of Christ (1986), a classic evangelical exposition.[116] However, Hocken advised Gumbel that Alpha's distinctive teaching about the cross was one of its special 'charisms' from the Holy Spirit, a key reason for Alpha's fruitfulness in evangelism, and must therefore be protected. Hocken also showed Gumbel that substitutionary atonement was, in fact, taught by the official *Catechism of the Catholic Church* (1992), even if often neglected in Catholic preaching.[117] On this contested question, therefore, Gumbel refused to revise Alpha's doctrine, and even strengthened it with a lengthy quotation from Raniero Cantalamessa about Jesus dying in the place of sinners and bearing the wrath of God. He added a reference to the *Catechism of the Catholic Church* for good measure.[118] On one further point, however, Gumbel did concede to the request of the French bishops. *Questions of Life* originally illustrated substitutionary atonement with a story from *Miracle on the River Kwai* (1963) about an innocent prisoner of war being brutally beaten to death by a Japanese guard, which seemed to equate God with a violent thug.[119] It was replaced in 2001 by another story from the Second World War of Father Maximilian Kolbe, who volunteered to die in the place of a fellow prisoner at Auschwitz. This was a better illustration, but was doubly appealing to Roman Catholic readers because Kolbe was a Catholic priest and martyr, canonised as a saint by Pope John Paul II in 1982.[120]

Similar sensitivities were apparent in other Catholic contexts, amplified by the complexities of translation. In English the word 'church', for example, covers a very broad lexical range, from local assembly to worldwide institution. However, when the Alpha materials were first translated into Polish, 'church' became *zbór* (congregation), an emphasis favoured among Protestants, and in 2003 the theological censor from the Roman Catholic diocese of Toruń requested this be corrected everywhere to *kościół* (church). Once again Peter Hocken was invited by Alpha International to advise on these theological nuances from a Catholic perspective.[121]

Speaking to an English Catholic newspaper about Alpha, Gumbel asserted: 'What I say to people is, if you can show me that something is wrong or unbalanced, I'll change it; but not just for the Catholics, I'll change it for everyone.'[122] Nevertheless, the vast bulk of his revisions were designed to appeal to Catholics, as Gumbel became increasingly alert to the importance of expanding beyond his Protestant homebase. In his other paperbacks pro-Roman revisions were also apparent. This was most obvious in the opening chapter to *Telling Others*, laying out the Alpha vision. The original 1994 version contained no Roman Catholic material at all, but during the early 2000s Gumbel added multiple quotations from Popes Paul VI, John Paul II and Benedict XVI.[123] He explained how some of the great evangelists from Christian history were 'filled with the Spirit' in dramatic ways, but all his exemplars in 1994 were famous evangelicals – John Wesley, George Whitefield, Charles Finney, D. L. Moody, Reuben Torrey and Billy Graham. After 2011 these were supplemented with two prominent Roman Catholics – St Philip Neri from the sixteenth century, and the ubiquitous Cantalamessa.[124] Gumbel also emphasised that any new converts through Alpha should join the congregation that had run the course – whether a Roman Catholic church in South America or a Coptic Orthodox church in North Africa.[125] He likewise explained that instead of the word 'evangelism' (popular among Protestants) he now preferred 'evangelisation' (popular among Catholics), because it conveyed the sense of conversion as the beginning of a lifelong process.[126] Gumbel was a careful diplomat, seeking to express himself in ways that would win Alpha the widest possible audience. All these revisions were designed to give the Roman Catholic community greater confidence in the Alpha project and thus to extend Alpha's sphere of influence and global impact.

Cardinals and Popes

As Alpha's reputation grew, it forged important relationships with leading members of the Roman Catholic hierarchy, including at the Vatican itself. A particularly fruitful friendship was the one with Raniero Cantalamessa, a prominent member of the Catholic Charismatic Renewal, who was frequently quoted in Gumbel's books. Cantalamessa's many writings included *Life in Christ* (1990), *The Holy Spirit in the Life of Jesus* (1994), *The Mystery of Pentecost* (2001) and *Sober Intoxication of the Spirit* (2005). Gumbel first heard him speak at the International Congress on World Evangelisation in Brighton in July 1991 and was especially impressed by his strong appeal for unity in the Holy Spirit. The papal preacher's declaration that 'what unites us is infinitely greater than what divides us' was adopted as one of Gumbel's personal mottos, written into Alpha.[127] The two men met for the first time in May 1999 when both were guest speakers at the interdenominational *Jesus 2000* conference in Nuremberg, attended by 4,000 delegates from across Germany, including 700 Catholics.[128] Four years later, Cantalamessa was a guest speaker at Focus, the first of his numerous contributions to HTB and Alpha events, where he charmed his audience with an exhortation to keep 'a keen Biblical devotion' to the Virgin Mary.[129] In June 2005, he opened the Alpha conference in London, and his address – published by Alpha International as *Faith Which Overcomes the World* – asserted that the theological issues that had provoked the Great Schism between East and West, and the Reformation between Protestant and Catholic, were no longer relevant. He called on all churches to proclaim Christ together, 'in fraternal accord', commending Alpha's role in helping people towards 'a personal encounter with Jesus'.[130] In a promotional film to advertise Alpha globally, Cantalamessa again praised Alpha's ecumenical spirit in urging participants not to join any particular denomination 'but just to join Jesus, to put Jesus at the centre'. He suggested that in a modern secularised context where Jesus was widely ignored, it was foolish for Catholics, Protestants and Orthodox to be arguing among themselves.[131] Gumbel called him 'one of my theological heroes' and recommended Cantalamessa's *Come, Creator Spirit* (2003) as his favourite book on the Holy Spirit.[132] Indeed, he claimed to have read all of Cantalamessa's English-language books, 'some of them many times over'.[133]

Gumbel frequently addressed European Catholic audiences, which helped to establish a network of wider relationships and boost Alpha's popularity. Another significant contact was Cardinal Christoph Schönborn, Archbishop of Vienna, a prominent Catholic churchman who had helped to write the *Catechism of the Catholic Church* and was tipped as a potential pope. Schönborn invited Gumbel to speak about Alpha at *Open the Doors to Christ!*, the first International Congress for the New Evangelisation (ICNE), a major event for European evangelists held in Austria in May 2003, hosted jointly by the cardinal archbishops of Brussels, Lisbon, Paris and Vienna.[134] The following year, in May 2004, Gumbel spoke on Alpha at *Together for Europe*, an interdenominational conference in Stuttgart attended by 10,000 people, at which church and political leaders outlined their visions for the future. Among the Catholic dignitaries were Queen Fabiola of Belgium, Henri, Grand Duke of Luxembourg, and Romano Prodi (president of the European Commission), alongside 55 Catholic bishops and cardinals.[135] It was also Gumbel's introduction to Cardinal Walter Kasper (president of the Pontifical Council for Promoting Christian Unity), who later invited him for talks at the Vatican.[136] At another ICNE congress, in Hungary in September 2007, Gumbel was the only non-Catholic to give a keynote address, at the invitation of Cardinal Péter Erdő, Archbishop of Esztergom-Budapest.[137] A few months later, he was with Schönborn at a smaller symposium in Rome on the role of the Catholic parish in evangelisation, attended by 80 priests and church leaders from around the world, organised by the Emmanuel Community and the Pontifical Redemptor Hominis Institute. Gumbel was again the only non-Catholic speaker at the event.[138] Although support for Alpha among the Catholic hierarchy at home in Britain was sometimes lukewarm, Gumbel was fêted among influential Catholics in continental Europe and globally.[139] These alliances were strengthened, in return, by frequent invitations to prominent Catholics to grace the platform of the HTB leadership conference in the Royal Albert Hall.

Through contacts at the Vatican, Gumbel also had the opportunity to meet three successive popes. In February 2004, he spent five days in Rome (with his wife Pippa, and with Kitty Arbuthnott) meeting with representatives of the Congregation on the Doctrine of the Faith, the Pontifical Council for Promoting Christian Unity, the Sant'Egidio Community, the Focolare Movement, and the Rome School of Evangelisation. As the capstone of the visit they joined a crowd of 6,000 at a General Audience with a frail John Paul II, in his wheelchair suffering with Parkinson's disease. Afterwards they were personally presented by Cantalamessa to the pope, to whom they gave one of Charlie Mackesy's specially commissioned paintings of the prodigal son (with the background writing in Polish, the pope's native tongue).[140] Gumbel later described John Paul II as a 'great spiritual hero'.[141]

In February 2005 Gumbel and Arbuthnott were back in Rome to meet with Cardinal Joseph Ratzinger at the Congregation for the Doctrine of the Faith, and told him about Alpha. Although it was just a brief 20-minute encounter, Gumbel saw it as another sign of the 'extraordinary providence of God', coming just months before Ratzinger's election as Pope Benedict XVI. He praised the new pope as 'very humble, very gracious, very loving, very Jesus-centred and enormously encouraged about what was happening with Alpha. It was further evidence of the extraordinary unity that God is bringing to us around the world.'[142] Alpha was invited to take part in the World Youth Day at Cologne in August 2005, when Pope Benedict gathered together a million young people from 200 countries for a giant Catholic festival. Seminars introducing Alpha were attended by Catholic youth from as far afield as the United States, Canada, India, Sri Lanka and Malaysia.[143]

A decade later, in June 2014, Gumbel was included in his friend Archbishop Justin Welby's delegation to meet Pope Francis at the Vatican.[144] In an article for the *Catholic Herald* entitled 'What I love about the Catholic Church', Gumbel explained that Roman Catholicism had 'hugely enriched my personal faith'. He especially praised Pope Francis's apostolic exhortation, *Evangelii Gaudium* (2013), for its emphasis on the love of God through Jesus Christ, evangelisation in the power of the Holy Spirit, and the unity of the Church.[145] These chimed closely with Gumbel's own passions and were central to the Alpha ethos.

Turning the Tide

As Alpha grew globally, it permeated many new Catholic contexts. Endorsements by Catholic dignitaries were always publicised loudly by *Alpha News*, including commendations from archbishops and cardinals in New Zealand, the United States, Canada, Japan, South Africa, France, Hong Kong, Poland, Singapore and Malaysia.[146] For example, André Vingt-Trois (Archbishop of Paris) praised Alpha in 2006 as 'a beautiful example' of ecumenism: 'People are always talking about the division between Christians . . . Now, for once, we are able to help show that the Bible and our Christian faith is the same.'[147] 'For those of us who are Catholic', announced an excited lay leader in Minneapolis, 'Alpha is the tool that is bringing into reality in our lifetime the church we have always dreamed of.'[148] In Spain, Alpha was first adopted in a Catholic context in 2005, after Monsignor Joaquin Garcia attended Alpha at a local Baptist church and decided to run it in his own parish.[149] It soon spread also to large Roman Catholic communities in Eastern Europe, India, South East Asia and Latin America. Garcia was a main speaker in April 2006 at the first Alpha conference in South America, held in Lima, Peru, with 350 delegates from 11 countries, mostly Roman Catholics.[150] As Alpha established itself on the continent there was a larger conference in Bogotá, Colombia, in October 2009, led by Nicky Gumbel, Sandy Millar and Marc de Leyritz, with delegates from Argentina, Colombia, Dominican Republic, Ecuador, Guatemala, Mexico, Nicaragua, Peru, Uruguay, Venezuela, and elsewhere. Catholic priests and nuns from across the continent spoke of how God was using Alpha in their nations, and the 24 Roman Catholic bishops and archbishops in attendance were all listed in *Alpha News* as a roll of honour.[151]

In Canada, one of the most eager Alpha adopters was Father James Mallon, a parish priest in Nova Scotia, who was passionate to see the Roman Catholic Church return to its fundamental missionary identity, called to evangelise and make disciples. From 2001, he placed Alpha at the centre of his parish evangelisation strategy and discovered that it was a very fruitful catalyst for renewal. His post-Alpha course was named 'Catholicism 201' because he viewed Alpha as 'Catholicism 101'.[152] Mallon laid out his broad vision in his bestselling *Divine Renovation: Bringing Your Parish from Maintenance to Mission* (2014), and *Divine Renovation: Beyond the Parish* (2020), while in *Unlocking Your Parish* (2019) he offered a practical analysis on how to embed Alpha in a Catholic context. 'Alpha is not a silver bullet', Mallon explained, but it was, in his experience, 'the best tool that I have found for jump-starting and sustaining parish renewal'. He believed there was no better way 'for reaching the unchurched and our own communities of faith with the life-changing power of the gospel'. Mallon celebrated: 'I have witnessed the power of God transforming the unlikeliest of people and bringing forth life in the most barren situations – on a regular basis. It's no lie to say that Alpha has changed my experience of the priesthood.'[153] By 2021 *Divine Renovation* had sold 103,000 copies, and the Divine Renovation Network encompassed 1,800 priests and 140 bishops, growing rapidly during the Covid-19 pandemic. Divine Renovation Ministry trained Roman Catholic leaders worldwide in parish renewal and by the end of 2021 had coached 432 priests, in 6 languages and 23 countries, from Mexico and Argentina to India and Malaysia. As part of this coaching, it offered an 'Alpha Boot Camp', to train priests in using Alpha as central to parish mission, with a global vision to see 35,000 Catholic parishes renewed and evangelising by 2028. In Britain, Divine Renovation also stimulated the resurgence of Alpha in a Catholic context – by 2021 it had connected with 662 Catholic parishes (23 per cent of the total) and 351 Catholic priests.[154] Divine Renovation's UK office was based at Alpha International's London headquarters, and Alpha organised and financed Divine Renovation's British conferences.

In the early years, Alpha had struggled to take root in a Roman Catholic context, but the tide turned. In a remarkable volte-face, even Cristina Odone, one of the most vociferous Alpha critics, changed her tune in a 2015 article for the *Catholic Herald* entitled, 'I was wrong about the Alpha course'. Twenty years after her first encounter with Alpha graduates, who she had found embarrassingly enthusiastic about their faith, she now welcomed Alpha as an 'essential ally' in the battle against aggressive secularism and praised the course for teaching Christians 'to stand up and speak out'.[155] Through years of patient advocacy, theological revision of the Alpha materials, and careful nurture of Catholic relationships, Alpha gradually persuaded its Catholic detractors. Having been born in English Protestantism, by the 2020s it was widely adopted by global Catholicism. Alpha's affection for Rome was permanent and mutual.

7

Transforming Society

ALPHA'S GLOBAL LAUNCH in spring 1993 was set against a back-drop of perceived cultural decline and moral degeneration. Britain was in the grip of a wave of 'moral panic', stoked by polit-icians and the media. The abduction and murder of two-year-old James Bulger in February 1993, just three weeks before the publica-tion of Nicky Gumbel's *Questions of Life*, led to widespread national grief and soul-searching. That autumn, Prime Minister John Major launched his ill-fated 'Back to Basics' campaign, a call for a return to conservative family values, widely ridiculed when numerous Tory MPs were exposed in sex scandals. But this popular trope of 'culture in crisis', beloved as much by the *Daily Telegraph* as the *News of the World*, was also picked up by the Christian churches. It was frequently heard from the HTB pulpit and was harnessed to market the Alpha materials. Addressing his congregation in March 1993, Sandy Millar asserted that Britain as a nation had 'turned our backs on God and over a thousand years of His grace – and in so doing have laid ourselves open increasingly to the merciless influence of evil'. The symptoms could be measured in socio-economic terms, such as rising crime and unemployment, but the underlying cause of the nation's ills, Millar insisted, was theological. The Christian church alone – and by impli-cation not the Tory government – possessed 'the key to the welfare of the nation'.[1]

Early editions of *Alpha News* maximised this theme to promote the need for Alpha. Millar and Gumbel lamented that over 90 per cent of the British population never darkened the doors of a church, even at Christmas or Easter. 'Following in the wake of the decline in Christian belief, there has been a decline in the moral climate. The fabric of our society has been unravelled as families break up.' As evidence they pointed to the rising number of divorces and children born to unmarried parents.[2] Another early Alpha advertisement offered hard statistics: every day in Britain at least 480 couples divorced, 170 babies were born to teenage mothers, and 470 babies were aborted. A new crime was committed every six seconds and a violent attack every two minutes. Although there were 30,000 Christian clergy in Britain, across all denominations, there were apparently over 80,000 registered fortune tellers and witches. 'How can the church change things for the better?' cried the promotional guide. 'One effective answer is Alpha.'[3]

This bleak cultural analysis pervaded Gumbel's paperbacks. In *Challenging Lifestyle*, he lamented, 'There is something very wrong with our society. We only have to open our newspapers to see a nation torn apart by strife' – violence, criminality, family breakdown, abortion. 'Traditional bases for morality are no longer accepted . . . There is a moral vacuum at the heart of our nation . . . Capitalism, with all its excesses, has been unable to restrain a society which is on the verge of moral bankruptcy.' This peril he traced to the national decline in Christian faith.[4] Similarly, in *The Heart of Revival*, Gumbel argued that modern Western culture at the end of the second millennium was undergoing an 'exilic experience', parallel to ancient Israel's Babylonian captivity. 'Our society has attempted to shut God out', he proclaimed, 'and in many ways has succeeded, with disastrous results.' Borrowing additional data from the government's 1996 *Social Trends* survey, Gumbel reported that every day in Britain 17 women were raped, 20 schoolgirls became pregnant, 90 children were taken into care, and 150 people were convicted of drugs offences. There were more prisoners in Britain per capita than any other European country, the pornography industry was worth £100 million annually, 65 per cent of videos depicted the occult, sex or violence, somebody called the Samaritans helpline every two minutes, and at least one homeless person died on the streets of London every week. As a trained barrister, Gumbel heaped evidence upon evidence to prove his claim that British culture was in 'exile' from God.[5] The antidote was 'revival', which meant far more than merely 'personal renewal'. As more and more individuals became Christians – perhaps through Alpha – the whole of society would soon feel the impact in demonstrable ways: 'Restitutions are made. Broken homes are reunited. Public moral standards improve. Integrity makes its way into government.'[6] Alpha therefore had the potential not only to change lives but to transform the very fabric of Western society, and reverse its rapid decline.

In this cultural analysis, the disintegration of family life loomed especially large. For example, Millar told a group of HTB leaders in 1994 that 'The greatest single threat to civilisation at the moment is the threat to the family.'[7] In *Challenging Lifestyle*, Gumbel lamented the prevalence of adultery, wrecked marriages and broken families, which were 'unravelling the very fabric of our society'. He warned that there were many forces at work 'eating away at the family'.[8] Likewise Nicky and Sila Lee's bestselling *The Marriage Book* (2000), published by Alpha International, opened with the startling words – in Gumbel's foreword – 'Marriage is under attack in our society.'[9] Nicky Lee used an identical phrase in a sermon to mark Valentine's Day in 2000: 'marriage is under attack'. As evidence, he pointed to the Labour government's scrapping of the Married Couple's Allowance, and to the refusal of Relate (formerly the National Marriage Guidance Council) to endorse marriage as 'the ideal basis for family life'. The 'single biggest crisis facing our society', Lee reiterated, was the breakdown of family relationships.[10] Again, Alpha was the proposed antidote, helping to restore marriages and strengthen families. *Alpha News* was filled with testimonies of Christian converts rescued from the destructive lifestyles most closely associated with HTB's cultural critique – alcoholism, violence, prison, prostitution, drug addiction, astrology, wicca, and much more. Alpha's advocates, observed Damian Thompson in *The Times*, 'attribute its success to the appeal of orthodox, biblically-based Christianity in a confused and fragmented society. Its critics, however, give warning of a new breed of fundamentalist zealots who feed on contemporary angst.'[11]

Morals and Moralism

The connection between spiritual and moral transformation was tightly drawn. Millar pictured the Christian community as 'a little island of purity in a sea of increasing secularism and unbelief'. 'The Christian faith is an ethical faith', he explained, 'and the ideal way to see the Christian faith is to see how we live.'[12] Preaching at HTB in January 1996, Millar criticised church leaders for being quick to decry the National Lottery, but slow to speak up about more important ethical questions:

> When did you last hear the church complaining about adultery? Or about divorce, which God hates? When did you last hear them speaking about fornication – heterosexual or homosexual? When did you last hear them speak about abortion, which is intrinsically as evil as anything has ever been in the history of mankind?

He urged that the church must be 'totally clear' on these subjects, on which God had spoken 'for our own good and our own health', because these sins 'damage us and damage other people and kill our relationship with God'.[13] A few months later, preaching from the prophet Amos, Millar reiterated: 'I have always felt, and I still feel, that it is the church's primary function to speak about ethical issues and to attempt to express what God feels about these things. We should not have to leave it to others.'[14] Elsewhere he criticised the Church of England's bishops for lecturing the government on unemployment while remaining silent on abortion – 'the wholesale murder of endless babies'.[15]

Millar himself led by example, refusing to shy away from complex or controversial moral questions. Sex was the hottest topic, especially for a congregation full of young adults. Preaching in 1992 on sexual purity, he lamented the 'steady drip-feed of poison' that was seeping into British culture through popular novels, films and television. Pornography, once the preserve of specialist suppliers in Soho, was now available on every newsagent's stand in Knightsbridge. Contemporary morals were being 'manipulated by commercial interests – fed by the Devil himself', and Millar warned of the sins of masturbation, fornication, homosexual sex, and the particular spiritual dangers of oral sex as a doorway to demonic oppression. This candid teaching was in such high demand at HTB that the cassette recording sold out multiple times.[16] Millar was frequently outspoken on these themes. He observed in 2004 that Christians were living in an increasingly pagan society, like the original apostles who had faced similar controversies over sex in the first century. A permissive 'new morality' had crept into the modern church disguised in 'pseudo theological babble', he declared, but it was simply the 'old immorality' reborn.[17]

One of the chief reasons that HTB so strongly prioritised personal holiness was a theological conviction that the Holy Spirit's blessing rested upon Christians who pursued God whole-heartedly. If they merely went with the flow of contemporary culture, and became entangled in sin, the Spirit's blessing would be removed. The success of Alpha was therefore understood to be dependent, in God's providence, on the willingness of HTB's clergy and congregation to seek sanctification. This was seen as one of the keys to revival. As Gumbel taught in *The Heart of Revival*, 'revival is always related to holiness'.[18] Repentance was a prerequisite to enjoying God's presence fully. He observed how confession and renunciation of sin, often with weeping, was widespread in revivals down the centuries from Northampton, Massachusetts, under Jonathan Edwards in the 1730s, to the recent 'visitation from the Holy Spirit' among students at Wheaton College, Illinois, in the 1990s.[19] 'Sin is a barrier to God's blessing', Gumbel wrote elsewhere, 'both in our individual lives and in the church.'[20] Likewise Millar explained: 'The sanctification of God's people is the necessary preparation for God to move.'[21]

Nevertheless, HTB drew a vital distinction – often lost in the public messaging – between speaking to Christians and speaking to the wider world. Addressing the Church of England specifically, Millar warned that it was impossible to 'hitch-hike into heaven as an immoral, unethical, unholy, ungodly, body'. Yet it was a 'heresy', he asserted, to expect non-Christians to behave like Christians. What the many millions of people outside the church most needed to hear was not moral criticism but the grace and love of Jesus.[22] Christians had a terrible reputation, Millar admitted, for being 'moralistic and judgmental and po-faced and hypocritical and always pointing our finger at everybody else'. They should be famous instead for proclaiming God's love and inviting everybody to come to Jesus and find forgiveness. He exhorted the HTB congregation to be

'Bible-believing, faith-talking, filled with the Spirit, ethically-aware, morally-aware, socially-aware Christians', ready to fulfil God's commission 'to pray, to work, to encourage, to smile, to speak where we can, to embrace, and by love, to win the world, starting with London'.[23]

These carefully nuanced distinctions between morals and moralism, and between grace and obligation, were often too subtle as a public message and easily misinterpreted. One radical leftist clergyman, Donald Reeves (rector of St James's, Piccadilly) lamented the rapid growth in the 1990s of 'happy-clappy' evangelical parishes for undermining the national Church of England and promoting 'Mickey Mouse religion – cheap, graceless and addictive'. In a fierce tirade, he assailed HTB for being un-Anglican:

> They are moralistic, sex-obsessed and unkind – more like a cult than a church. I've no objection to people holding those beliefs. But they are hijacking the Church of England, our buildings and our vicarages. If people want to listen to Sandy Millar, they can do so in a tent for all I care – but not in an Anglican church.[24]

This accusation was deeply ironic, given that Reeves and his liberal congregation were themselves famous for sitting loose to traditional Anglican dogma.[25] But it highlighted a major dilemma facing Alpha. How could abundant grace for non-Christians and radical holiness for Christians be taught at the same time without confusing and complicating the message? It was easy for hostile critics (both secular and Christian) to deride HTB's teaching for being unbalanced in one direction or another, especially if they only listened to one sermon or read one newspaper report. Some of the Alpha resources, especially *Searching Issues* and *Challenging Lifestyle*, laid out the ethical and moral implications of Christianity. But since Alpha itself was intended for those outside the church, grace and love was the keynote.

Homosexuality

Of all social and moral questions, the most contested was homosexuality. Some Christian commentators saw the multiplication of gay relationships as emblematic of cultural crisis and decline. During Sandy Millar's two decades as vicar of HTB between 1985 and 2005 the question was addressed publicly from the pulpit, but Nicky Gumbel's strategy as vicar from 2005, in a very different and fast-moving moral climate, was a studied silence. This regime change at the start of the new millennium was therefore highly significant for Alpha's cultural adaptation.

Initially, HTB took a conservative line. For example, in November 1987 the Church of England's General Synod debated a motion brought by Essex clergyman Tony Higton that affirmed that sex belonged only within heterosexual marriage, that 'fornication, adultery and homosexual acts' were sinful in all circumstances, and that Christians should demonstrate 'Christ-like compassion' for those who fell into sexual sin while also calling upon them to repent.[26] HTB's church council felt so strongly on the matter that they wrote to all the London representatives on General Synod urging them to vote for the motion, and also sent a gift of £500 to Higton to encourage him in his work.[27] Millar's own views were published occasionally in HTB's monthly newspaper. In 1992, for example, in his catalogue of sexual sins he included homosexual relationships as 'sterile, uncreative and not of God'.[28] Three years later, during a campaign by Outrage to force the Church of England to accept gay clergy – using what were widely viewed as intimidatory tactics by 'outing' ten allegedly gay bishops – Millar again addressed the subject directly. Responding to Outrage, the Bishop of Southwark announced in March 1995 that he would consider ordaining gay clergy, provided they were in a 'stable relationship', to which Millar replied:

> Church leaders are called to lead and any attempt to buy off any party with specious sub-biblical or heretical views can only lead in the long run to the deep discouragement and ultimate disaffection of the loyal flock who are trying to lead a biblically Christian life ... Of course

practising homosexuals should not be ordained. Of course those in Christian leadership who are involved in immoral relationships (hetero *or* homo) should resign or be removed . . . This is nothing to do with homophobia – it is to do with a proper phobia of sin. A so-called 'stable relationship' that is immoral is after all only one that has gone on for longer than any other one.

Although obviously controversial, Millar insisted that the church 'must teach clearly and unambiguously' about homosexuality.[29]

By 2003 this question was dividing Christian denominations across the globe. Within the Anglican Communion the fractures were deepening. In the diocese of Oxford, gay clergyman Jeffrey John was announced as the new Bishop of Reading, to rejoicing or consternation on different sides of the theological divide. In the diocese of New Westminster, Canada, a liturgy for blessing same-sex relationships was formally authorised. In the diocese of New Hampshire, in the United States, gay clergyman Gene Robinson was elected as the new bishop. In his analysis of these events, Stephen Bates described the Anglican Communion as 'a church at war'.[30] In autumn 2003, in an address to HTB leaders on the pursuit of holiness, Millar criticised those in the wider Church who had not only given up battling against sexual sin but were now redefining it as not sinful after all.[31] Then, on the very morning of Robinson's consecration in Durham, New Hampshire, Millar preached on the topic, 3,000 miles away in Kensington. He reiterated, as many times before, that all sexual activity outside marriage, whether heterosexual or homosexual, was inconsistent with the Christian call to holiness. But he described Robinson's consecration as 'a wake-up call on an alarm clock without a snooze button'. It was not a fight against 'flesh and blood', he declared, but against 'a new demonic ideology that is attacking the very fabric of the church', often cloaked in theological language. 'Somebody said to me the other day that the Church should be inclusive, and draw everybody in. Of course! Jesus drew all people to himself, *but he commanded them to repent*. He didn't tell them to stay as they were.' Millar urged his hearers to be willing, like the martyred saints of old, to stand for God in a hostile world and to speak with courage from the Holy Spirit. He especially commended African

Anglicans for their vocal witness in the Anglican Communion, and pointed to the Ugandan martyrs of 1886 who were killed for refusing the homosexual advances of their king.[32] Millar's sermon was not intended only for his congregation, but was widely disseminated through *UK Focus*, published in association with *Alpha News*. Two months later, in January 2004, Millar was in Kampala to preach at the enthronement of Henry Orombi (a long-time friend of HTB) as the new Archbishop of Uganda.[33] When Millar retired from HTB the following year, he was consecrated by Orombi in Uganda (with the consent of the Archbishop of Canterbury and the Bishop of London) as a missionary bishop for England.[34]

Alpha was created within this HTB environment and naturally reflected a similar viewpoint. Although homosexuality was never mentioned in Alpha itself, Gumbel's *Searching Issues* included a chapter on 'What is the Christian attitude to homosexuality?' It was published in 1994 under the assumption that it was possible to describe '*the* Christian attitude', but within a decade any broad consensus among the churches had disappeared, in the Anglo-American world at least. The first edition argued concisely that homosexual practice was a sin that needed to be repented, and that homosexual orientation could be healed by 'the supernatural power of the Spirit' or by psychiatric therapies. Gumbel, like Millar, proclaimed that the church must speak out against homosexual practice: 'It is wrong to promote a homosexual lifestyle in schools. It is wrong to ordain unrepentant practising homosexuals into Christian leadership.'[35] The 2001 edition of *Searching Issues* carried substantially the same argument, though with some softening of tone. Gumbel was now at pains to make clear that 'We should reject and resist all forms of irrational prejudice', and that sins like greed and dishonesty were equally condemned by the Apostle Paul.[36] References to the destruction of Sodom and the Old Testament condemnation of homosexual practice as 'detestable' were deleted, as was Gumbel's criticism of 'the defiant attitude of some of the leaders of the gay movement today'. Leanne Payne's controversial book, *The Healing of the Homosexual* (1984), was likewise removed from Gumbel's recommended reading list, though his basic teaching did not change.[37] For enquirers who wanted to understand HTB's position on homosexuality, Millar recommended Gumbel's chapter where the matter was set out 'sensitively and clearly'.[38]

However, *Searching Issues* generated considerable negative publicity for Alpha, more than any other topic. In 2000, All Saints' Episcopal Church in Beverly Hills, California, launched 'Gay Alpha', seeking to use the Alpha materials to reach the gay community. One of the organisers described it as a safe place 'to integrate your spirituality with your sexuality', though *Searching Issues* was deliberately kept off the bookstall.[39] But watching on from the United Kingdom, the *Gay Times* was unimpressed:

> Gay Alpha, unless it abandons the evangelical fervour of the British original, will require its participants to refrain from having sex. And in that case, is it any different really to the ex-gay movement? If it arrives in this country, give it a wide berth. It has nothing to offer but unhappiness.[40]

Two years later, in February 2002, students at the University of York tried to prevent Alpha taking place on campus because of the teaching in *Searching Issues*. The president of the Student Union, Ffion Evans, denounced Alpha as 'homophobic' and 'threatening', and advocated a 'No Platform' policy on the grounds that 'Freedom of speech should not apply on campus.'[41] The proposed ban was overwhelmingly defeated by the wider student body, though the case was taken up publicly by the Gay and Lesbian Humanist Association (GALHA) and by a campaign group called Gay Men Against Alpha (GMAA).[42] Popstar Will Young came out as gay in March 2002, soon after releasing his debut single, but he was strongly criticised when he began attending Alpha a few months later. GALHA warned that Young's example was damaging to young people struggling with their sexuality, and that the gay community would be justified in boycotting his records and concerts because of his Alpha links.[43]

Gumbel was often made to squirm uncomfortably in media interviews, and his position was lampooned by journalists like Jon Ronson.[44] In a scathing assessment in *The Times*, Cristina Odone lambasted Alpha as 'a world full of no-nos: no sex before marriage, no feminism, no abortion and no gay sex'. She claimed that Alpha had 'made homophobia respectable' at the heart of the Church of England, and that it delighted in 'the metaphorical stoning of the wicked, while overlooking the compassionate Christ of the Gospels'. 'The Alpha course has clout', she concluded; 'A shame it uses it to hound rather than heal, and to exclude rather than embrace.'[45] These hostile journalistic attacks were deeply damaging to the Alpha brand.

By the time Gumbel succeeded Millar as vicar of HTB in 2005, he had grown more circumspect. On contentious questions, he refused to be pinned down. As one journalist observed, he had grown 'adept at deflective answers'.[46] A 2008 profile by Deborah Orr for *The Independent* noted how Gumbel 'studiously avoids controversy'. He declined, for example, to appear on *Question Time* 'because they'll ask me questions, and if I say certain things I'll alienate half the churches running Alpha quite unnecessarily . . . It does no good at all for me to express my views on certain things, and potentially does a lot of harm.'[47] Top of the list of those euphemistic 'certain things' was sexuality.

The new 2010 edition of *Questions of Life* continued – in its closing chapter, the rousing finale of Alpha – to emphasise the need for Christians to remain distinctive and not be conformed to the world's view of sex. 'Rather than indulging in sexual immorality', Gumbel declared, 'we should be demonstrating the blessing of keeping God's standards.'[48] Likewise, the new 2010 edition of *The Jesus Lifestyle* urged readers to have 'courage to swim against the tide' in their attitudes to sex, and to live in a 'radically different' way to the rest of society. Gumbel called them to repent of any sexual relationship outside marriage.[49] However, for the new 2013 edition of *Searching Issues*, the chapters on homosexuality and sex before marriage were both deleted. Alpha withdrew previous editions of the book from sale from all its worldwide distributors in its multiple translations, because the subject had become toxic and was injuring the Alpha brand and its ecumenical appeal. HTB and Alpha's attitude to the rights and wrongs of homosexuality was now a deliberate silence. Gumbel was often interrogated on the question, but worked hard to change the focus of debate. He argued that Alpha guests were not much interested in the furore over sexuality that obsessed the media and internal church divisions. Instead they were concerned about issues like 'poverty and homelessness, drug addiction, finding meaning in their lives, dealing with guilt, building meaningful relationships'.[50] Even Millar in his retirement, when pushed by the media on the question of homosexuality, was more reticent. He replied:

> The real burning issue for the C of E is mission. That is what matters, and it is desperate the way we seem to be willing to talk about anything else. The people out there aren't really interested in our internal little discussions. They just go round in ever-decreasing circles. A centre for bickering is not very attractive.[51]

Abortion

Another particularly sensitive moral and pastoral question was abortion, which Nicky Gumbel decried in *The Heart of Revival* as 'the killing of innocent babies'.[52] Its prevalence in modern Britain was frequently referenced in his cultural analysis. In 1994 – at the same period as Alpha was launched – HTB began the Post-Abortion Course, 'not as a political platform, but simply to serve men and women who have been through abortion'.[53] Membership was kept highly confidential, and the venue and times of the meetings were never advertised. Unlike Alpha, which was marketed everywhere, the Post-Abortion Course remained deliberately under the radar. Yet both courses formed part of HTB's coordinated response to the perceived cultural crisis.

The Post-Abortion Course was initiated by HTB member Jonathan Jeffes (a former helicopter pilot) whose girlfriend had had an abortion in the early 1980s with his encouragement. He had made a conscious effort to forget about it, but it deeply troubled his conscience. In 1985 at an exhibition of seventeenth-century Italian artwork at the Louvre in Paris, he was viewing a painting of Jesus standing outside the empty tomb when suddenly, according to Jeffes' testimony, it seemed that Jesus himself appeared – a 'very frightening' experience because Jesus looked at him with 'eyes of fire' and showed him that he was 'going to hell'. As he contemplated hell, Jeffes' conviction was, 'You have the blood of your child on your hands.' At that moment, standing in the Louvre gallery, he sneezed and a single large drop of blood came out of his nose onto the handkerchief in his hand. Seven years later, in 1992, Jeffes was invited to Alpha at HTB and became a Christian. At the Alpha weekend he committed his life to Jesus, and was filled by the Holy Spirit 'so much so that I felt I was pumped up like a balloon'. He felt God speak clearly to him that his guilt concerning abortion was now finished and forgiven.[54] One of his first responses was to launch the Post-Abortion Course, which later expanded from its HTB roots to be offered by other churches and pregnancy advice centres across Britain.[55] Jeffes' testimony was promoted by *UK Focus*, the *Alpha News* supplement.

Abortion was also addressed elsewhere in the Alpha publicity. For example, it was a major theme in the Alpha testimony of Marijke Tapson, a businesswoman in south-west London. She fell pregnant in 1997, aged 42, with her third child and planned a termination. However, her husband had become a Christian the previous year through Alpha at HTB and tried to dissuade her. Tapson herself joined Alpha at St Stephen's, Twickenham, and during the Holy Spirit weekend at Rye in East Sussex, as she lay in the bath contemplating her life and the sacrifices of having a baby, she believed she heard God say more than once, 'Trust me'. The following day she committed her life to Christ and decided against abortion, provided the baby was healthy. Yet as Tapson lay in hospital preparing for an amniocentesis test for Downs Syndrome, again she suddenly heard the words, 'Trust me', very insistently, so she walked away from the test at the last moment. Her healthy son was born a few months later.[56] These narratives helped to build Alpha's public messaging; that it was not only enabling individuals to make better life choices but was also thereby acting as a bulwark against Britain's social and moral decline.

Saving Marriages

Sandy Millar celebrated that all over the world, through Alpha, God was 'bringing people to a faith that is not just living but throbbing with life'. As evidence, he pointed to 'lives changed, marriages saved, churches grown and people renewed'.[57] This emphasis on 'marriages saved' was another major Alpha motif. If the spiralling divorce rate was a symptom of cultural malady, then Alpha was promoted as the antidote. *Alpha News* was filled with numerous testimonies of marriages restored and broken families mended.

HTB's marriage and family life ministries were overseen by Nicky and Sila Lee. They pioneered the Marriage Course, covering practical topics such as resolving conflict, communication, good sex, forgiveness, and the in-laws, published in 2000 as *The Marriage Book*. It became another Alpha International bestseller and borrowed much of the standard Alpha methodology and marketing. There was branded merchandise including guest manuals, leaders' guides, audio cassettes and videos. Like Alpha, the Marriage Course took place over food – not at a banqueting table, but at a candle-lit dinner for two, designed to encourage intimate conversation.[58] By 2003 there were 280 Marriage Courses running in 17 countries, and a parallel Marriage Preparation Couse was launched for engaged couples.[59] Numbers grew rapidly. By 2008, there were over 3,000 Marriage Courses in 70 countries, and *The Marriage Book* had sold nearly 150,000 copies.[60] Building on this success, Alpha International published *The Parenting Book* (2009), also by Nicky and Sila Lee, with a parallel Parenting Course and Parenting Teenagers Course marketed on DVD from 2011.[61] By the end of 2020, cumulative global sales stood at 338,700 for *The Marriage Book* in 31 languages, and 54,800 for *The Parenting Book* in 12 languages.[62]

There was a symbiotic relationship between Alpha and the Marriage Course, often run in tandem, and guests moved from one course into the other. *Alpha News* again published many examples. For instance, in 2002 Steve Rice, chief financial officer for a London hedge fund, and his wife Rachael, were invited by Christian friends in Bedford to join the Marriage Course. They enjoyed it but were irritated by the Christian content, especially the call to put God at the centre of their marriage, so signed up for Alpha at Christ Church, Bedford, to find out more. Both became Christians on the Alpha day away, and Steve celebrated that 'Jesus has completely turned my life upside down'.[63] It was the reverse process for fitness instructors Kim Santino and his girlfriend Emma. While working in the Canary Islands, they began in 2002 to attend South Tenerife Christian

Fellowship (STCF) in Los Cristianos, where Emma rediscovered the Christian faith of her youth. Kim attended Alpha and decided 'to ask God into my life', after watching the Gumbel videos 'sitting on the edge of my seat all the time, taking in every word like a sponge absorbing water'. The pastor of STCF gave them *The Marriage Book*, which they read together on the beach. On returning to England, they attended the Marriage Course in 2004 at New Life Christian Centre (Assemblies of God) in Derby, and were married three months later.[64]

As with other *Alpha News* conversion testimonies, stories of 'marriages saved' were normally published in the first fresh flush of renewed marital bliss. Alpha did not research the extent to which the couples they profiled in their publicity were still happily married five or ten years afterwards. Christian couples, even those 'saved' by Alpha, were not immune from breaking up. In 2000, the same year that HTB launched the Marriage Course, they rolled out another new course, Recovering from Divorce and Separation, with videos and guest manuals. It grew out of HTB's 'divorce recovery' seminars, led by congregation member Christopher Compston, a barrister and circuit judge, himself a remarried divorcee, author of *Recovering from Divorce: A Practical Guide* (1993) and *Breaking Up without Cracking Up* (1998).[65] The programme – which later evolved into the Restored Lives course – was designed to help people through the trauma of relationship breakdown, and was marketed by *Alpha News* among the growing suite of 'Alpha resources'.[66] Although Gumbel mourned over broken marriages and continued to view divorce as a symptom of Britain's departure from its Christian heritage, his new 2010 edition of *The Jesus Lifestyle* was alert to the fact that divorce was endemic not only in wider society, but now also within the Christian community itself. 'To those who are badly hurt by divorce', he proclaimed, 'the church is a hospital. To those who acknowledge that they were responsible for such pain, the church is a community of forgiven sinners. Divorce is not an unforgivable sin.'[67] Alpha wanted to build a society where strong marriages and happy families were fundamental building blocks, but had to temper its ambitions to the pastoral realities of modern life.

Privatised Religion and Social Justice

Although Alpha was marketed in the 1990s by harnessing widespread concerns over cultural crisis and moral decline in Western society, the early editions contained surprisingly little positive teaching about social transformation, or indeed about social involvement of any sort. The topic was addressed only very briefly, towards the end of the course, in the session on evangelism, which exhorted new converts to live 'a radically different lifestyle' from the rest of the world so that they would be effective witnesses as 'salt and light'. Building on these metaphors, Gumbel explained that it was the vocation of Christians 'to stop society going bad', by speaking up about 'moral standards', creating better social structures, working for justice and freedom, abolishing discrimination, caring for the 'casualties of our society', and contributing to local or national politics. As exemplars, he pointed to the ministry among the poor and marginalised by Mother Teresa in Kolkata and Jackie Pullinger in Hong Kong.[68] But this was all compressed into one short paragraph in *Questions of Life*, hardly a major theme.

Critics of Alpha homed in on this weakness. Some mocked the social privilege of the Kensington set who dominated HTB. Their Holy Spirit weekend in the 1990s was not in a hotel or luxury resort, but usually at a cheap Pontins holiday camp at Chichester, on the Sussex coast, where guests shared rooms. This itself seemed a comic irony, given the wealth of the congregation. 'HTB is the only place', quipped Dominic Kennedy in *The Times*, 'where people pay for a Pontins weekend with a Coutts chequebook kept in the pocket of a Harrods overcoat.'[69] The *Ship of Fools* website published a spoof in 1998, announcing that Gumbel and Millar had launched Beta, a 'below stairs' version of Alpha to reach 'our friends in less prosperous areas'. It had its own working–class acronym:

B – Bring a mate
E – Eastenders
T – TV dinners
A – Ask anything

The spoof had Millar offering to cook 'pie and mash' instead of pasta, if it would 'bring more into the kingdom', and Gumbel declaring at a greyhound track in Haringey: 'They're a super bunch of chaps, the working class. All those Lees and Deans have got something very special to offer to the church.'[70] This parody was intended in good humour, but others were less kind. One cynical college chaplain who tried running Alpha for his students caustically suggested it was designed for those who believed 'Saint Gumbel of Wealthydom is the ultimate Guru to lead you to world peace, prosperity and happiness.'[71] *The Tablet* jibed that they were more likely to meet Alpha converts at 'black-tie balls and polo matches' than as volunteers combatting global poverty and climate change.[72]

Another outspoken cleric, Kenneth Wakefield (vicar of Launceston, Cornwall), likened Alpha to a fizzy glass of Coca-Cola: 'But once the fizz has gone, what have you got left? You can't live on bubble and froth all the time . . . It's Noddy theology. It feeds privatised religion. It's all about "me and my God".'[73] A Methodist superintendent likewise asserted that whereas Jesus Christ emphasised community, Alpha bred individualism.[74] Others castigated the huge sums of money spent every year on Alpha marketing. A clergywoman at St James's, Piccadilly, for example, said that if her congregation had a spare £1 million, they would use it to set up day centres or campaign against Third World debt.[75] Stephanie Merritt, a secular humanist writing in *The Observer*, complained that the Alpha advertising budget would be better spent feeding the poor in Niger than in encouraging 'predominantly middle-class people to sit around talking about whether or not they feel fulfilled'.[76]

Some critics offered a more sustained academic assessment. Philip Kingston, a Roman Catholic and former lecturer in social work at the University of Bristol, was puzzled at the apparent dichotomy in the 1990s between charismatic renewal and social activism. Although he acknowledged that care for the poor and marginalised did make a brief appearance in Alpha, it was not properly integrated as a Christian essential. Alpha focused on personal and individual, not structural, sins. Kingston concluded that Gumbel showed an excellent understanding of human psychology, but not of sociology, ecology, economics or politics.[77] Likewise Martyn Percy argued that Alpha mirrored too much the upper-middle-class background of its authors. For example, Alpha emphasised the Holy Spirit's personal, therapeutic work in the life of the individual Christian, but ignored the Spirit's wider work in creation, justice, peace and reconciliation. Therefore, Percy lamented, Alpha provided 'no real social mandate' and 'no prophetic witness'.[78]

Alpha's association in the public imagination with the wealth and privilege of Kensington's social elite was a difficult narrative to break. Early Alpha publicity worked hard to demonstrate its adaptability in other social contexts, where the idea of a 'supper party' or a 'weekend away' was entirely foreign. For example, *Renewal* magazine profiled Alpha's success in working-class communities such as the parish of West Bowling in Bradford, a non-book culture with high unemployment and low literacy levels. The Bradford church found some of Gumbel's teaching too intellectual and the Alpha manual too imposing, but they persevered and adapted the resources for their own context.[79] The Anglo-Catholic parish of St Francis, Mackworth, a housing estate on the outskirts of Derby, was another early adopter of Alpha, and first ran the course as a follow-up to evangelist J.John's city-wide mission to Derby in 1994. 'No – we are not a happy-clappy middle-class suburban evangelical parish!' reported the vicar, Father Bryan Hackney.[80] He celebrated that Alpha was drawing people back to Mass, and praised it as a 'very effective tool for communicating the basics of orthodox Catholic faith in an ordinary non-eclectic parish'.[81] *Alpha News* promoted 'Inner City Alpha', with reports of the course's fruitfulness in Middlesborough, Hull, Toxteth, Canvey Island and Tower Hamlets.[82] Even at HTB itself, contrary to the stereotype, Alpha guests came from surprisingly diverse social backgrounds. One Roman Catholic noted that his Alpha small group at HTB included a lorry driver, a primary school teacher, an alcoholic living in a hostel, and a man who had spent much of his life sleeping on the streets – not the typical clientele of polo matches.[83]

Gumbel also set about revising his Alpha paperbacks in response to the critics, increasingly alert to the Christian gospel's social imperatives. For example, the original edition of *Questions of Life* expounded the phrase 'Your kingdom come' from the Lord's Prayer (Matthew 6:10), as meaning the growth of God's kingdom through individual conversions to Christ. Gumbel gave the examples of the fourth-century African saint Monica praying for the conversion of her son Augustine of Hippo, and the nineteenth-century American evangelist D. L. Moody praying for the conversion of 100 people.[84] But the second edition offered a more holistic interpretation:

> We are praying not simply for God's rule and reign in individuals' lives but ultimately for the transformation of society. We are praying for God's peace, justice and compassion. We are praying for those often marginalised by society but for whom God cares especially, such as widows, orphans, the lonely and prisoners.[85]

This emphasis was echoed in *Challenging Lifestyle*, where Gumbel explained 'Your kingdom come' as a prayer for the nation to be transformed in the areas of politics, economics, social justice, crime and education.[86] He urged Christians to take action to combat poverty, the spread of AIDS, marriage breakdown and child abuse.[87] He reiterated that they must not 'withdraw from the world into a Christian sub-culture', but must get involved in society with a global mandate to tackle chronic food shortages, the violation of human rights, and the widespread oppression of the poor. Building on the teaching of John Stott's *Issues Facing Christians Today* (1984), Gumbel also argued that environmental destruction was perhaps the greatest threat to the human race and that Christians had a responsibility to be 'ecological stewards'.[88] *Telling Others* likewise affirmed Alpha's conviction that 'evangelism is fundamentally linked to social responsibility'.[89]

These themes were addressed most fully in *The Heart of Revival*, where Gumbel warned against the dangers of 'privatised religion'. He called for Christian involvement in social structures to remove the scourge of injustice, inhumanity and inequality, applauding campaigners like William Wilberforce, Mother Teresa, Martin Luther King, Nelson Mandela and Desmond Tutu, and humanitarian organisations like World Vision, Habitat for Humanity, Operation Smile, and the hospice movement.[90] Drawing lessons from church history, Gumbel praised John Wesley as not only a preacher but also 'a prophet of social righteousness'. The eighteenth-century Evangelical Revival,

Gumbel argued, had given Britain a 'social conscience', leading to the abolition of slavery, legislation to protect women and children from dangerous working conditions, better care for prisoners and the mentally ill, and improved housing for the poor. Likewise, he suggested that the Welsh Revival of 1904–5 had led to a reduction in drunkenness and criminality. 'True and lasting revival changes not only human hearts', Gumbel concluded, 'but also communities and institutions. Love for God and love for neighbour go hand in hand.' Therefore, Christians were called to usher in revival not only by proclaiming the gospel message but also by 'attacking the causes of human need by social action, and the direct relief of human need by social service'.[91]

The new 2010 edition of *Questions of Life* showed another leap forward in the maturing of Gumbel's social theology. 'We experience the Holy Spirit not just so that we have a warm feeling in our hearts', he declared, 'but so that we go out and make a difference to our world.'[92] As a model of Spirit-empowered leadership, he deleted his original illustration of his Bash-camp mentor, E. J. H. Nash, who ran Bible-teaching camps for public-school boys, and replaced him instead with the civil rights activist Martin Luther King.[93] In the chapter on evangelism, earlier editions focused exclusively on proclaiming the gospel with words, but now Gumbel urged Christians also to 'fight for social justice', to campaign for the abolition of 'exploitation, inequality and inhumanity', and to join practical projects to relieve 'hunger, homelessness, and poverty'.[94] In the chapter on the church, earlier editions encouraged new believers to develop their spiritual gifts within midweek small groups and pastorates, especially by giving talks, leading worship, praying for the sick, and learning to prophesy and pray out loud. But these could be pietistic and inward-looking activities, so Gumbel added a new emphasis, calling small groups also to go out and serve their communities, by visiting the sick and elderly, painting the house of a person in need, or volunteering at a homeless shelter or youth group.[95] Compared with the early 1990s, by the 2010s Alpha's teaching on social and cultural transformation had matured substantially and itself been radically transformed, now a fully integrated priority. The language of 'culture in crisis' had given way to friendly and practical engagement. Alpha's early alarmist criticism of the trajectory of Western society was replaced by collaborative community spirit.

Fighting Poverty and Exploitation

Alpha's emphasis on social transformation, and care for the poor and marginalised, was evidenced in practice by some of HTB's wider ministries. Sandy Millar's original call to ordination in the mid-1970s was stimulated by his weekly outreach with the London City Mission among the homeless and urban poor. This became a congregational priority. In 1986, soon after his appointment as vicar, HTB joined forces with YWAM to launch the Earl's Court Project. Although adjacent to the plush homes of Kensington and Chelsea, the bustling district of Earl's Court had high levels of social deprivation and drug addiction. The Project aimed to communicate the Christian faith by combining evangelism on the streets, and in local pubs and bars, with practical help for those in need. It offered medical and legal advice, accommodation referrals, connection to drug rehabilitation centres, care for those dying from AIDS (including basic nursing support), and late-night outreach to prostitutes and transvestites.[96] Other activities included a women's drop-in centre, a coffee bar, meals for the homeless, counselling, and a 12-step recovery programme for addicts.[97] In 1992 the Project opened a safe house in Battersea for those who wanted to 'break free' from prostitution and addiction.[98]

From the Earl's Court Project grew an outreach to the World's End Estate, the less attractive corner of Chelsea, dominated by seven tower blocks built in the 1970s upon the old Victorian slums. It was home to between 2,500 and 3,000 people, and around 50 languages, including large numbers of Spanish, Portuguese, Moroccans, Tunisians, Egyptians, Iranians and Iraqis. HTB planted a church on the estate in 1997, in a disused photography studio at the foot of one of the tower blocks, ministering to the marginalised – though, as its pastor joked, 'World's End Community Church' sounded like a millenarian cult preparing for Armageddon![99] Another local initiative was Grandma's, founded in 1991 by HTB member Amanda Williams, who had become a Christian through Alpha three years earlier. The charity supported families and children affected by HIV and AIDS, and most of its volunteers were from the HTB network.[100]

Another compassionate ministry closely connected with HTB was the Besom Foundation, established in 1987 by London banker James Odgers, who had recently become a Christian and was deeply impressed by visiting Pullinger's ministry among heroin addicts and triad gangs in Hong Kong.[101] The Besom connected donors and volunteers with people and places in need. It helped to find the finance, for example, to plant trees in Botswana, to lay a new water supply for a mountain village in Albania, to purchase a jeep for a drugs rehabilitation centre in Russia, and to provide medical equipment and bunkbeds for an orphanage in Colombia. Closer to home, the Besom encouraged London churches to serve their local communities in practical ways through volunteer projects such as painting, gardening, cooking and cleaning. It also acted as a clearing house for distributing second-hand clothes and furniture to those in need, such as women fleeing domestic violence.[102] In 2004 Odgers launched *Simplicity, Love and Justice*, a practical ten-week course covering topics such as consumerism, community and care for creation. As other churches caught the vision, a flourishing Besom network multiplied across Britain, which by 2020 numbered over 20 local hubs.

These social ministries were strongly promoted by *Alpha News*, which also carried testimonies of Christians driven to compassionate outreach after their conversions through HTB or Alpha. For example, in November 1987 Sarah Jarman, a 27-year-old BBC television producer, was invited to HTB by her cousin. She went reluctantly and sat in the gallery, ready to make a quick escape. But as the band led the congregation in a new Graham Kendrick song, 'Such Love', Jarman experienced instantaneous conversion:

> Suddenly it was as though my whole body became flooded with a warm heat, a heat that seemed to wash through me from my head to my feet over and over again. And I knew I had been touched by God. I knew instantly that Jesus was real. I knew that this was what I had been searching for all these years . . . I sat down and wept and wept. They weren't tears of sadness, they were tears of relief, of joy, of repentance.

When Gumbel preached on the forgiveness of sins and union with God through the death of Jesus Christ, Jarman 'knew it was the truth. It was as though his every word cut through into my heart.' She attended Alpha, and in 1990 gave up her television career to work among street children in the *favelas* of Brazil, where she founded *Ministerio Programa Crianca Feliz* (Happy Child Mission).[103]

Louise Strajnic was brought up in a Christian family, but drifted away from church as a teenager for a hedonistic lifestyle. Her father gave her a copy of Gumbel's *Questions of Life* and encouraged her towards HTB, where she attended Alpha in 1999 and began to reconnect with her childhood faith. After three weeks of the course she concluded, 'That's it, I'm giving my life to God', and prayed the *Why Jesus?* prayer of repentance and faith. 'I fell in love with Jesus completely', she testified. Strajnic felt called by God to India in 2003, where she helped to establish a refuge in Delhi for young women, especially those caught in the sex trade.[104] Shona Stewart began work as a prostitute in Vancouver in 1982, aged 22, and did not escape for 16 years. She was pimped and trafficked across various cities in western Canada and the United States, forced to work on the streets, in massage parlours, and for escort agencies, facing violence and abuse. Like many in the sex industry, she was an alcoholic and developed a cocaine habit. In 1999 Stewart attended Alpha in Victoria, British Columbia, and testified that during the Alpha weekend, 'The Spirit of the Lord came upon me.' She prayed a prayer of repentance and her life moved in a new direction. In 2011 she founded Setting The Captives Free, a ministry to women facing sexual exploitation.[105]

Alpha News drew special attention to these narratives of social endeavour. It also actively promoted debt-counselling agency Christians Against Poverty (CAP), founded in 1996. Many churches ran Alpha and CAP side by side, combining evangelistic proclamation with practical assistance. For example, when Peter and Nicole Wright in Fleetwood, Lancashire, defaulted on their mortgage payments in 2006, their house was due to be repossessed and their family evicted. They saw an advertisement in the local newspaper for CAP, being run by Emmanuel Church around the corner, who helped them slowly to manage their debt crisis. The family began to attend church, then

Alpha, and became Christians.[106] Alpha International also joined forces in 2004 with Soul Survivor youth ministry for 'Soul in the City', when 20,000 young people congregated in London for a two-week summer mission, again seeking to demonstrate God's love through evangelism and practical service.[107]

Globally, Alpha International put its weight in 2005 firmly behind Make Poverty History, a coalition of charities and campaign groups calling for trade justice and the cancellation of unpayable debts owed by the poorest nations.[108] Nicky Gumbel declared that extreme poverty was 'arguably the greatest moral and ethical issue of our day'. He set this urgent call for action within a theological framework, arguing that 'One of the first marks of the experience of the Spirit is a desire to make a difference to the poor.'[109] Drawing lessons from the example of William Wilberforce, to mark the bicentenary of the abolition of the slave trade in 2007, Gumbel exhorted Christians to engage in politics, especially to 'speak up for the voiceless', such as the homeless, the elderly, prisoners and unborn babies.[110] He became a vice-president of Tearfund, an overseas evangelical relief agency, and reiterated his passion for tackling the issues of poverty, disease, universal primary education and the environment.[111] In an HTB sermon, he highlighted the dangers of global warming, deforestation and species extinction, calling Christians to be at the forefront of environmental campaigning – again as an act of love for the poor and marginalised who often suffer the brunt of environmental destruction.[112]

Nevertheless, these emphases on societal transformation always went hand in hand with evangelism. The two could not be separated. Preaching at HTB on the need to be 'born again', Millar explained:

> Of course we must feed the hungry; of course we must minister to the poor; of course we will serve and help all that we can – all humanity, all faiths, all races. Of course we should support Make Poverty History, Soul in the City and Besom – but we do it as children of God. Our aim, our priority, our ultimate service to humanity, is to *preach Christ*, to be the life of Christ in the world and to bring everyone to the knowledge of God that they may be born from above as a gift.[113]

Similar motivations underpinned the Love Your Neighbour (LYN) campaign, initiated by HTB in March 2020 in response to the Covid-19 pandemic. The LYN network harnessed the energies of churches and charities across Britain to offer crisis support and community care, including food provision, mental health groups and drop-in cafes.[114] They also delivered one million 'Bags of Kindness' to people in need during the 2021 'Love Christmas' initiative.[115] But these compassionate ministries ran in tandem with the more explicit proclamatory and conversionist work of Alpha.

Unchaining Prisoners

One unexpected context for Alpha's expansion was in prisons, where the consequences of social deprivation and relational breakdown were often seen at their most raw. HTB had long taken an interest in this area of Christian ministry, especially through HTB members Sylvia Mary Alison and her politician husband Michael Alison. In 1979, the Alisons founded the Prison Christian Fellowship (later renamed Prison Fellowship England and Wales), the British arm of Chuck Colson's Prison Fellowship International, a growing network seeking to bring the Christian message to jails worldwide.[116] From the mid-1990s, Alpha became a major new player in global prison ministry.

HTB staff member Emmy Wilson, a former nurse who helped lead the Earl's Court Project, was also involved in prison ministry from 1991, initially with great reluctance. Sandy Millar was on the Board of Visitors at Holloway Prison in north London, the largest women's prison in Britain, and recommended she join the part-time chaplaincy team there. She was eventually persuaded by two factors. First, when the so-called 'Kansas City Prophets' visited London from the United States in 1990, they had given Wilson a prophecy that she would become 'a key to many, unchaining and unshackling those who cannot any longer free themselves'.[117] Next, she read a couple of prison autobiographies by incarcerated Christian women, Jenny Davis's *Rescued By Love* (1991) and Sabina Wurmbrand's *The Pastor's Wife* (1970). 'I wept my way through the first and the second shocked me', she recalled. 'Who was I to say I could not go inside a prison?'

After cutting her teeth in Holloway Prison, Wilson was asked to initiate Alpha's prison ministry. Her courage increased during the early days of the Toronto Blessing in 1994, when she was 'powerfully touched' by the Holy Spirit and 'fell in love with Jesus all over again, saying: "I don't mind where you send me or what you want me to do." All fear of man left me.'[118]

Alpha was not, of course, designed with prisons in mind. Indeed, it was hard to find a social and educational context more distant from the leafy neighbourhood of Kensington. There could be no prison dinner parties, and no 'weekend away' in the countryside – much as that might have been popular among inmates. Numbers in chapel were often tightly controlled by prison governors, especially in light of the riot at Manchester's Strangeways prison in April 1990, which began in the chapel. Inmates had little control over their own timetables and the population was always in a state of high flux, so attendance at a 10-week course was frequently disrupted by sudden lockdowns, or prison transfers to another part of the country, or by parole. A special 'fast-track Alpha' was recommended for remand centres and detention centres, which had particularly high turnover rates, by squeezing all 15 sessions into two and a half weeks.[119] One convict in Exeter, who was released early, asked permission to stay for a few extra days so he could finish the course.[120] Alpha in a prison context faced many limitations, but was unexpectedly successful. It typically involved a small group of inmates watching Gumbel on video, with tea and biscuits. Despite Gumbel's Etonian background and lengthy monologues, prisoners often warmed to his humour and his illustrations from the law court.[121]

As early as 1994, Alpha was pioneered by chaplains at Gartree Prison, Leicestershire, and Winson Green Prison, Birmingham. When Glen Parva young offender institution began running the course in 1995, they were given 200 copies of *Questions of Life* by the publishers, Kingsway.[122] Exeter Prison was also an early adopter of Alpha. One of the Exeter inmates, Michael Emmett, had been arrested by armed police in November 1993, aged 35, at Bideford in Devon while trying to import four and a half tons of cannabis with a street value of about £13 million. He shared a cell with his father, Brian Emmett, part of the same drug smuggling gang. Michael experienced panic attacks in prison, brought on by his cocaine addiction, but one morning in June 1994 while reading his Gideon's Bible, he was struck by a verse in the New Testament: 'If you have faith as small as a mustard seed ... nothing will be impossible for you' (Matthew 17:20). 'Wow, I want that', he thought. 'That is what I need if I want to be well.'[123] He began to attend prison chapel, where he publicly repented of his sins. Emmett's girlfriend in London had been invited to HTB by the popstar Samantha Fox (a recent Alpha graduate), and he read in the *Mail on Sunday* of the long queues for HTB's Sunday services in the wake of the Toronto Blessing, so Emmett persuaded the Exeter prison chaplain, Bill Birdwood, to telephone Nicky Gumbel and request a team visit. Gumbel dispatched Emmy Wilson to Exeter in December 1994, with six other HTB members. They met with about 20 prisoners in the chapel – 'hardened criminal', said Emmett, 'tough kids, who could rip your head off', whereas he likened Wilson with her upper-class accent to Mary Poppins or Princess Diana. There was a sharp clash of cultures and the HTB team were 'totally out of their comfort zone'. After teaching the prisoners a children's 'action song' – 'Jesus, I Need You, Deep Down in My Heart' – they prayed, 'Come Holy Spirit'. The results were dramatic. 'Everyone had an experience with the Holy Spirit,' Emmett recalled, 'all twenty inmates, just in twenty different ways.' His father fell to the floor laughing, and the guards thought he was high on drugs.[124]

After a year on remand, the Emmetts were sentenced in December 1994 to twelve and a half years in prison (reduced to nine years on appeal), but they became keen Alpha advocates. Birdwood ran Alpha at Exeter Prison for the first time in spring 1995. 'There was just such an extraordinary presence of God,' he exclaimed, 'the prisoners couldn't believe what was happening to them. Men coming into the chapel at the beginning of the course proclaiming to be atheists, would be giving their lives to Christ at the end.'[125] He then moved to Dartmoor Prison and began Alpha there in 1996. The Emmetts were also transferred to other jails – first in June 1995 to Swaleside Prison, on the Isle of Sheppey in Kent – and wherever they were incarcerated they began a Bible study and encouraged their fellow inmates to attend Alpha. Michael Emmett was released on parole in May 1998, and became a regular speaker at Alpha prison events, and on the HTB platform, as a celebrity convert. His story was strongly promoted by *Alpha News*, though he continued for some years to struggle with Christian discipleship – or as he put it, 'to slip in my spiritual walk' – returning initially to cocaine and adultery. He described his relationship with God, and paying his taxes, as 'a continuous fight'.[126]

As Alpha's prison ministry expanded, Wilson headhunted 41-year-old Paul Cowley in 1997 as director of the new 'Prison Alpha' department. Cowley was the first ex-offender and divorcee to join the HTB staff – in fact, he was twice divorced, though he kept that detail secret and only confessed to it later.[127] Cowley had served three months in a young offenders institution in 1973, aged 17, for theft. He then joined the British Army for 16 years, including seeing service in Northern Ireland during the Troubles and as an army physical training instructor, before becoming manager of a private health club in Mayfair. He became a Christian through the witness of a friend and joined HTB in 1993. At Alpha that year, he received the gift of tongues on the Holy Spirit weekend away, while sitting in the bath after returning from a long run.[128]

A significant inspiration for Alpha's prison ministry came from the revival sweeping through Argentina, further evidence of the dynamic flow of ideas across a network of global Christian relationships. In June 1997, Wilson and Cowley visited Los Olmos maximum security prison, on the outskirts of the city of La Planta, near Buenos Aires.[129] It was designed to hold 1,728 prisoners, but was overcrowded with about 3,200, and had been notorious for violence, drugs and murder. But in the early 1980s, Pentecostal pastor Juan Zuccarelli of the Assemblies of God began a fruitful evangelistic ministry in Los Olmos, and revival swept through the cells. By 1997 about 45 per cent of the prison population had professed faith in Christ and were members of Christ the Only Hope Church, a Pentecostal congregation within the prison. There were over 300 baptisms of new converts every year.[130] This transnational experience gave the British visitors a bolder vision for what revival might look like in British prisons. Wilson reported: 'We came back saying that if that can happen in Argentina then we are going to pray it happens here!'[131]

Out of 160 prisons in the United Kingdom, the number running Alpha grew rapidly – two in 1995, eight in 1996, 38 in 1997, 100 in

1999, 121 in 2000, and 134 in 2002 – reaching over 80 per cent of these institutions.[132] When evangelist Michael Green joined an Alpha team on a three-day mission to Dartmoor Prison in December 1999, he was left amazed at the 'remarkable work of God' taking place in the British prison system. In the previous four years, at Dartmoor alone, over 300 prisoners had professed faith in Christ and the chapel was packed for the mission with 70 people. 'The response was incredible', Green exclaimed. 'These tough men with blood on their hands were responding to Jesus Christ in a way I never see outside.'[133] High conversion rates – much higher than Alphas in other contexts – were frequently reported. When Geoff Phillips, prison chaplain at Shepton Mallet in Somerset, led Alpha for 20 prisoners, 18 professed faith by the end of the course. 'We have seen men constantly coming to Christ', he celebrated. 'It is staggering . . . We haven't argued them into a faith but they are touched by the power of the Holy Spirit.'[134] At Albany Prison, on the Isle of Wight, the chaplain reported a threefold rise in chapel attendance.[135] By 2005, an estimated 35,000 prisoners had attended Alpha in Britain.[136]

As inmates became Christians, and their behaviour improved, Alpha won favour among prison governors. There were anecdotal reports of a decline in prison violence, and the arrival of Alpha coincided with the Prison Service's strategy from the late 1990s of promoting 'Offending Behaviour Courses' to change prisoner attitudes and long-term outcomes. Alpha rode this wave of secular prison policy, attractive to the authorities not as Christian evangelism but as an effective method for transforming criminals into model citizens and thereby reducing reoffending rates. As *The Observer* suggested in its profile of Christian prison ministries, 'Jesus can save not just fallen souls, but, crucially, taxpayers' cash.'[137] Vice-Admiral Sir Peter Woodhead (the first Prisons Ombudsman) admitted in 1999 that he had strong doubts about Alpha's ability to reach prisoners, because it was designed for a different context and was 'far too middle class'. 'But I was wrong,' he confessed, 'I was completely and utterly wrong.' He believed that Alpha had made a significant contribution to the reduction of crime.[138] Alpha itself was committed to long-term rehabilitation, not just temporary conversions. In 1998 it launched the 'Caring for Ex-Offenders' initiative (later called 'Caring for Prison

Leavers'), to help prisoners who had completed Alpha connect with local Alpha-friendly churches on their release. Churches aimed to meet them at the prison gates, integrate them into the Christian community, and help them find accommodation and employment.[139] Within the first three years of the scheme, it linked 330 ex-prisoners with Alpha churches.[140]

This 'religious turn' in British prisons in the 1990s and early 2000s soon attracted the attention of the secular media. Alpha was easy to sell to 'bored inmates at Her Majesty's Pleasure', observed Scottish journalist Tom Morton, but he warned of the conversionist intensity generated by a prison environment: 'In jail, they don't encourage seaside breaks, but the hothouse atmosphere is easy to cultivate.'[141] The *Sunday Telegraph* offered a positive profile, but noted the problems of cynicism in jail, where sham conversions at Alpha might be faked to impress the parole board.[142] Likewise, in an article for *The Freethinker*, atheist prisoner Charles Hanson (a convicted murderer serving a life sentence) argued that Alpha was only interested in 'indoctrination' not rehabilitation. He suggested that prisoners who attended Alpha were not motivated by a genuine desire to explore Christianity, but they only went along because the course provided variety in the midst of monotony, guaranteed a favourable reference from the chaplain, and enabled inmates to engage in 'illicit activities' away from the vigilance of prison guards.[143] Other commentators, however, had little doubt that many prison conversions were authentic.[144]

Alpha's own publicity trumpeted the success of its prison ministry. *Alpha News* carried numerous testimonies from convicts who had found Christ behind bars. For example, a heroin addict and alcoholic was sentenced to prison on multiple occasions for crimes such as burglary, armed robbery, and grievous bodily harm. In June 1998, aged 36, he committed his life to Jesus while watching Christian dance band World Wide Message Tribe on satellite television, but he found it difficult to live consistently as a Christian and soon returned to his old patterns of behaviour. After being jailed again in 2000 for burglary, he completed Alpha twice in prison, at Shepton Mallet and at The Verne in Dorset, an important part of his rehabilitation.[145] Likewise, notoriously violent criminal Shane Taylor was jailed in 2000, aged 19, for stabbing two men. Suffering from paranoia, he frequently attacked prison officers and fellow inmates, and incited riots, but he began to consider Christianity after a 'born again' convicted murderer gave him a copy of Gumbel's *Why Jesus?* Taylor attended Alpha at Long Lartin maximum security prison in Worcestershire, initially only for the coffee and cake, and became a Christian on the Holy Spirit day, praying, 'Jesus Christ, I know you died on the cross for me. Please, I don't like who I am, please forgive me, please.'[146]

Ex-convicts, who attended Alpha after prison, were also often profiled by *Alpha News*. For example, Gram Seed from Middlesbrough had been in and out of prison for theft and violence. He became an alcoholic beggar, living on a bench, hoping to die, but in 1996, aged 31, was befriended by two young Christians who invited him to Alpha at Emmanuel Fellowship, Eaglescliffe (later Tees Valley Community Church). Seed was converted during the Holy Spirit weekend and went on to found Sowing Seeds Ministries, bringing the Christian message to young prisoners.[147] Bob Hughes-Burton, a member of a violent motorcycle gang, was sentenced to seven years in prison, aged 25, for grievous bodily harm after attacking a man he found in bed with his fiancée. He became a Christian after attending Alpha in 1998, in his mid-40s, and joined the Christian Motorcycle Association, an evangelistic group that hands out Bibles and tracts at motorcycle rallies.[148] Former soldier Dave Blakeney worked as a violent mercenary in Angola in the 1970s, robbing gold and diamond mines, and abducting and selling children into slavery. On his return to Britain, he smuggled guns and drugs, and served seven years in prison in the 1990s for manslaughter. By his early 50s he was a homeless drug addict, living on the streets, but in 2002 attended Alpha at the South Manchester Christian Fellowship with about 20 other homeless men and women. Blakeney did the course twice, initially only for the free meal, but the Christian message made sense and he prayed, 'Jesus, I want you in my life . . . Come into it and straighten me up.' He stopped injecting heroin, without withdrawal symptoms, and was baptised on Easter Sunday 2003.[149]

This style of Alpha testimony, from criminality to Christ, was highly marketable, especially to men. Mark Elsdon-Dew's testimony highlights from *Alpha News*, including of several former prisoners, were published as *Life Change: Fifteen Men Tell Their Extraordinary Stories* (2011). Some wrote book-length autobiographies, marketed with dramatic titles: Gram Seed's *One Step Beyond: One Man's Journey from Near Death to New Life* (2008), Darrell Tunningley's *Unreachable: One Man's Journey Through Drugs, Violence, Armed Robbery and a Miraculous Encounter with God in Prison* (2011), Shane Taylor's *Shane: The True Story of One of the Most Dangerous Men in Britain's Prisons* (2019), Paul Cowley's *Thief, Prisoner, Soldier, Priest* (2020), and Michael Emmett's *Sins of Fathers: A Spectacular Break from a Dark Criminal Past* (2020). Alpha generated more literature from ex-convicts than from any other group of converts.

In parallel with its success in British prisons, Alpha was pioneered in prisons globally. In September 1996 a young Baptist pastor at Bartoszyce, in northern Poland, launched Alpha at the high-security Kamińsk prison, after he heard about the course on a visit to England. In January 1997, it was introduced to the Westgate Correctional Facility, Bermuda, in the North Atlantic, by the Anglican chaplain.[150] By 1999 Alpha was also running in prisons in Australia, Canada, Denmark, Finland, Morocco, New Zealand, Norway, Peru, Romania, South Africa, Sweden, Switzerland, Uganda, the United States and Zambia.[151] There were further enquiries from Fiji, Greece, Kazakhstan and Kenya.[152] In Texas – with more people incarcerated than in any other American state – Alpha's roll-out through the prison system was approved by Governor George W. Bush, a year before his election as President.[153] At the first Alpha conference for American prison chaplains – led by Emmy Wilson in Austin, Texas, in August 1999 – delegates were brought to tears as two female convicts, dressed in their white prison uniforms and flanked by two prison guards, testified to their new faith in Jesus Christ through Alpha's ministry.[154] A month later, in Sofia, Bulgaria, the Prison Fellowship International's triennial convocation urged all its national affiliates to adopt Alpha – a major boost to Alpha's global reach.[155]

Testimonies began to emerge from prisons across the world. Paul Swala, a junior soldier in the Zambian Army, was caught up in a failed coup attempt in October 1997 to overthrow President Frederick Chiluba, who was accused of political corruption. The coup, code-named 'Operation Born Again', managed to broadcast on Zambia's state-run radio station but was crushed within just a few hours. Swala was arrested, tortured, charged with treason, and detained in cramped conditions in Lusaka Central Prison. There he read Gumbel's *Why Jesus?* and attended Alpha, committing his life to Christ. The Alpha team gave him a Bible in which he read the account of Daniel rescued from the lions' den, and wondered, 'Can God do these things today?' Swala prayed: 'Jesus, if you release me out of this situation, I will know that you are the king and you are answering prayers. This cannot be done by a man, but by yourself.' At trial in 1999, Swala was the only one acquitted – 59 fellow soldiers were sentenced to death for their part in the coup plot (later commuted to life imprisonment). Released from custody, he became a pastor and preacher, helping to take the Christian message into Zambia's 53 prisons.[156] In nearby South Africa, cabinet minister Ben Skosana (Minister of Correctional Services) praised Alpha's impact in reducing levels of reoffending. At Leeuwkop Prison in Johannesburg, 900 inmates were released between 2000 and 2002 – of the 73 who had done Alpha, none reoffended, whereas over half the others were back in prison within a few months.[157] By 2014, an estimated 250,000 prisoners had completed Alpha worldwide, and towards the end of the decade over 900 prisons were running Alpha, with 45,000 annual participants.[158] Ministry among incarcerated offenders was not only a pathway to social transformation but a significant means by which Alpha permeated the globe.

8

Reaching the Globe

SOON AFTER HIS Christian conversion as a Cambridge undergraduate, Nicky Gumbel discovered a passion for global, transcultural mission. In the mid-1970s, during his student years, he twice visited the Soviet Union on holiday with his parents. His father, Walter Gumbel, had a lifelong ambition to pay tribute to the Russians for the costly stand they had taken during the Second World War at the Battle of Stalingrad, a key turning point in the fight against Hitler and Nazism. The family toured Moscow, and later returned to Leningrad on the Baltic Sea, and to Samarkand and Bukhara in Uzbekistan, historic centres of Islamic culture on the old Silk Road between East and West. In preparation for the trip, Gumbel wrote to Open Doors, who coordinated Bible smuggling operations behind the Iron Curtain, and a few days later a supply of Russian Bibles was left anonymously on his doorstep.[1] In the Soviet Union, he attended local churches (often infiltrated by the KGB) and tried to identify people who seemed genuine Christians, in order to deliver his contraband. At one location, in Bukhara, he followed a man in his 60s down the street after the service:

> Glancing round to check nobody was there, I went up to him and tapped him on the shoulder. I took out one of my Bibles and handed it to him. For a moment he had an expression of disbelief. Then he took from his pocket a New Testament, which was probably 100 years old, the pages so threadbare they were virtually transparent. When he realised he had received a whole Bible, he was elated. He didn't speak any English, I didn't speak any Russian. We hugged each other and started dancing up and down the street jumping for joy.[2]

Stimulated by this global engagement, Gumbel was attracted to the idea of becoming a missionary, though he never settled on one particular country. At first, he had 'a passionate desire to go to Russia'. Next, after reading a biography of Victorian missionary pioneer James Hudson Taylor (founder of the China Inland Mission), he wanted to go to China.[3] He was also deeply impressed by the exploits of C. T. Studd and the 'Cambridge Seven' in China and Africa – Studd, like Gumbel, was educated at Eton and Trinity College, Cambridge, so there was an added resonance. With a voracious appetite to learn about the global church, especially Christians undergoing contemporary persecution, Gumbel hoovered up literature such as Brother Andrew's *God's Smuggler* (1967), Richard Wurmbrand's *In God's Underground* (1968), Michael Bourdeaux's *Faith on Trial in Russia* (1971), Myrna Grant's *Vanya* (1975), and G. P. Vins's *Three Generations of Suffering* (1976). His interests flipped between Uganda, Iran, Eastern Europe, the Soviet Union, India, China, and elsewhere.[4]

'I felt called to all these places', Gumbel announced, and yet he could not imagine how to reach them.[5] Unexpectedly, he remained permanently settled in London, rooted in one place and one congregation at Holy Trinity Brompton (just a few hundred yards from his childhood home) for his entire working life from graduation in 1976 to retirement as vicar in 2022. And yet from this fixed base, Alpha flourished into a global movement and Gumbel did become a missionary, after all, much to his own surprise, not to one nation but to many nations across the world. In 1995, in the first flush of Alpha's expansion beyond the British Isles, he remembered his early missionary longings and began to see, in the providence of God, 'how all these things can fit together and I consider it the most amazing privilege'.[6]

When Alpha was launched in May 1993, Gumbel's dream was that there would be 5,000 courses running somewhere in the world by the turn of the millennium. This seemed so far-fetched that he feared ridicule for suggesting it.[7] Yet Alpha's early exponential growth far exceeded all expectations and outstripped even HTB's most optimistic forecasts. By mid-1996, Alpha was running in 50 countries, on five continents, and *Alpha News* celebrated that 'the course looks set to explode all over the world'.[8] It had cruised past the 5,000 target by the end of the year, and Gumbel began privately to sketch out bolder projections, imagining what would happen if Alpha continued to double every year. At first, he mapped out annual turnover. If there were 5,000 courses worldwide in 1996 with an annual turnover of £1 million, then by 2006 there would be over five million courses with an annual turnover of over £1 billion.[9] The next year, he calculated Alpha's potential in people. If a cumulative total of one million people attended Alpha by the end of 1997, and numbers continued to double, then eight billion people would have attended Alpha by 2010, more than the entire world population. Although Gumbel knew these projections were wildly unrealistic, his vision in 1997 (as recorded privately in his diary) was that within 15 years every person on the planet would have had the opportunity to attend Alpha, or a similar evangelistic course.[10] In the same year, he published *The Heart of Revival*, proclaiming: 'God's vision is so often bigger than our own. It is a worldwide one. We should not settle for anything less. We thank God for local revivals and national revivals but we should not be satisfied until we see a worldwide revival.'[11] Gumbel's ambition for Alpha was truly global.

Conference Fuel

At first, Alpha was planted into new contexts haphazardly, through individual enterprise. By the end of 1994 it had been picked up by congregations not only in the Anglophone world (Australia, New Zealand, South Africa, Canada and the United States of America), but was running at Utrecht in the Netherlands, Bern in Switzerland, Zaragoza in Spain, Kampala in Uganda, Arequipa in Peru, and elsewhere.[12] When this global potential was recognised, HTB began to invest heavily in international training conferences, a central plank in Alpha's multiplication strategy and one of the major drivers for its growth. The very first Alpha conference, at HTB in 1993, proved to be the catalyst for its British explosion, so the model was duplicated worldwide, directed by Tricia Neill's professional expertise as an events organiser. Conferences generated courses, and courses generated demand for conferences, in a virtuous cycle of expansion. During a two-day event in a strategically located city, Alpha International could train hundreds of local church leaders to use the course in their own contexts, disseminating the Alpha vision and Alpha resources to Christians hungry for help in evangelism.

The inauguration of Alpha's conference ministry in North America did not have auspicious beginnings, however. In the first week of September 1995, an HTB team led by Nicky Gumbel and Nicky Lee was scheduled to lead conferences in Canada at Toronto Airport Vineyard (recent birthplace of the Toronto Blessing) and in the United States at Truro Episcopal Church in Fairfax, Virginia, near Washington DC. The events ran back-to-back, separated by a long weekend for the Labor Day public holiday. Despite meticulous preparation, 'almost everything that could go wrong did go wrong'. It seemed to Gumbel that they were 'under attack' and that 'the devil did not want Alpha to take off in America'. First, the Alpha videos, cassettes and books that had been shipped from England were impounded by Canadian customs and did not arrive in time. Next, Gumbel woke on the first morning of the conference, a Thursday, to discover his hotel bedroom had been burgled. The thieves took his briefcase, inside which were his wallet with all his credit cards and almost all his cash, his driving licence, his diary with the schedule for the year, his Bible with 13 years of annotations, his Filofax with his conference talk notes, his address book, prayer diary, mobile telephone, Dictaphone, and travel documents, including his passport. The burglars even stole some of Gumbel's clothes from his suitcase. Without his passport, he would never reach the United States, and the passport office was about to close for the long weekend. There were frantic calls to the police and to Gumbel's bank in England, and after delivering his first Toronto address he rushed away to have a new passport photograph taken. Early on Friday morning, he flew to Ottawa to the British High Commission for a replacement passport, but the necessary documentation had not arrived. Gumbel had to dash to a local bank for a 'reverse charge' call to his wife Pippa in London, asking her to persuade every influential person they knew in England to contact Sir Nicholas Bayne (the British High Commissioner to Canada, an Old Etonian) and 'besiege him with phone calls'. While Gumbel ran from pillar to post, including to the American

Embassy, there were emergency prayer meetings at HTB and Toronto. 'Everyone was praying like mad.' Gumbel was granted a new passport and, despite missing his intended flight, was back in Toronto in time to deliver the afternoon conference address. To the Alpha team this seemed like a miraculous intervention. Gumbel interpreted the episode as 'spiritual warfare' but also as evidence that 'God is sovereign and no weapon formed against us can prevail'. As a thank you gift, he sent the British High Commissioner a copy of *Alpha News* and *Questions of Life*.[13]

A month later, in October 1995, Gumbel was on the move again, leading Alpha's first African conferences, in Zimbabwe at Harare, and in South Africa at Johannesburg, Bloemfontein and Cape Town, while Nicky Lee was dispatched to Stavanger in Norway and to Hong Kong. The 1996 conference itinerary included Germany, Kenya, Denmark, Finland, New Zealand, Australia and Ireland; 1997 added Switzerland, the Netherlands, Sweden and Russia, plus multiple return visits to many of these countries in response to increasing demand. The events were most fruitful when hosted by local churches, though not all went smoothly. The first Alpha training conference in St Petersburg, in May 1999, took place in a former military arms factory on 'an industrial wasteland', surrounded by disused buildings and cement. There were 54 Russian delegates, most of whom were living on the poverty line, and 'two-thirds had no idea why they were there'.[14] In better circumstances, conferences were a catalyst for Alpha's extension into new domains, beyond the host city. The first Alpha training conference in Central Asia took place for a thousand church leaders in Almaty, Kazakhstan, in May 2002, led by Sandy Millar. It was hosted at a Russian-speaking congregation that hoped to start Alpha in neighbouring Kyrgyzstan and Uzbekistan, with a vision ultimately to export the course to all the countries along the old Silk Road from Turkey in the west to the Uyghurs in the Xinjiang region of China.[15]

The way in which training conferences fuelled Alpha's ministry in new territories is illustrated well by Zimbabwe. English clergyman Nick Crawley attended the first Alpha conference in London in May 1993 and introduced the course to Zimbabwe a few months later when he became rector of Avondale in Harare. His parish hosted the first two national Alpha conferences, in October 1995 and September 1996, and became headquarters of the Zimbabwe Alpha national office. The inaugural conference, led by Nicky Gumbel and Jeremy Jennings from HTB, was attended by 200 Christian leaders from 70 congregations, with many from Harare but also large contingents from Banket, Nyanga and Penhalonga, and elsewhere across the country. At the end of the conference, 46 churches indicated their intention to start Alpha.[16] *Zimbabwe Alpha News* was launched a month later, to resource this new growth.

The Alpha participants manual was translated into Shona and Ndebele, and some of the earliest courses were in rural areas. Near Lake Kariba, for example, on Zimbabwe's border with Zambia, the Kariba Lakeshore Mission ran Alpha at Gache Gache (an area best known for its hippo and crocodiles) from which a small church was planted. At nearby Charara there was an Alpha mission to a local banana farm, where the course was run in Shona by evangelist Shamisa Nyamasoko in the farm compound for the labourers, and separately for the farm manager and his wife using the English videos.[17] On the other side of the country in Manicaland, near the border with Mozambique, Alpha was run by a farmer's wife for migrant labourers in the Middle Sabi region. She played the videos in a hall on the farm, attracting a sizeable crowd, though perhaps largely from curiosity rather than a desire to hear Gumbel's oratory – many of the labourers had never seen a television before.[18]

Alpha worked in friendly collaboration with African Enterprise, a mission agency founded in 1962 by South African evangelist Michael Cassidy, with a vision to reach the whole continent with the Christian message. At the cessation of the Rhodesian Bush War, and the election in 1980 of Robert Mugabe as Zimbabwe's first black prime minister, African Enterprise sent out teams of rural evangelists across the nation in 'Operation Foxfire'. Two decades later, in 1999, Alpha copied the idea for their own initiative, called 'Alpha Mwenje-Ukukhanya' ('Alpha Light'). The national office recruited young men from Bible colleges, on a one-year contract, trained them in Alpha, and sent them out to the rural districts. They were supplied with a bicycle, rucksack, sleeping bag, change of clothes, First Aid kit, diary (to record their experiences), Bible, and Alpha resources in Shona or Ndebele. They travelled usually in pairs – New Testament style – and were sometimes fed and housed by a local church, but often lived on a farm or mining compound, working alongside the labourers.[19] The initial concept was for Alpha to be run with perhaps only five people, 'sitting round a fire or in a hut', but the evangelists aimed to train others in leading the course and thus it would 'spread like a bush-fire'.[20]

The first Alpha Mwenje team was deployed to the Chipangayi district of the Middle Sabi, where there were as many as 20,000 migrant workers on the farms during the cotton-picking season. Initially the evangelists were treated with suspicion and presumed to be policemen because they rode bicycles. The labourers mostly spoke Ndau, which made communication in Shona difficult, and they had little time to attend Alpha because of long hours in the fields. Nevertheless, the evangelists joined in the regular activities of the labourers, helping to pick cotton and citrus fruit, and taking part in farm sports, and were gradually accepted. They ran four Alphas in Shona before returning to Harare.[21] In 2000, the Alpha Mwenje teams ran 33 courses across the country, mostly on farms, but also in the capital itself in the slums of Mabvuku suburb, where many residents were affected by AIDS, and in the wealthier Gun Hill suburb among domestic workers. In rural areas, 'war veterans' and Mugabe loyalists often disrupted the Alpha outreach, abusing and threatening the evangelists.[22] As political violence escalated, so did the dangers. Anderson Mudhara, director of Alpha Zimbabwe, and his co-workers were arrested and imprisoned seven times in 2007–8. One of the Alpha evangelists was beaten so badly that he was left permanently paralysed; another was killed.[23]

From Zimbabwe, Alpha spread to neighbouring territories. Among the attenders at the original Alpha conference in Harare in 1995 was a Brethren couple from Kitwe, in the Zambian Copperbelt, who took the course back to their local church. Their inaugural Alpha dinner was traditional Zambian cooking, with chicken relish and *nshima* (mealie meal porridge), and one young mother was so eager to attend that she walked two kilometres to Alpha every week with her toddler on her back.[24] Alpha was also used among white Zambian farmers in the districts of Mkushi and Mazabuka, before reaching the capital Lusaka.[25] From Zambia, Alpha then spread to the neighbouring Democratic Republic of the Congo.[26] By the time Zambia held its first Alpha conference – led by Gumbel in Lusaka in July 2004 – there was enough interest in the region to attract 400 delegates from 11 countries, further fuelling growth.[27] This also gave new impetus for translating Alpha materials into Bemba and Nyanja, two of Zambia's seven official local languages.[28] This pattern of multiplication was repeated in other parts of the globe.

National Infrastructures

Another key part of Alpha's multiplication strategy was the formation of national offices. Some were small affairs – perhaps an enthusiastic Alpha volunteer, or clergy couple, answering emails and posting out resources from their spare bedroom. Other offices had proper premises and full-time staff. Their creation frequently followed a successful conference, and one of their responsibilities was in turn to organise further conferences and foster local courses. By 1999, there were already 14 Alpha offices across the globe, from Vancouver to Moscow and Stravanger to Sydney.[29] Some produced their own bulletins in magazine or newspaper format, containing local testimonies and conference reports. For example, there was *Alpha Nieuws* in the Netherlands, *Alpha Nytt* in Norway, *Alfa Uutiset* in Finland, *Альфа Новости* in Russia, *Алфа Инфо* in Bulgaria, *Berita Alpha* in Malaysia, and *Oz Alpha* in Australia. By 2002, Alpha was running in 24,000 churches in 132 countries, with materials published in 46 languages.[30] By 2011, there were 55,000 courses in 169 countries and 112 languages.[31]

The most sophisticated national Alpha infrastructure, after the United Kingdom, was in the United States, led initially by McKinsey management consultant Alistair Hanna (1945–2014). Hanna was raised in Northern Ireland, before migrating to England for a doctorate in nuclear physics, and then to America for an MBA at Harvard Business School. In 1974 he joined McKinsey and Co., a global management consultancy, rising through the ranks to become a partner and then a director. By the mid-1990s there were 7,000 McKinsey staff worldwide, with 150 directors, and Hanna managed the office in Stamford, Connecticut.[32] He had been raised within Belfast Protestantism, but stopped attending church at age 18 and stayed away for two decades. When his wife Nancy (later an ordained Episcopalian minister) went to church, Hanna remained in the car reading the newspaper. But he was gradually drawn back to Christian faith and by 1991 felt called to a change of career. 'I was lying in bed', he reflected, 'when I heard a very clear message that I should be doing something different. It was really weird. I thought it was a voice. I felt as though I had been spoken to by an external agent.' At first, Hanna believed it was God speaking audibly to him, but he concluded it was probably a dream.[33]

The Hannas were based in England for six months in 1995, while Nancy (chair of the evangelism committee for the diocese of New York) was on sabbatical at Wycliffe Hall, Oxford, and Alistair divided his time between the McKinsey offices in London and New York. They became regular attenders at HTB where they discovered Alpha and resolved to promote it back in America.[34] They organised the first Alpha conference in New York – held at St Bartholomew's Episcopal Church in Manhattan in September 1996 – and Gumbel invited Hanna to leave McKinsey and head up America's national Alpha office. There were clear parallels with Gumbel's recruitment of Tricia Neill from big business in 1994 – both Neill and Hanna were 'Gumbeled' (an affectionate verb in HTB circles for Gumbel's repeated pattern of identifying talented individuals and persuading them to join the Alpha team). Hanna's strategic expertise was a key asset. 'An infectious enthusiasm, entrepreneurial spirit, and a bold plan for growth are all trademarks among Alpha's top leaders', suggested American magazine *Christianity Today*, in a profile entitled 'The Alpha-Brits are coming'.[35] Hanna's plans were certainly bold. In an interview with *Forbes* magazine, he announced his expectation that Alpha in the United States would reach between 8 and 10 million people in the first three years.[36] By 2000, he wanted to see 50,000 churches running Alpha.[37]

The American investment in organisational strategy paid quick dividends, though not the enormous returns for which Hanna hoped. The number of registered Alpha churches in the United States rose from 200 in 1997 to 2,300 in 2000. In the same period, the number of staff in the national office tripled, from 5 to 14, and they moved from a cramped room at St Bartholomew's to the ninth floor of an office block owned by another Episcopalian congregation in Manhattan, Trinity Church Wall Street, the wealthiest parish in the Anglican Communion. There were 40 Alpha conferences forecast for 2001 and Hanna's vision was to move to a satellite model where 100 conferences might be held in different cities across the United States on the same two days. 'The time has now come when the concept of Alpha is proven and we have to build a world-class organisation', he declared.[38] He also led a push to establish self-funding regional Alpha offices throughout the country, beginning with Houston in 2001, followed by Chicago, Minneapolis, Boston and Philadelphia, and rising to 16 cities by 2004.[39]

The United States was the globe's largest Christian marketplace, with vast potential. By the end of 2002 Alpha USA was generating an annual turnover of $5.4 million, and had registered 6,000 courses (a rise of 65 per cent on the previous year), but this was still only a drop in the ocean compared with the nation's 300,000 churches. Its initial growth was among the old mainline denominations: of the 6,000 courses the largest take-up was among Methodists (1,257), Episcopalians (1,082), Lutherans (643) and Presbyterians (527), plus smaller numbers of Baptists (233), Vineyard (200), Assemblies of God (162) and Roman Catholics (142).[40] In 2004, the number of registered courses in the United States overtook the number in the United Kingdom for the first time, becoming Alpha's largest global market.[41] However, ambition exceeded reality. Alpha's American infrastructure grew too quickly. It was in deep financial crisis and risked insolvency. After the initial flurry of activity, the number of training conferences declined (as did the average number of delegates), leading to reduced sales of Alpha resources, while donor gifts that had kept the ministry afloat in earlier years were unpredictable and could no longer bridge the growing gulf between income and expenditure. After a shortfall for three years in succession, and serious problems with cash flow, Alpha USA needed to find $850,000 in a hurry, to pay its staff salaries and most urgent bills. Its largest creditor, the company that printed and warehoused Alpha resources, was owed $200,000. Some smaller vendors threatened to quit their links with Alpha over the slow payment of debts, which they deemed a lack of Christian integrity.[42] Alpha regional offices were also distressed to discover that the funds they had raised and sent to New York for safe keeping had been spent on national bills.[43] This loss of momentum and confidence coincided with a loss of organisational focus. Hanna tried to reassure his trustees on the Alpha USA board in November 2004: 'The building was on fire for the third year in a row, but it is not widespread, and the fire is now contained. I hope it will be out by the end of the year.'[44] Nevertheless, he stood down from his American leadership and was replaced by Todd Hunter, previously national director of John Wimber's Vineyard network and later a bishop in the Anglican Church in North America.[45] After these challenges to Alpha's viability in the United States, when retreat looked inevitable, it returned to a more secure footing and continued to grow steadily.

Elsewhere across the globe, Alpha offices aimed to increase their visibility with national marketing campaigns, seeking to emulate HTB's sophisticated annual advertising, sometimes using local celebrities. New Zealand, an early adopter of Alpha from 1995, soon boasted more courses per head of population than any other country in the world. Their first national advertising initiative in April 2000 was supported by 700 churches across the whole length of the country, from Kaitaia in the far north to Invercargill in the far south. Between them, they distributed 50,000 posters designed by Saatchi and Saatchi, 40,000 car stickers, and 600,000 dinner invitations, which resulted in 47,000 dinner guests watching Gumbel's video address, 'Christianity: boring, untrue, and irrelevant?', with 17,000 signed up for the full course (one-third of them unchurched).[46] Gumbel's polished English accent – a hindrance in some parts of Britain – was welcomed as an asset in New Zealand, because although he was a foreigner at least he was not an American.[47] The Moderator of the Presbyterian Church of New Zealand purred that Gumbel's 'superb' communication skills and winsomeness 'would give any pastor pulpit envy'. Alpha's famously laid-back style, he suggested, was especially attractive to 'the average Kiwi bloke', an ideal tool for 'the making of casual Kiwis into committed Christians'.[48]

There were similar advertising campaigns in the early 2000s in Australia, Norway, Denmark, Canada, Switzerland and Hong Kong. Some national offices focused their efforts on particular regions or cities. In September 2010, for example, Germany's first Alpha campaign took place across the state of Baden-Württemberg, supported by 120 churches, and South Africa's first campaign was focused on Cape Town, supported by 100 local churches, with street posters, billboards and radio messaging.[49] Alpha Canada took the unusual step of incentivising church participation in their national advertising with material inducement. In 2007, they launched Canada's 'Alpha Car Flag Challenge', to raise the course's profile, encouraging Christians to fly an Alpha flag on their vehicles. Anyone who emailed a photograph of themselves with car and flag was entered into a weekly prize draw to win a free iPod. And for every church member entered in the iPod draw, their local Alpha course administrator was entered in a second prize draw, for a free trip for two to England, including tea with Nicky Gumbel. 'The more entries, the more chances to win', urged the Canadian edition of *Alpha News*.[50] This coveted prize of tea with Gumbel, a global Christian celebrity, was won by a married couple from the small town of Kindersley in Saskatchewan, an agricultural district where they ran Alpha in the winter months to avoid the harvest and planting seasons, even though temperatures could fall to minus 40 degrees.[51]

Global Flows

Alpha's worldwide expansion was driven not only by strategic infrastructure, conferences, resources and campaigns, but also in less premeditated ways through the continual global flow of ideas and people. Alpha's origins in the centre of London – a vibrant capital city and global transportation hub, which stands at the nexus of numerous interconnected transnational relationships – gave it natural advantages for dissemination. At an Alpha prayer event in St Paul's Cathedral in 2003, Bishop Chartres declared: 'This is a world city, a world crossroads. Whatever we do here reverberates for good or for ill throughout the entire globe.'[52] As many millions of individuals passed through London, for business, study or holiday, some of them encountered HTB and Alpha, carrying news of the course back to their own nations. These natural global flows were as important as any deliberate expansion strategy.

For example, a Presbyterian visitor from Jakarta, Indonesia, attended Alpha at HTB and on her own initiative started running it in 1994 in her homeland, after painstakingly translating the Alpha manual and *Questions of Life* into Indonesian. Within three years, the course was established on most of the larger islands, including at Bogor in West Java, and Manado, Ujung Pandang and Soroako in Sulawesi.[53] Mike and Cheryl Frith carried Alpha with them from England to Madagascar, when Mike was posted there as a pilot and engineer with the Mission Aviation Fellowship. They ran the course in 1996 in their home in Antananarivo, for ten Malagasy and four expats, watching Gumbel's English videos.[54] In 1998, the decennial Lambeth Conference brought over 700 bishops to London, many of whom travelled back to their dioceses across the Anglican Communion with Alpha resources. More than 400 bishops visited the Alpha stall at the conference, and Gumbel was invited by Archbishop Carey to deliver an Alpha evening seminar, which was attended by 60 bishops.[55] Drexel Gomez, Bishop of Nassau and the Bahamas, and Archbishop of the West Indies, was one of those who first encountered Alpha at Lambeth and enthusiastically promoted it across his entire province. Within months, the course was established among Bahamians, running for 80 people on New Providence Island and 40 people on Exuma Island.[56]

Some global travellers came to England to study. The Anglican Bishop of Ruaha in central Tanzania, Donald Mtetemela (primate of Tanzania from 1998 to 2008), first discovered Alpha while on sabbatical at Wycliffe Hall and was impressed by its evangelistic potential in his own East African context. He invited Sharing of Ministries Abroad (SOMA), a mission agency that emphasised ministry in the power of the Holy Spirit, to send a team in January 1997 from England to Ruaha diocese, a region of extreme poverty and high levels of illiteracy. Led by Warwickshire rector Justin Welby, the visitors worked intensively for five days at Iringa, training 15 Maasai church leaders in Alpha, though they inadvertently left behind the specially translated Kiswahili course manuals on the carousel at Dar-es-Salaam airport. Further north, near the Kenyan border, Alpha was also launched in January 1997 at Moshi, at the foot of Mount Kilimanjaro, before spreading to Arusha, Korogwe and Dar-es-Salaam.[57] In later years it reached the nomadic Maasai community at Narok, near Nairobi, where the local Alpha evangelist had to follow the group from place to place while they herded cows.[58]

Global flows were also stimulated by economic migrants attracted by the City of London's commercial and banking sector. Roman Catholic Marc de Leyritz worked in the City as an investment banker before taking Alpha back to his homeland in France (as seen in Chapter 6). A similar global migrant was New Zealander Chris Sadler, who grew up in Masterton, near Wellington, but 'walked away from God' and church, aged 10, after his sister died. He moved to New York in 1984 to study for an MBA in finance and became an investment banker, first on Wall Street and then for SG Warburg in the City of London, working on mergers and acquisitions. Before the age of 30 he had achieved his life's ambition to accrue wealth, with a smart apartment in Notting Hill, transatlantic flights on Concorde, and weekends in the south of France, but 'deep down in my heart something was not quite right'. Then his boss at SG Warburg, Ken Costa, invited him to an Alpha dinner at HTB in 1991. Sadler and his wife both became Christians through Alpha, where Nicky Gumbel was their small-group leader, and Sadler carried enthusiasm for the course back to the Antipodes when he transferred to Melbourne, Australia, as a director at J. P. Morgan and then Deutsche Bank. In 2004, he was 'Gumbeled', persuaded to abandon his banking career to work *pro bono* as executive director of Alpha in the Asia-Pacific zone, where he spoke of his passion for 'the critical role that Alpha can play in sharing the Good News of Jesus with everyone in this vast region'.[59]

Alpha's global flows ran in multiple directions, increasingly independent of London. At the other end of the economic spectrum was Thelunius Nkomo, a Xhosa witchdoctor from the Eastern Cape in South Africa, who had spent much of her life living in squatter camps. In 2004, aged 44, she travelled to New Zealand to work temporarily as a family maid at Bucklands Beach in the Auckland suburbs. There she was invited to Alpha and on the Holy Spirit weekend experienced deep internal conflict. She found herself stuck in her chair with 'roaring in her ears', and then unable to speak and lying on the floor. According to the report circulated by Alpha New Zealand, this was spiritual warfare. When the Alpha leaders prayed for Nkomo, 'she heard the spirits shouting "We are going" – and she prayed with all her might that they would go'. The report rejoiced that at Alpha, 'her witchdoctor spirit was confronted by God's Holy Spirit – and the Holy Spirit won!!' This economic migrant then returned to South Africa. It was an unusual transcultural encounter for the quiet suburban congregation, but illustrated again the potential of transnational flows to extend Alpha's reach.[60]

International tourism was another means by which Alpha migrated, as local churches aimed at innovative outreach to transient visitors. For example, in North America, Alpha was run in 2000 on board the *Vision of the Seas* cruise liner, operated by Royal Caribbean International with capacity for over 3,000 passengers and crew, during its seven-day trip down the Alaskan coast.[61] On the other side of the globe, Alpha was run regularly in the early 2010s for tourists on the *Sun Princess*, during its cruises around Australia.[62] In New Zealand, the South Island resort town of Wanaka had a population boom for two months every winter, when skiers, snowboarders and backpackers from across the world converged on the area to enjoy the mountains, glaciers and alpine lakes of Mount Aspiring National Park. Therefore the Wanaka churches in 2007 launched 'Alpha for Travellers', with advertisements featuring a snowboarder, distributed in English and Japanese. The offer of free food was a particular incentive to young tourists on a budget.[63]

Global military manoeuvres also pushed Alpha into new territories, including war zones. At Paderborn Garrison in Germany, for example, where Major Arthur Norman-Walker and his wife Anna were posted with the British Army, they hosted Alpha in 1996 for members of their regiment. When soldiers from their Alpha small group were sent on exercises to Belize in Central America for six weeks, they took Gumbel's audio cassettes with them, to listen and discuss in the jungle. Alpha was also soon pioneered among British troops at Osnabrück, another German garrison town.[64] It was likewise carried onboard ship. For example, in 1999 an Alpha group was established on USS *Kearsarge*, an amphibious assault ship and aircraft carrier, deployed in the Adriatic Sea off the Balkans during the Kosovo War.[65] At the same period, Alpha was run within the Royal Canadian Navy, on HMCS *Protecteur* during its 15-week deployment in the Pacific Ocean and on HMCS *Regina* during its six-month deployment in the Persian Gulf.[66] The Royal Australian Navy also agreed to adopt Alpha as 'an advanced character training course' and it was launched in 2002 at HMAS Stirling, a naval base off the coast of Western Australia, on Garden Island in the Indian Ocean.[67] During the American-led 'war on terror' in the Middle East, Alpha was pioneered in Afghanistan at Camp Julien (the main Canadian military base) near Kabul, for soldiers and civilian workers.[68] In Iraq, the course was run at the US army base at Fallujah and among US paratroopers stationed near Baghdad.[69]

Alpha hopped from country to country, without London's involvement. When an Anglican minister from the Seychelles witnessed Alpha working successfully in South Africa, he transported it back to the Indian Ocean archipelago, launched at St Paul's Cathedral, Victoria, on Mahé Island in 1997.[70] From Singapore, where Alpha was established among Anglicans as early as 1993, the vision of the local churches was to carry Alpha throughout South East Asia to Brunei, Cambodia, Indonesia, Laos, Malaysia, Myanmar, the Philippines, Thailand and Vietnam.[71] From Australia, Alpha jumped to neighbouring Papua New Guinea. Senior judge Sir Mari Kapi (chief justice of the supreme court of Papua New Guinea from 2003) ran a seminar in his home village of Keapara in 2002, educating residents on the anti-corruption laws surrounding the national elections. Realising that the Bible had much to say on public life, the village requested a follow-up Bible study, so Kapi introduced Alpha, having recently bought the Alpha resources from the Koorong chain of Christian bookstores in Australia. The course was run in the Keapara language for 88 people, and then spread to the neighbouring villages of Alukuni and Karawa. Kapi gained further inspiration from a small Alpha training conference he attended at Surfers Paradise on Australia's Gold Coast. He and his wife promoted Alpha across Papua New Guinea, including in the capital Port Moresby, and as founder of the local branch of Prison Fellowship International, he also helped to introduce it to the nation's prisons.[72]

In a mobile global population, Alpha's many translations were often used outside their countries of origin. Sometimes this was due to enforced migration. For example, in Finland, Alpha was run in

Albanian for 40 Muslim refugees from the Balkans who had been granted asylum by the Finnish government after escaping the ethnic cleansing of the Kosovo War.[73] In Egypt, Alpha was run in the early 2000s for the many Sudanese refugees fleeing the civil war in their homeland.[74] During the huge surge of refugees into Europe in 2015–16 from Syria, Iraq and Afghanistan, Alpha was frequently used to reach the new arrivals with the Christian message. In Germany, which welcomed more asylum seekers under Angela Merkel than anywhere else in Europe, over 60 Alpha courses combined German with Arabic or Farsi, thus helping to integrate refugees with local churches.[75] Translations were also embraced in nations with more settled multi-ethnic communities. In New Zealand, for example, Alpha was running in 2007 not only in English, but in Arabic, Chinese (Mandarin and Cantonese), French, Hindi, Japanese, Korean, Portuguese, Spanish and Russian.[76]

Global Alpha Training

Honduras in Central America was devastated in October 1998 by Hurricane Mitch, the deadliest Atlantic hurricane for two centuries, which wreaked havoc, killing 7,000 inhabitants and leaving another 1.5 million homeless. In the wake of this catastrophe, new evangelistic initiatives were born. Eduardo Monzón, a local Episcopalian clergyman and church planter, was praised by *Alpha News* in 1999 for his 'astonishing feat of stamina' in running five Alphas simultaneously, in five different parts of the country. He delivered the Alpha talks in Spanish each week on Tuesday evenings at the Catedral del Buen Pastor (Cathedral of the Good Shepherd) in San Pedro Sula; on Thursday mornings in the small village of Ojo de Agua, in the mountains near the border with Nicaragua; on Thursday evenings in the capital Tegucigalpa; on Friday evenings in Siguatepeque, also in the mountains; and on Saturday afternoons in Puerto Cortés on the Atlantic coast. Monzón covered 5,000 miles on this evangelistic enterprise and spoke in total to 300 people. Many were poor Honduran villagers, who travelled to Alpha with their babies and young children in the back of borrowed pick-up trucks, 12 per vehicle.[77]

Nevertheless, because Monzón focused on delivering Alpha, rather than training others to deliver Alpha, this model exhausted his energies and did not multiply. An alternative approach was advocated from the United States by Christ Church, Kansas City, a suburban Episcopalian congregation that had run Alpha in Missouri since 1997 and experienced considerable growth as a result. In response to Hurricane Mitch, they began humanitarian missions to Honduras, at first sending small teams to Siguatepeque to help rebuild homes, in partnership with the local Episcopalian parish. However, in 2002 the Christ Church rector, Ron McCrary, received 'a prophetic picture from the Lord' during his morning prayers, with an impulse to take Alpha to other churches, even 'to the ends of the earth'. Christ Church received permission from Alpha International in London to 'adopt' Honduras, with authority to multiply Alpha there via annual training conferences.[78]

This localised method of Alpha extension became particularly popular during the early 2000s, as congregations carried Alpha with them on short mission trips, often from Global North to Global South, or from West to East. For example, an Anglican congregation from Duncan, British Columbia, established mission links over a number of years with a small village outside the Mexican city of Tijuana, just south of San Diego. The Canadian visitors built homes for local families, ran Vacation Bible Study programmes for children, and in summer 2000 helped the local church to launch Alpha. On the mission trip they took a television, video player, and the Spanish Alpha video cassettes. One of the Canadian team celebrated: 'Who would have thought that a "Spanish dubbed Nicky Gumbel" would be so powerful in a slum village in Mexico!? Only God!'[79] In Europe, a small group of Christians from Russia, England and the Netherlands combined in 2005 to form the 'Trans-Siberian Alpha Express', an 11-day mission trip, travelling by train across Siberia to lead Alpha conferences in the cities of Omsk, Novosibirsk, Tomsk and Krasnoyarsk.[80] It became an annual event, and in 2009 a regional Alpha office opened in Vladivostok, the terminus of the Trans-Siberian Railway, on the Sea of Japan. When the railway stretched no further, the Alpha team flew by aeroplane to run training events in the cities of Magadan and Petropavlovsk-Kamchatsky, in the very far east of Russia, over 4,000 miles from Moscow.[81]

These sorts of initiatives gave birth to a new multiplication strategy, Global Alpha Training (GAT). For several years, GAT teams were promoted strongly by Alpha International as an ideal way for Christians to enjoy cross-cultural mission while extending Alpha's sphere of influence. They were self-funding and self-organised, creating a global web of inter-church relationships from El Salvador to Ethiopia and Mongolia to Mauritius, though the teams almost all hailed from wealthy nations who could afford the holiday and the international flights.[82] During 2008, 53 GAT teams were deployed across the world, rising to 510 in 2010, with 2,300 planned in 2012, acting as Alpha conduits to new regions.[83] However, indigenisation required local knowledge, not just youthful missionary zeal from Western visitors. In India, which received many GAT teams, it was local Christians who pioneered Alpha among transvestites in Bangalore, in leper colonies in Tamil Nadu, in the slums of Kolkata, and among prostitutes in Kolkata's red-light district.[84] Alpha was also launched in 2010 as part of a 'train ministry' among Kolkata commuters, onboard local trains departing from Sealdah station, the second busiest railway terminal in India. Since the trains took over two hours to reach their destinations, there was plenty of time to run Alpha groups 'on the move'.[85] These innovative enterprises were designed by Indians for Indians. Although GAT teams from the Global North sometimes displayed crass naivety in their cross-cultural missionary tourism, once Alpha was properly indigenised and contextualised by local Christians it had the potential to reach deeply into a culture.

Global Attendances

Alpha International interpreted its continual global expansion theologically, not only as a sign of the generous blessings of God, but as a vindication of their resolution never to hold on tightly to resources for themselves (whether ideas, publications, money, ministry models, or people) but to release them freely to others. Jackie Pullinger from Hong Kong particularly emphasised this spiritual principle of investment, during a global Alpha conference at HTB in 2003:

I believe that one of the reasons that God has so richly blessed Alpha is because Nicky Gumbel and others have always given away what they had. They've not kept it and, I tell you, if they had it would have gone off. With passion they have gone on sharing, gone to new tents, gone to new countries where they are lacking. If you don't keep giving away your surplus, it goes mouldy. That's exactly how Alpha has been blessed. They've blessed and blessed and given away and given away . . . and they haven't run out. They've got more. That's how it works.[86]

Nevertheless, quantifying Alpha's global impact was a complicated task. Christian conversions, however numerous, were often contested and difficult to count. Alpha attendance figures were a safer measurement, though even these proved highly perplexing.

Although Alpha was birthed in London, participation in the rest of the world overtook the United Kingdom within just four years. Attendances in the United Kingdom peaked between 1998 and 2000, coinciding with the early years of the national advertising campaigns, when over 225,000 people attended Alpha for three years in succession. Numbers then fluctuated downwards, perhaps due to market saturation, before peaking again over 200,000 for four years in a row in the early 2010s (see Table 1). Meanwhile in the rest of the globe, the trend was steadily upwards, driven initially by strong growth in the United States, which by 2005 already accounted for a third of Alpha's global market.[87]

To keep track of global growth, Alpha International assiduously collected data from national offices and from 2004 to 2014 employed Christian Research (an independent research organisation led by statistician Peter Brierley) to analyse the annual figures and estimate attendances. It was not a straightforward exercise. Although there were national registers of Alpha churches, in some regions many churches ran Alpha without registering. National attendance was therefore estimated by extrapolating from the probable number of churches, to the probable number of courses, multiplied by the probable average number of participants (including host and helpers, not only Alpha guests). Where no national register existed, attendance was estimated by the sales of Alpha participant manuals, reckoning that for every eight attenders, five manuals were sold in the Global North compared to three manuals in the Global South (where there were higher levels of poverty and illiteracy). Of course, Alpha manuals might be sold in one year but used in the next (or never used at all), or purchased from one country but shipped to another, which could skew the data.[88] There was a myriad of variables in these complex calculations and considerable guesswork.

Numbers were always a key feature in Alpha's publicity and the Christian Research estimates generated impressive headlines in *Alpha News* – for example, that over 1.5 million people attended Alpha across the globe in 2007, and another 2 million people in 2009.[89] A major new driver for this growth appeared to be Asia. In 2011, India claimed 843,000 Alpha participants and South Korea claimed another 399,000, accounting between them for more than half the Alpha participants worldwide. It put those two nations far out in front at the top of the Alpha league tables, outpacing even the United States.[90] Upon closer investigation, however, Alpha International concluded that these estimates were hugely inflated, so they were forced to re-evaluate their published global data and methods of calculation. There were some embarrassing discoveries. For example, Christian Research had estimated 2.8 million Alpha participants in 2012, but Alpha International's recalibrated figure was 1.7 million.[91] The Alpha International statistics department resolved in future to err on the side of caution, only counting registered courses, though the tighter methodology still required high levels of estimation and was never a precise measurement. Furthermore, over-counting continued in the cumulative totals, because the same hosts and helpers often participated year after year so were included multiple times.

With these caveats, Alpha International's recalibrated estimates reveal some significant broad trends. Alpha was reaching over a million participants a year within a decade of its global launch and maintained that level of engagement every year thereafter (see Table 1). Taking a snapshot from 2019 – the last full year before the Covid-19 pandemic – Alpha was running in 114 countries (down from a peak of 169) and attendances were heavily weighted towards a few nations. North America remained the biggest market, encompassing nearly half of Alpha participants worldwide. Four English-speaking countries – the

United States, Canada, the United Kingdom and Australia – accounted for 60 per cent of the global coverage. In Africa, more than half the Alpha participants were in South Africa (see Table 2). Worldwide, more than half the nations with registered courses were small-scale, with fewer than a thousand participants (see Table 3). Despite Alpha's Anglo-American centre of gravity, however, the statistics also reveal strong take-up in parts of South East Asia, Latin America and Europe, such as Malaysia, Colombia, Mexico and Poland. Coverage was uneven, but Alpha by the 2020s had taken root in multiple cultures and languages across the globe.

Time to Accelerate

Although Alpha was numerically successful, Gumbel was never satisfied. By the start of 2008 – fifteen years after its global launch – Alpha had already reached over 10 million people worldwide. But Gumbel announced that it was 'time to accelerate'. His dream was for Alpha to reach a cumulative 100 million people 'at the very minimum' within the next decade. That would require a new strategy for the 2010s. It would need closer partnerships, especially with the Roman Catholic Church, the largest global denomination with one billion members. It would also mean empowering the regions to translate Alpha's suite of resources into every language and innovating with new methods of digital distribution. Gumbel's desire was to see Alpha freely available for download 'at the press of a button on a computer', in every village in the world, in the local language, and he declared this to be Alpha's main strategic priority. 'This is a global vision because our God is a global God', he proclaimed. Yet it also required local initiative: 'We've got to think global, but we've got to act local, act small, one by one, because it's one by one that this world will be changed.'[92]

Gumbel's vision for acceleration encompassed not just millions of individuals converted to Christianity through Alpha, but also the creation of many new vibrant Christian congregations to nurture and disciple them. Since the mid-1980s HTB had been famous as pioneers in church planting, launching approximately 20 congregations across London in 20 years, but Gumbel wanted to see a much faster rate of multiplication, aiming for 20 new churches every year. For this to be possible, there was an urgent need for buildings and leaders, and a vision that stretched beyond the boundaries of the capital. Gumbel declared:

> All we're saying to the Church of England is, 'Please don't close any more churches – please give us those churches and we will plant into them wherever they are, in London, around the country, Newcastle, Chester, Halifax, doesn't matter where, just let us have the churches!'[93]

This vision to resurrect dying churches was initially dubbed 'Project Lazarus'.[94] The diocese of Chichester was the first to rise to the challenge, offering HTB the use of St Peter's, Brighton, a Grade II listed building that could seat 800 but had a congregation of only 20 and was facing closure. Archie Coates (HTB's associate vicar) led a church plant to St Peter's in 2009, with a team of about 80, HTB's first plant outside London.[95] The revitalised congregation then itself planted multiple times in quick succession, within Brighton and also further afield to Hastings, Portsmouth, Crawley and Bognor Regis. As the HTB network accelerated its church planting initiatives during the 2010s and early 2020s, there were soon revitalised Church of England congregations in places such as Birmingham, Blackpool, Bournemouth, Bristol, Coventry, Derby, Exeter, Gateshead, Grimsby, Lincoln, Liverpool, Norwich, Nottingham, Plymouth, Preston, Southampton and Swindon, plus Cardiff and Wrexham in the Church in Wales. Some were in strategic city-centre buildings, others were on neglected urban estates. The Church Revitalisation Trust (CRT) was created in 2017, with Gumbel as chairman, to further catalyse and coordinate this growth. Not everyone welcomed the trend, however, and HTB church plants were often criticised, especially by other churches, for expansionist attitudes, privileged financing, or fundamentalist theologies.[96]

This multiplication strategy also required a ready supply of ordained leaders, schooled in the Alpha ethos. Many trained through St Mellitus College, or joined HTB's large group of curates, before being deployed across the country. CRT pioneered new models of training, in partnership with St Mellitus, seeking to diversify the talent pool. The Peter Stream (launched in 2018) encouraged people from less advantaged social or educational backgrounds to pursue ordination, and the Caleb Stream (launched in 2021) trained older leaders, aged over 55, to revitalise rural parishes.[97] CRT's Accelerator Programme, a one-year intensive for church-planting curates, was another fruitful initiative. By 2022, the HTB network encompassed over 100 congregations plus 30 larger resource churches, embedding Alpha principles throughout the Church of England. Yet the network also had global aspirations. HTB's first church plant beyond British shores was Holy Trinity Bukit Bintang (HTBB), located in a fashionable retail district of Kuala Lumpur, Malaysia, launched in 2014 by HTB's associate vicar Miles Toulmin. Its weekly congregation grew from 20 to 2,000 within five years and it became a key hub for Alpha in the Asia-Pacific region.[98] Also part of the network were Vintage Church in Los Angeles, St Jax Church in Montreal, and Renewal Church in Nairobi, all planted by clergy who had close connections with HTB and boosted Alpha in their cities.

Another way in which Gumbel promoted Christian nurture, and reached a growing global audience, was through the 'Bible in One Year' project. He himself came to Christian faith through encountering the New Testament, and every year afterwards he endeavoured to read the whole Bible from cover to cover. 'Reading the Bible is not an academic exercise', Gumbel observed, 'but the expression of a relationship. Faith is about putting our trust in the God who speaks to us through his Word. God has revealed himself in the Bible.'[99] In *Questions of Life*, he described Scripture as 'a love letter from God' – authoritative, reliable, powerful, and without error. 'Scripture is God speaking', he explained.[100] The Bible was therefore essential to healthy Christianity:

> If we stay close to Jesus Christ through his word, we will not dry up or lose our spiritual vitality. It is not enough to have great spiritual experiences, although they are very important and very wonderful. Unless we are deeply rooted in Jesus Christ, in his word and in that relationship with him, we won't be able to withstand the storms of life.[101]

One of Gumbel's chief strategies in nurturing new Christians was to help them develop daily patterns of Bible reading. The Alpha resource,

30 Days: A Practical Introduction to Reading the Bible (1999), was his first foray into scriptural commentary, enough for one month.

As a young curate, Gumbel was an early adopter of *The Bible in One Year* (1988), published by Hodder & Stoughton and given to him as a Christmas present by Sandy Millar in 1990.[102] It subdivided the whole Bible into 365 readings, with a portion from the Old Testament, New Testament, and Psalms or Proverbs every day. This became Gumbel's Bible of choice for his personal devotions, and in January 2009 he launched the 'Bible in One Year Challenge' for the HTB congregation. The aim was to stimulate regular Bible study, and to build congregational unity, by all reading the same passages every day alongside Gumbel's emailed commentary. Initially 1,400 people signed up for the experiment, and it was soon broadened to the worldwide Alpha community by posting the commentary online.[103] By 2011 there were 9,200 subscribers and Hodder & Stoughton published a branded Alpha version of *The Bible in One Year*, with the Alpha logo on the front cover and an introduction by Gumbel.[104] He especially recommended it to Alpha graduates, so that by reading together *The Bible in One Year*, they could continue to discuss biblical themes with their Alpha friends after the course had ended.[105]

As this Scripture project gathered momentum, it was launched as a digital app in 2015, with audio commentary from Gumbel added the following year. There was also a published volume from Hodder & Stoughton, for those who preferred books to apps, plus digital 'Youth' and 'Express' versions. In 2021, 493,000 people downloaded the Bible in One Year app (with an average 40,000 users each day, across the year), 28,000 subscribed to the daily email, and another 1.1 million people subscribed to the plan via YouVersion (an online Bible platform). This brought Gumbel's Bible teaching, which often included anecdotes and testimonies from Alpha, to a new global audience. By 2022 the commentary was available in nine languages – Arabic, Chinese, English, French, German, Hindi, Indonesian, Spanish and Thai – with plans for further translations into Czech, Danish, Finnish, Italian, Polish and Swedish.[106] This enterprise was another example of Gumbel's, and Alpha's, appetite to embrace a global vision.

The Digital Revolution

Gumbel's ambition for Alpha acceleration into the 2010s and 2020s required new digital technologies and an entire refreshing of the brand. One of Alpha's foundational principles was that although the content of the Christian gospel never changes, the packaging must continually change in order to remain attractive to contemporary culture. Yet by 2013, Alpha's packaging was already two decades old and looking tired. Gumbel therefore asked 35-year-old Al Gordon (later rector of Hackney) to head up a new initiative called 'Alpha Innovation', seeking to bring fresh vitality and energy to the long-established product.

After graduating from the University of Edinburgh in 2000, Gordon had served a six-month internship with the HTB worship department, before moving into the British film industry as a script editor and talent agent. In 2005 he returned to the HTB staff full-time, and the following year launched Worship Central with fellow musician Tim Hughes. They toured the world, training worship leaders and playing concerts for thousands of Christian young people. Gordon had creative talent and a long track-record for urging HTB to think outside the box. The first focus of his Alpha Innovation team was to reconnect the Alpha brand with contemporary youth culture and thus reclaim its primary target audience. Gordon observed:

> Alpha is aimed at a 24-year-old urban male Christian leader and his non-Christian friend. This is the hardest demographic to reach, and it is also the most digitally connected tribe – and it is the same tribe all over the world, in Canada or the US or Bombay or Africa. It is not that Alpha doesn't want to reach 78-year-old rural women, but the way to do so is to reach the 24-year-old urban male.[107]

For branding advice, Alpha approached Wolff Olins, a leading creative consultancy that had designed the controversial logo for the London 2012 Olympics. Wolff Olins would have been far beyond Alpha's price bracket, but a junior employee happened to be a member at St Paul's, Onslow Square, and connected Gordon with the head of the London office, Ije Nwokorie (CEO of Wolff Olins worldwide from 2014). Nwokorie, a Christian, took a particular interest in the Alpha project and gathered a small team to work on it in their spare time.[108]

This creative exercise led to two significant branding changes. First, the 'Alpha Course' was rebranded simply as 'Alpha'. In earlier years, the idea of joining a course was part of Alpha's attraction. 'People like the idea of going on a course', Mark Elsdon-Dew suggested in 2000. 'Whether it's yoga, cookery or Christianity.'[109] But the cultural mood soon shifted. 'Young people don't want to sign up for a course', Gordon declared in 2015, 'it makes them think of tuition fees and a £20k debt.'[110] Second, the famous Alpha logo – Charlie Mackesy's cartoon man carrying a question mark – was dropped. It was created in the early 1990s and had served well for two decades, but a cartoon sketch seemed out of step with the new digital age, and the image of a white man was not appropriate for a global product. Therefore the new Alpha logo was a simple red question mark. Nwokorie explained that in the world of competitive brands, a logo suggesting uncertainty was normally off-limits, but by reducing Alpha to its essence (exploring life's big questions), the question mark was 'incredibly powerful and unique'.[111]

Alpha Innovation generated abundant ideas, some of which were short-lived. For example, there was a brief experiment called 'Alpha Labs', a move away from old-style Alpha training events towards relational hubs. The idea was for young Alpha pioneers to meet together every six months in a regional Alpha Lab, for specialist coaching and the mutual sharing of wisdom – pitched as 'a community of innovation, strategy and encouragement'. Alpha Labs would 'inspire a new generation of leaders to see Alpha as relevant to their own communities and workplaces', leading to 'an exponential rise' in the number of young people coming to Christian faith, but the project failed to fly.[112] Another brief experiment from 2014 was Alpha TV, using internet technology to stream HTB's Alpha talks live each week from London to the rest of the world. Friends in any nation could gather for a meal, tune in, and discuss.[113] Rejuvenation sometimes required cancellation. The plug was pulled on the old tabloid newspaper, *Alpha News*, after two decades of long service and 53 issues, replaced from

2013 to 2016 by *Alpha Life*, a high-end, artistic, annual magazine. This change of format was in keeping with Alpha Innovation's shift towards 'uber-cool' branding, but one dimension that remained constant was the prominent use of Alpha testimonies. *Alpha Life* carried stories from Argentina, Brazil, Egypt, Hong Kong, Kenya, the Netherlands, the Philippines, Rwanda, Sicily, Trinidad and Tobago, and elsewhere. Alpha was running, for example, among the homeless on the streets of Kuala Lumpur, among Indigenous communities in the Australian outback, and among Greek Catholics in the Beqaa Valley in Lebanon.[114] Testimonies of lives changed across the globe remained a consistent feature of Alpha's publicity from the 1990s to the 2020s, although instead of being recorded by Dictaphone and typed up for the newspaper they were now often filmed by iPhone and posted on social media.

Alpha's core product also needed significant rejuvenation. Gumbel's Alpha talks had travelled the world first as audio cassettes, then videos, then DVDs, but in an age of multimedia his monologues no longer appealed to a young audience. To bridge this widening cultural gap, two Canadian youth workers, Jason Ballard and Ben Woodman, experimented in 2013 by re-filming Alpha in fast-moving, often comic, segments, to reach a new generation of teenagers.[115] The Alpha Youth Film Series was so popular that by 2016 it had spread beyond Canada to 49 countries in 19 languages. It was refreshed and relaunched the following year, with new animations and testimonies from across the world, aiming to be 'a truly global resource . . . more global, more diverse and more relevant than ever'.[116] Unlike Gumbel's set-piece talks to camera, this multimedia format had the potential to embrace diverse voices. For example, the Alpha Africa team re-filmed the 'vox pop' interviews on the streets of Nairobi, Lagos and Johannesburg to contextualise the series for Africa's urban youth.[117]

Alpha Innovation built on this concept for the Alpha Film Series, shot on location around the globe and launched in April 2016. Each session was less than 30 minutes, constantly dynamic, with multiple voices and creative visuals, presented by Gemma Hunt (a children's television presenter with CBBC and CBeebies) and Toby Flint (one of HTB's curates). Filming took place from the mountains of Vancouver to the beaches of Normandy and the desert of Judea, via the bustling streets of Hong Kong, New York, Paris and London. There were numerous testimonies and interviews, from personalities such as hip hop artist Propaganda, geneticist Francis Collins, sportsman Ugo Monye, and theologian Raniero Cantalamessa, alongside regular 'vox pop' segments. However, careful continuity was maintained with classic Alpha because Gumbel still presented the bulk of the teaching, sometimes on vintage footage cut from the original 1990s Alpha videos. Gordon (the project's executive producer) described it as 'a documentary for the soul' and explained: 'We wanted to take Alpha completely apart and rebuild it for the next generation.'[118]

By the end of 2017, the Alpha Film Series was translated into 26 languages (via dubbing and subtitles), including Mandarin, Hindi, Spanish and Arabic, the four most widely spoken global languages after English, with plans for many more.[119] As with earlier Alpha products, these translations had potential usages in multiple contexts, among mobile global populations. For example, in 2018, the first African translation of the Alpha Film Series was into Amharic, one of the official languages of Ethiopia, which enabled its use not only in that nation but also among the Ethiopian diasporic communities in Dubai, Sweden, Luxembourg and the United States.[120] By 2022, the series was available in 53 languages and plans were at an advanced stage for new regionally contextualised editions. Alpha's global translation strategy was called 'Project Pentecost', because on the original Day of Pentecost, according to the Acts of the Apostles, the Holy Spirit enabled people from all over the world to hear the Christian message in their own tongues.[121]

It was not only Alpha's content that needed reimagining, but also its global dissemination. Alpha and the internet were both born in the same era, in the early 1990s, but by the 2010s Alpha had fallen significantly behind the digital curve. New technologies transformed evangelistic possibilities. Alpha International took the strategic decision to make the Alpha Film Series available online, for everyone, for free. It was no longer necessary to purchase an expensive DVD box set to run Alpha. The material was now more attractive, accessible and affordable than ever before. It could be downloaded on to a mobile device anywhere on the planet. 'That's an awesome thought', Gordon celebrated, 'most of the world one click away from exploring the meaning of life.'[122] This digital revolution also generated new possibilities for reconceiving the Alpha community, especially the discussion group. For example, in 2014 five friends met weekly on Google Hangouts to discuss the Alpha material, though they were scattered across the globe in San Francisco, Hong Kong, Thailand, Switzerland and India.[123]

When the Covid-19 pandemic led to widespread global shutdowns in 2020, Alpha's digital resources allowed it to pivot quickly to meet the new situation. There were 40,000 courses across the globe that year, almost 15,000 of them online.[124] Gumbel was initially reluctant, because offering personal hospitality, building close friendships and sharing food were key parts of the Alpha brand. 'But I have been proved wrong', he confessed. 'Alpha works *far better* online than we ever believed possible, not least because of the simple convenience of engaging from home.'[125] In the United Kingdom, Alpha attendance jumped by 81 per cent from 117,000 in 2019 to 212,000 in 2020, while in the United States it rose 35 per cent in the same period, from 426,000 to 575,000 participants.[126] This unexpected growth was due to a multiplicity of factors. During lockdown many people had extra time on their hands, without competing commitments, and had the mental space to explore Christianity. Alpha Online typically lasted only an hour, without the additional time required to travel to a physical venue and share dinner beforehand. Busy parents did not need to find babysitters, and those housebound by illness or disability could also access the course. It was easier to invite friends and family, especially those living at a distance, who could meet at the same Alpha event from anywhere in the world, via their laptops. Alternatively, those who felt isolated from friends and family by the lockdowns were offered an instant new community at Alpha Online. Furthermore, Gumbel acknowledged, many people preferred to explore Christianity 'anonymously' and online engagement enabled them to do so without the barrier of crossing the threshold of a church.[127] There were also reports from some parts of the world of Muslims logging into Alpha, who would not have been free to attend a course in person.[128] The global pandemic, with high death rates in many countries, may also have provoked spiritual anxieties and a search for meaning.[129]

Alpha's other digital products showed a similar uptick in attendance. The Marriage Course and Pre-Marriage Course were relaunched as film series in January 2020, shortly before the pandemic took hold, which proved to be fortuitous timing. There was a massive surge in online take-up during the lockdowns. During 2020, there were over 6,000 Marriage and Pre-Marriage Courses running in 90 countries, with over 100,000 participants.[130] At HTB alone, more than 5,500 couples attended the courses that year, smashing previous records.[131] Accessibility and anonymity were key attractions.

Not only were pandemic numbers up, but Alpha Online enabled new depths of relationship. This appeared counterintuitive, in a famously impersonal medium, with participants separated from each other by computer screens. Nevertheless, Alpha International observed that guests often seemed more open and relaxed, and quicker to 'let their guard down' because they were attending from the security of their own homes.[132] There was a lower drop-out rate than usual, and Gumbel noticed deeper levels of personal vulnerability and engagement in the small groups. At Alpha Online, he concluded, 'the conversation on week 2 is like what it would normally be on week 6'.[133] There were also higher levels of attendance at online Holy Spirit weekends. 'What happened was extraordinary', announced Alpha International: 'as Alpha weekends ran online, we began to hear stories of people being filled with the Holy Spirit by themselves in their living rooms or in their bedrooms. People were moved to tears just on a laptop, responding to a prayer online of "Come Holy Spirit".'[134] 'The Holy Spirit is not confused by Zoom,' Gumbel celebrated, 'he still works powerfully remotely and at a distance! People have been healed, found faith and been filled with the Spirit at their kitchen tables.'[135]

Gumbel likened this modern 'digital revolution' to a previous leap forward in global communications, the invention of movable-type printing presses that were utilised by sixteenth-century Reformers like Martin Luther to disseminate biblical Christianity far and wide. Some were prophesying that the pandemic would be a catalyst for accelerated decline in church attendance, but Gumbel proclaimed at the HTB Leadership Conference in May 2021 that, on the contrary, it was 'the greatest moment of opportunity for acceleration in the growth of the church for over 500 years'. Digital technologies enabled 'everyone on the planet to hear the good news about Jesus' for the first time. 'This really is the greatest opportunity of our lifetime', he rejoiced.[136]

'Out of the tragedy of 2020', Alpha International suggested, 'something exciting has begun. A new digital wave of evangelisation has been set in motion that has the potential to see the spread of the gospel beyond anything we've seen before.'[137] In India, for example, the Alpha national office was able to reach remote rural communities with digital Alpha, beyond their normal range of influence, using the comparatively slow 2G mobile network.[138] In Kenya, when secondary schools were shut by the pandemic, 208 churches launched an 'Alpha Youth Marathon', using the Alpha Youth Film Series to reach 2,600 young people.[139] In Latin America, a social media campaign ran with the Spanish and Portuguese hashtags #AlphaEnCasa and #AlphaEmCasa ('Alpha at Home').[140] In Britain, the advertising slogan was 'Pause Netflix, Try Alpha.' In some regions, this digital revolution was hindered by high data costs and poor connectivity, but in Venezuela, where the internet was notoriously unreliable, one pastor's solution was to deliver Alpha USB sticks by bicycle.[141] Local Alpha advocates were forced to innovate and adapt like never before. Many ran Alpha on Zoom, while others watched the Alpha Film Series on YouTube and then met for small-group discussion on Facebook or WhatsApp.[142] In 2022, Alpha International launched AlphaNow, a custom-built video-conferencing platform, to enable smoother running of Alpha Online via laptops, tablets and mobile phones anywhere in the world. The future was ripe with digital possibilities. 'From now on', Gumbel declared, 'our church will always offer Alpha online, even when we are back running physical courses.'[143] Much of this technology had been available for several years, but it took a pandemic to jolt Alpha into properly recognising the potential of online platforms for reaching new global audiences.

A New Chapter

Nicky Gumbel's retirement from the leadership of HTB in 2022, aged 67, marks a major moment of transition and the opening of the next, unwritten, chapter in Alpha's story. Always looking for new and creative ways to propagate the Christian gospel, Gumbel's energies have already begun to turn to the evangelistic potential of the year 2033, to be celebrated by churches worldwide as the 2000th anniversary of the Resurrection of Jesus Christ, and how Alpha can help to maximise the anniversary's impact. By 2033, Alpha itself will have been a significant player in the global Christian marketplace for four decades, if it continues to innovate, a story yet to be told.

Innovation and cultural adaptability are built into Alpha's DNA, one of the chief reasons for its longevity and influence. Since the publication of *Questions of Life* and the launch of Alpha in 1993, the movement has evolved from 'supper party evangelism' in the Kensington suburbs into a global brand of Christian outreach, contextualised into multiple cultures and languages across the planet. The teaching itself has matured, after the heady days of the Toronto Blessing, adopting a more profound commitment to social transformation and a deeper ecumenical spirit. Although born in English Anglicanism, Alpha now embraces every part of the global church from Peruvian Pentecostals to Japanese Catholics, and from Bulgarian Orthodox to Zambian Brethren. It has been pioneered in multiple contexts from prisons in Papua New Guinea to schools in Ghana, and from villages in Nicaragua to executive boardrooms in Hong Kong. From the original audio and video cassettes, via marketing billboards and television broadcasts, Alpha has joined the multimedia and digital revolutions. Instead of flyers and flags, it is now promoted globally via Instagram and Twitter. Yet at its core, Alpha remains the same: an opportunity to explore Christianity, repackaged in a convivial, informal, experiential environment. Over a million people attend Alpha every year and it is securely rooted in manifold contexts in every region of the globe, well placed in the 2020s to reach new generations, in new ways, with the message of Jesus Christ.

Tables

Table 1: Global Estimates of Alpha Participants, 1993–2021
Information from Alpha International, rounded to nearest 1,000

Year	United Kingdom	Rest of the World	Annual Total
1993/4	25,000	—	25,000
1995	67,000	13,000	80,000
1996	129,000	126,000	255,000
1997	181,000	225,000	406,000
1998	228,000	319,000	547,000
1999	253,000	440,000	693,000
2000	238,000	583,000	821,000
2001	190,000	733,000	923,000
2002	153,000	758,000	911,000
2003	147,000	886,000	1,033,000
2004	175,000	918,000	1,093,000
2005	182,000	949,000	1,131,000
2006	168,000	1,138,000	1,306,000
2007	192,000	1,182,000	1,374,000
2008	186,000	1,153,000	1,339,000
2009	183,000	1,231,000	1,414,000
2010	188,000	943,000	1,131,000
2011	203,000	1,062,000	1,265,000
2012	204,000	1,504,000	1,708,000
2013	244,000	1,456,000	1,700,000
2014	258,000	971,000	1,229,000
2015	186,000	1,121,000	1,307,000
2016	186,000	1,007,000	1,193,000

2017	146,000	987,000	1,133,000
2018	118,000	1,032,000	1,150,000
2019	117,000	1,075,000	1,192,000
2020	212,000	1,171,000	1,383,000
2021	128,000	977,000	1,105,000
Total	**4,887,000**	**23,960,000**	**28,847,000**

Table 2: Regional Estimates of Alpha Participants, 2019
Information from Alpha International, rounded to nearest 100

Region	Estimated Participants	Global Proportion
United Kingdom	117,400	10%
North America	547,700	46%
United States	*426,200*	
Canada	*121,500*	
Latin America	106,600	9%
Colombia	*30,100*	
Mexico	*23,900*	
Brazil	*14,400*	
Argentina	*13,000*	
Costa Rica	*8,800*	
Asia Pacific	190,400	16%
Australia	*49,500*	
Malaysia	*28,000*	
South Korea	*22,900*	
Philippines	*6,400*	
New Zealand	*6,300*	
Europe, Middle East and North Africa	178,000	15%
France	*35,000*	
Poland	*31,700*	
Netherlands	*18,100*	
Germany	*17,300*	
Sweden	*12,500*	

Africa	52,200	4%
South Africa	27,700	
Uganda	6,200	
Kenya	6,100	
Zambia	3,200	
Nigeria	3,000	

Table 3: National Distribution of Alpha Participants, 2019
Information from Alpha International

Estimated Participants	Number of Countries
Over 125,000	1
100,000–124,999	2
50,000–99,999	0
35,000–49,999	1
30,000–34,999	3
25,000–29,999	2
20,000–24,999	2
15,000–19,999	5
10,000–14,999	5
5,000–9,999	7
1,000–4,999	27
Fewer than 1,000	59

Notes

Acknowledgements

1. Stephen Hunt, *The Alpha Enterprise: Evangelism in a Post-Christian Era* (Aldershot: Ashgate, 2004); Andrew Brookes (ed.), *The Alpha Phenomenon: Theology, Praxis and Challenges for Mission and Church Today* (London: Churches Together in Britain and Ireland, 2007); James Heard, *Inside Alpha: Explorations in Evangelism* (Milton Keynes: Paternoster, 2009); Stephen Brian, *Assessing Alpha: Does the Alpha Course Explore the Meaning of Life?* (Chisinau, Moldova: Lambert Academic Publishing, 2010).

2. *Alpha News* ran for 53 issues between 1993 and 2011. HTB's monthly newspaper ran for 234 issues, under several titles: *HTB in Focus* (1992–5), *Focus* (1995–2006), and *HTB News* (2007–11). *Focus* should not be confused with *UK Focus* (1996–2011), a monthly *Alpha News* supplement.

Chapter One: Rebirth and Renewal

1. 'Did you know?', *Brompton Magazine* (June 1981), 9, Kensington Central Library.

2. John Morris, 'The vicar's letter', *Brompton Broadsheet* (October 1975), Kensington Central Library.

3. Charles Patterson, 'The healing ministry at Holy Trinity', *Brompton Broadsheet* (February 1976).

4. 'The church's ministry of healing', *Brompton Broadsheet* (June 1969); *Brompton Broadsheet* (July/August 1972; May 1973; January 1974).

5. *Brompton Broadsheet* (May 1970; May and September 1971; March 1973; October 1975).

6. Rodney Radcliffe, 'A church on fire!', *Brompton Broadsheet* (May 1975).

7. Rodney Radcliffe, 'An eventful trip to the USA', *Brompton Broadsheet* (February 1975).

8. Jenny Cooke, *Upon This Rock: The Story of Nicholas Rivett-Carnac and St Mark's Church, Kennington* (London: Hodder & Stoughton, 1989).

9. 'One of the kindest men you could hope to meet', *Focus* 149 (June 2004), 5; the words of Sandy Millar from Rivett-Carnac's memorial service.

10. Details in this section are taken, unless stated, from Sandy Millar's interviews with Mark Elsdon-Dew (8 January 2014, transcript) and Andrew Atherstone (19 May 2020).

11. Sandy Millar, 'Best of times, worst of times', *Sunday Times Magazine* (24 March 2002), 11–12. See also, Christian Tyler, 'The vicar with a flock in a frenzy', *Financial Times* (3–4 June 1995), FT Weekend, 24.

12. Sandy Millar, 'Tough questions in the rush hour', *HTB in Focus* 37 (March 1995), 10.

13. Sandy Millar, *All I Want Is You: A Collection of Christian Reflections* (London: Alpha International, 2005), 30.

14. Millar, *All I Want Is You*, 36–8.

15. Nicholas Rivett-Carnac, 'Love and humour', in 'Jean Darnall's 25 years of ministry in Britain: her friends pay tribute', *Renewal* 186 (November 1991), 15.

16. *You'll Go to London: The Autobiography of Lionel Ball* (Fearn, Ross-shire: Christian Focus, 2008), 70–83.

17. Rivett-Carnac, 'Love and humour'.

18. Sandy Millar, 'Foreword', in *You'll Go to London*, 7–9.

19. Larry Eskridge, *God's Forever Family: The Jesus People Movement in America* (New York: Oxford University Press, 2013), 202–5.

20. 'Christ is alive in London', *Church of England Newspaper* (8 September 1972), 3, 16.

21. Circular by Mark Brooke, Mickie Calthorpe, Melinda Dewar (later Marchioness of Reading), Sarah Dulley, Phil Lawson-Johnston, Annie Rice and Ann Sargent (January 1974), John Reynolds papers (in possession of Andrew Atherstone).

22. 'The Calthorpes and Birmingham', in David Cannadine, *Lords and Landlords: The Aristocracy and the Towns, 1774–1967* (Leicester: Leicester University Press, 1980), 79–225.

23. Circular by Mark Brooke et al. (signed by Calthorpe).

24. Mickie Calthorpe, 'Kitchen aspects', Stewards' Trust newsletter (30 October 1975); Kitty Tilea, 'Kitchen aspects', Stewards' Trust newsletter (25 February 1976), John Reynolds papers.

25. Stewards' Trust steering committee minutes, 3 October 1974, John Reynolds papers.

26. Stewards' Trust annual report 1974–5, John Reynolds papers.

27. Circular by Mark Brooke et al.

28. 'Every Cloud has a singer lining', *Meeting Point: St Paul's Magazine* (April 1977), 2, 10, Kensington Central Library; Philip Lawson-Johnston, *The Song of the Father's Heart* (Bradford on Avon: Terra Nova Publications, 2004), 29–31.

29. Lawson-Johnston, *The Song of the Father's Heart*, 22–4.

30. Lawson-Johnston, *The Song of the Father's Heart*, 25.

31. Interview with Chuck and Carol Butler, 1 June 2020. With his next Californian band, Parable, Chuck Butler wrote a song entitled '16 Petersham Place', about the Kitchen, for their album *More Than Words* (1975).

32. Philip Lawson-Johnston, 'Power in praise: worship, "Cloud", and the Bible', in Robin Sheldon (ed.), *In Spirit and Truth: Exploring Directions in Music in Worship Today* (London: Hodder & Stoughton, 1989), 168.

33. 'Lord Luke: Greenbelt's genial host', *Crusade* 26 (September 1980), 38–40.

34. Stewards' Trust newsletter (16 December 1975), John Reynolds papers.

35. Stewards' Trust steering committee minutes, 12 February 1975, John Reynolds papers.

36. St Paul's, Onslow Square, PCC Minutes, 10 October 1971, London Metropolitan Archives [LMA], P84/PAU/088.

37. St Paul's, Knightsbridge, baptism register (1955–86), entry for 11 February 1956.

38. Arthur D. Brenner, *Emil J. Gumbel: Weimar German Pacifist and Professor* (Leiden: Brill, 2001).

39. For the Gumbel family context, see for example: Ruth Gledhill, 'The magnet of Alpha', *The Tablet* (27 June 1998), 840; Gyles Brandreth, 'The prime minister', *Sunday Telegraph* (29 July 2001), Review, 2; Jonathan Aitken, *Heroes and Contemporaries* (London: Continuum, 2006), 224–5.

40. Nicky Gumbel, 'Profile', *Brompton Magazine* (March 1981), 6.

41. John Capon, 'The lawyer who lost his case against Christ', *Baptist Times* (19 May 1994), 8.

42. Nicky Gumbel, *Questions of Life* (Eastbourne: Kingsway, 1993, revised 2010), 21; interview with Nicky and Pippa Gumbel, 3 March 3021.

43. Mark Elsdon-Dew, 'The vision and the power for God's purpose', *Renewal* 218 (July 1994), 14.

44. Nicky Gumbel, *Questions of Life*, 69.

45. Gumbel, 'Profile', 6.

46. Interview with Nicky and Sila Lee, 22 April 2021.

47. Nicky Lee and Sila Lee, 'A love story (with God in the middle)', *UK Focus* (October 1997), 4.

48. Lee and Lee, 'A love story', 4, 7.

49. Interview with Nicky and Sila Lee, 22 April 2021.

50. Information from David MacInnes, February 2021.

51. Nicky Lee and Sila Lee, *The Marriage Book* (London: Alpha International, 2000), 7.

52. Lee and Lee, 'A love story', 7.

53. Elsdon-Dew, 'The vision and the power', 14.

54. Gumbel, *Questions of Life*, 70.

55. Interview with Nicky and Pippa Gumbel, 3 March 2021.

56. Elsdon-Dew, 'The vision and the power', 15.

57. Gumbel, 'Profile', 6.

58. Lee and Lee, 'A love story', 1, 4–7.

59. Aitken, *Heroes and Contemporaries*, 227.

60. Charles Moore, 'Why it needs an Alpha male to save the Church of England', *Daily Telegraph* (10 November 2012), 28.

61. Gumbel, *Questions of Life*, 185–6.

62. Interview with Nicky and Pippa Gumbel, 3 March 2021.

63. Interview with Henry Montgomery, 17 January 2022; Nicky Gumbel, *A Life Worth Living* (Eastbourne: Kingsway, 1994), 18–19.

64. Gumbel, *Questions of Life*, 193.

65. Michael Skapinker, 'Alpha male', *Financial Times Magazine* (2–3 February 2008), 12–13.

66. Caroline Merrell, 'The banker who does business by the Good Book', *The Times* (16 October 2004), 58.

67. Ken Costa, 'Portrait of the pastor as a young man', *Brompton Magazine* (November 1980), 3–4.

68. Ken Costa, *God at Work: Living Every Day With Purpose* (London: Continuum, 2007), 1–3.

69. Andrew Atherstone, *Archbishop Justin Welby: Risk-taker and Reconciler* (London: Darton, Longman and Todd, 2014), 30–2.

70. John Eddison (ed.), *Bash: A Study in Spiritual Power* (Basingstoke: Marshall, Morgan and Scott, 1983).

71. Gumbel, *A Life Worth Living*, 97.

72. Gumbel, *Questions of Life*, 144.

73. Nicky Gumbel, *The Jesus Lifestyle* (London: Alpha International, 2010), 18.

74. Ian Randall, 'Charismatic renewal in Cambridge from the 1960s to the 1980s', in Andrew Atherstone, Mark Hutchinson and John Maiden (eds), *Transatlantic Charismatic Renewal, c.1950–2000* (Leiden: Brill, 2021), 134–8.

75. Atherstone, *Archbishop Justin Welby*, 36–7.

76. 'The way we have come, 1829–1979', *Brompton Magazine* (June 1979), 6.

77. Church Commissioners Board of Governors, Pastoral Measure 1968, St Paul's Onslow Square / HTB, report of the Pastoral Committee (14 June 1978), Lambeth Palace Library [LPL], RC 23/330.

78. Raymond Turvey, 'The vicar's letter', *Brompton Broadsheet* (June 1976).

79. 'St Paul, Onslow Square SW7: report on the fabric of the church' (February 1973), LPL, Advisory Board of Redundant Churches, ABRC/2/1239.

80. Letter from Raymond Turvey, *Meeting Point* (August/September 1975).

81. 'And the next item is . . .', *Meeting Point* (February 1974).

82. Letter from Raymond Turvey, *Meeting Point* (August/September 1975).

83. Dorothy Stroud to Desmond Mandeville (Council for the Care of Churches), 22 May 1974, LPL, CARE 23/530.

84. Robert Swan to Sir John Betjeman, 14 March 1974, LPL, CARE 23/530.

85. John Morris, 'The vicar's letter', *Brompton Broadsheet* (September 1975).

86. *Deployment of the Clergy: The Report of the House of Bishops' Working Group* (London: Church Information Office, 1974), GS205.

87. Raymond Turvey, 'The vicar's letter', *Brompton Broadsheet* (September 1976).

88. Interview with Phil Lawson-Johnston, 18 January 2019.

89. Letter from Raymond Turvey, *Meeting Point* (July 1976).

90. 'Cross-Pew', *Meeting Point* (July 1977), 10.

91. 'A time to dance', *Brompton Magazine* (January 1979), 3; Anne Atkins, 'Acting in the aisle', *Brompton Magazine* (April 1979), 3; Carolyn Richardson, 'The experience of worship at HTB', *Renewal* 116 (April/May 1985), 12–15.

92. Raymond Turvey, 'Sizing it all up', *Meeting Point* (November 1976), 8.

93. Turvey, 'Sizing it all up'.

94. Details in this and the following paragraphs are largely drawn from Charles and Tricia Marnham's interview with Mark Elsdon-Dew (January 2014, transcript).

95. Charles Marnham to Andrew Atherstone, 29 May 2020.

96. 'The Alpha Group' (3 November–8 December 1977), Charles and Tricia Marnham papers.

97. 'The Alpha Group' (18 May–22 June 1978), Alpha International Archives.

98. Letter from Raymond Turvey, *Brompton Magazine* (October 1978), 1.

99. 'The Alpha Group' (5 June–10 July 1980), Alpha International Archives.

100. Richard Kirby to Tricia Marnham, 20 January 2021.

101. Elsdon-Dew interview with Charles and Tricia Marnham, January 2014.

102. Letter from Raymond Turvey, *Brompton Magazine* (May 1979), 1.

103. HTB PCC minutes, 14 February 1979.

104. Raymond Turvey to Nick McKinnel, May 1979, Nick McKinnel papers.

105. Letter from Raymond Turvey, *Brompton Magazine* (July/August 1979), 1–2.

106. Letter from Raymond Turvey, *Brompton Magazine* (November 1979), 1.

107. Turvey to McKinnel, 31 October 1979, Nick McKinnel papers.

108. Letter from Raymond Turvey, *Brompton Magazine* (December 1979), 1.

109. Steve Williams, 'Who cares for who?', *Brompton Magazine* (March 1980), 3.

110. Patrick Whitworth, 'To London with Love', *Brompton Magazine* (March 1980), 6.

111. Patrick Whitworth, 'To London with Love', *Brompton Magazine* (April 1980), 8.

112. HTB PCC minutes, 12 December 1979.

113. Peregrine Worsthorne, 'When free men should bow to God', *Sunday Telegraph* (25 May 1980), 16.

114. 'To London with Love: A report for the Chelsea Council of Churches' (June 1980), with HTB PCC minutes.

115. HTB PCC minutes, 11 June 1980.

116. Letter from Sandy Millar, *Brompton Magazine* (September 1980), 1.

117. Letter from Raymond Turvey, *Brompton Magazine* (February 1980), 1.

118. Letter from Sandy Millar, *Brompton Magazine* (September 1980), 1.

119. HTB PCC minutes, 10 October 1979.

120. Charlie Colchester and David Orton, 'Presentation' (7 November 1979), with HTB PCC minutes.

121. HTB PCC minutes, 14 November 1979.

122. David Sheppard, *Steps Along Hope Street: My Life in Cricket, the Church and the Inner City* (London: Hodder & Stoughton, 2002), 21–5; Andrew Bradstock, *David Sheppard: Batting for the Poor* (London: SPCK, 2019), 42–7; David Watson, *You are My God* (London: Hodder & Stoughton, 1983), 17–23.

123. Peter Hocken, *Streams of Renewal: The Origins and Early Development of the Charismatic Movement in Great Britain* (Exeter: Paternoster, 1986), 99–103; Ian Savile, 'Canford Magna parish church', in Eddie Gibbs (ed.), *Ten Growing Churches* (London: MARC Europe, 1984), 173–87.

124. Ken Stewart, 'A local look', *Brompton Magazine* (June 1982), 6.

125. HTB PCC minutes, 13 February 1980.

126. Letter from John Collins, *Brompton Magazine* (March 1982), 1.

127. Letter from John Collins, *Brompton Magazine* (January 1982), 1.

128. Letter from John Collins, *Brompton Magazine* (December 1980), 1; Ken Stewart, 'Report on AGM', *Brompton Magazine* (June 1983), 2.

129. Helen Perrott, 'HTB – is there life over 40?', *Brompton Magazine* (January 1983), 10.

130. Letter from John Collins, *Brompton Magazine* (November 1981), 1.

131. Letter from John Collins, *Brompton Magazine* (November 1982), 1.

132. Patrick Whitworth, 'Lighthouse', *Brompton Magazine* (July 1980), 11–12.

133. Letters from John Collins, *Brompton Magazine* (May 1981), 1, (February 1982), 1.

134. Letter from John Collins, *Brompton Magazine* (April 1982), 1; Issy Cooper, 'Festival of Christ: a retrospect', *Brompton Magazine* (July 1982), 3–4.

135. Letters from John Collins, *Brompton Magazine* (February 1983), 1, (June 1983), 1.

136. Ken Stewart, 'Blueprint for a breakthrough', *Brompton Magazine* (November 1982), 2.

137. Letter from John Collins, *Brompton Magazine* (May 1983), 1; Teddy Saunders, 'The final years', in Edward England (ed.), *David Watson: A Portrait by His Friends* (Crowborough: Highland Books, 1985), 187–8, 195.

Chapter Two: Californian Catalyst

1. Tory K. Baucum, *Evangelical Hospitality: Catechetical Evangelism in the Early Church and its Recovery for Today* (Lanham, MD: Scarecrow Press, 2008), 75.

2. 'Tributes to John Wimber', *Focus* 71 (December 1997), 1.

3. David Watson, *Fear No Evil: A Personal Struggle with Cancer* (London: Hodder & Stoughton, 1984), 52.

4. David Pytches, *Living at the Edge: Recollections and Reflections of a Lifetime* (Bath: Arcadia, 2002), 256.

5. Nigel Wright, 'Weighing up Wimber', *Renewal* 152 (January 1989), 22.

6. Nigel Wright, 'A pilgrimage in renewal', in Tom Smail, Andrew Walker and Nigel Wright, *Charismatic Renewal: The Search for a Theology* (London: SPCK, 1993), 27.

7. Nigel Wright, in John Gunstone (ed.), *Meeting John Wimber* (Crowborough: Monarch, 1996), 47.

8. HTB PCC minutes, 9 June 1982.

9. Letter from John Collins, *Brompton Magazine* (July 1981), 1.

10. Letter from John Collins, *Brompton Magazine* (May 1982), 1.

11. Millar, *All I Want Is You*, 41–2.

12. Bill Jackson, *The Quest for the Radical Middle: A History of the Vineyard* (Cape Town: Vineyard International Publishing, 1999), 107–25.

13. Interview with Edward Wright, 1 March 2021.

14. Millar, *All I Want Is You*, 43.

15. John and Andrea Irvine interview with Mark Elsdon-Dew (January 2014, transcript).

16. 'Does God heal today?', Alpha Film Series, episode 15 (2016).

17. For a critique, see Martyn Percy, *Words, Wonders and Power: Understanding Contemporary Christian Fundamentalism and Revivalism* (London: SPCK, 1996).

18. Elsdon-Dew, 'The vision and the power', 16.

19. Gumbel, *Questions of Life* (revised 2010), 98–9.

20. Elsdon-Dew, 'The vision and the power', 16.

21. Tom Freeman, 'Practising what they preach', *Legal Business* (November 1997), 43; Brandreth, 'The prime minister', 2.

22. Letter from John Collins, *Brompton Magazine* (October 1982), 1.

23. HTB PCC minutes, 27 October 1982.

24. Letter from John Collins, *Brompton Magazine* (December 1982), 1.

25. Letter from John Collins, *Brompton Magazine* (April 1983), 1.

26. Letter from John Collins, *Brompton Magazine* (February 1983), 1.

27. Letter from John Collins, *Brompton Magazine* (April 1983), 1.

28. *Brompton Magazine* (September 1983), 9.

29. Atherstone, *Archbishop Justin Welby*, 53.

30. Sandy Millar, 'Re-inspiring, cleansing and envisioning God's church', *HTB in Focus* 25 (March 1994), 2.

31. Sandy Millar, 'I am laying before us as a church the opportunity to *do* something', *HTB in Focus* 22 (December 1993), 4.

32. Sandy Millar, 'A friend's recollections', in David Pytches (ed.), *John Wimber: His Influence and Legacy* (Guildford: Eagle, 1998), 269–87.

33. Andrew Atherstone, 'John Wimber's European impact', in Andrew Atherstone, Mark Hutchinson and John Maiden (eds), *Transatlantic Charismatic Renewal, c.1950–2000* (Leiden: Brill, 2021), 215–39.

34. HTB PCC minutes, 22 February 1984.

35. John Collins to HTB PCC, 28 January 1985.

36. Sandy Millar interview with Mark Elsdon-Dew (8 January 2014, transcript).

37. '1,700 celebrate HTB plants at Westminster Central Hall', *Focus* 46 (December 1995), 3.

38. John McClure, 'How seriously are you taking your race for Jesus Christ?', *HTB in Focus* 14 (April 1993), 6.

39. Sandy Millar, 'Preparing our church building for the future', *HTB in Focus* 3 (May 1992), 5.

40. Sandy Millar, 'Let's hang on to what God spoke to us, and go for it together', *HTB in Focus* 18 (August 1993), 2.

41. C. Peter Wagner, *Strategies for Church Growth: Tools for Effective Mission and Evangelism* (Ventura, CA: Regal Books, 1987), 168–9.

42. Sandy Millar, 'The way ahead' (June 1990), with HTB PCC minutes.

43. Letter from Sandy Millar, *HTB in Focus* 2 (April 1992), 7.

44. Sandy Millar, 'New joy, colour, diversity . . . in us *and* our building', *HTB in Focus* 15 (May 1993), 7.

45. Damian Thompson, 'Church rift as rebel bishops break away', *Daily Telegraph* (31 January 1992), 18. See also, David Pytches and Brian Skinner, *New Wineskins: Defining New Structures for Worship and Growth Beyond Existing Parish Boundaries* (Guildford: Eagle, 1991).

46. HTB PCC minutes, 15 January 1986.

47. John and Andrea Irvine interview with Mark Elsdon-Dew (January 2014, transcript).

48. Charlie Colchester, 'Secretary's report 1987' (April 1988), with HTB PCC minutes. See further, 'Planting from Holy Trinity, Brompton', in Bob Hopkins (ed.), *Planting New Churches* (Guildford: Eagle, 1992), 84–100.

49. Jonathan Petre, 'Church reopens as the flock returns', *Daily Telegraph* (29 February 1988), version at LPL, RC23/330.

50. Derek Hayward to Michael Davies (Church Commissioners), 26 October 1988, LPL, RC23/330.

51. 'Reunion fervour', *HTB in Focus* 1 (March 1992), 1.

52. 'Our fourth child is born', *HTB in Focus* 32 (October 1994), 3.

53. Sandy Millar, 'Church planting – the most exciting development in Anglican strategy for years', *HTB in Focus* 17 (July 1993), 5.

54. Sandy Millar, 'The Lord is giving us a bigger vision than we have ever had before', *HTB in Focus* 42 (August 1995), 2.

55. Sandy Millar, 'Perspectives on church planting', in Roger Ellis and Roger Mitchell (eds), *Radical Church Planting* (Cambridge: Crossway, 1992), 201–10.

56. George Lings and Paul Perkin, *Dynasty or Diversity? The HTB Family of Churches* (Sheffield: Church Army, 2002).

57. Brandreth, 'The prime minister', 1.

58. Bill Saunders, 'A strange cry from Kensington', *Midweek* (10 July 1995), 9.

59. M. C. Barrow et al. to John Klyberg (archdeacon of Charing Cross), 13 April 1994, LMA, DL/A/K/01/11/029.

60. R. F. Bushau (area dean of Westminster) to John Klyberg, 23 March 1994, LMA, DL/A/K/01/11/029.

61. John Klyberg to John Brownsell, 29 March 1994, LMA, DL/A/K/01/11/029.

62. Ruth Gledhill, 'Heaven's door', *The Times* (28 December 1996), Weekend, 9.

63. Nicky Gumbel, *The Bible in One Year: A Commentary* (London: Hodder & Stoughton, 2019), 387.

64. Gumbel, *Challenging Lifestyle* (Eastbourne: Kingsway, 1996), 15; Gumbel, *A Life Worth Living*, 21.

65. Gumbel, *A Life Worth Living*, 21.

66. Nicky Gumbel, 'It was so difficult to encourage each other', *HTB in Focus* 3 (May 1992), 4–5.

67. 'Getting an ordination sensation', *HTB in Focus* 15 (May 1993), 6–7.

68. Elsdon-Dew, 'The vision and the power', 16.

69. Gumbel, *Questions of Life*, 186–7.

70. Interview with Nicky and Pippa Gumbel, 3 March 2021.

71. Interview with Nicky and Pippa Gumbel, 3 March 2021.

72. Gumbel, *A Life Worth Living*, 23.

73. Aitken, *Heroes and Contemporaries*, 236.

74. HTB register of services (1985–90), LMA, P84/TRI2/192.

75. John Irvine, 'How the weekend became part of Alpha', *Focus* 108 (January 2001), 4.

76. Charlie Colchester, 'Secretary's report 1987' (April 1988), with HTB PCC minutes.

77. Nicky Lee, 'The Alpha course: report of the year 1988' (March 1989), with HTB PCC minutes.

78. 'Graham hints at a final farewell', *The Times* (10 July 1989), 5. For the impact on Alpha, see Charlie Colchester, 'Secretary's report 1989/90' (April 1990), with HTB PCC minutes.

79. 'HTB's Alpha course grows across Britain', *HTB in Focus* 2 (April 1992), 3.

80. Nicky Gumbel, *Telling Others* (Eastbourne: Kingsway, 1994, revised 1997), 66.

81. Gumbel, *Telling Others*, 11.

82. Nicky Gumbel, 'Next stop: the world', *HTB in Focus* 42 (August 1995), 13.

83. Nicky Gumbel, 'How to stop worrying and start living', *HTB in Focus* 39 (May 1995), 8.

84. 'HTB's Alpha course grows across Britain'.

85. 'It's Alpha time again!', *HTB in Focus* 7 (September 1992), 3; 'Hundreds come to Alpha', *HTB in Focus* 8 (October 1992), 3.

86. 'HTB re-fit plans get go ahead', *HTB in Focus* 12 (February 1993), 1.

87. Sandy Millar, 'Building up the people and the place', *HTB in Focus* 12 (February 1993), 7.

88. 'HTB's Alpha course grows across Britain'; 'The Holy Spirit in Buckinghamshire', *HTB in Focus* 4 (June 1992), 9.

89. '100 Alpha courses ready to start all over Britain', *HTB in Focus* 16 (June 1993), 1.

90. 'Alpha takes off as church leaders praise "inspiring" conference', *HTB in Focus* 16 (June 1993), 4.

91. All Saints Chilvers Coton PCC minutes, 19 July 1993; Justin Welby to Nicky Gumbel, 21 May 1993, Alpha International Archives.

92. '400 Alpha courses now running all over Britain', *Alpha News* 3 (April 1994), 1; 'More than 750 Alpha courses now running all over UK', *Alpha News* 5 (December 1994), 3.

93. David Pytches to Nicky Gumbel, 4 November 1993, Alpha International Archives.

94. Millar, 'Re-inspiring, cleansing and envisioning'.

95. 'Tricia joins HTB staff to take charge of events', *HTB in Focus* 24 (February 1994), 3. Further details in these paragraphs are from Tricia Neill, *From Vision to Action: Practical Steps for Church Growth* (new edition, London: Alpha International, 2013), 19–30; Tricia Neill interview with Mark Elsdon-Dew (7 May 2018, transcript).

96. Sandy Millar, 'Foreword', in Neill, *From Vision to Action*, 12.

97. David Hilborn, 'A chronicle of the Toronto Blessing and related events', in David Hilborn (ed.), *'Toronto' in Perspective: Papers on the New Charismatic Wave of the Mid-1990s* (Carlisle: Acute, 2001), 129–330.

98. 'A mighty wind from Toronto', *HTB in Focus* 28 (June 1994), 3.

99. 'A day-by-day diary of what we have seen', *HTB in Focus* 28 (June 1994), 3.

100. Emmy Wilson, 'What happened to me', *HTB in Focus* 28 (June 1994), 5.

101. Mike Fearon, *A Breath of Fresh Air* (Guildford: Eagle, 1994), 115.

102. Tricia Neill interview with Mark Elsdon-Dew (7 May 2018, transcript).

103. Eleanor Mumford, 'This whole move of the Lord is all about Jesus', *HTB in Focus* 28 (June 1994), 4–5.

104. 'A day-by-day diary'.

105. Sandy Millar, 'It is all so excitingly reminiscent of accounts of early revivals', *HTB in Focus* 28 (June 1994), 2.

106. 'Revival breaks out in London churches', *Church of England Newspaper* (17 June 1994), 1; Ruth Gledhill, 'Spread of hysteria fad worries Church', *The Times* (18 June 1994), 12; Damian Thompson, 'Evangelical congregation shows signs of the Spirit', *Daily Telegraph* (18 June 1994), 3; Nicholas Monson, 'Congregation rolling in the aisle', *Sunday Telegraph* (19 June 1994), 5; Tony Halpin, 'Rolling in the aisles at church of laughter', *Daily Mail* (20 June 1994), 20.

107. 'Queuing for church', *HTB in Focus* 31 (September 1994), 1.

108. 'HTB starts two Sunday evening services', *HTB in Focus* 32 (October 1994), 1.

109. Ken Costa, 'Surprised by joy', *HTB in Focus* 30 (August 1994), 9.

110. R. T. Kendall, *In Pursuit of His Glory: My 25 Years at Westminster Chapel* (London: Hodder & Stoughton, 2002), 115–21.

111. Glenda Waddell, 'Those strange animal noises and what God showed me', *HTB in Focus* 32 (October 1994), 12.

112. John Arnott, 'The river of the Holy Spirit is taking us downstream, flowing faster and deeper and wider', *HTB in Focus* 33 (November 1994), 4–5; 'John Arnott reflects on Toronto's first year of blessing', *HTB in Focus* 37 (March 1995), 4–7.

113. Richard N. Ostling, 'Laughing for the Lord', *Time* 144 (15 August 1994), 38.

114. 'The Father's Day Outpouring' (18 June 1995), Brownsville, Florida, video recording, https://www.youtube.com/watch?v=tNecA_t1TZk (accessed 3 May 2022). See also, ' "Revival" hits Florida after evangelist Steve receives prayer at HTB', *Focus* 53 (July 1996), 3.

115. Steve Rabey, *Revival in Brownsville: Pensacola, Pentecostalism, and the Power of American Revivalism* (Nashville, TN: Thomas Nelson, 1998).

116. 'When God visited a leaders' weekend', *HTB in Focus* 34 (December 1994), 4.

117. Christian Tyler, 'The vicar with a flock in a frenzy', *Financial Times* (3–4 June 1995), FT Weekend, 24.

118. Colin Moreton, 'Neighbour accuses Holy Trinity, Brompton, of "intellectual vacuity"', *Church Times* (27 January 1995), 4.

119. Robert Jeffery, 'Review of the year 1994', in *Church of England Yearbook* (1995), xxvi.

120. Letter from Lesslie Newbigin, *Church Times* (3 February 1995), 11.

121. Sandy Millar, 'Be open and honest with God – and he will do the rest', *HTB in Focus* 41 (July 1995), 2.

122. Sandy Millar, 'We have been asking the Holy Spirit to come for the last 20 years – and He comes', *HTB in Focus* 44 (October 1995), 2.

123. Sandy Millar, 'The best witness? What Jesus has done for *us*', *Focus* 49 (March 1996), 2.

124. Sandy Millar, 'Staying in the flow of the river of God', *HTB in Focus* 31 (September 1994), 2.

125. Sandy Millar, 'God is giving us joy – and let's drink all we can', *HTB in Focus* 29 (July 1994), 2.

126. Sandy Millar, 'Answering the questions posed by Toronto', *HTB in Focus* 33 (November 1994), 2.

127. Elizabeth McDonald, *Alpha: New Life or New Lifestyle? A Biblical Assessment of the Alpha Course* (Cambridge: St Matthew Publications, 1996), 4–8; K. B. Napier, 'The Alpha heresy' (1996), in *Alpha, the Omega of the Gospel: Biblical Criticism of the Alpha Course* (Swansea: Bible Theology Ministries, second edition, 2007), 10–12; Chris Hand, 'Tasting the fruit of the "Toronto Blessing"', in Peter Glover (ed.), *The Signs and Wonders Movement Exposed* (Bromley: Day One Publications, 1997), 55.

128. Nicky Gumbel, 'The Spirit and evangelism', *Renewal* 228 (May 1995), 15.

129. Testimony of Richard Ward, *HTB in Focus* 43 (September 1995), 6, 8.

130. Ted Harrison, 'Not falling for blessings ploy', *Church Times* (12 May 1995), 10.

131. Heard, *Inside Alpha*, 17.

132. 'Alpha follow-up manuals launched as demand for resources grow', *Alpha News* 10 (July 1996), 1.

133. Jon Ronson, 'Catch me if you can', *Guardian Weekend* (21 October 2000), 19.

134. Sandy Millar, 'It's time to go!', *HTB in Focus* 39 (May 1995), 6–7.

135. 'Hunt for more staff as HTB mounts "expansion in faith"', *HTB in Focus* 41 (July 1995), 3.

136. John Wimber, 'Catch the disease folks!', *HTB in Focus* 42 (August 1995), 4.

137. John Wimber, 'God is calling you to shake this city', *HTB in Focus* 42 (August 1995), 5.

138. Millar, 'The Lord is giving us a bigger vision'.

139. Gumbel, 'Next stop: the world'.

Chapter Three: Building a Brand

1. Annabel Miller, 'God's human touch', *The Tablet* (19 August 1995), 1050–1.

2. Gumbel, *Questions of Life*, 231.

3. Gumbel, *Searching Issues* (Eastbourne: Kingsway, 1994), 31, 39.

4. Gumbel, *A Life Worth Living*, 31.

5. Gumbel, *Telling Others* (revised 1997), 30.

6. Rachel Harden, 'Hold the potting shed – this man has a mission', *Church Times* (10 March 2006), 21.

7. Sandy Millar, 'Foreword', in Gumbel, *Telling Others*, 10.

8. Michael Green interview with Mark Elsdon-Dew (2014, transcript).

9. Gumbel, *Telling Others* (revised 2011), 61.

10. Gumbel, *Telling Others*, 39.

11. Jon Ronson, 'The saviour of Christianity', *Evening Standard Magazine* (19 May 2000), 21.

12. Gumbel, *Telling Others*, 46.

13. Gumbel, *Telling Others*, 121.

14. Damian Thompson, 'The born-again old boys', *Telegraph Magazine* (21 September 1996), 31.

15. Olivia Stewart-Liberty, 'Alpha female', *Evening Standard Magazine* (18 June 2004), 26.

16. Damian Thompson, 'Discovering God among the teacups', *The Times* (2 February 1998), 20.

17. Ronson, 'The saviour of Christianity', 21.

18. Gumbel, *Telling Others*, 100.

19. Gumbel, *Telling Others*, 81.

20. *What Do You Think? Alpha Team Guide* (new edition, London: Alpha International, 2016), 13.

21. Review by Hugo and Sharon Anson, *Christianity* (June 2008), 56.

22. Steve Waring, 'The smiling face of Alpha: an interview with Nicky Gumbel', *Living Church* (19 January 2003), 10–11.

23. Debra Bendis, 'Beginning with Alpha: ABCs of faith', *Christian Century* (9 March 2004), 24.

24. Douglas Todd, 'The joy of proselytizing', *Vancouver Sun* (7 July 2000), A15.

25. Mark Elsdon-Dew, 'So just what *is* so special about Alpha?', *Alpha News* 3 (April 1994), 2.

26. Chris Hand, *Falling Short? The Alpha Course Examined* (Epsom: Day One, 1998), 70, 72–3.

27. 'Pewburner's 1999 almanac', *New Christian Herald* (2 January 1999), 27.

28. Jim Herrick, 'Beta is better', *New Humanist* (Autumn 2001), 6.

29. A. A. Gill, 'Would you want to tuck him in?', *Sunday Times* (5 August 2001), Culture, 13.

30. Madeleine Bunting, 'Happy, clappy . . . and zappy', *The Guardian* (4 March 1998), G2, 2–3.

31. Nikolai Segura, 'The respectable face of fundamentalism', *The Freethinker* 123 (October 2003), 6.

32. Testimony of Mike Norris, *UK Focus* (June 1999), 1, 4–5.

33. Peter Clark, 'What's it all about, Alpha?', *Evening Standard* (30 July 2001), 33.

34. Herrick, 'Beta is better', 6.

35. Sue Arnold, 'Now God is cool', *The Observer* (11 June 2000), Review, 2.

36. Brandreth, 'The prime minister', 2.

37. Clark, 'What's it all about, Alpha?'

38. Darren E. Grem, *The Blessings of Business: How Corporations Shaped Conservative Christianity* (New York: Oxford University Press, 2016), 63.

39. Quoted in Grem, *Blessings of Business*, 63.

40. Michael McKinley, 'Salvation in Aisle 7', *National Post* (6 April 2002), Saturday Post, 3.

41. Nicky Gumbel appointment diary 1990–1.

42. Mary Killen, 'Back-seat driver', *House & Garden* 57 (January 2002), back page.

43. 'Alpha tapes launched nationally', *HTB in Focus* 25 (March 1994), 1.

44. 'Alpha video is launched', *Alpha News* 4 (September 1994), 1.

45. 'Take two! Course video is completely re-filmed', *Alpha News* 13 (July 1997), 1, 3.

46. John Leonard (vicar of St Theodore's Church, Rushey Mead, Leicester) to Nicky Gumbel, 5 July 1995, Alpha International Archives.

47. 'Launch of new Alpha worship pack meets demand from courses', *Alpha News* 12 (February 1997), 3.

48. 'Youth manual launched', *Alpha News* 9 (March 1996), 1; 'Student Alpha', *Alpha News* 18 (March 1999), 6–7.

49. Roger Simpson, 'The successful businessman who said to me, "Roger, I am so empty . . .",, *Alpha News* 27 (March 2002), 21; Shaila Visser, 'How Alpha is now up and booming in the workplace', *Alpha News* 34 (July 2004), 11; '20-min Alpha talks now on DVD', *Alpha News* 37 (July 2005), 1.

50. '"Senior Alpha" manuals are launched', *Alpha News* 36 (March 2005), 4.

51. Martyn Percy, 'Assessing Alpha', *Church Times* (4 April 1997), 12.

52. Letter from Sandy Millar, *Daily Telegraph* (11 September 1999), 25.

53. 'Alpha's new logo', *Alpha News* 2 (December 1993), 1.

54. Charlie Mackesy, 'From drinking and streaking – to painting for Jesus Christ', *HTB in Focus* 40 (June 1995), 10, 12.

55. 'Sunday television and radio', *The Times* (1 December 1990), 29; 'Sunday television', *Sunday Telegraph* (2 December 1990), Review, 28.

56. Gumbel, *A Life Worth Living*, 10.

57. Nicky Gumbel appointment diaries 1993–4, 1995–6 and 1996–7.

58. Nicky Gumbel appointment diary 1997–8.

59. '30 Days Bible study book is a big seller', *Alpha News* 19 (July 1999), 9.

60. Gledhill, 'The magnet of Alpha', 838.

61. Gumbel, *Telling Others*, 41; Tricia Neill, 'How to keep Alpha growing', *Alpha News* 18 (March 1999), 14.

62. 'Nine new home groups get going after Alpha 2', *Focus* 50 (April 1996), 3.

63. *Alpha II Manual* (London: HTB, 1998), Alpha International Archives. For an earlier provisional syllabus, see 'HTB to start "Alpha Two" in October', *HTB in Focus* 39 (May 1995), 3.

64. Sandy Millar, 'Mission-minded and adaptable', *Focus* 90 (July 1999), 6.

65. Gumbel, *Challenging Lifestyle*, 8; Gumbel, *Telling Others* (revised 1997), 64; Gumbel, *Telling Others* (revised 2011), 102.

66. '30 Alpha course regional advisers await your calls', *Alpha News* 6 (April 1995), 3.

67. 'Regional advisers', *Alpha News* 8 (December 1995), 28.

68. '120 UK advisers meet in London', *Alpha News* 21 (March 2000), 36; '200 Alpha advisers meet in London', *Alpha News* 27 (March 2002), 8.

69. 'How the Alpha register came to change a window cleaner's life', *Alpha News* 5 (December 1994), 10.

70. *The Alpha Course Directory* (July–October 2002). There were further instalments in November 2002 and March 2003, before the directory moved online.

71. 'New resource centres being planned for 1995', *Alpha News* 4 (September 1994), 11; Tricia Neill, 'Four priorities facing all of us involved with Alpha in 2003', *Alpha News* 29 (November 2002), 17.

72. Ric Thorpe, *Resource Churches: A Story of Church Planting and Revitalisation across the Nation* (London: Gregory Centre for Church Multiplication, 2021).

73. Neill, 'Four priorities'.

74. Gumbel, *Telling Others* (revised 1997), 25.

75. Pete Ward, 'Alpha – the McDonaldization of religion?', *Anvil* 15 (1998), 279–86.

76. Letter from Sandy Millar, *Church Times* (15 January 1999), 9.

77. Gumbel, *Telling Others*, 51; Tricia Neill, 'Seven tips on making the most of your course', *Alpha News* 21 (March 2000), 9.

78. 'Alpha copyright: a statement to clear up any confusion', *Alpha News* 10 (July 1996), 5.

79. Percy, 'Assessing Alpha'.

80. Tony Roake, 'To crack a nut', *New Directions* 2 (June 1997), 9.

81. Sandy Millar and Nicky Gumbel to Mark Ireland, 12 December 2000, Alpha International Archives.

82. Mike Booker and Mark Ireland, *Evangelism – Which Way Now? An Evaluation of Alpha, Emmaus, Cell Church and Other Contemporary Strategies for Evangelism* (London: Church House Publishing, 2003), 20.

83. Roger Arguile, 'Needed: proper nourishment', *Church Times* (19 July 2002), 16.

84. 'Battle of faith', *The Times* (18 May 2000), 22.

85. 'A chance to be a Friend of Alpha', *Alpha News* 10 (July 1996), 2.

86. *Holy Trinity Brompton: Annual Report 1997–98*.

87. *Holy Trinity Brompton: Annual Report 1998–99*; Victoria Combe, 'Church's income is doubled by Alpha', *Daily Telegraph* (27 January 1999), 4.

88. 'Partners for Alpha', *Alpha News* 24 (March 2001), 17; *Alpha International Annual Report 2002*.

89. *Alpha International Annual Report 2003*; *Alpha Annual Review 2007*; *Alpha Annual Review 2010*; *Alpha International Annual Review 2019*.

90. *Holy Trinity Brompton Annual Report 2003; Holy Trinity Brompton Annual Review 2010*.

91. Interview with Mark Elsdon-Dew, 18 November 2019.

92. *Alpha News* 13 (July 1997), 23.

93. Letter from Kenneth Wakefield, *Church Times* (13 July 2001), 9.

94. Michael Marsden, 'Alpha male', *New Humanist* (July/August 2006), 18.

95. John Pridmore, 'We few, we unhappy few', *Church Times* (16 August 1996), 7.

96. Letter from W. J. McIlroy (Sheffield Humanist Society), *Evangelicals Now* (May 2000), 16.

97. Grant Wacker, *One Soul at a Time: The Story of Billy Graham* (Grand Rapids, MI: Eerdmans, 2019), 37.

98. Letter from Philip Foster, *Church Times* (15 January 1999), 9.

99. 'Fourth volume of popular Alpha series is out', *Alpha News* 35 (November 2004), 8.

100. Testimony of Ben Freeman, *UK Focus* (October 2002), 1–5.

101. 'Ben Freeman: a statement', *Alpha News* 33 (March 2004), 6.

102. 'From drugs to God', *Reading Evening Post* (20 September 2002), 18.

103. 'Born-again thief raided churches', *Reading Evening Post* (26 April 2004), 1, 5.

104. Gumbel, *A Life Worth Living*, 18.

105. Gumbel, *Questions of Life* (revised 2010), 217.

106. Percy, 'Assessing Alpha'.

107. Martyn Percy, '"Join-the-dots" Christianity: assessing Alpha', *Reviews in Religion and Theology* 4 (August 1997), 17. For a response, see Markus Bockmuehl, '"Dotty" Christianity: assessing Percy on Alpha', *Reviews in Religion and Theology* 5 (February 1998), 10–12.

108. Letter from Andrew Davison, *The Tablet* (11 August 2001), 1145.

109. Andrew Billen, 'Pushed away from God', *The Times* (14 January 2003), T2, 5.

110. Letter from Laurie Gibson, *Guardian Weekend* (28 October 2000), 7.

111. Marsden, 'Alpha male', 18.

112. Charles Spencer, 'Stimulating religious thriller is hokum – but enjoyable none the less', *Daily Telegraph* (26 October 2000), 25.

113. Letter from Malcolm Brown, *Guardian Weekend* (28 October 2000), 7.

114. Letter from Alan Smith, *Methodist Recorder* (9 January 1997), 16.

115. Letter from Richard J. Bradshaw, *Methodist Recorder* (11 October 2001), 6.

116. Matthew Lawrence, 'Letter to an Alpha friend: a skeptical priest looks at the Alpha course', *Living Church* (15 December 2002), 12–13.

117. Letter from R. Campbell Paget, *The Times* (16 September 1998), 17.

118. Stephen Overell, 'Christianity for the "me" generation', *Financial Times* (10 November 2000), 20.

119. Katie Grant, 'Religion is not a teacup for sale from a leaflet', *The Herald* (Glasgow) (25 October 1999), 13.

120. Fiona Campbell, 'Alpha's salvation motorway', *The Tablet* (4 August 2001), 1106–7.

121. Rico Tice, 'Winning hearts', *Christian Herald* (13 July 2002), 15.

122. Rico Tice, 'We can't distort the word of God', *Christianity* (July 2011), 21–3.

123. 'Marketing the gospel', *Movement: Magazine of the Student Christian Movement* 113 (Spring 2003), 18.

124. 'Beta treads in Alpha's footsteps', *Church Times* (27 February 2004), 3; 'From Alpha to Beta', *The Tablet* (6 March 2004), 17; Sara Savage, 'The second step for Christian disciples', *Church of England Newspaper* (1 July 2005), 12.

125. 'Liberal Episcopalians unveil modified Alpha', *Christian Century* (9 March 2004), 18.

126. Liz Hogarth, 'Bringing the church into a new age', *Baptist Times* (12 December 2002), 8–9.

127. Mark Woods, 'Extraordinary start to evangelism course', *Baptist Times* (22 May 2003), 4.

128. 'The Y Course', *Inspire* 40 (July/August 2009), 22–3. See further, Peter Meadows and Joseph Steinberg, *Beyond Belief?* (Milton Keynes: Authentic Media, 1999).

129. Naomi Starkey, 'Chat show is, sadly, a turn-off', *Church Times* (22 January 2010), 22.

130. Ken Costa, 'A vision for London' (February 1993), with HTB executive committee minutes (1 March 1993) and HTB PCC minutes (19 May 1996).

131. Costa, 'A vision for London'.

132. George Carey, 'There'll be a big party going on', *Reader's Digest* 138 (March 1991), 43.

133. Costa, 'A vision for London'.

134. Costa, 'A vision for London'.

135. 'London's Christian Centre' (November 1995), with HTB PCC minutes.

136. HTB PCC minutes, 10 December 1995.

137. Dominic Kennedy, 'Millennium will be a Christian event, Bottomley pledges', *The Times* (2 December 1996), 8.

138. Prince Charles, 'A vision for the millennium', *Perspectives on Architecture* 21 (February/March 1996), 33.

139. *Hansard*, House of Commons (18 November 1996), vol. 285, column 682.

140. HTB PCC minutes, 7 October 1996.

141. Sandy Millar, 'Is having a flutter on the lottery unbiblical?', *Focus* 48 (February 1996), 10.

142. Martin Wroe, 'Bottomley backs "Christian village" for millennium', *The Observer* (8 December 1996), 3; *Hansard*, House of Commons (18 November 1996), vol. 285, column 681.

143. Sarah Oliver, 'Why Charles is praying Lottery money will back this £123m super church', *Mail on Sunday* (29 December 1996), 8–9.

144. Ken Costa, 'Why I believe so strongly that God is in this project', *UK Focus* (January 1997), 2–3.

145. Sandy Millar, 'A vision for a church of the third millennium', *Focus* 52 (June 1996), 2.

146. Sandy Millar, 'The church's need for unity and visibility', *UK Focus* (September 1996), 2.

147. 'The Millennium Village' (fund-raising report, May 1997), Alpha International Archives.

148. 'What will make up the Millennium Village?', *UK Focus* (January 1997), 5.

149. Catherine Osgerby, 'Prince backs HTB's mega-church', *Church Times* (3 January 1997), 1.

150. 'A national focus for Christianity', *UK Focus* (January 1997), 4.

151. Oliver, 'Why Charles is praying'.

152. 'Charles and his church', *The Times* (30 December 1996), 15.

153. Letter from L. D. Deal, *Mail on Sunday* (5 January 1997), 39; letter from Norman Churcher, *Evening Standard* (6 January 1997), 47.

154. Letter from Ivor Smith-Cameron and Alan Gadd, *Church of England Newspaper* (10 January 1997), 11. See also Alan Gadd to Sandy Millar, 23 January 1997; Roy Williamson (Bishop of Southwark) to Sandy Millar, 24 January 1997, HTB Archives.

155. Roger Ryan (vicar of St Mary's, Summerstown) to Martin Wharton (Bishop of Kingston), 9 December 1996, HTB Archives.

156. A. N. Wilson, 'Bring Swampy to Battersea', *Evening Standard* (7 February 1997), 11.

157. Cristina Odone, 'Diary', *The Spectator* (25 October 1997), 9.

158. Dominic Kennedy, 'Prince's plan for Christian village is turned down', *The Times* (6 February 1997), 4.

159. *Hansard*, House of Commons (19 March 1997), vol. 292, column 1049.

160. 'Diana Millennium Village' (memorandum, 29 September 1997), Alpha International Archives.

161. HTB PCC minutes, 5 February 2005.

162. 'St Paul's plans', *Focus* 158 (March 2005), 3.

163. 'Alpha International campus: project update' (6 April 2006), Alpha International Archives.

164. 'New video plans for St Paul's', *Focus 160* (May 2005), 5.

165. Alex West, 'Church fails to convert', *Kensington and Chelsea News* (10 August 2006), 1–2; Ed Caesar, 'Alpha's Kensington crusade', *The Independent* (12 August 2006), 10–11; Rashid Razaq, 'Celebrity church ditches plan for "happy clappy" worship centre', *Evening Standard* (14 August 2006), 17.

166. Keith Dovkants, 'Onslow Square's holy war', *Evening Standard* (2 March 2007), 18–19.

167. Celia Walden, 'Spy: Von Bulow's hullabaloo', *Daily Telegraph* (27 February 2007), 23.

168. Mira Bar-Hillel, 'Christian centre is axed after opposition from locals', *Evening Standard* (8 March 2007), 27.

169. 'Breakthrough as Alpha buys headquarters', *Alpha News* 43 (March 2008), 2.

170. 'Book of Alpha's "big seven" questions to be published', *Alpha News* 2 (December 1993), 6.

171. 'Sales of Nicky Gumbel's four Alpha books continue to rise', *Alpha News* 3 (April 1994), 3.

172. Brian Davies (Kingsway managing director) to Nicky Gumbel, 5 April 1995, Alpha International Archives.

173. Tricia Neill to John Paculabo (Kingsway managing director), 13 March 1995, Alpha International Archives.

174. Neill to Richard Herkes (Kingsway publishing director), 19 March 1997, Alpha International Archives.

175. Gumbel to Neill, 23 February 1998, Alpha International Archives.

176. Neill to Herkes, 2 March 1998, Alpha International Archives.

177. Paculabo to Sandy Millar, 8 July 1998, Alpha International Archives.

178. Paculabo to Millar, 8 July 1998.

179. Millar to Paculabo, 30 July 1998, Alpha International Archives.

180. Herkes to Neill, 27 October 1997, Alpha International Archives.

181. Draft letter to Paculabo, 16/18 December 1998, Alpha International Archives.

182. Paculabo to Alistair Hanna, 3 February 1999, Alpha International Archives.

183. Neill to Peter Fenwick (chairman of Kingsway), 11 August 2000; Fenwick to Neill, 31 May 2001, Alpha International Archives.

184. 'The Kingsway relationship' (memorandum, 2006), Alpha International Archives.

185. Toria Gray to Mark Elsdon-Dew et al., 1 November 2006, Alpha International Archives.

186. Paculabo to Lisa Carlson (Alpha International publishing director), 4 February 2008, Alpha International Archives.

187. Paculabo to Rebecca Stewart (Alpha UK national director), 6 May 2008, Alpha International Archives.

188. 'Holy Trinity holds Alpha conference', *HTB in Focus* 9 (November 1992), 1; 'Four Alpha books in Top 20 best sellers', *Alpha News* 6 (April 1995), 3; 'Alpha follow-up manuals launched as demand for resources grow', *Alpha News* 10 (July 1996), 1; 'Why Jesus tops 7 million', *Alpha News* 45 (November 2008), 21.

189. 'Alpha follow-up manuals launched'; 'The book of the Alpha course has sold more than 500,000 copies – and now it's hitting the UK high streets', *Alpha News* 25 (July 2001), 3; 'Course book tops 1m', *Alpha News* 39 (May 2006), 2; 'New books launch publishing deal', *Alpha News* 50 (July 2010), 6.

190. Information from Alpha International, January 2022.

Chapter Four: Experiencing the Holy Spirit

1. Gumbel, *Telling Others*, 18–20.

2. Gumbel, *Telling Others* (revised 2011), 33.

3. Gumbel, *Searching Issues*, 125.

4. Gumbel, *Telling Others*, 17.

5. Gumbel, *Questions of Life*, 121.

6. Christopher Noble, 'Article of faith? An empirical study of the tract *Journey Into Life* in the development of British evangelical identity between 1963 and 1989' (PhD thesis, King's College London, 2018).

7. Norman Warren, *Journey Into Life* (Eastbourne: Kingsway, 1991), 14.

8. Nicky Gumbel, *Why Jesus?* (Eastbourne: Kingsway, 1991), 14.

9. Warren, *Journey Into Life*, 13.

10. Gumbel, *Why Jesus?*, 20.

11. Gumbel, *Questions of Life*, 54–5; Gumbel, *Telling Others*, 116.

12. Nicky Gumbel, *The Heart of Revival* (Eastbourne: Kingsway, 1997), 202.

13. Sandy Millar, 'More Holy Spirit – more of Jesus', *HTB in Focus* 40 (June 1995), 2.

14. Testimony of Andy Green, *UK Focus* (October 1998), 4–5.

15. Testimony of Jamie Hinde, *UK Focus* (March 2006), 4–5.

16. Gumbel, *Questions of Life*, 112.

17. Gumbel, *Telling Others* (revised 2011), 44.

18. Gumbel, *Questions of Life*, 132–3.

19. Gumbel, *Telling Others*, 119–20.

20. See, for example, letter from Ric Harvey, *Alpha News* 15 (March 1998), 4.

21. Gumbel, *Questions of Life*, 135.

22. Gumbel, *Questions of Life*, 136.

23. Testimony of Derek Fox, *Focus* 47 (January 1996), 10, 12.

24. Testimony of Carolanne Minashi, *UK Focus* (January 1999), 4–5.

25. Testimony of Mark Minashi, *UK Focus* (January 1999), 5.

26. Testimony of Philippa Deane, *Alpha News* 15 (March 1998), 14.

27. Testimony of Sandy Meaney, *HTB in Focus* 11 (January 1993), 8.

28. Testimony of Sandy Meaney, *HTB in Focus* 45 (November 1995), 12.

29. Testimony of Keith Prestridge, *UK Focus* (February 1998), 5.

30. Information from Nigel Skelsey, October 2020.

31. Testimony of Nigel Skelsey, *HTB in Focus* 25 (March 1994), 6, 8.

32. '350 attend Edinburgh conference', *HTB in Focus* 25 (March 1994), 3.

33. Nigel Skelsey, 'What I say to my work colleagues when they say, "Call yourself a Christian?"', *UK Focus* (January 1999), 2.

34. John Chapman, '"Alpha" no world-beater', *Southern Cross* (April 1996), 15; republished as John Chapman, 'First things first', *The Briefing* 184 (August 1996), 8–10.

35. David Richardson, 'Alpha – the omega in evangelism?', *Prophecy Today* 13 (September/October 1997), 7.

36. Hand, *Falling Short?*, 77.

37. Hand, *Falling Short?*, 79. For similar criticisms, see G. Richard Fisher, 'The Alpha course: final answer or fatal attraction?', *Quarterly Journal: The Newsletter Publication of Personal Freedom Outreach* 18 (October 1998), 4–9; William D. Scholes, '"A" is for Alpha, "B" is for Berean', *Churchman* 112 (Winter 1998), 294–312; Gordon R. Lewis, 'Evaluating Alpha', *Christian Research Journal* 23 (2001), 26–31, 47–9.

38. Gumbel, *Telling Others* (revised 2011), 71.

39. Tricia Neill, 'Five tips for leaders', *Alpha News* 14 (November 1997), 8.

40. Gumbel, *Questions of Life*, 139–47.

41. Sandy Millar, 'Do you want to be built up as a Christian? Here's a way of doing it', *Focus* 137 (June 2003), 2, 6.

42. Gumbel, *Questions of Life*, 147.

43. Gumbel, *Questions of Life* (revised 1995), 173.

44. Ronson, 'Catch me if you can', 21.

45. Gumbel, *Telling Others*, 118.

46. *Youth Alpha Manual* (London: HTB Publications, 1996), 29.

47. Gumbel, *Telling Others*, 121.

48. *UK Focus* (February 1998), 4–5.

49. Testimony of Donna Matthews, *UK Focus* (April 2003), 4–5, 7.

50. Testimony of Damian McGuinness, *UK Focus* (October 2005), 1–3, 6.

51. Dominic Kennedy, 'Smart route to the Lord', *The Times* (14 December 1996), Weekend, 2.

52. Julia Llewellyn Smith, 'How I fell for the crash course in Christianity', *The Express* (16 November 1998), 28–9; Julia Llewellyn Smith, 'Upwardly mobile to God', *The Times* (21 July 2001), Weekend, 13.

53. Victoria Moore, 'Beyond belief?', *Daily Mail* (10 January 2002), 47.

54. Michael Hodges, 'Want to cast the first stone? Join the queue', *Time Out London* (4–11 October 2006), 10.

55. Howard Davies, 'The words of the Alpha course', *The Banner of Truth* 418 (July 1998), 18.

56. Letter from David Copley, *Guardian Weekend* (28 October 2000), 7.

57. Letter from Jim Hamilton, *Baptist Times* (19 November 1998), 13.

58. Gumbel, *Telling Others* (revised 2011), 72.

59. Gumbel, *Telling Others*, 117.

60. Alex Preston, 'The Alpha set', *Evening Standard Magazine* (14 December 2012), 43.

61. Alex Preston, *The Revelations* (London: Faber and Faber, 2012), quotations at 17, 35, 174–5, 181.

62. Gumbel, *Questions of Life*, 58, 166, 244.

63. Gumbel, *Questions of Life*, 63.

64. Gumbel, *Questions of Life*, 47.

65. Gumbel, *A Life Worth Living*, 119.

66. Gumbel, *Questions of Life* (revised 2010), 179.

67. Gumbel, *Searching Issues* (revised 2013), 87.

68. Gumbel, *Questions of Life*, 136–7.

69. Gumbel, *Telling Others*, 26–7.

70. Gumbel, *Questions of Life*, 121–2.

71. Hand, *Falling Short?*, 67.

72. Hand, *Falling Short?*, 65.

73. Hand, *Falling Short?*, 68–9. For similar criticisms, see Robin Weekes, 'Review article: the Alpha and Christianity Explored courses', *Foundations* 47 (Autumn 2001), 36–44.

74. Gumbel, *Questions of Life*, 44; Gumbel, *Questions of Life* (revised 1995), 46.

75. Gumbel, *Questions of Life*, 30.

76. Gumbel, *Questions of Life*, 46.

77. Gumbel, *Questions of Life*, 202.

78. Hand, *Falling Short?*, 59–60, 69.

79. Gumbel, *Challenging Lifestyle*, 55.

80. Gumbel, *Heart of Revival*, 51.

81. Gumbel, *Heart of Revival*, 195–7.

82. Gumbel, *Questions of Life* (revised 2001), 40.

83. Gumbel, *Questions of Life* (revised 2003), 64.

84. Gumbel, *Questions of Life* (revised 2010), 45.

85. Gumbel, *Jesus Lifestyle*, 53.

86. Gumbel, *Jesus Lifestyle*, 247.

87. Testimony of Michaela Flanagan, *Alpha News* 15 (March 1998), 12–13.

88. *Memoirs of Rev. Charles G. Finney, written by himself* (New York: A. S. Barnes, 1876), 20.

89. Gumbel, *Questions of Life*, 150, 158, 161.

90. Gumbel, *Telling Others* (revised 1997), 163.

91. 'Dracula fans lose stake in cemetery', *The Times* (10 February 1997), 8; 'Whitby aims to drive the stake into Stoker', *Daily Telegraph* (22 February 1997), Weekend, 21.

92. 'The day the president of the vampires read *Questions of Life*', *UK Focus* (June 1997), 7.

93. 'Best-selling author: Alpha inspired me', *Alpha News* 37 (July 2005), 11.

94. Gumbel, *Questions of Life*, 152–3; Gumbel, *Questions of Life* (revised 2010), 154–5.

95. Gumbel, *Searching Issues*, 63.

96. Testimony of Lee Duckett, *HTB in Focus* 23 (January 1994), 7–8.

97. Testimonies of Fatimah and Iain Murray, *Focus* 53 (July 1996), 10–12.

98. Testimony of Christine Woodall, *UK Focus* (June 2001), 4–5.

99. Testimony of Claire Jerath, *UK Focus* (February 2008), 6–7.

100. Gumbel, *Telling Others*, 21–4, 31.

101. Gumbel, *Telling Others*, 124–5.

102. Testimony of Francie Lygo, *HTB in Focus* 8 (October 1992), 12.

103. Testimony of Seonaid Fresson, *HTB in Focus* 8 (October 1992), 12.

104. Testimony of Judy Cahusac, *UK Focus* (November 1997), 4–5.

105. 'Alpha guests: "We have been healed"', *HTB News* 215 (December 2009), 2; Gumbel, *The Bible in One Year*, 374.

106. Testimony of Jean Smith, *UK Focus* (June 2000), 5.

107. Testimony of Sally van Wyk, *Alpha News* 13 (July 1997), 5.

108. Testimony of Steve Downes, *UK Focus* (June 2001), 6–7; Steve Downes, 'Miracle child', *Christianity* (August 2007), 12–15.

109. Gumbel, *Questions of Life*, 212.
110. Gumbel, *Questions of Life* (revised 1995), 222.
111. Gumbel, *Questions of Life* (revised 2010), 185.
112. Patrick Pearson Miles, 'Living with kidney failure – but drawing closer to Jesus', *HTB in Focus* 36 (February 1995), 11–12; John Wimber, 'God's promised us we'll live forever', *HTB in Focus* 41 (July 1995), 4–5; Patrick Pearson Miles, 'People have asked, "Are you angry at God?"', *UK Focus* (March 2001), 3–5; Patrick Pearson Miles, 'I've never liked needles very much', *UK Focus* (February 2003), 4–5.
113. Tribute edition to Mick Hawkins, *Focus* 54 (August 1996).
114. Zilla Hawkins, 'I've never felt bereft', *UK Focus* (July 1997), 3.
115. Gumbel, *Questions of Life* (revised 2001), 91.
116. Mark Smith, 'Take your seat at the first supper', *Glasgow Herald Magazine* (15 February 2003), 17.
117. Gumbel, *Questions of Life* (revised 2010), 72.
118. 'Tragedy as three HTB members are in accident', *Focus* 104 (September 2000), 4.

Chapter Five: Marketing the Gospel

1. '"Trendy" vicar sacks choir', *Kensington and Chelsea Post* (27 September 1990), 3.
2. Mark Palmer, 'Christ is risen in the Brompton Road', *Sunday Telegraph* (11 April 1993), Review, 1.
3. Tricia Neill, 'How to attract young people to an Alpha course', *Alpha News* 27 (March 2002), 17.
4. Theo Hobson, 'Don't call us evangelicals', *Church Times* (2 January 2004), 12.
5. Sam Cash, 'O come all ye faithful', *Harpers & Queen* (December 1996), 89.
6. Viv Groskop, 'Is this the hottest ticket to heaven?', *You Magazine: Mail on Sunday* (25 September 2005), 31.
7. Andrew Carey, 'Alpha: some questions to answer', *Church of England Newspaper* (20 May 1994), 12.
8. Llewellyn Smith, 'How I fell for the crash course', 28.
9. Brandreth, 'The prime minister', 1.
10. Preston, 'The Alpha set', 43.
11. Bryan Appleyard, 'Answering the call of God and Gucci', *Sunday Times* (29 July 2001), News Review, 8.

12. 'Why so happy? Booze? Men? No, it's God', *New Woman* (November 2001), 229.

13. *Elle* (December 2002), 11, and Jenny Dyson, 'Jesus loves me', *Elle* (December 2002), 186.

14. *Cosmopolitan* (October 2006), 136.

15. Arnold, 'Now God is cool'.

16. Saunders, 'A strange cry from Kensington', 8.

17. Tom Morton, 'Leap of faith', *The Scotsman* (27 September 2000), S2, 2–3.

18. Michael Hodges, 'Faith, hope, clarity', *Time Out London* (1–8 June 2005), 34.

19. Mike Purton, 'A ticket to God for Thatcher's children', *The Guardian* (1 December 2001), 24.

20. Pete May, 'Holy Rollers', *Midweek* (17–20 February 1997), 4.

21. Imogen Stubbs, 'We need solace to help us brave the secret, undiscovered road ahead', *Daily Telegraph* (16 December 2000), Weekend, 2.

22. Dyson, 'Jesus loves me', 185–6.

23. Danny Kruger, 'Diary', *The Spectator* (20 November 2004), 9.

24. Stubbs, 'We need solace', 2.

25. Mary Wakefield, 'Giving sight to the bland', *The Spectator* (23 January 1999), 19.

26. Celia Walden, 'It sure beats The Priory', *The Spectator* (7 August 2004), 22.

27. Brigit Grant, 'Where to pick up a perfect partner', *Sunday Express* (5 June 1994), London, 2–3.

28. Barnaby Jameson and Stephen Gibbs, 'Godspell: How the rich and the beautiful are finding religion – and each other', *Evening Standard* (20 January 1992), 15.

29. Katherine Miller, 'Marriage, sex and the single Christian', *The Times* (1 August 1998), 17.

30. Testimony of Vanessa Rayne, *UK Focus* (April 2005), 4–5.

31. Testimony of Natalie Joannou, *UK Focus* (May 2010), 4–5.

32. Pete Greig, 'How to build authentic relationships', *UK Focus* (September 2007), 3.

33. Catherine Osgerby, 'Christmas ad sparks angry reaction', *Church Times* (6 September 1996), 1.

34. Glyn Paflin, 'Che posters revolutionise Easter push', *Church Times* (8 January 1999), 1–2; David Kunzle, *Chesucristo: The Fusion in Image and Word of Che Guevara and Jesus Christ* (Berlin: De Gruyter, 2016), 290–4.

35. Ruth Gledhill, 'Churches turn to Mammon for the millennium', *The Times* (16 September 1999), 1.

36. *Adscene* (12 September 1997), Margate, Ramsgate and Broadstairs edition, 38; 'When 23 Kent churches joined together to advertise their Alpha courses in a newspaper, word got out', *Alpha News* 15 (March 1998), 5.

37. Information from Mark Elsdon-Dew, February 2019.

38. 'Nation responds to UK initiative', *Alpha News* 17 (November 1998), 1.

39. 'Nation responds to UK initiative'.

40. 'Getting the word out', *Alpha News* 17 (November 1998), 11.

41. '4,000 churches join together', *Alpha News* 17 (November 1998), 12–13.

42. 'Non-churchgoers up by 100%, survey reveals', *Alpha News* 18 (March 1999), 9.

43. 'From the accountants', *Alpha News* 18 (March 1999), 9.

44. Stephen Hoare, 'Steps to heaven', *Evening Standard* (2 November 1998), Professional Secretary, 17.

45. 'Alpha plus', *The Economist* (7 November 1998), 35.

46. Richard Askwith, 'God's own spin doctor', *The Independent* (17 September 1998), Thursday Review, 1.

47. Clifford Longley, 'A younger generation without any religion', *Daily Telegraph* (25 September 1998), 31.

48. *The Guardian* (13 October 1998), G2, 18.

49. 'New Alphayed course fails to win converts', *Private Eye* (2 October 1998), 23.

50. Kristina Cooper, 'Faith with extra cheese', *The Tablet* (5 February 2005), 22.

51. 'Oh, what a party', *Alpha News* 20 (November 1999), 3.

52. 'Launching across the UK', *Alpha News* 20 (November 1999), 4–5.

53. 'Learning the meaning of life for the millennium', *Solihull News* (10 September 1999), 14.

54. 'Alpha's new face', *Focus* 101 (June 2000), 3.

55. Vanessa Thorpe, 'Pin-up girl sells God to Britain', *The Observer* (3 September 2000).

56. Overell, 'Christianity for the "me" generation'.

57. Stephen Overell, 'Turn up, look good, find God', *Financial Times* (10 November 2000), 20.

58. 'The face of Alpha?', *Christianity* (August 2000), 6–7.

59. 'Biggest ever UK poster initiative', *Alpha News* 25 (July 2001), 1.

60. 'Buses, tubes and poster sites', *Alpha News* 25 (July 2001), 20–1.

61. 'Introducing the posters set to cover the UK this September', *Alpha News* 28 (July 2002), 4.

62. 'How can YOU get involved?', *Alpha News* 16 (July 1998), 12–13; 'Millennium Alpha initiative: How can you get the word out in YOUR area this September?', *Alpha News* 19 (July 1999), 18–19.

63. 'E-mails reveal how poster brought people to Alpha', *Alpha News* 26 (November 2001), 23.

64. Testimony of Ann Hughes, *UK Focus* (June 2000), 4–5.

65. Testimony of Chris Green, *UK Focus* (April 2001), 6–7.

66. 'Bus backs, billboards, tubes and radio ads . . .', *Alpha News* 29 (November 2002), 6.

67. 'Church curate warned for flyposting in parish', *Cumberland News* (24 August 2007), 1.

68. For details in these paragraphs, see 'Events across the nation', *Alpha News* 23 (November 2000), 18–19; 'Inviting the country to supper', *Alpha News* 26 (November 2001), 22–3; 'Bus backs, billboards, tubes and radio ads . . .', 6–7; 'Inviting the UK to supper', *Alpha News* 32 (November 2003), 4–5; 'UK Christians join biggest campaign', *Alpha News* 34 (July 2004), 6–7; 'Inviting the nation to supper' and 'Text message theme takes off', *Alpha News* 35 (November 2004), 2–4; 'Serving supper to the nation', *Alpha News* 38 (November 2005), 4–5; 'UK hosts its big Alpha party', *Alpha News* 45 (November 2008), 4–5.

69. 'Comedian Bobby: "Alpha is fantastic"', *Alpha News* 48 (November 2009), 2. See also testimony of Bobby Ball, *Alpha News* 49 (March 2010), 18–19.

70. Shane Lynch, *The Chancer* (Littlehampton: Canaan Press, 2008), 196–210.

71. 'Bear and Shane join in the big invitation', *Alpha News* 40 (November 2006), 4.

72. 'Just who converted St Samantha?', *Daily Mail* (5 September 1994), 20–1.

73. Mike Rimmer, 'Naughty girls need loving too', *Cross Rhythms* 23 (October 1994), 34.

74. 'Sexy Sam has found religion', *Daily Mirror* (25 January 1994), 11; 'My heavenly bod is just for God', *The Sun* (7 February 1994), 16–17.

75. 'Sam Fox finds God', *The Sun* (25 January 1994), 1; 'Now Sam's all body AND soul!', *Daily Star* (25 January 1994), 6.

76. Rimmer, 'Naughty girls', 35. See also, 'Samantha Fox lays bare her new faith in God', *Sunday Telegraph* (28 August 1994), 8; 'And lo, the Foxy Lady had them screaming for more', *Daily Mail* (30 August 1994), 5; 'Sam's a real bible smasher', *The Sun* (30 August 1994), 15; Ruth Gledhill, 'A celebrity bares her soul', *The Times* (31 August 1994), 11.

77. Amanda Mitchison, 'Fox hunting', *Sunday Telegraph Magazine* (10 January 1999), 13.

78. Harriet Lane, 'She's still up front', *The Observer* (2 February 2003), Review, 3.

79. Samantha Fox, *Forever* (Milwaukee, WI: Backbeat Books, 2017), 216.

80. Jonathan Aitken, *Pride and Perjury* (London: HarperCollins, 2000), 26. See further, Luke Harding, David Leigh and David Pallister, *The Liar: The Fall of Jonathan Aitken* (second edition, London: The Guardian, 1999).

81. Aitken, *Pride and Perjury*, 341.

82. Aitken, *Pride and Perjury*, 11.

83. 'Jonathan Aitken speaks: "Alpha put me on the right road to God and I am so grateful"', *Alpha News* 29 (November 2002), 9.

84. Gareth Sturdy, 'Journey in the limelight for "an audience of one"', *Church Times* (31 March 2000), 5.

85. Aitken, *Pride and Perjury*, 270–3.

86. Jonathan Aitken, *Porridge and Passion* (London: Continuum, 2005), 72.

87. Aitken, *Pride and Perjury*, 274–5.

88. Jonathan Aitken, 'Now I understand the Christmas story', *The Spectator* (20/27 December 1997), 14.

89. Nigel Dempster, 'Good God, now look who's here', *Daily Mail* (9 October 1997), 37; 'Jonathan's trial', *Evening Standard* (19 December 1997), 11.

90. Hodges, 'Want to cast the first stone?'

91. Aitken, *Porridge and Passion*, 72–3.

92. 'Inviting the UK to supper'.

93. 'Hello, good evening (and welcome . . .)', *Alpha News* 23 (November 2000), 2–3.

94. Andy Peck, 'Alpha on your TV', *Christianity + Renewal* (August 2001), 13.

95. Harry Powell, 'It made a very big difference to our wedding day', *Alpha News* 26 (November 2001), 7.

96. James Bann, 'My knee has been completely healed', *Alpha News* 26 (November 2001), 5.

97. Testimony of Tony Bolt, *UK Focus* (November 2001), 1–3.

98. 'We've changed', *Alpha News* 43 (March 2008), 3.

99. Terence Blacker, 'Welcome to the new, exclusive moral health club', *The Independent* (31 July 2001), Review, 4.

100. James Delingpole, 'The sublime and ridiculous', *The Spectator* (18 August 2001), 45; Andrew Billen, 'God makes another sell', *New Statesman* (13 August 2001), 35.

101. Kathryn Flett, 'If you go down in the woods . . .', *The Observer* (5 August 2001), Review, 20.

102. Peter Clark, 'What's it all about, Alpha?', *Evening Standard* (30 July 2001), 33.

103. Flett, 'If you go down in the woods . . .'

104. Catherine Fox, 'Alpha's TV exposure', *Church of England Newspaper* (3 August 2001), 17.

105. Billen, 'God makes another sell'.

106. Keith Porteous Wood, 'The Alpha experience', *The Freethinker* 121 (September 2001), 5.

107. *Alpha: Will It Change Their Lives: Ratings* (2001), Alpha International Archives.

108. For example, 'Alpha series ditched for two weeks', *Baptist Times* (9 August 2001), 3; 'Alpha on TV: ITC steps in', *Baptist Times* (16 August 2001), 1; letter from Andrew Palfreyman, *Church of England Newspaper* (3 August 2001), 15; letter from John Steer, *The Scotsman* (4 August 2001), 15; letter from Nigel Holmes, *Church of England Newspaper* (24 August 2001), 17.

109. Richard Porter to ITV, 12 August 2001, Alpha International Archives.

110. Letter from A. C. Smith, *Baptist Times* (23 August 2001), 6.

111. 'The book of the Alpha course has sold more than 500,000 copies'.

112. 'Alpha at HTB', *Holy Trinity Brompton Annual Report 2002*, 5.

113. 'Alpha at HTB', *Holy Trinity Brompton Annual Report 2003*, 4.

114. 'Alpha at HTB', *HTB Review 2003–2004*, 7; 'Alpha at HTB', *HTB Annual Review 2005*, 8.

115. 'MORI poll shows 45% growth in Alpha awareness', *Alpha News* 26 (November 2001), 15; 'MORI poll finds that 10 million know Alpha', *Alpha News* 38 (November 2005), 2; 'National survey: millions have interest in Alpha', *Alpha News* 40 (November 2006), 1; '4m have interest in Alpha', *Alpha News* 49 (March 2010), 1.

116. 'Are you coming to supper?', *Evangelicals Now* (April 2000), 1.

117. Andrew Burnham, 'Alpha, Bisto and omega', *The Door* (September 2005), 8 (Oxford diocesan newspaper).

118. 'After Scientology and Buddhism Geri tries God', *Heat* (8–14 December 2001), 4–5.

119. 'It's Geri Holywell', *The Sun* (22 November 2001), 19; 'Geri Halliwell charts path to becoming a Christian', *Daily Telegraph* (23 November 2001), 5; 'Geri's conversion', *Daily Mail* (24 November 2001), 17.

120. 'Will's Alpha date upsets gay group', *Church of England Newspaper* (18 July 2002), 28.

121. 'Sally: Bible teacher has rescued me', *Sunday Mirror* (7 April 2002), 3.

122. Andrew Billen, 'CDs? They're for chopping out a line', *The Times* (29 May 2007), Times 2, 13; 'Kabbalah Guy was a "secret" holy rolla', *Evening Standard* (14 April 2009).

123. Testimony of Laura Michelle Kelly, *Alpha News* 32 (November 2003), 6–7.

124. Testimony of Ugo Monye, *Alpha News* 44 (July 2008), 8–9, 20.

125. Ian Stafford, 'Heavens above', *Rugby World* 583 (February 2009), 47.

126. 'Alpha people', *Alpha News* 49 (March 2010), 4.

127. Testimony of Charlie Simpson, *UK Focus* (April 2008), 1–3; 'Life after Busted' (28 August 2007), https://www.crossrhythms.co.uk/articles/news/Life_After_Busted/28842/p1/ (accessed 4 March 2022).

128. Testimony of Rhydian Roberts, *UK Focus* (July 2011), 4–5.

129. 'Bus backs, billboards, tubes and radio ads . . .', 6–7.

130. Linvoy Primus, *Transformed* (Fareham: Legendary Publishing, 2007), 204–5.

131. Testimony of Kim Johnson, *UK Focus* (October 2005), 4–6.

132. Maev Kennedy, 'God gets glitzy as Christians hit silver screen', *The Guardian* (10 September 2005), 5.

133. Stephen Tomkins, 'By your adverts ye shall be known . . .', BBC News website (14 September 2005), http://news.bbc.co.uk/1/hi/magazine/4244958.stm (accessed 4 March 2022).

134. 'Alastair, 23, celebrates viral victory', *Alpha News* 40 (November 2006), 5.

135. 'Now Alpha advert is set to go on TV', *Alpha News* 41 (May 2007), 1, 5.

136. 'Well, what would YOU ask?', *Alpha News* 44 (July 2008), 2–3.

137. Katie Aston, 'United Kingdom: all publicity is good publicity, probably', in Steven Tomlins and Spencer Culham Bullivant (eds), *The Atheist Bus Campaign: Global Manifestations and Responses* (Leiden: Brill, 2017), 334–68; Lois Lee, 'Vehicles of New Atheism: the atheist bus campaign, non-religious representations and material culture', in Christopher R. Cotter, Philip Andrew Quadrio and Jonathan Tucker (eds), *New Atheism: Critical Perspectives and Contemporary Debates* (Cham, Switzerland: Springer, 2017), 69–86.

138. Quoted in Aston, 'United Kingdom', 353.

139. 'Come and see . . .', *Alpha News* 48 (November 2009), 2–3.

140. 'There is no God say 96%', *The Sun* (23 October 2009), 47.

141. Bear Grylls, *Mud, Sweat and Tears: The Autobiography* (London: Channel 4 Books, 2011), 112–14.

142. Grylls, *Mud, Sweat and Tears*, 131–3.

143. Grylls, *Mud, Sweat and Tears*, 451.

144. 'From youngest Briton on Everest to Arctic racer', *Alpha News* 37 (July 2005), 2.

145. 'Alpha hits the headlines', *Alpha News* 38 (November 2005), 2.

146. Kate Corney, 'Born again survivor', *Christianity* (June 2008), 42.

147. 'From youngest Briton on Everest'.

148. 'The UK's big car sticker challenge', *Alpha News* 39 (May 2006), 1.

149. 'Bear films video ad for Alpha', *Alpha News* 48 (November 2009), 5.

150. 'Global Alpha campaign', *Alpha International Annual Review 2016*, 32–3; 'Global Alpha invitation', *Alpha International Annual Review 2017*, 50.

151. '1,000 attend Bear event in London', *Alpha News* 48 (November 2009), 4–5.

152. 'Bear's Alpha launch', *Alpha News* 51 (November 2010), 4–5, 19.

153. 'Adventurer Bear Grylls: on life, fame, TV, and Alpha', *Alpha News* 45 (November 2008), 6–7, 18.

154. Bear Grylls, *Never Give Up: A Life of Adventure* (London: Bantam Press, 2021), 248.

155. 'Bear Grylls: faith isn't about being weird but being loved', *Alpha News* 39 (May 2006), 3.

156. 'Adventurer Bear Grylls', 18; 'Alpha people', *Alpha News* 53 (November 2011), 13.

157. Bear Grylls, *With Love, Papa* (Oxford: Lion, 2009); Shara Grylls, *Marriage Matters* (Oxford: Lion, 2009); *Alpha News* 48 (November 2009), 5.

158. Bear Grylls, *Soul Fuel: A Daily Devotional* (London: Hodder & Stoughton, 2019).

159. Sandy Millar, 'Revival brings judgement too', *Focus* 64 (June 1997), 2.

160. Gumbel, *Questions of Life*, 88.

161. Gumbel, *Heart of Revival*, 186.

162. Sandy Millar, 'Characteristics of God's church', *Focus* 96 (January 2000), 5.

163. '150 pray for revival on HTB weekend', *HTB in Focus* 36 (February 1995), 3.

164. Jeremy Jennings, 'Why do we go on doing this?', *Focus* 51 (May 1996), 4.

165. Jeremy Jennings, *The Church on Its Knees: Dynamic Prayer in the Local Church* (London: HTB Publications, 1998), 95.

166. 'More than 100 go away to pray', *HTB in Focus* 24 (February 1994), 1; 'Learning to pray – by doing it', *HTB in Focus* 25 (March 1994), 4–5.

167. Jennings, *The Church on Its Knees*, 78.

168. '900 at the big prayer party', *HTB News* 216 (January 2010), 4; 'New Year's Eve prayer party', *HTB News* 228 (January 2011), 5.

169. Jennings, *The Church on Its Knees*, 88–9. For reports, see 'Prayer from the Thames', *Focus* 46 (December 1995), 4–5; '260 join river boat prayers', *Focus* 70 (November 1997), 1.

170. Michael Lloyd, 'Prayer may be a lonely slog at times – but it brings heaven a little closer to earth', *UK Focus* (September 2003), 6–7.

171. '230 gather to pray', *Focus* 145 (February 2004), 8.

172. Tricia Neill, 'Our 10-part strategy for the next five years', *Alpha News* 26 (November 2001), 16.

173. '158 prayer events across the country', *Alpha News* 17 (November 1998), 13.

174. '18,700 attend initiative prayer meetings', *Alpha News* 26 (November 2001), 22.

175. '7,000 churches get set for September', *Alpha News* 31 (July 2003), 6–7.

176. '2,400 pack St Paul's for Alpha prayers', *Alpha News* 32 (November 2003), 1–2.

177. 'And it all began as 4,000 prayed . . .', *Alpha News* 35 (November 2004), 6–7.

178. '24/7 Pete Greig to lead Alpha prayer', *Alpha News* 44 (July 2008), 4.

Chapter Six: Embracing Rome

1. 'London for Jesus', *HTB in Focus* 33 (November 1994), 3.

2. Millar, 'The Lord is giving us a bigger vision'.

3. Millar, 'The church's need for unity and visibility'.

4. Nicky Gumbel, 'God is able to do far more than we can imagine – just look at the Sombrero galaxy', *UK Focus* (January 2004), 7.

5. 'Nicky Gumbel is installed as vicar of Holy Trinity Brompton', *Alpha News* 38 (November 2005), 6.

6. Gumbel, *Questions of Life*, 127; Gumbel, *Questions of Life* (revised 2010), 133.

7. Gumbel, *Challenging Lifestyle*, 217.

8. Gumbel, *Telling Others*, 114.

9. Ruth Gledhill, 'Bishop of Durham denies Bible story of Christmas', *The Times* (20 December 1993), 1–2.

10. 'Sandy speaks for the Christian gospel to TV, radio and newspaper', *HTB in Focus* 23 (January 1994), 3.

11. Sandy Millar, 'Don't let us be fooled by all this modern liberalism', *HTB in Focus* 23 (January 1994), 2.

12. See chapter 7.

13. Nicky Gumbel, 'Why does unity matter so much to Jesus?', *UK Focus* (August 2010), 6–7.

14. C. S. Lewis, *Mere Christianity* (London: Geoffrey Bles, 1952), vi, viii. See further, George M. Marsden, *C. S. Lewis's Mere Christianity: A Biography* (Princeton, NJ: Princeton University Press, 2016).

15. 'Alpha to issue invitations to all', *Church of England Newspaper* (6 March 1998), 5.

16. Hand, *Falling Short?*, 92.

17. Andy Peck, 'The Alpha phenomenon', *Christianity* (May 2000), 16.

18. David Coffey, 'Foreword', in Rob Warner, *Baptism and Belonging* (Didcot: Baptist Union of Great Britain, 2001); letter from Derek Allan, *Baptist Times* (1 March 2001), 6.

19. 'Are you coming to supper?'

20. Letter from Alan Howe, *New Christian Herald* (26 September 1998), 6.

21. Letter from Mike Guddat, *New Christian Herald* (14 November 1998), 6.

22. Letter from C. J. Schorah, *New Christian Herald* (17 October 1998), 6.

23. Michael Lloyd, *Café Theology: Exploring Love, the Universe and Everything* (London: Alpha International, 2005), back cover.

24. Review by Wendy Bray, *Christianity* (September 2005), 58.

25. Lloyd, *Café Theology*, 10.

26. Steven Croft, 'Let's have a bit of cut-and-thrust', *Church Times* (11 November 2005), 23.

27. 'Bishop: I have felt the Holy Spirit', *Focus* 139 (August 2003), 2–3.

28. Nicky Gumbel appointment diary 2004–5.

29. 'Top man to lead HTB theology centre', *Focus* 158 (March 2005), 1, 5; Jonathan Aitken, *The St Mellitus Story* (privately published, 2017).

30. 'Graham Tomlin made dean of new theological college', *Alpha News* 45 (November 2008), 25.

31. Graham Tomlin and Nathan Eddy (eds), *The Bond of Peace: Exploring Generous Orthodoxy* (London: SPCK, 2021); Graham Tomlin, *Navigating a World of Grace: The Promise of Generous Orthodoxy* (London: SPCK, 2022).

32. Peck, 'The Alpha phenomenon', 18.

33. Hobson, 'Don't call us evangelicals', 12.

34. Nicky Gumbel, 'Alpha plus', in Caroline Chartres (ed.), *Why I am Still an Anglican: Essays and Conversations* (London: Continuum, 2006), 96.

35. 'Alpha goes from strength to strength', *Christianity* (May 1998), 5.

36. Sandy Millar, 'Why it is so important to bring people to faith', *Focus* 78 (July 1998), 5, 8.

37. *The Nottingham Statement* (London: Church Pastoral Aid Society, 1977), 44. See also, John Maiden, 'Evangelicals and Rome', in Andrew Atherstone and David Ceri Jones (eds), *The Routledge Research Companion to the History of Evangelicalism* (London: Routledge, 2019), 93–109.

38. Andrew Atherstone, 'Archbishop Carey's ecumenical vision', *Theology* 106 (September 2003), 342–52.

39. Atherstone, 'John Wimber's European impact', 220–2, 236–7.

40. Adam Zamoyski, 'Feelin' groovy down at HTB', *Catholic Herald* (9 April 1993), 5.

41. For correspondence, see *Catholic Herald* (23 and 30 April 1993), 4.

42. Letter from Francis Holford, *Catholic Herald* (11 June 1993), 4.

43. Valentina Ciciliot, 'The origins of the Catholic Charismatic Renewal in the United States: the experience of the University of Notre Dame and South Bend (Indiana), 1967–1975', in Andrew Atherstone, Mark Hutchinson and John Maiden (eds), *Transatlantic Charismatic Renewal, c.1950–2000* (Leiden: Brill, 2021), 144–64.

44. Joan Le Morvan, 'The Alpha course feedback', *Goodnews* 113 (September/October 1994), 4; 'Alpha success at Catholic church', *Alpha News* 4 (September 1994), 11.

45. David Payne, *Alive* (St Albans: CaFE, 2009), 5, 22, 36–9. On the Upper Room community, see 'Zapped in the Spirit' *Goodnews* 68 (March/April 1987), 4–5; 'The URPG story', *Goodnews* 84 (November/December 1989), 4–5.

46. David Payne, 'Alpha for Catholics', *Goodnews* 126 (November/December 1996), 1–2.

47. Kristina Cooper, 'Catholics get the message about Alpha', *The Tablet* (24 May 1997), 688.

48. Eldred Willey, 'The Alpha phenomenon in its user-friendly form', *The Universe* (4 January 1998), 20.

49. 'Roman Catholic bishops applaud Alpha as course spreads through church', *Alpha News* 13 (July 1997), 1.

50. Dominic Elliot to Basil Hume, 13 May 1997, Westminster Diocesan Archives [WDA], Basil Hume papers.

51. 'Catholic Alpha goes to Rome', *Alpha for Catholics: News Update* (5 March 1998); 'Another visit to the Vatican', *Alpha for Catholics: News Update* (Spring 1999), Peter Hocken papers.

52. Gledhill, 'The magnet of Alpha', 838.

53. Willey, 'The Alpha phenomenon'.

54. Kristina Cooper, 'Total marketing approach marks new evangelism', *Catholic Times* (28 May 2000), 7.

55. Richard Barrett, 'Doubts and queries', *Catholic Herald* (30 June 2000), 10.

56. Interview with David Payne, 13 December 2018.

57. Peter Berners-Lee, 'Alpha in a Catholic context', *Catholic Gazette* 88 (November 1997), 9.

58. Charles van der Lande, 'Alpha: some thoughts and reflections' (unpublished typescript, January 1998), WDA, Basil Hume papers.

59. 'Papal preacher gives Alpha follow-up talks', *Alpha News* 19 (July 1999), 1.

60. 'Catholic follow-up to Alpha', *Alpha News* 21 (March 2000), 17.

61. Interview with David Payne, 13 December 2018.

62. Roger Fay, 'Alpha courses and Catholicism', *Evangelical Times* (March 1998), 13.

63. Neil Richardson, 'Unmasked: Nicky Gumbel – "a tale of two cities". Part 1: Rome', *Vanguard* 2 (January 1997), 22–31, copy at Alpha International Archives.

64. 'Ecumenical Alpha', in E. S. Williams, *Ecumenism: Another Gospel – Lausanne's Road to Rome* (London: Belmont House Publishing, 2014), 115.

65. 'Toronto Blessing branded "blasphemous" at Omagh meeting', *Tyrone Constitution* (9 May 1996), 2.

66. Noel McAdam, 'Alpha bid to focus on common ground', *Belfast Telegraph* (24 January 1998), 16; letter from Robert McFarland, *Belfast Telegraph* (7 February 1998), 8. See further, 'Alpha in Ireland', *Alpha News* 15 (March 1998), 10–11.

67. 'Doctrinal differences', *Impartial Reporter and Farmers' Journal* (15 October 1998).

68. Paul Fitton, 'The Alpha course: Bible-based or hell-inspired?', *The Battle Standard* 1 (April 1998), 4–7. For similar criticisms, see Colin Mercer, *The Alpha Course Examined: The Alpha Course Weighed in the Balances of Holy Scripture* (Kilkeel, County Down: Mourne Missionary Trust, 2001); Mary Danielsen and Chris Lawson, *The Alpha Course: An Evangelical Contradiction* (Eureka, MT: Lighthouse Trails Publishing, 2016).

69. 'The Alpha course: Satan's latest device to deceive believers', *The Burning Bush* 31 (November 2000), 3.

70. Paddy Monaghan, 'Say you hate Jesus or I'll kill you', in Paddy Monaghan and Eugene Boyle (eds), *Adventures in Reconciliation: Twenty-nine Catholic Testimonies* (Guildford: Eagle, 1998), 165–72.

71. Atherstone, 'John Wimber's European impact', 220–3.

72. Paddy Monaghan, 'The Alpha course', *Irish Catholic* (18 August 2005), 13.

73. Julie Waters, 'Seven Bangor churches unite for Alpha season', *County Down Spectator and Ulster Standard* (13 September 2007), 2; letter from David Priestley, *County Down Spectator and Ulster Standard* (20 September 2007), second section, 10.

74. Caroline Farey, 'Questions about Alpha', *The Sower* 20 (September 1998), 22–3.

75. *Christian Order* 40 (January 1999), 1, 3, 18.

76. Gillian van der Lande, 'Should Alpha be used in a Catholic context?', *Christian Order* 40 (January 1999), 19.

77. Gillian van der Lande to Basil Hume, 24 April 1999, WDA, Basil Hume papers.

78. Bess Twiston Davies, 'Is Catholic Alpha simply Protestantism with optional extras?', *Catholic Herald* (1 October 1999), 5.

79. '"Catholic" Alpha: a warning', *The Flock: Newsletter of Pro Ecclesia et Pontifice* 3 (Winter 1999), 3.

80. Twiston Davies, 'Is Catholic Alpha simply Protestantism with optional extras?'

81. Letter from Edith Caversham-Hope, *Catholic Herald* (1 June 2001), 7.

82. Letter from Graham Moorhouse, *Catholic Herald* (22 September 2000), 7.

83. Letter from Graham Moorhouse, *Catholic Herald* (1 September 2000), 7.

84. Letter from Sîon Cowell, *The Tablet* (25 January 2003), 16.

85. 'Cathedral opts for Alpha', *Catholic Herald* (6 December 2002), 2; letter from Tom Mahon, *Catholic Herald* (20 December 2002), 9.

86. William K. Kay, 'Peter Hocken: his life and work', *Pneuma* 37 (2015), 82–110.

87. Peter Hocken, 'Alpha and the Catholic Church', *The Sower* 20 (September 1998), 21.

88. Letter from David Palmer, *Catholic Herald* (25 August 2000), 7.

89. Letter from Christopher Peake, *The Tablet* (5 July 1997), 867.

90. Letter from Peter Kraushar, *Catholic Herald* (8 October 1999), 7.

91. Letter from M. M. Heley, *Catholic Herald* (15 October 1999), 7.

92. 'The Catholic school where it's "cool" to do Alpha', *UK Focus* (June 1998), 2.

93. Justin Trudeau, *Common Ground: A Political Life* (London: Oneworld, 2017), 138–9.

94. Cristina Odone, *A Perfect Wife* (London: Orion, 1997), quotations at 86, 192.

95. 'Londoner's diary: unhappy clappy', *Evening Standard* (23 July 1997), 10.

96. 'Church maverick Odone attacks happy-clappy set', *Sunday Times* (19 October 1997), 11.

97. Cristina Odone, 'A contagious case of HTB', *The Spectator* (20 September 1997), 11–12.

98. Letter from Mark Elsdon-Dew, *The Spectator* (27 September 1997), 28.

99. Cristina Odone, 'Diary', *The Spectator* (25 October 1997), 9.

100. 'Cristina picks a fight', *Church of England Newspaper* (31 October 1997), 6.

101. Andrew Brown, 'Hitting at HTB', *Church Times* (24 October 1997), 17.

102. Cristina Odone, 'My church? Dan Brown hasn't seen the half of it', *The Observer* (21 May 2006), 27.

103. Alice Thomas Ellis, 'God . . .', *The Oldie* 188 (November 2004), 26.

104. Marc de Leyritz, 'We're seeing God at work in France', *Alpha News* 21 (March 2000), 4–5.

105. De Leyritz, 'We're seeing God at work in France', 5, 33.

106. Charlie Cleverly, 'How the French are warming to the evangelicals', *Church of England Newspaper* (20 April 2000), 12.

107. De Leyritz, 'We're seeing God at work in France', 33.

108. Marc and Florence de Leyritz to Nicky Gumbel and Tricia Neill, 30 November 2000, Peter Hocken papers.

109. Peter Hocken to Nicky Gumbel, 23 December 2000, Peter Hocken papers.

110. Gumbel, *Questions of Life*, 76.

111. Gumbel, *Questions of Life*, 218.

112. See, however, Gumbel, *Questions of Life*, 128, where the reference to Roman Catholics as a 'denomination' was retained.

113. Gumbel, *Questions of Life*, 227–8.

114. Gumbel, *Questions of Life*, 229. Nicky Gumbel, *Les Questions de la Vie* (Burtigny: Jeunesse en Mission, 1998), 172.

115. Willey, 'The Alpha phenomenon'.

116. Gumbel, *Questions of Life*, 47.

117. Hocken to Gumbel, 23 December 2000.

118. Gumbel, *Questions of Life* (revised 2001), 45, 234.

119. Gumbel, *Questions of Life*, 47–8.

120. Gumbel, *Questions of Life* (revised 2001), 43–4. The Kolbe illustration was previously used in an earlier chapter, *Questions of Life*, 19–20.

121. Tricia Neill to Peter Hocken, 22 January 2003, Peter Hocken papers.

122. Willey, 'The Alpha phenomenon'.

123. Gumbel, *Telling Others* (revised 2001), 39; Gumbel, *Telling Others* (revised 2011), 23, 27, 31–2, 49.

124. Gumbel, *Telling Others* (revised 2011), 45, 49.

125. Gumbel, *Telling Others* (revised 2011), 24–5.

126. Gumbel, *Telling Others* (revised 2011), 29.

127. Gumbel, *Heart of Revival*, 162; Gumbel, *Questions of Life* (revised 2010), 133.

128. 'Nicky Gumbel speaks to 4,000 in Germany', *Focus* 89 (June 1999), 5.

129. 'Raniero on hope, commitment . . . and Mary', *UK Focus* (September 2003), 4–5.

130. Raniero Cantalamessa, *Faith Which Overcomes the World* (London: Alpha International, 2006), 7–11.

131. 'Raniero: why I love Alpha', *HTB News* 188 (September 2007), 5.

132. Nicky Gumbel, 'What I love about the Catholic Church', *Catholic Herald* (16 January 2015), 22.

133. Nicky Gumbel, 'Foreword', in Cantalamessa, *Faith Which Overcomes*.

134. 'Cardinal's welcome for Alpha', *Alpha News* 31 (July 2003), 1.

135. Austen Ivereigh, 'Europe of the heart', *The Tablet* (15 May 2004), 35–6; 'On Europe's stage', *Alpha News* 34 (July 2004), 3.

136. 'Nicky meets cardinal', *HTB News* 191 (December 2007), 5.

137. 'A cardinal honour', *Alpha News* 42 (November 2007), 8–9.

138. 'Nicky Gumbel invited to Rome to speak on evangelisation', *Alpha News* 43 (March 2008), 6.

139. 'Vatican's warm welcome for Nicky and Pippa Gumbel', *Alpha News* 53 (November 2011), 10.

140. 'Meeting the pope', *Focus* 146 (March 2004), 3, 6; 'Papal audience as cardinals speak out', *Alpha News* 33 (March 2004), 7.

141. Gumbel, 'What I love about the Catholic Church', 22.

142. 'Alpha for Catholics', *Alpha News* 37 (July 2005), 15.

143. 'News in brief', *Alpha News* 38 (November 2005), 6.

144. Christopher Lamb, 'Two traditions, one holy ground', *The Tablet* (21 June 2014), 5.

145. Gumbel, 'What I love about the Catholic Church', 22–3.

146. 'Cardinal praises Alpha as he attends conference saying "I'm here to learn"', *Alpha News* 14 (November 1997), 1; 'Why I welcome Alpha, by cardinal', *Alpha News* 19 (July 1999), 6–7; 'Catholic archbishop: this "source of hope"', *Alpha News* 23 (November 2000), 7; 'Bishops lead drive all across Asia', *Alpha News* 30 (March 2003), 24–5; 'News in

brief', *Alpha News* 36 (March 2005), 4; 'The cardinal and the archbishop', *Alpha News* 41 (May 2007), 1; 'News in brief', *Alpha News* 43 (March 2008), 6; 'Thousands attend Singapore events', *Alpha News* 44 (July 2008), 10–11; 'I have prayed for this day', *Alpha News* 50 (July 2010), 14–15.

147. 'Archbishop of Paris speaks at French event', *Alpha News* 39 (May 2006), 19. See also, André Vingt-Trois, 'Why I support Alpha so strongly', *Alpha News* 44 (July 2008), 13.

148. 'Papal audience as cardinals speak out'.

149. 'Alpha in Europe', *Alpha News* 36 (March 2005), 23.

150. '350 attend first South American conference', *Alpha News* 40 (November 2006), 9.

151. '24 Catholic bishops join Alpha event in Bogota', *Alpha News* 48 (November 2009), 10–11.

152. 'Alpha and Catholicism 201: a complete package for the Catholic Church', *Alpha News: Canadian Edition* 26 (Summer 2007), 7.

153. Ron Huntley and James Mallon, *Unlocking Your Parish: Making Disciples, Raising Up Leaders with Alpha* (Frederick, MD: The Word Among Us Press, 2019), 28, 34, 147.

154. *Divine Renovation: A Review of Our Ministry* (annual report 2021), https://www.divinerenovation.org/annual-report (accessed 3 May 2022).

155. Cristina Odone, 'I was wrong about the Alpha course', *Catholic Herald* (2 January 2015), 15.

Chapter Seven: Transforming Society

1. Sandy Millar, 'The remarkable effect of going on holiday together', *HTB in Focus* 13 (March 1993), 7.

2. Sandy Millar and Nicky Gumbel, 'Why we believe this course to be a work of God in our generation', *Alpha News* 2 (December 1993), 2.

3. *Alpha News* 6 (April 1995), 7.

4. Gumbel, *Challenging Lifestyle*, 24.

5. Gumbel, *Heart of Revival*, 21.

6. Gumbel, *Heart of Revival*, 17–18.

7. 'When God visited a leaders' weekend'.

8. Gumbel, *Challenging Lifestyle*, 69, 82.

9. Nicky Gumbel, 'Foreword', in Lee and Lee, *The Marriage Book*, vii.

10. Nicky Lee, 'Looking to God in relationships', *UK Focus* (March 2000), 6.

11. Thompson, 'Discovering God among the teacups'.

12. Sandy Millar, 'At the heart of our faith is the heart', *UK Focus* (November 2000), 2–3.

13. Millar, 'Is having a flutter on the lottery unbiblical?'

14. Sandy Millar, 'New Labour? Isn't it time for "New Church"?', *UK Focus* (November 1996), 3.

15. Monica Furlong, *C of E: The State It's In* (London: Hodder & Stoughton, 2000), 275.

16. 'Sandy Millar on sex', *HTB in Focus* 4 (June 1992), 4–5.

17. Sandy Millar, 'As we face the same challenges as Timothy and Paul, my three suggestions for 2004', *Focus* 144 (January 2004), 5. Elsewhere Millar described the 'new morality' as 'the old immorality re-cycled for a new generation'; see Sandy Millar, 'A warning from the Greek ruins', *Focus* 93 (October 1999), 2.

18. Gumbel, *Heart of Revival*, 185.

19. Gumbel, *Heart of Revival*, 117.

20. Gumbel, *A Life Worth Living*, 25.

21. Sandy Millar, 'Faith requires us to stick closely to God', *Focus* 98 (March 2000), 5.

22. Sandy Millar, 'The amazing approachability of Jesus', *UK Focus* (November 2002), 4–5.

23. Millar, 'New Labour?', 3.

24. Damian Thompson, 'I hate the happy clappies', *The Times* (11 April 1998), Weekend, 21.

25. Letter from Nicholas Masterson-Jones, *The Spectator* (27 September 1997), 28. See further, Donald Reeves, *Memoirs of a Very Dangerous Man* (London: Continuum, 2009).

26. *General Synod: Report of Proceedings* 18 (November 1987), 913–56.

27. HTB PCC minutes, 28 October 1987; HTB executive committee minutes, 25 November 1987. For earlier commentary at HTB on the Church of England report, *Homosexual Relationships: A Contribution to Discussion* (1979), see Nick Miller, 'Homosexuality', *Brompton Magazine* (December 1979), 10; John Gladwin, 'Homosexuality and the church', *Brompton Magazine* (February 1980), 10–11; letter from Bob Porter, *Brompton Magazine* (March 1980), 8; 'Marriage', *Brompton Magazine* (December 1980), 2–3.

28. 'Sandy Millar on sex', 5.

29. Sandy Millar, 'Let's offer the world a better way of life', *HTB in Focus* 38

(April 1995), 2.

30. Stephen Bates, *A Church at War: Anglicans and Homosexuality* (London: I.B. Tauris, 2004).

31. Sandy Millar, 'The intense desire for purity and holiness that comes from God', *UK Focus* (October 2003), 7.

32. Sandy Millar, 'A new bishop: What are we to think?', *UK Focus* (November 2003), 1–2.

33. Sandy Millar, 'To the new Archbishop of Uganda – with love', *UK Focus* (February 2004), 4–5.

34. 'Sandy's big day', *Focus* 167 (December 2005), 2–3; Giles Fraser, 'Is Sandy Millar a Trojan horse?', *Church Times* (4 November 2005), 11; Andrew Carey, 'A "Ugandan" bishop for Britain', *Church of England Newspaper* (4 November 2005), 18.

35. Gumbel, *Searching Issues*, 86, 90.

36. Gumbel, *Searching Issues* (revised 2001), 71, 73.

37. Gumbel, *Searching Issues*, 78–9, 91.

38. Millar, 'A new bishop', 2.

39. 'Next: the Gay Alpha course', *Church Times* (16 June 2000), 4; 'Adaptable Alpha course draws praise and worry', *Christianity Today* 45 (12 November 2001), 29.

40. Terry Sanderson, 'Using my religion', *Gay Times* (August 2000), 68.

41. Adrian Butler, ' "Cultish" bible group slammed by Union', *York Vision* (12 February 2002), 1; Ffion Evans, 'Re: freedom of speech should not apply on campus', *York Vision* (5 March 2002), 13. For letters in response, see *York Vision* (5 March 2002), 12. For undergraduate commentary, see John Rose, 'A critique of the Alpha course's attitude towards homo-sexuality' (January 2002), Nicky Gumbel papers; abridged as John Rose, 'Alphabet soup: how words can mangle meaning', *Gay and Lesbian Humanist* 21 (Spring 2002), 8.

42. 'Campus Alpha: the voice of one crying in the wilderness', *Gay and Lesbian Humanist* 21 (Spring 2002), 4.

43. ' "Idol" threat?', *Christian Herald* (8 June 2002), 3; 'Will's Alpha date upsets gay group', *Church of England Newspaper* (18 July 2002), 28.

44. Ronson, 'Catch me if you can', 15–16.

45. Cristina Odone, 'Church war on gays', *The Times* (24 February 2005), 20.

46. Sholto Byrnes, 'Why am I here? What is life? Is there a God? Just ask Nicky', *Independent on Sunday* (29 July 2001), 17.

47. Deborah Orr, 'The meaning of life', *Independent Magazine* (13 December 2008), 19.

48. Gumbel, *Questions of Life* (revised 2010), 213.

49. Gumbel, *Jesus Lifestyle*, 73, 77.

50. Hobson, 'Don't call us evangelicals', 12.

51. Harden, 'Hold the potting shed', 20–1.

52. Gumbel, *Heart of Revival*, 135.

53. Jonathan Jeffes, 'God told me "It's all over"', *UK Focus* (March 2000), 3.

54. Jeffes, 'God told me "It's all over"', 1–2.

55. https://postabortioncourse.com. See further, Jonathan Jeffes, *Abortion: Breaking the Silence in the Church* (Chichester: Lean Press, 2013); Jonathan Jeffes, *What Happens After an Abortion? The Other Side of the Story* (Chichester: Lean Press, 2014).

56. Testimony of Marijke Tapson, *UK Focus* (May 2000), 1, 4–6.

57. Sandy Millar, 'Let's not be overtaken in zeal by our brothers and sisters elsewhere', *Focus* 143 (December 2003), 2.

58. 'The marriage feast', *Focus* 111 (April 2001), 3.

59. '"Marriage Prep" launched at HTB', *Focus* 141 (October 2003), 5.

60. 'Marriage Course news', *Alpha News* 45 (November 2008), 25.

61. 'Parenting Course is filmed for DVD', *Alpha News* 51 (November 2010), 29.

62. Information from Alpha International, February 2022.

63. Testimony of Steve Rice, *UK Focus* (October 2003), 4–5.

64. Testimony of Kim Santino, *UK Focus* (April 2005), 1–3.

65. 'Divorce recovery', *Alpha News* 23 (November 2000), 9.

66. 'Alpha resources', *Alpha News* 26 (November 2001), 43; Erik Castenskiold, *Restored Lives: Recovery from Divorce and Separation* (Oxford: Monarch, 2013).

67. Gumbel, *Jesus Lifestyle*, 88.

68. Gumbel, *Questions of Life*, 188.

69. Kennedy, 'Smart route to the Lord', 2.

70. 'New "Alpha" course for Eastenders' (1998), http://ship-of-fools.com/1998/Beta.html (accessed 4 March 2022).

71. 'Marketing the gospel', 18.

72. Campbell, 'Alpha's salvation motorway', 1107.

73. 'Alpha sets out to save souls with £1m campaign', *Sunday Telegraph* (22 July 2001), 12.

74. Letter from David Copley, *Guardian Weekend* (28 October 2000), 7.

75. Dominic Kennedy, 'Church spreads word with £1m ad campaign', *The Times* (9 September 1998), 9.

76. Stephanie Merritt, 'Having a chat won't make poverty history', *The Observer* (18 September 2005), Review, 2.

NOTES

77. Philip Kingston, 'Alpha is only a start', *The Tablet* (17 May 1997), 624–5.

78. Percy, 'Assessing Alpha'.

79. Alex Welby, 'The Alpha course in the inner city', *Renewal* 220 (September 1994), 26–9. See also, Peter Byron-Davies, 'An Alpha course in the countryside', *Renewal* 212 (January 1994), 21–3; Paul Hamilton, 'The Alpha course on an Essex housing estate', *Renewal* 230 (July 1995), 38–40.

80. Bryan Hackney, 'Alpha course for Catholics', *New Directions* 1 (July 1995), supplement. Alpha Course Update Form (September 1995), St Francis, New Mackworth, Alpha International Archives.

81. Bryan Hackney, 'More about Alpha for Catholics', *New Directions* 1 (August 1995), supplement.

82. 'How Alpha is working in . . . the Inner City and Urban Priority Areas', *Alpha News* 12 (February 1997), 10; 'Inner City Alpha', *Alpha News* 13 (July 1997), 14–15; Paul Hamilton, 'The Alpha course has been crucial for our growth', *Alpha News* 14 (November 1997), 10; 'It's no surprise Alpha works in the inner city, says pastor', *Alpha News* 36 (March 2005), 19.

83. Letter from Peter Kraushar, *The Tablet* (11 August 2001), 1145.

84. Gumbel, *Questions of Life*, 97–8.

85. Gumbel, *Questions of Life* (revised 1995), 104.

86. Gumbel, *Challenging Lifestyle*, 151.

87. Gumbel, *Challenging Lifestyle*, 198.

88. Gumbel, *Challenging Lifestyle*, 33–5.

89. Gumbel, *Telling Others*, 21.

90. Gumbel, *Heart of Revival*, 129–37.

91. Gumbel, *Heart of Revival*, 143–6.

92. Gumbel, *Questions of Life* (revised 2010), 116.

93. Gumbel, *Questions of Life* (revised 2010), 114–15.

94. Gumbel, *Questions of Life* (revised 2010), 172.

95. Gumbel, *Questions of Life* (revised 2010), 200.

96. Emmy Wilson, 'The Earl's Court Project' (July 1989), with HTB PCC minutes.

97. 'What the Project is doing . . .', *Focus* 52 (June 1996), 11.

98. 'Earl's Court Project safe house opened', *HTB in Focus* 4 (June 1992), 1.

99. Mark Perrott, 'To World's End with love', *Focus* 61 (March 1997), 5; Mark Perrott, 'Beware the barriers which put people off church', *UK Focus* (October 1999), 6–7.

100. 'Grandma's love – reaching out to be the hands and feet of Jesus', *Focus*

289

49 (March 1996), 8–9; 'Grandma's sounds such a cuddly thing to do, but it is all about taking life into death', *UK Focus* (January 1998), 1, 4–5.

101. James Odgers, 'I stood between these two heavily-tattooed gangsters and said in my best dinner party speak, "And what do you do?"', *UK Focus* (February 1998), 6–7.

102. James Odgers, 'Is there *anything* you would like to give?', *UK Focus* (March 1998), 6–7.

103. Sarah de Carvalho, *The Street Children of Brazil: One Woman's Remarkable Story* (London: Hodder & Stoughton, 1996), quotations at 27–8.

104. Testimony of Louise Strajnic, *UK Focus* (February 2009), 4–6.

105. Testimony of Shona Stewart, *UK Focus* (May 2011), 1–2.

106. Testimony of Peter and Nicole Wright, *UK Focus* (April 2008), 4–5.

107. Mike Pilavachi, 'Alpha and Soul Survivor: the joint initiatives', *Alpha News* 32 (November 2003), 14–15.

108. 'Alpha joins Make Poverty History drive', *Alpha News* 36 (March 2005), 4. See further Nicolas Sireau, *Make Poverty History: Political Communication in Action* (Basingstoke: Palgrave Macmillan, 2009).

109. Nicky Gumbel, *Make Poverty History* (London: Alpha International, 2005), 2, 12.

110. Nicky Gumbel, *Wilberforce: The Challenge for Today* (London: Alpha International, 2007), 12–13.

111. '60 seconds with . . . Nicky Gumbel', *Tear Times* (Autumn 2008), 30.

112. Nicky Gumbel, 'A Christian attitude to the environment', *UK Focus* (March 2006), 1–3.

113. Sandy Millar, 'Why did Jesus say it was so vital that we should all be "born from above"?', *UK Focus* (May 2005), 7.

114. 'Love your neighbour', *Revitalise* 4 (December 2020), 20–9.

115. 'Compassionate communities', *Revitalise* 5 (December 2021), 22.

116. Kendrick Oliver, 'The origin and development of Prison Fellowship International: pluralism, ecumenism and American leadership in the evangelical world 1974–2006', *Journal of American Studies* 51 (2017), 1221–42; Sylvia Mary Alison, *God is Building a House* (second edition, Alresford: John Hunt Publishing, 2002).

117. Emmy Wilson, 'A key to many', in *Inspiring Women: Making the Most of the Christian Life* (Farnham: CWR and *Woman Alive*, 2002), 135.

118. 'Looking out from inside', *Woman Alive* (November 1998), 7.

119. *Alpha in Prisons: Training Manual* (London: Alpha Publications, 2000), 24–5.

120. 'Prisoners set Alpha trend in Britain's jails', *Alpha News* 9 (March 1996), 36.

121. Peter Tullett, 'Alpha in prisons', *Alpha News* 13 (July 1997), 6.

122. 'Alpha takes off in UK prisons', *Alpha News* 7 (August 1995), 3.

123. Testimony of Michael Emmett, *UK Focus* (July 2004), 1–3.

124. Michael Emmett, *Sins of Fathers: A Spectacular Break from a Dark Criminal Past* (London: HarperCollins, 2020), 149–52.

125. Bill Birdwood, 'Alpha in prisons', *Alpha News* 12 (February 1997), 34.

126. Testimony of Michael Emmett, 3–4.

127. Paul Cowley, *Thief, Prisoner, Soldier, Priest* (London: Hodder & Stoughton, 2020), 174, 178–82.

128. Cowley, *Thief, Prisoner, Soldier, Priest*, 151.

129. Emmy Wilson, 'The Argentinian prison where 1,400 inmates worship and pray every day', *UK Focus* (July 1997), 4–5.

130. Juan Zuccarelli, 'God's kingdom in Olmos Prison', in C. Peter Wagner and Pablo Deiros (eds), *The Rising Revival: Firsthand Accounts of the Incredible Argentine Revival, and How it Can Spread Throughout the World* (Ventura, CA: Renew Books, 1998), 171–84.

131. 'Looking out from inside', 7.

132. 'Alpha now running in 100 prisons across UK', *Alpha News* 18 (March 1999), 3; 'Prison chief to speak at Alpha day', *Alpha News* 21 (March 2000), 13; '43 prisoners attend three day event at Highpoint Prison', *Alpha News* 28 (July 2002), 21.

133. Michael Green, 'Reflections on a three-day mission in Dartmoor Prison' (2000), in Alison, *God is Building a House*, 114–18.

134. '350 attend "Caring for Ex-Offenders" day', *Alpha News* 27 (March 2002), 9.

135. Peck, 'The Alpha phenomenon', 16.

136. Jean Hatton, 'If you're there God – help me!', *Christian Herald* (24 September 2005), 13.

137. Jamie Doward, 'Faith groups spreading the word on the wings', *The Observer* (26 October 2008), 28.

138. 'Alpha cuts crime, says chief', *Alpha News* 20 (November 1999), 6–7.

139. 'Helping ex-offenders join the church family on their release', *Alpha News* 15 (March 1998), 9; *Caring for Ex-offenders: A Handbook for Churches* (London: Alpha International, 2001).

140. 'Ex-offenders video launched for UK churches', *Alpha News* 29 (November 2002), 9.

141. Morton, 'Leap of faith', 2.

142. Jonathan Petre, 'Criminals find courage of conviction as religion sweeps jails', *Sunday Telegraph* (27 September 1998), 12.

143. Charles Hanson, 'Alpha courses in prison: who's kidding who?', *The Freethinker* 121 (July 2001), 8–9.

144. Mian Ridge, 'Spirit in the cells', *The Tablet* (14 December 2002), 10–11; Charlie Burton, 'Alpha males', *GQ* (June 2014), 198–203.

145. *UK Focus* (June 2003), 1–3.

146. Testimony of Shane Taylor, *UK Focus* (December 2008), 1–5.

147. Testimony of Gram Seed, *UK Focus* (February 2001), 1–3.

148. Testimony of Bob Hughes-Burton, *UK Focus* (October 2010), 1–3, 8.

149. Testimony of Dave Blakeney, *UK Focus* (July 2008), 1–3.

150. 'Double murderer writes a letter', *Alpha News* 13 (July 1997), 7.

151. 'Alpha in prisons', *Alpha News* 19 (July 1999), 15.

152. 'Demand for Alpha at Bulgaria conference', *Alpha News* 20 (November 1999), 6.

153. 'Governor George Bush Jnr gives OK to Alpha in Texas prisons', *Alpha News* 18 (March 1999), 15.

154. 'The Texas women prisoners who brought tears to delegates', *Alpha News* 20 (November 1999), 7; Deann Alford, 'Prison Alpha helps women recover their lost hopes', *Christianity Today* 43 (4 October 1999), 28.

155. 'Demand for Alpha at Bulgaria conference'.

156. Testimony of Paul Swala, *UK Focus* (July 2011), 1–3; 'The impossible life of Paul Swala', *Alpha Life* 3 (2015), 66–71; 'Zambia loyalists thwart army coup', *The Times* (29 October 1997), 15; '59 soldiers sentenced to death over chaotic coup in Zambia', *Daily Telegraph* (18 September 1999), 16.

157. 'The 73 who didn't come back', *Alpha News* 28 (July 2002), 3. See further, 'Jesus behind bars', *Alpha News: South Africa* 8 (July 2003), 1.

158. Burton, 'Alpha males', 202; 'Alpha prisons', *Alpha International Annual Review 2016*, 24; 'Lasting impact', *Alpha International Annual Review 2017*, 7.

Chapter Eight: Reaching the Globe

1. Interview with Nicky and Pippa Gumbel, 3 March 2021.

2. Gumbel, *Questions of Life* (revised 2010), 79.

3. Gumbel, 'Next stop: the world'.

4. Information from Nicky Gumbel, January 2022.

5. Gumbel, 'Next stop: the world'.

6. Gumbel, 'Next stop: the world'.

7. 'Where next for Alpha?', *Alpha News* 9 (March 1996), 6.

8. '4,000 courses now running worldwide', *Alpha News* 10 (July 1996), 1.

9. Nicky Gumbel appointment diary 1995–6.

10. Nicky Gumbel appointment diary 1996–7.

11. Gumbel, *Heart of Revival*, 107.

12. 'How Alpha is growing around the world', *Alpha News* 5 (December 1994), 9.

13. Gumbel, *Heart of Revival*, 102–6; Nicky Gumbel, 'How Nicky Gumbel lost his trousers . . . and his passport and money and diary and talk notes . . . and what happened next', *HTB in Focus* 44 (October 1995), 4–5.

14. 'Siberia hosts one of Russia's conferences', *Alpha News* 19 (July 1999), 17.

15. 'Changing lives along Asia's old Silk Route', *Alpha News* 28 (July 2002), 22–3; 'Witness to hope: how Alpha is spreading all over the world', *Alpha News* 29 (November 2002), 14.

16. 'Zimbabwe's first Alpha conference', *Zimbabwe Alpha News* 1 (November 1995).

17. Bill Humphreys, 'GatcheGatche to Mahombekombe', *Zimbabwe Alpha News* 4 (November 1996).

18. 'International Alpha', *Alpha News* 16 (July 1998), 16–17.

19. Edward Nyamuda, 'World first for Zimbabwe Alpha?', *Zimbabwe Alpha News* 10 (November 1998).

20. 'Alpha Mwenje', *Zimbabwe Alpha News* 10 (November 1998).

21. Forster Mushure, 'Rise up and walk!', *Zimbabwe Alpha News* 12 (July 1999).

22. 'Alpha Ministries Zimbabwe annual report 2000', Alpha International Archives.

23. 'Zimbabwe's Anderson is lifted up in prayer after year of persecution', *Alpha News* 50 (July 2010), 5.

24. 'Alpha introduced to Zambia', *Alpha News* 9 (March 1996), 33.

25. 'Alpha introduced to Zambia'; 'International Alpha', *Alpha News* 15 (March 1998), 16.

26. 'Witness to hope', 14.

27. 'Other international news', *Alpha News* 35 (November 2004), 11.

28. 'Transforming lives around the world', *Alpha News* 35 (November 2004), 22.

29. 'To the ends of the earth . . .', *Alpha News* 19 (July 1999), 3.

30. 'Witness to hope', 14.

31. 'The Alpha course', *Alpha News* 53 (November 2011), 14.

32. 'New York consultant is to spread Alpha across North America', *Alpha News* 11 (November 1996), 31.

33. Susan Lee, 'Filling the God-hole', *Forbes* (6 October 1997), 148–9.

34. 'Proposal for Alpha New York office and conference' (February 1996), Nicky Gumbel papers.

35. Timothy C. Morgan, 'The Alpha-Brits are coming', *Christianity Today* 42 (9 February 1998), 37.

36. Lee, 'Filling the God-hole', 149.

37. *Alpha Notes USA: A Publication of Alpha North America* 1 (Fall 1997).

38. 'US Alpha office moves as 2,500 courses are registered', *Alpha News* 23 (November 2000), 4.

39. 'Alpha USA annual report 2002', Nicky Gumbel papers; 'Alpha advisers gather from 53 countries', *Alpha News* 35 (November 2004), 11.

40. 'Alpha USA annual report 2002'.

41. 'News in brief', *Alpha News* 34 (July 2004), 4.

42. 'Organizational concerns with Alpha USA' (November 2004), Nicky Gumbel papers; Alistair Hanna to Alpha USA board, 22 November 2004, Nicky Gumbel papers.

43. Phil Jeansonne (New Orleans) to Tricia Neill, 29 November 2004, Nicky Gumbel papers.

44. Hanna to Alpha USA board, 22 November 2004.

45. Todd D. Hunter, *The Accidental Anglican: The Surprising Appeal of the Liturgical Church* (Nottingham: Inter-Varsity Press, 2011).

46. 'Nation invited to Alpha dinner', *Challenge Weekly* (21 March 2000), 1; 'Nation celebrates Alpha', *Alpha Update: New Zealand* (June 2000), 3; '50,000 to supper in New Zealand', *Alpha News* 22 (July 2000), 17; 'Inviting the nation to dinner', *Alpha Update: New Zealand* (October 2000), 1.

47. Vic Francis, ' "Astonishing" growth, big surprise', *Rise Up* (December 1999), 4.

48. Rob Yule, 'Gumbel to gumboots', *Alpha Update: New Zealand* (July 2001), 2.

49. 'News in brief', *Alpha News* 51 (November 2010), 6, 19.

50. 'Join the Alpha car flag challenge', *Alpha News: Canadian Edition* 26 (Summer 2007), 1.

51. 'Car flag challenge winners', *Alpha News: Canadian Edition* 27 (Fall 2007), 4.

52. 'St Paul's Cathedral prayers', *Alpha News* 32 (November 2003), 2.

53. 'Indonesian women's group starts Alpha', *Alpha News* 9 (March 1996), 33; 'International Alpha', *Alpha News* 13 (July 1997), 17.

54. Information from Mike Frith, February 2022.

55. 'World bishops speak of their need of Alpha', *Alpha News* 17 (November 1998), 3.

56. Marie Roach, 'Our archbishop says he wants Alpha all over the W. Indies', *Alpha News: USA Edition* 4 (August 1999), 8–9.

57. Atherstone, *Archbishop Justin Welby*, 85; 'Tanzania', *Alpha News* 12 (February 1997), 33.

58. 'News from the nations', *Alpha News* 50 (July 2010), 5.

59. 'Kiwi heads Alpha in Asia Pacific region', *Alpha New Zealand Update* (October 2006), 4.

60. 'Thelunius Nkomo: God's work in progress', *Alpha New Zealand Update* (February 2006), 4–5.

61. 'Alaskan cruise', *Alpha News: Canadian Edition* 5 (Summer 2000), 3.

62. 'Alpha afloat', *Alpha Life* 1 (2013), 36.

63. 'Alpha goes to extremes', *Alpha New Zealand Update* (October 2007), 1–2.

64. Anna Norman-Walker, 'Changing lives in the army', *Alpha News* 12 (February 1997), 7.

65. 'Course running on US navy ship', *Alpha News* 19 (July 1999), 4; Stephen Powers, 'Alpha in a combat zone', *UK Focus* (November 1999), 7.

66. 'Alpha joins the navy', *Alpha News: Canadian Edition* 3 (Winter 1999), 2.

67. 'Another first for the Royal Australian Navy', *Alpha News Australia* 1 (April 2003), 1–2.

68. 'Alpha goes to Afghanistan', *Alpha News: Canadian Edition* 15 (Fall 2003), 7.

69. 'Alpha takes off at army base in Iraq', *Alpha News: USA Edition* 19 (September 2004), 4; 'Alpha in Baghdad', *Alpha News (USA)* (Summer 2009), 14.

70. 'International Alpha', *Alpha News* 15 (March 1998), 16.

71. '56 countries report progress', *Alpha News* 32 (November 2003), 17.

72. Mari Kapi, 'The Alpha course in Keapara village', *Alpha News Australia* 1 (April 2003), 2.

73. 'Alpha Finland annual report 2001', Nicky Gumbel papers.

74. 'Country reports', *Alpha News* 38 (November 2005), 13.

75. 'Alpha with refugees', *Alpha International Annual Review 2016*, 17.

76. 'Alpha in many languages', *Alpha New Zealand Update* (October 2007), 3.

77. 'Honduras cleric drives 5,000 miles to lead five courses', *Alpha News* 20 (November 1999), 17.

78. Ron McCrary, 'Our church's link with the growth of Alpha in Honduras has brought us so much excitement', *Alpha News* 32 (November 2003), 23.

79. 'Church brings Alpha to Mexican village', *Alpha News: Canadian Edition* 7 (Spring 2001), 7.

80. 'Aboard the Trans-Siberia Express', *Alpha News* 38 (November 2005), 13.

81. 'News in brief', *Alpha News* 51 (November 2010), 6.

82. 'Global Alpha Training events 2012', *Alpha News* 53 (November 2011), 35.

83. 'GAT in over 500 locations worldwide', *Alpha News* 52 (March 2011), 2–3; '2300 GATs planned in 2012', *Alpha News* 53 (November 2011), 13.

84. 'Alpha course in Kolkata red-light district', *Alpha India News* (April 2009); 'Alpha course among transvestites', *Alpha India News* 2 (July 2011), 4; 'Alpha in the slums', *Alpha India News* 2 (July 2011), 8; 'Alpha course runs in leprosy communities', *Alpha India News* 2 (October 2011), 7.

85. Dilip Debnath, 'Alpha course in Kolkata local train', *Alpha India News* 2 (April 2011), 4.

86. '56 countries report progress'.

87. Peter Brierley, *International Alpha Courses in 2005: Evaluation Report* (Christian Research, May 2006), Alpha International Archives.

88. Peter Brierley, *International Alpha Courses in 2002 and 2003: Evaluation Report* (Christian Research, July 2004), Alpha International Archives.

89. '1.5 million did Alpha in 2007', *Alpha News* 44 (July 2008), 1; '1.6m did Alpha course last year', *Alpha News* 47 (July 2009), 19; 'Survey: 2m went on Alpha in 2009', *Alpha News* 50 (July 2010), 6.

90. Michael Hudson, *International Alpha Courses in 2011: Report for Holy Trinity Brompton* (Christian Research, August 2012), Alpha International Archives.

91. Michael Hudson, *International Alpha Courses in 2012: Report for Holy Trinity Brompton* (Christian Research, May 2013), Alpha International Archives.

92. Nicky Gumbel, 'It's time to accelerate', *HTB News* 194 (March 2008), 5.

93. Gumbel, 'It's time to accelerate', 5.

94. 'Project Lazarus' (2008), Nicky Gumbel papers.

95. 'Archie to lead Brighton plant' and 'We're off to Brighton', *HTB News* 208 (May 2009), 1–3; Archie Coates, 'Winning a city for God', *UK Focus* (June 2009), 6–7.

96. Madeleine Davies, 'Exporting the Brompton way', *Church Times* (21 April 2017), 19–20, 28.

97. 'New training for a new kind of vicar', *CRT News* [*Revitalise*] 2 (Summer 2019), 20–1; 'Revitalising rural parishes', *Revitalise* 4 (December 2020), 37; 'Raising up leaders', *Revitalise* 5 (December 2021), 41.

98. 'Holy Trinity Bukit Bintang: a story of growth and impact', *CRT News* 2 (Summer 2019), 8.

99. Gumbel, *Searching Issues* (revised 2013), 78.

100. Gumbel, *Questions of Life*, 73, 79.

101. Gumbel, *Questions of Life*, 85.

102. Gumbel, *The Bible in One Year*, preface.

103. '1400 sign up for HTB's One Year Bible initiative', *Alpha News* 46 (April 2009), 24.

104. 'Thousands follow daily commentary as Alpha's Bible in One Year is published', *Alpha News* 53 (November 2011), 10.

105. Nicky Gumbel, 'Introduction', in *NIV Bible in One Year* (London: Hodder & Stoughton, 2011), vii.

106. Information from Alpha International, January 2022.

107. Mark Ireland and Mike Booker, *Making New Disciples: Exploring the Paradoxes of Evangelism* (London: SPCK, 2015), 80.

108. Interview with Al Gordon, 6 May 2021.

109. Ronson, 'The saviour of Christianity', 21.

110. Ireland and Booker, *Making New Disciples*, 80.

111. Ije Nwokorie, 'The rejuvenation of Alpha', *Alpha Life* 2 (2014), 21.

112. Tim May, 'A taste of the future', *Alpha Life* 1 (2013), 19.

113. 'Innovating Alpha', *Alpha Life* 2 (2014), 17.

114. 'Kuala Lumpur, Malaysia', 'Melbourne, Australia', and 'Beirut, Lebanon', *Alpha Life* 2 (2014), 52–3, 57.

115. 'Listening to a global generation', *Alpha Life* 2 (2014), 26–8.

116. 'Alpha Youth Series', *Alpha International Annual Review 2016*, 36.

117. 'Youth', *Alpha Africa* (May 2019).

118. Al Gordon, 'The vision', *Alpha Life* 4 (2016), 72.

119. 'Alpha Film Series', *Alpha International Annual Review 2017*, 48.

120. 'Alpha Film Series translated in Ethiopia', *Alpha Africa* (May 2019).

121. 'Serving the church in a time of turmoil', *Alpha International Annual Review 2020*, 11.

122. Gordon, 'The vision', 72.

123. Vincent Cheng, 'A global experiment', *Alpha Life* 3 (2015), 59–61.

124. 'Pioneering in a pandemic', *Revitalise* 4 (December 2020), 32.

125. Nicky Gumbel, 'Letter from the chairman', *Alpha International Annual Review 2020*, 3.

126. Information from Alpha International, February 2022.

127. Nicky Gumbel, 'Reimagining a post-pandemic world' (HTB Leadership Conference, May 2021), www.youtube.com.

128. 'What's different about Alpha Online?', *Alpha International Annual Review 2020*, 7.

129. For further analysis, see Susie Triffitt, ' "The only person who is not confused by Zoom is the Holy Spirit": the growth of the Christian Alpha course during the pandemic' (MPhil thesis, University of Cambridge, 2021).

130. 'The Marriage Course', *Alpha International Annual Review 2020*, 24.

131. Gumbel, 'Letter from the chairman'.

132. 'What's different about Alpha Online?'

133. Gumbel, 'Reimagining a post-pandemic world'.

134. 'What's different about Alpha Online?'

135. Gumbel, 'Letter from the chairman'.

136. Gumbel, 'Reimagining a post-pandemic world'.

137. 'What's on the horizon?', *Alpha International Annual Review 2020*, 8.

138. 'Overcoming distances in India', *Alpha International Annual Review 2020*, 9.

139. 'Kenya spotlight', *Alpha International Annual Review 2020*, 13.

140. 'Latin America', *Alpha International Annual Review 2020*, 18.

141. 'Delivering Alpha USB sticks by dirt bike in Venezuela' (24 May 2021), https://alpha.org/blog/ (accessed 4 March 2022).

142. 'Africa', *Alpha International Annual Review 2020*, 12.

143. 'Pioneering in a pandemic', 32.

Index